THE GREAT D

From the Era of Hope and Progress to the Age of Fear and Rage

John Bone

BRISTOL
UNIVERSITY
PRESS

First published in Great Britain in 2024 by

Bristol University Press
University of Bristol
1–9 Old Park Hill
Bristol
BS2 8BB
UK
t: +44 (0)117 374 6645
e: bup-info@bristol.ac.uk

Details of international sales and distribution partners are available at bristoluniversitypress.co.uk

British Library Cataloguing in Publication Data
A catalogue record for this book is available from the British Library

ISBN 978-1-5292-1302-7 hardcover
ISBN 978-1-5292-1303-4 paperback
ISBN 978-1-5292-1306-5 ePub
ISBN 978-1-5292-1305-8 ePdf

Cover design: Nicky Borowiec
Front cover image: Adobe Stock/Haruki Yui
Bristol University Press uses environmentally responsible print partners.
Printed and bound in Great Britain by CPI Group (UK) Ltd, Croydon, CR0 4YY

FSC
www.fsc.org
MIX
Paper | Supporting
responsible forestry
FSC® C013604

Contents

Acknowledgements

For my wife Arlane, for her patience and support throughout. For my children Laurie, Jenny, Erin and Ethan. With many thanks to my colleagues and friends past and present in the School of Social Sciences, University of Aberdeen, and to my colleagues and compatriots at the Aberdeen Just Transition Lab for making the last couple of years particularly interesting and fun.

Finally, in memory of my old and sadly missed mentor Chris Wright who always indulged my disruptive speculations with great humour and encouragement.

Introduction: The New Age of Angst

I think it's fair to say that, emerging from the first decades of the 21st century, many of us have had a feeling that life was becoming ever more hectic, insecure and to some extent overwhelming. A slow-burning malaise that has been steadily encroaching since the late 1970s has appeared to have reached a critical stage, as evidenced in a wide range of tensions and deep uncertainties spanning the personal, communal, political and geopolitical, to the extent that in some ways we seem to be experiencing a period of upheaval broadly reminiscent of the late 19th and early 20th centuries. This has been an era where a brief period of relative calm has given way to recurrent economic crises, a global pandemic, the growing effects of climate change, as well as rising social problems and an increasingly febrile politics emerging across numerous nations that were until recently considered to be stable democracies. It comes as no surprise then that the *Collins Dictionary* of 2022 cited 'permacrisis' as its top word for the year, defined as 'an extended period of instability and insecurity'.[1] Adding to the dispiriting lexicon of this era, the term 'food bank' has gone from being virtually unknown before the financial crisis of 2007/2008 to entering common parlance, latterly joined by the so-called 'warm banks' in the UK that emerged during the energy crisis of 2022/2023. Perhaps one of the most disturbing developments in this regard has been the emergence of so-called 'baby banks' to provide essential support and foodstuffs for impoverished mothers and their babies, something that had once been taken for granted in terms of state provision.

These developments are emblematic of a growing tide of insecurity, inequality, destitution and desperation pervading our times, providing a stark illustration of just how far states like the UK, as one of those which most enthusiastically embraced neoliberalism, have retreated from responsibility for their citizens' welfare and wellbeing over a number of decades. Not so long ago, confident predictions of a relatively prosperous, stable and settled future proposed that we were moving towards a world dominated by liberal democracies and greater personal autonomy, with nations becoming more closely bound together by global consumerism, trade and free markets. This vision of the 'end of history'[2] now seems wildly off the mark from

1

the standpoint of the present as darker aspects of our history appear to have re-emerged with a vengeance: 'Noam Chomsky has warned that the world is at the most dangerous moment in human history owing to the climate crisis, the threat of nuclear war and rising authoritarianism.'[3]

If there is a political trend that characterizes this era, it is a movement towards greater division, populism and authoritarianism, as radical leaders largely of the right have challenged longstanding political norms. The emergence of Trump's right-wing 'Make America Great Again' (MAGA) movement in the US, threatening insurgency and the undermining of American democracy, has been symptomatic of this growing wave, from the Far East through a swathe of previously solidly democratic European nations, including the UK, where authoritarian populism, hard-right extremism and even neo-fascism have become an unnervingly realistic concern. The chaotic scenes witnessed during the storming of the US Capitol on 6 January 2021 appeared surreal by previous standards, like scenes from some far-fetched dystopian movie of just a decade or so earlier. Now they are features of a creeping and darkening reality echoed in various guises elsewhere.

In post-Brexit Britain, the new febrile politics destabilized the so-called 'mother of parliaments', with former conventions, probities and practices seemingly being eroded by the populist tide. The spectre of grassroots right-wing nationalist movements has also grown in the UK and is no longer securely confined to the radical fringe. Much as in the 1930s, this seems to be a recurrent symptom of economic troubles, of insecurity and inequity. Of particular issue, however, is that such destructive social and political trends now tend to proliferate and intensify at an unprecedented pace, fuelled by the algorithms and filter bubbles of contemporary social media.

Consistent with the angry political divisions within nations, strident nationalisms and associated resurgent geopolitical undercurrents and enmities have undermined international cooperation and the relative calm that emerged after the end of the Cold War. The latter has been underlined by the fact that we have witnessed the return of open warfare in Europe on a scale not seen since 1945, as well as the resurgence of serious conflict in the Middle East. There is also the pervasive sense that the fractious state of the international order may offer even worse in the future.

As I argue here, feeding these global problems at the local and personal levels, everyday life has been marred by a growing sense of anxiety and anger, as people rail against the fact that, for the majority, circumstances keep getting worse and when troubles strike, people seem to feel less supported by mainstream politicians than was once the case, feeling that their concerns and needs fail to be addressed. Even among those who have little experience of the worst in terms of the growing poverty, insecurity and inequality that now pervades many societies, there is the fear of losing out in future; a situation turbo-charged by an ever rising cost of living and stagnating incomes.

Paradoxically, despite all of this, the popular zeitgeist that emerged with neoliberalism has dictated that we should be constantly enthusiastic, upbeat and 'together'; consistently exuding the 'right stuff' to make it in hypercompetitive, goal-driven, aspirational societies. To successfully demonstrate our worth, amid the pressure to find approval in many of the workplaces on which our insecure livelihoods are sustained, an air of faux chutzpah, a fragile self-confidence and an unflagging appetite for industriousness are often demanded of us while we sustain a persistent concern of falling short. There has been a persistent fear of failing to reflect the correct attitude or to hit ubiquitous targets, the short- to medium-term 'key performance indicators' we are routinely presented with, or indeed our own longer-term life goals. In our socially mediated world, our home lives, activities, personalities, appearance and personal relationships are also constantly evaluated, and self-evaluated, measured against peers and, often unrealistically, against the ubiquitous Photoshopped lifestyles of those 'achievers' who appear to have risen above the fray and who we might hope to emulate at some distant point in the future if we just stick to the plan or, otherwise, good fortune intervenes. The strain of aspirational desire for a lifestyle that is realistically beyond the reach of most, as inequality has become an ever-widening gulf, is compounded by a growing fear of failure in societies that are increasingly unforgiving. While these private concerns regarding numerous aspects of everyday living, and our own and our families' futures, might harry our thoughts during the day and even keep us awake at night, they are compounded by the aforementioned global issues that intrude on our peace. Little wonder then that many people have experienced a well-documented rise in personal distress. Compounding this sense of angst, and against all evidence, we are informed that emotional responses to living this life are actually due to individual infirmity, as opposed to the increasingly toxic societal conditions to which we are subjected. As we know, this has spawned a whole therapeutic industry that, albeit largely well intended, is engaged in persuading us that something inherently defective in us is at the root of our troubles, rather than the world that we confront, while the solution is to patch us up, through self-help, counselling or pharmaceuticals, sufficiently to return us to the fray.

For someone of my own vintage, this observable deterioration in lived experience has seemed a long-running process that has cast a shadow over memories of youth in a world that, looking back, and while far from ideal, had once seemed much more optimistic and secure. In most areas of contemporary life, however, the world we have created has seemed an increasingly meaner, darker, unjust and, broadly, less human place, squeezing the space for creativity, enriching experiences and fulfilling relationships, together with a thinning of our better nature. Now clearly most generations will tend to have a rosier picture of the past when looking back on the era of their youth than was really the case, understandably aside from those whose formative years may have been blighted by conflict, deprivation and economic turbulence. It's also clear that, from a more objective standpoint, it is very easy to overplay the cosiness of the past when living through a troubled present. However, as is argued here, while the past of my own youth may have been a long way from being the golden age that many have imagined it to be, given numerous troubles and continuing injustices and inequities, this was a time of growing equality and security in many societies by design, while there was much less of a sense that the future was as blighted as it appears at present. Despite the problems of that era, there was a belief that they could be fixed and that society was gradually moving forward, rather than the current view that, for many, things are falling apart in an angry, selfish and uncaring world. In qualification here, there has been some ongoing progress in terms of rolling back some of the social conservatism that persisted, but which was beginning to be successfully challenged at that time, albeit that even this is now coming under increasing pressure from an emboldened reactionary right. The question then is how did we get here? How did a brief awakening of measured confidence and hope that emerged in the middle of the last century dissolve so swiftly and easily? How did the stuttering progress that many commentators once regarded as being our broad direction of travel – where interpersonal conduct and wider social organization was deemed to be at least broadly on a course towards increasing stability, confidence, equity and order – seemingly dissolve in a regressive ferment of fear, injustice, anger and growing disarray?

These are, of course, some of the most compelling questions of the late modern era, understandably spawning a multitude of accounts. Here, however, I am approaching these issues from a new direction, to offer a different take on the problems that currently confront us. In general, my own view as to *why* we have experienced such a dramatic decline in our hopes, expectations and experience is not particularly novel. The simple answer is that the turning away from the social democracy and measured progressive politics of the mid-20th century towards the neoliberal economic and political ideology of recent decades is a key source of our recent instabilities and discontents. By pulling apart the fragile, fledgling stabilizing features of postwar democracies, which were put in place precisely to confront some broadly similar issues to those that we face at present – of poverty, inequality, insecurity, instability, injustice, anger, discord and conflict – we have simply disinterred some perennial and familiar societal ills. We appear to have forgotten the lessons of the recent past and have once more allowed a minority to pursue what they believe to be in their own narrow interests at the expense of everyone else, persuading enough of us that we'll also benefit from their ascendancy and largesse. Many have also been persuaded to believe that, while the system may seem harsh at times, it holds out the prospect that they can 'make it' with a little effort and good fortune, despite all evidence to the contrary as widening inequalities have become more entrenched. In terms of these divisions, a minority who have greatly benefited from the recent status quo continue to do whatever is necessary to sustain 'normal' service, beguiling and co-opting as many as they can to their cause, with sadly a multitude of the victims of the harsh societies they are forging among them.

Of course, as suggested, I am very far from alone in coming to these broad conclusions. There are clearly screeds of copy and polemic proposing that neoliberalism has been bad for us economically, socially, politically and personally. However, despite the abject failure of this credo, the debate is far from over, with the champions of neoliberalism largely retaining the upper hand, insisting that a market-led approach is the only pragmatic way for the economy and society to be organized, and that attempts to thwart the operation of markets goes against both common sense and, as they often assert, against our 'nature'. It is in terms of both of these contentions that the problem with neoliberalism lies. Firstly, as will be argued in the succeeding chapters, contrary to the vehement denials of its apologists, the neoliberal model has been seen to fail ever more obviously and drastically on its own terms. The abandoning of business and financial regulation reintroduced a variant of capitalism that is pervaded with risk. Financial markets returned to a form of pre-Keynesian casino capitalism, turbo-charged by globalization and new technology, enriching a few while producing little benefit to the wider economy and society. Rather, as is discussed in the later chapters, the neoliberal deregulation of finance has delivered stagnating wages, unaffordable housing, economic instability and crises, together with fantasy profits for its financial alchemists, whose losses have been underwritten by governments, central banks and taxpayers across a number of nations. We have seen insipid economic growth, although it has to be recognized that given the damage to the planet being caused by even our current levels of consumption, that might not be an issue in itself, as a radical change of direction here may prove essential to our survival. What is troubling, however, is that growing inequality within and between nations is now reaching eye-watering and largely indefensible proportions, despite a good deal of self-serving rhetoric. And while there has been limited economic advancement in developing economies, the exploitative model under which this has occurred, via sweatshop outsourcing of manufacturing and rapacious and occasionally violent appropriation of resources, suggests that a much more equitable and consensual approach to humanity's collective wellbeing is both possible and necessary. The alternative, of continuing burgeoning inequality and injustice, provides the incipient rage that fuels disorder and conflict within nations and around the world, much as it has in the past. However, it is in understanding the underlying reasons why we have experienced such a seemingly cataclysmic breakdown in the order of things where I wish to present a new approach, outlining why we are so ill-suited to the world that has been imposed on many of us. At the root of this is nothing less than a fundamental re-appraisal of who we are and how we relate to the world. We have been sold an idea over the last few decades that nature has designed us to thrive on relentless competition, adversity and risk taking, often expounded by those who are largely insulated from these conditions by the wealth derived from imposing them on others. Just as the 'leisure classes' of the Gilded Age of the late 19th century advocated relentless hard work, self-denial and thrift for the lower orders, while setting aside these principles for themselves, their inheritors among the contemporary elite prescribe similar measures for contemporary 'hardworking' citizens, while ensuring they and their offspring are not similarly burdened. What is argued here is that the vision of what we are, as currently presented, is well off the mark. Firstly, it is largely through cooperation and collective support that human beings became successful, as opposed to the sharp-elbowed competitive individualism that is currently encouraged.[4] More broadly, we have fundamental needs based on our innate predispositions and propensities that are undermined by current arrangements. A key problem, as is discussed throughout this book, is that neoliberal societies tend to operate in opposition rather than in concert with these. A modicum of interesting diversion and occasional calculated risk taking and competition is indeed part of our repertoire, but only where this is measured and contained for the greater good and is approached from conditions that offer a good deal of security, stability, sociability and predictability. Put plainly, we don't mind raising our heads above the parapet at times, but for most people, security and solidarity trumps insecure, atomized achievement. There are very good reasons for all of this, and for understanding the observable consequences of our needs not being met.

Previous accounts have tended to simply chart the inequalities and insecurities that I've discussed and point towards some of their consequences, but, as argued here, with an incomplete account of how all of this arises or an understanding of its deeper ramifications. The aim here is to offer a more rounded understanding of where we're at and where we are going, while providing a solidly grounded and evidenced argument for challenging the current direction of travel. As implied from the preceding discussion, I also intend to approach these issues from a broad perspective, addressing the conditions of our times as they have arisen, but also considering where we are within a wider historical and, to an extent, evolutionary perspective, to make the albeit controversial case that how we deal with the current crises we confront may not only affect our wellbeing in the present, but may potentially influence the future development of our species over the short or even the longer term. In short, it is argued that we have reached a crisis point in our development and there is now evidence to suggest that the stakes are far higher than have been understood thus far. This is approached by exploring the consequences neoliberalism has wrought, principally in the West and with a particular focus on the UK and the US.

While neoliberalism emerged among the exclusive academic circles of the Mont Pelerin Society on the European mainland, its progenitor was surely the exploitative and unforgiving laissez-faire capitalism advanced by Britain, particularly during the 19th century.[5] The exportation of this model and its culture to the US, and with its further intensification as America emerged as the dominant economic and cultural powerhouse of the 20th and early 21st centuries, saw both of these nations, and particularly their elites, embrace and advance neoliberalism as a return to their preferred normal conditions of capitalism that they then extended to the world. As the most ardent exponents of neoliberalism, within and beyond their borders, they also provide an exemplar as to how and why some of our most developed and leading societies and democracies have now rapidly deteriorated, socially and politically, as a consequence of the adoption and promotion of a credo that continues to produce casualties both large and small across the planet. In short, as I will argue throughout this book, Britain and America provide laboratories for exploring the deeply corrosive consequences of the neoliberal model on advanced developed societies, in terms of its traducing of the fleeting progressive advances once experienced by the citizens of these nations, and as a socially, politically, environmentally and economically destructive influence that has been extended globally since the late 1970s.

While several chapters focus on a range of specific areas of current concern, from the nature and development of contemporary work, the economy and politics to climate change and the role of psychotherapy in dealing with the individual fallout in neoliberal societies, Chapter 1 introduces the original explanatory framework that informs this work, one aim of which is to also draw connections between some of the ostensibly discrete issues that are addressed. The chapter sets out an original biosocial model of the individual and how we relate to each other and to the societies we inhabit. This approach has featured in a number of peer-reviewed and published articles over the last two decades, in papers outlining the thesis itself and its application to understanding a range of social, economic and political processes, with its key elements drawing upon and being consistent with a broad range of works, including current and emerging evidence from sociology, psychology, neuroscience and social epigenetics.

The main features and implications of my approach (*The Social Map*) are set out here, in as nontechnical language as is possible, explaining how and why human evolution has produced a species which, as suggested, enjoys an element of stimulation and diversion, but also has a highly limited tolerance to complexity, change and unpredictability. It is explained here that this is an effect of the limited processing capacities of the 'conscious' areas of the brain, a condition that has been attributed to our species evolving in small-scale communities.[6] One of the key consequences of this is that our cognition and emotions become vulnerable to chronic overstimulation in a world where urbanization and social atomization, technological advances, expanding information and constant change persistently stretch our coping capacities. This provides the basis for what follows, including a whistlestop re-appraisal of key stages of the historical developments that led to the emergence of the modern world, before focusing on the difficulties we have in adapting to this through the nitty gritty of living in our societies in the here and now, in the UK, the US and beyond, and what this may entail for our future development.

One final point that needs addressing at the outset is that having identified the turn to neoliberalism in the late 1970s as the key instigator of societal regression and a range of contemporary woes, it is important how we understand this. As with many ideas and concepts, some commentators are prone to arguing endlessly over definitions, dare I say, often in a pedantic manner. I suppose that this is a particular irritation of my own as, in my view, while not always the case but often, nit picking over definitions regularly gets in the way of discussing real ideas. As to neoliberalism, in avoiding such digression, my view is that we know it when we see it and its key features are pretty well understood. For me, Bob Jessop's very concise definition, as indicated in Chapter 4, captures the key features of the marketization of society that was imposed in the neoliberal era.[7] In addition to definitional debates, there are also arguments over variants of neoliberalism and, of late, suggestions that the neoliberal era may even have passed, with a move towards governments more assiduously championing their own national economies and pulling back from global markets. However, and while conceding that there may be some evidence of this, for a number of reasons such arguments are largely incidental to the issues presented here. Firstly, with respect to neoliberalism, aside from debates around the extent to which it has evolved or morphed over time, it seems clear that its legacy and logic continues to dominate political thinking, economic and social planning in the UK, the US and across much of the world. The critical point is that it is the under-regulated capitalism associated with the neoliberal model and its privileging of free markets as the primary form of socioeconomic organization, no matter how finely tuned, that continues to govern the societies and lives of the majority of citizens. Critically, the economy, business interests and profit continue to be privileged and take clear precedence over social and environmental concerns and human wellbeing. While sectors of the political establishment in neoliberal societies regularly expound their prosocial credentials, much of this appears to be more about rhetoric than meaningful action. Hence, the gross inequities and insecurities that the neoliberal turn have generated very much remain and have intensified over time, producing disturbing social, political and personal consequences regardless of what minor tinkering has occurred. In fact, I would tend to argue that if there has been a shift with respect to neoliberalism, aside from that outlined in the preceding discussion, it is in terms of its application and implications becoming ever more extreme – in short, questions around definitions and semantics others might well take up. However, what is important for the arguments that are set out here is how the general socioeconomic and political environment that we have created since the late 1970s continues to negatively affect who and what we are – and, not least, as I argue, what we might become.

Notes

[1] https://blog.collinsdictionary.com/language-lovers/a-year-of-permacrisis/

[2] Fukuyama, F. (2006) *The End of History and the Last Man*, New York: Simon & Schuster.

[3] 'Noam Chomsky: the world is at the most dangerous moment in human history', *New Statesman*, 17 September 2020, https://www.newstatesman.com/politics/2020/09/noam-chomsky-the-world-is-at-the-most-dangerous-moment-in-human-history

[4] Hare, B. (2017) 'Survival of the friendliest: homo sapiens evolved via selection for prosociality', *Annual Review of Psychology*, 68(1): 155–186.

[5] Bone, J.D. (2010) 'Irrational capitalism: the social map, neoliberalism and the demodernization of the West', *Critical Sociology*, 36(5): 717–740; Lansley, S. (2021) 'Why luxury capitalism is the enemy of social progress', *Discover Society: New Series*, 1(4), https://doi.org/10.51428/dsoc.2021.04.0002

[6] Dunbar, R.I. (1993) 'Coevolution of neocortical size, group size and language in humans', *Behavioral and Brain Sciences*, 16(4): 681–694.

[7] Jessop, B. (2002) 'Liberalism, neoliberalism, and urban governance: a state–theoretical perspective', *Antipode*, 34(3): 452–472, at 461.

PART I

Being Human in an Evolving World

1

Who Are We and Why Does It Matter?

This chapter sets out some of the key ideas that inform the analysis in the book. The theoretical framework *The Social Map* is the culmination of a long period of work, a range of which has been presented elsewhere. However, with a view to making this as open and accessible as possible, some details have been set aside in favour of clearly outlining the key concepts and their development, with a particular focus on the ideas that will be applied to the social, economic and political issues addressed in the subsequent chapters. This theoretical model, together with the evidence and ideas that have informed it, is presented to offer a novel approach to understanding what has gone wrong in our societies. The argument presented here is that in order to challenge the ideas and self-interest that continues to support the favouring of markets over people and the planet, we need to be able to point to more than the fact that our societies and citizens are, to say the least, not at ease with themselves. Rather, there is a need to provide a solid basis and evidence as to why this is the case and what the implications are of letting this set of social and economic arrangements persist. Without this, debates as to where we are and where we're going can be dismissed as simple differences of opinion, reduced to debate and rebuffs relating to so-called 'culture wars' or calls for greater equity dismissed as the 'politics of envy', with the most powerful voices winning out as they have done over the last few decades. As such, the aim here is to present a firmly grounded case that strips such self-serving arguments of their legitimacy, while offering an unequivocal case as to why fundamental change is not only preferable but also essential.

Being human

As noted in the Introduction, whenever we're talking about how we relate to the world, we must take account of who we are, our capabilities and so on. While this might seem very obvious, for many in the social sciences and other areas of academia, it remains highly problematic. For a variety of reasons, some of which are very sound and some much less so, social scientists have tended to skirt around the issue of what it means to be human in its most fundamental sense, as fully social *and* biological beings, as the latter comes loaded with a significant element of political baggage. As a consequence, there is a strong lobby that presents our identities, personalities and behavioural tendencies as being, more or less, wholly shaped by life experiences, crucially with little regard to our physical capacities and so on. The problem, as argued here, is that this position is not tenable. On pain of being facetious, just as human beings cannot fly and arms and legs tend to operate in particular ways, there are some fundamental aspects of who we are that are defined, or where at least variability is limited, by our biological constitution and inheritance. Yet, to be clear, this does not in any way imply that the human condition and conduct are determined by our genes and innate tendencies.

The question of the relationship between our biological inheritance and the role of experience in shaping who we are and how we engage with the world is of course a perennial issue. For many, it is sufficient to let the matter rest on the fairly obvious proposition that 'it's a bit both', with little elaboration on that point, and to simply set this issue aside in further discussion. A few bold outliers, of course, do continue to remain wedded to the position that we are creatures with a nature largely determined by our genetic inheritance, albeit that this has been a significantly diminishing perspective over time.[1] As suggested, however, there are a very large number of commentators who position themselves at the other end of this divide, often rejecting wholesale any notion of our biology as a meaningful concern when trying to come to an understanding of what it is to be human in a social sense.[2] As noted in the Introduction, this is a view that I do not hold, albeit conceding that there are very understandable, if not justifiable, reasons as to why many would wish to adhere to this position and reject any notion of biological innateness. Firstly, many writers, a legion of social scientists among them, are uneasy with the notion that there are limits to the malleability of the human constitution, perhaps in part because this would also tend to place limits on what can be imagined for the future. This makes sense if one's standpoint is one where a wholly open-ended present and future is a desirable or necessary condition for sustaining a particular stance on some issue or another. Conversely, recognizing that there are limits to human variability may mean that some difficult and uncomfortable constraints have to be contemplated, explored and understood. This would also make the business of thinking and writing about society harder in some respects, not just for social scientists but perhaps also for some journalists and other commentators if they were called upon to engage with aspects of human biology in their writings. Importantly, however, a major reason for suspicion of accounts of human 'nature' more generally is that many of those that have gained currency have been highly flawed to say the least and were often devised and cynically employed to advance unsavoury positions of one form or another. From religiously based claims regarding the innate superiority of particular social, ethnic and economic groups, to misapplied Darwinian ideas to claim effectively the same thing, the misuses of biological 'knowledge' have been profound, and not without serious consequences at times.[3] In fact, across Western societies, and imposed on a host of others, a conflation of pseudobiological and religious doctrine shaped, and continues to a great extent to shape, a hierarchical definition of peoples that long supported the self-serving interests of exploitative Western elites, a point to which I will return in Chapter 3.

Across medieval Europe, it's easy to see how religion supported the position of a feudal aristocracy as divinely appointed and, as such, innately superior. In this view, those favoured were rightful rulers, producing a veneer of respectability and legitimation that over time created a particular image of 'nobility' in the public imagination, one that detracts from the fact that the origins of many, if not all, aristocratic lineages were forged in violence in what was effectively, it might be argued, a form of medieval gangsterism. From the 19th century onwards, in an era transformed by the scientific and industrial revolutions, Social Darwinism – the notion that some humans are inherently 'fitter' due to having biologically 'superior' ancestors – began to replace religious ideology as a means of justifying high levels of social inequality. This provided the foundations for the currently widely accepted view that social positions, wealth and power are simply reflections of individual 'merit'. It's often overlooked that arguments legitimating the neoliberal order of the current era have implied more than a whiff of Social Darwinism. In effect, as suggested earlier, neoliberalism has reinvoked 19th-century ideas of human beings as being inherently conflictual and competitive, with the winners decided by personal qualities and attributes, as a means of justifying ever more unequal social and economic arrangements.

Similar arguments were employed to justify racial discrimination and domination, including European imperialism, colonialism and the dark chapters of the slave trade, and later other forms of discrimination and domination, even to the point of genocide. Given the tendency in the modern era for the mask of (bad) science and biology to be used to justify horrific injustice, it is perhaps unsurprising that any claims regarding human biological capacities and tendencies are treated with considerable suspicion by the progressive and liberally minded.

Suspicion regarding the misapplication of biology has, of course, not been confined to concerns relating to class, race and ethnicity, as gender relations have also featured prominently in the reasons for an aversion to biological accounts of the human condition. Again, the dovetailing of religious and pseudoscientific legitimation was also prevalent in ideas widely promulgated regarding the differences between men and women, depicting the latter as the weaker and less rational gender. As we know, this perspective was employed (and variants still are in many parts of the world) to justify the effective ownership and domination of women by men as well as more contemporary inequalities. Given this fact, once more there is no great mystery in understanding the women's movement's adoption of an affirmed anti-biological stance, at least at a point when the battle for gender quality began to really gain traction. As Linda Birke notably observed:

> 'biological experiences do form a part of the way in which we understand concepts of gender. But that belief was heresy to the W.L.M. in the mid-1970s ... The problem was then, and remains, that the belief that gender is socially constructed was the only alternative to a belief in biological determinism. If you did not agree with one, then by implication, you must believe in the other. This opposition has had dire consequences, both for feminism and for the Left in general.'[4]

This comment also aptly illustrates the binary thinking that, as was noted earlier, has often governed this debate, on the one side essentialism and biological determinism and on the other the position (so-called strong social constructionism) that insists that everything we are is a shifting product of our experiences. However, the evidence has long suggested that neither of these polarized positions has ever stood up to more than cursory scrutiny, while growing developments in neuroscience and genetics, particularly since the 1990s, have presented an ever greater challenge to neat binary ideas on nature and nurture.

Bridging binaries

As far as my own journey along this path is concerned, this began when I was an undergraduate studying both psychology and sociology. I began to see apparent connections between ideas and concepts that seemed to remain unacknowledged by many of my teachers. In particular, I was interested in the way in which concepts and evidence I was presented with in neuropsychology seemed to connect with and clarify ideas I was being presented within sociology, and to some extent vice versa.

However, one very clear qualification must be noted here. I'm in no sense attempting to assert that I'm remotely qualified to engage in any broadly based critique of these rich bodies of knowledge, nor is this intended as a criticism of either. This would be clearly well beyond anyone's reach and should be beyond their ambition. What I'm saying is simply that in their approach to understanding particular aspects of the relationship between the individual and society, both psychology (including its biological aspects) and sociology seemed to me to offer somewhat one-sided and incomplete perspectives. Much of this seeming interdisciplinary myopia in certain areas is, of course, almost impossible to avoid, as boundaries are invariably erected between academic disciplines as a response to practical considerations – principally, the fact that bodies of knowledge may inevitably grow to exceed the limits of what students and their professors within universities can be reasonably expected to learn. In this way, over time, disciplines develop subdisciplines that further down the line may emerge as disciplines in their own right. These limitations are, as it happens, a central feature of the arguments that inform this book. Given this fact, it would be no surprise to see some of the currently familiar disciplines and faculties within universities break down further over time. Another means by which disciplinary volume is kept in check is for ideas to be challenged and rejected, and for others to simply fall out of fashion, many quite rightly so, which is also an aim here.

Returning specifically to the matter at hand, of particular interest to me was the way in which key aspects of brain structure and function I was presented with seemed to 'flesh out' and more adequately explain important features of social development, where some sociological explanations had seemed to me as being somewhat vague and unconvincing. Looking back, I must have been quite an annoying undergraduate, having the temerity to question my teachers regarding key aspects of what had been delivered in their lectures, while much of this book is testimony to the fact that this is a tendency that I haven't lost in the intervening years.

Why was it that we could not answer some of the central questions that we addressed in classes and lectures? For example, social scientists would talk a great deal about how societies generally tended towards being structured and orderly in one form or another. However, on questioning this, the means by which this happened was usually explained by a range of rather unsatisfactory terms as far as I was concerned. And yet, thinking across the areas I studied, I began to consider that the answers to these questions might be simpler than some of the vague and convoluted explanations I was often offered when seeking clarity.

One of the main issues I was concerned with related to such questions regarding social order and how this was understood. In qualification, it is important to stress at this point that this is not to suggest that society is orderly in the sense that it tends towards stability and tranquility, as history and experience for the most part clearly indicate otherwise. What's argued throughout the book is a testament to that. Rather, social order within the social sciences is understood from the perspective that societies often exhibit longstanding regularities in terms of their established institutions and in terms of the flow of everyday activity, often even in societies that might appear superficially chaotic or are riven by internal conflict. What is important is that discernible and relatively predictable patterns of relationships present themselves and persist over time. These are learned and understood, and allow people to make sense of and confront everyday life with a degree of confidence that what they will experience, good or ill, will broadly fit with their socially acquired expectations. In short, social life is rarely chaotic for very long, despite appearances, even if it falls well short of providing a form of regularity that suits many of its inhabitants.[5]

This issue goes to the heart of how we understand the nature of the relationship between the individual and society, and also, as will be made clear later on, is central to understanding a broad range of issues addressed in this book. As to my recollection here, I was often told that social order emerged from society, but was never quite clearly informed how this happened. If pressed, my teachers would usually refer to 'emergent properties' of society ('it kind of just happens spontaneously when people come together en masse'), but with no reference to our individual or, even more certainly, innate biological capacities or limitations.

Social scientists' avoidance of biological explanations with respect to social issues was not always so emphatic. As Renwick notably pointed out,[6] until the early part of the 20th century, many sociologists did engage with biology and evolutionary ideas. Over time, however, the desire to demarcate clear terrain for this emerging discipline saw an increasing marginalization of biological and, to a lesser extent, psychological ideas in favour of social explanations for societal phenomena, a trend that became further consolidated over time by a turn to philosophy as a key source of social thought and by the anti-biologism informed by the political concerns and sensibilities outlined earlier. This led to a scenario where social scientists have tended to advance a range of different formulations pointing to external sources in order to account for the apparent regularities of everyday life.

Again, there is a further qualification here, in that one set of psychological ideas was and continues to be embraced by many social scientists, namely the Freudian and neo-Freudian concepts that were also taken up by the arts and humanities, adopted and transformed by continental philosophy, notably in the work of Jacques Lacan and a legion of other continental thinkers, despite Freudian notions now tending to be viewed as being somewhat anachronistic and largely irrelevant within contemporary psychology.

Having been exposed to this heady mix of ideas, and moving on to postgraduate study, I began to entertain the notion that an adequate and clear understanding of the relationship between individual and society could not be provided by much of the theory I had encountered, worthy though much of that was, and would certainly not be revealed via many of the evidence-free and, as have been regarded, often self-consciously pretentious philosophical musings of postmodern theory that were increasingly in vogue at that time. I, therefore, turned to the 'dark side', wondering whether the answer to some fundamental questions might be much simpler than much of the tortuous and opaque writings on such matters suggested.[7,i] In terms of social order, I came to the straightforward conclusion that we are individually and collectively driven to impose order on our everyday and ongoing experience simply as we tend to find its absence inherently distressing – that is, without a significant sense of clarity and predictability, the world becomes too stressful to navigate for a species ill-equipped to deal with too much complexity and flux.

The idea that there might be something driving us towards imposing some sort of regularity in our experience seems self-evident and, as was noted previously, has been widely understood, with sociologists who did cite psychological sources (again, mainly Freudian) tangentially reasoning that human beings appear to have a preference for life to be at least relatively predictable, where socially acquired expectations will be met and where they can plan ahead with some confidence that the world will correspond to their understanding of it.[8] However, once again, even among those who tentatively pointed towards human tendencies, there was a clear reticence to engage with biology.

As was argued earlier, my own view is that this has been shortsighted at best. In particular, given the growing knowledge of human capacities and tendencies emerging from advances in neuroscience and related disciplines, there is now a wealth of very well-founded evidence that can inform a deeper understanding of the human condition and the societies we have created. Over the last decade or so, this is a pursuit that has begun to engage a small number of social and natural scientists,[9] while key aspects of my own voyage into this emerging field are set out in what follows.

Mapping the world

A starting point for exploring a fresh approach to understanding the relationship between the individual and society, and the processes underlying social regularities and institutions, begins from the very simple premise that in order to adaptively engage with the world, we need to retain an internal representation of what it's like and how we relate to what's out there. The brain, together with the sensory input and physical output of the body, is where we human beings reside. We are in essence our brains and bodies.

---

i   This refers to my long-held suspicion that when academics have run out of good ideas, or had none in the first place, they either resort to theory-free empiricism or will otherwise engage in elaborate and obscure language games to conceal their absence. See also Billig, M. (2013) *Learn to Write Badly: How to Succeed in the Social Sciences*, Cambridge: Cambridge University Press.

Despite that, numerous social scientists persistently go to great lengths to challenge the notion that there is nothing more to us than this, and also to undermine the constraints and tendencies that follow from observing that we are inherently biological entities. This is a position that has been motivated by some of the aversion to biological explanation noted earlier, and by a consequent unwillingness to accept that what we can be has biological limitations and bounds. In short, for many there must be something more, a notion that has informed a wide range of positions in many guises, which have sought to present us as something more than the sum of our biological parts or to externalize processes that are rooted within us.

Firstly, of course, there is the longstanding religious view that we are in essence *souls* that have a kind of quasi-tether to the body and brain that concludes when we die and the soul moves on, to the celestial plain or, for some, to inhabit another body. Later propositions tended to draw a distinction between *mind* and brain, implying that the two were, once more, related but not the same thing. While the vagueness of the concept of mind (a more scientific formulation of the soul?), and the emergence of greater understanding of the brain has challenged these types of ideas, they continue to emerge in other forms.

While some would undoubtedly argue with my characterization of these latter-day escapes from the human = brain/body position, my view is that a new form of this kind of thinking has re-emerged with what has been referred to as '4e' cognition (embodied, embedded, enacted and extended cognition).

'4e' cognition: from the moderate to the 'out there'

Effectively, 4e cognition is a further step, albeit one taken seriously by the scientific community, in arguing that we are more than our brains. It is a set of ideas that are often difficult to pin down, given the broad range of perspectives that have been advanced in this area. In its more moderate formulations, as will be discussed later on, some premises of the so-called 4e approach are compatible with the ideas I'm presenting here, particularly those that do not appear to depart very substantially from standard cognitive science understandings of the human condition. However, more contentiously, the approach has produced a broad spectrum of perspectives that seek to argue that not only does the mind extend beyond the brain, which in some limited senses is perfectly plausible, but also call into question the notion of internal representations in the brain as being central to our engagement with the world.[10]

Firstly, in terms of *embodied* cognition, there is absolutely no argument with the notion that the body contributes to what we're thinking, as emotion and sensory experiences evidently generate bodily states that affect cognition and vice versa. For example, when we feel angry, anxious or happy, it is evidently the interaction between brain and body that contributes to our overall experience. It is also the case that this connection between brain and body runs deep, as there is an important bidirectional pathway between the brain and gut, mainly via the *vagus nerve*.[11] In a sense, we really do have *gut feelings*, as what we think can affect the gut and its microbiome (the vast collection of micro-organisms that inhabit the digestive tract), while the composition of our microbiome can reciprocally influence our thoughts and emotions by affecting the chemical neurotransmitters that stimulate activity in the cells of the brain and body: 'Gut bacteria both produce and respond to the same neurochemicals – such as GABA, serotonin, norepinephrine, dopamine, acetylcholine and melatonin – that the brain uses to regulate mood and cognition.'[12]

This is an important discovery that placed new focus on our experiences and our diet, as this can affect the way we think and feel in ways not previously contemplated. Crucially, it has implications for understanding the way in which the gut/brain axis interacts in response to stress.[13] However, this does not dispense with the fact that we build, understand and reflect on such experiences via the construction and application of internal representations.

The second aspect of 4e cognition, *embedded* cognition, relates to the fact that our cognition is closely bound up with the environments in which we find ourselves. Once more, in its milder form, this proposition seems relatively uncontroversial, in that our thinking and experiences can often be understood to be 'situated'. Again, my view is that this is pretty self-evident and, in fact, as I will argue later on, the relationship between how we think about the world and the physical environment we occupy may be understated, a situation that has further interesting implications for understanding how our worldview and sense of who we are can shift depending on where we are located.

Enactivism, in turn, is a position – in fact, more a range of positions – that further advances the notion that our cognitive processes emerge from our dynamic, physical interaction with the world, shaping our understanding of it and, in turn, impacting on that environment. Some aspects of this way of thinking also seem plausible to a limited extent and are broadly consistent with ideas related to evolutionary niche construction discussed later on, and with some aspects of my own approach as outlined subsequently. That being said, however, the more controversial enactivist notion that we might dispense with the need for internal models (representations) of the world in order to engage with it seems much less persuasive, particularly when applied to higher-order thought processes and reflection.[14]

Perhaps the most contentious aspect of 4e cognition is *extended cognition*, the claim that the mind extends beyond the brain and body, into the environment, other people and the various props/tools we use to aid our thinking. In terms of the environment and other people, as was noted earlier, of course there is a constant ongoing dialogue between us, where we are and who and what we encounter, which constantly impacts on what we're thinking and shapes us over time. However, this does not alter the fact that there is a distinction between our internal thought processes and reflections and what happens externally. Having a dialogue does not mean that those engaged in it are no longer separate entities, as even those closest to us are not privy to many if not most of our internal, subjective thoughts. Even more contentious is the notion that the tools/supports we use can be considered as part of the mind, the *extended* mind thesis (EMT), a proposition notably espoused by Andy Clark and David Chalmers in 1998, and which can be regarded as an important contribution to the 4e cognition debate as a whole.[15]

The argument here is that when we use props to augment our thinking, the latter may be regarded as being in a sense part of the mind. For example, if we can imagine part of a computer being implanted in our skulls and attached to the brain, then we might consider this to be part of mind and, thus, it follows that just because props to mind and cognition are external, this is no reason to insist that we should not regard them in much the same way. However, I would argue that the problem lies with the suggested parity between the external and internal, in that it misrepresents the nature of the relationship here, falling foul of the same problem suggested earlier by understating the distinction between and nature of what's outside and what's going on inside our heads.

As Jerry Fodor has argued, the connectedness between tools and supports and what's going on internally is incorrectly overstated. Here he argues that using notebooks or external devices such as smartphones to record and store information does not make the latter parts of mind, given that they lack the internal intentionality and representations that are its essential components. As Fodor suggests: 'Externalism needs internalism; but not vice versa. External representation is a side-show; internal representation is ineliminably the main event.'[16]

It is only fair to suggest that Clark and Chalmers draw a distinction between cognition and consciousness, as it would surely be a nonsense to imply that the external environment, and other people, could also be regarded as being part of our consciousness. In this way, the mind can only be seen to be extended in a limited sense, while the idea does not seem to stand up to closer scrutiny. This is a view that was reinforced when viewing a 2018 interview with Andy Clark in conversation with Robert Lawrence Kuhn on the latter's YouTube channel, 'Closer to Truth'.[17] The impression gained from their discussion was that Andy Clark seemed more equivocal regarding the defence of his own ideas than expected. His concluding point, citing the example of a patient with memory impairment who used a mobile phone to record and recount important information, was to seemingly propose that regarding the latter as an example of extended mind rather than just tool use might be an ethical issue. While in a sense this is admirable and compassionate, and on those grounds is a position with which I might have some sympathy, but from a purely objective standpoint it does not alter the ontological distinction between the subject and object of use, and the fact that it is the subject's internal and intentional deployment of acquired representations that employs external sources simply as a prop and aid to the latter. Given the foregoing, it is perhaps no surprise that the model set out here departs from at least the more contentious claims of this overall approach.

The Social Map

My own approach starts from a few basic considerations, placing the brain and representations at the centre of our engagement with the world, while also recognizing the important contribution of embodiment discussed earlier. The starting point is the recognition that the human brain did not develop anew, but was built on earlier capacities (this will be discussed in more depth later on) through the long process of our evolution and, as such, some of the capabilities we currently employ have foundations we share with species further down the evolutionary chain:

> [B]rain evolution is basically conservative, and certain systems, especially those that have been generally useful for our survival and have been around for a long time, have been preserved in their basic structure and function.[18]

> … each species has its own specializations that enable it to fit into its unique ecological niche; but common ancestry results in structural (e.g., brain) and functional (e.g., memory) processes that are remarkably similar between humans and nonhumans.[19]

One initial assumption concerned how we create the internal representations of the world discussed earlier. I approached this from the point of view of what we, and indeed other animals, primarily need to do in order to adapt to and negotiate the physical world. Evidently, basic to survival is a requirement for us to recall a map of our environment, and it's now clear that many other animals do this – even honeybees are suggested to retain a cognitive map of their local area to find their way around.[20]

I initially became interested in how we managed this very basic aspect of cognition and memory formation as an undergraduate on discovering that the hippocampus, a key structure of the brain's limbic system, is centrally involved in both locating and allowing us to negotiate physical space, and is also a key structure involved in the formation and recall of the episodic and sematic memories that constitute our inner worldview.[21] From this I came to the view that both of these functions were likely to be inextricably linked to the extent that our understanding and recall of who we are and how and where we fit in was likely a vastly elaborate extension of the foundational capacity to map our environment. It was with this in mind that I called my own model *The Social Map*. This is a perspective that is now supported by a growing body of evidence.[22]

Feel for the game

Emotion clearly also plays a pivotal role in our everyday functioning and memory formation, social and otherwise, and in humans this is also founded on early adaptive capacities. One structure,[ii] the amygdala, among the emotional areas located in the brain's limbic system, plays a key role in our adaptive responses and memory formation. The amygdala was once thought to be mainly associated with fear, anger and preparing the body for appropriate action (invoking the so-called 'fight or flight' response). However, this structure is also understood to have a wider function in assisting in the appraisal of experience and associated responses. The amygdala is centrally involved in an emotion system that mediates both *emotional arousal*, our degree of physiological stimulation, and *emotional valence* (the extent to which stimulation provokes pleasant or unpleasant feelings), the inherent function of which, as was noted earlier, is to assist us in safely and advantageously adapting to experience.[23]

The amygdala is also present in other mammals, ranging from rodents to other primates, underlining that human emotional capacities also have long evolutionary roots. The amygdala functions in conjunction with associated areas of the brain (see Figure 1.1), stimulating the hippocampus in the forming of long-term memories relating to significant experiences that should be recorded for future reference.[24] Initially, this would have been in the form of adding survival relevant memories to the map. In humans, however, these capacities have once more been extended, bringing into play other regions of our more developed neurological capacities to build an inner world of rich topographic, semantic, episodic as well as procedural memories that involve other brain regions and that enable our engagement with a complex world.

As we know, human beings also have a rich conscious awareness and ability to manipulate internalized information, reflecting on their inner and outer experiences and coordinating their action purposefully. A number of brain regions contribute to this capacity for conscious awareness and attention, which is described as involving a 'concerto' of neural engagement.

[ii] In fact, the amygdala is actually comprised of two bilateral structures, but it is customary to refer to them as one structure.

Figure 1.1: Key neural structures associated with *The Social Map* model

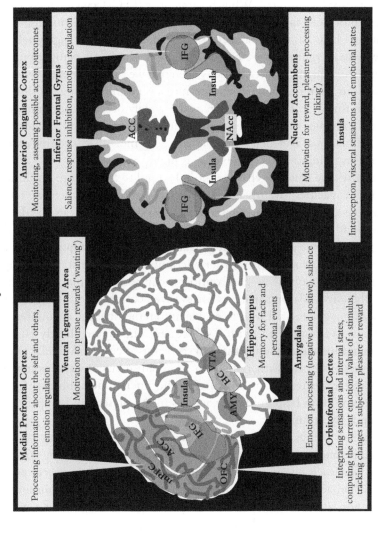

Source: Dolcos, S., Moore, M. and Katsumi, Y. (2018) 'Neuroscience and well-being', in E. Diener, S. Oishi and L. Tay (eds), *Handbook of Well-Being*. Salt Lake City, UT: DEF Publishers.

The hippocampus (episodic and semantic memory formation, recall and spatial orientation) and the amygdala and the other areas indicated previously (emotion, action, and evaluating experience and memory) and, critically, the neocortex and the prefrontal cortex (PFC), with the PFC thought to be the central locus of working memory, the 'executive', where conscious attention, thought and planning are centrally located, all appear to be particularly important (see Figure 1.1).[25] While the executive (PFC) facilitates higher-level thought processes, there is a critical issue in terms of its functioning which it is argued here has manifest social significance, and is also highly relevant to the central arguments presented throughout the book. Simply put, the executive has a highly limited capacity such that we can only hold a few items in conscious awareness and pay attention to a very limited range of things at any given time.[26] For example, there is the widely observed notion that we can hold only plus or minus seven numbers/digits in working memory at a time.[27] Similarly, as is evident, our ability to keep more than a couple of ideas or thoughts in mind at any given time is highly restricted.[28]

This raises the issue of what we should attend to and devote our limited conscious capacities towards at any given time, and this is where we return to the role of emotion and memory. The amygdala helps us to identify and respond to likely candidates for future attention and stimulates that attention when we encounter them again, while also prompting the recall of memories associated with earlier encounters. In our past, for example, the emotions involved in confronting a dangerous animal would have led to the amygdala preparing us for evasive action while stimulating the hippocampus and related areas to enable us to remember the encounter, and likely how we responded, with a subsequent encounter quickly eliciting similar emotions and bringing these to conscious attention. A similar process also comes into play with respect to more advantageous and potentially pleasurable experiences (also involving the nucleus accumbens). In this way our emotions help guide our actions in the present and prepare us to act adaptively in future.

As human beings also have the capacity to draw connections between experiences and to generalize, the type of scenario just described by no means implies that each encounter would need to be identical in every respect, but only broadly similar. In this way, human beings identify meaningful information and encounters based on past experience building a general template of their world and how they might engage with it, with the latter having important implications of its own that are addressed in what follows.

Communication, categorization and mapping

As we know, our highly developed ability to communicate also allows us to short circuit first-hand, trial-and-error methods of acquiring knowledge, as we gain understanding of features of our world vicariously from our parents and a range of others from birth. In the modern world, of course, this process involves engaging with a much broader and more varied range of social and cultural threats and opportunities than were presented to our ancestors, the implications of which will be discussed in relation to many of the topics in the following chapters. It is also the case that the particular perspectives we internalize will be shaped by our personal experiences and by our culture, religion, ethnicity, gender and socioeconomic (class) background. It is in this way that we begin to build the elaborate inner representation of our world in long-term memory, *The Social Map*, that enables us to identify what is meaningful and to deal with what we encounter without dealing with it anew. In addition, it is not only our perspectives on the world and our view of how we fit in that are shaped via this process, but also the particularities of how we move, our physical postures and gestures, and the accent with which we speak.

Of course, there is nothing novel in any of these observations in and of themselves, as there are numerous depictions as to the way in which we identify, classify, categorize, internalize and deploy our stock of knowledge. We learn and remember what's important in our world, including what to avoid or fight what's unpleasant or dangerous, and to pursue and also recall and accommodate what's potentially pleasant and enjoyable, building a rich framework to guide our experience and action; so what? The reader may be forgiven at this point for questioning the need to engage with biology at all to understand what's going on here. However, and as I hope will be made clear as we progress, approaching an understanding of some of the biological mechanisms facilitating our social development and engagement not only offers potential for more grounded explanation, while avoiding some of the prior and current misconceptions discussed earlier, but also opens us up to potential new insights regarding many aspects of social, economic and political life that have remained relatively opaque or highly contested thus far.

Relating to the world: habit, routine and control

A key issue here relates to the limited capacity of the PFC noted earlier, in that the demands on our attention are always in danger of being overwhelmed and, as will be discussed in the subsequent chapters, this has been particularly the case since the onset of modernity. The processing demands placed on the executive are what psychologists often refer to as cognitive load.[29] It is the case that we are constantly managing our limited capacity for conscious attention. The way in which we do this is that well-practised routines, familiar practices and experiences build such strong neural circuitry that they can operate on the verges of conscious awareness, if we're aware of them at all.

This is what I think the more enthusiastic enactivists misconceive, where they cite highly habitualized thought and action as evidence that we don't require internalized models of the world to engage with it, when in fact the speed at which we can call upon the latter and the assumed lack of conscious attention required may simply reflect the fact that what started as something that required conscious attention has become so neurologically *engrained* that it operates at the periphery of conscious awareness. For example, we learn to walk and once that initial learning takes place, we may instigate the action consciously or semi-consciously while we don't need to think about the mechanics of the action itself.

On pain of labouring this point, activities that are more specific and picked up much later – for example, learning to type, playing a musical instrument or driving a car – follow a similar process. Driving provides a good example. As learners, we have to concentrate and pay very close attention to the complex set of actions involved, to the extent that (and particularly with European manual gearshifts) many of us feel that we'll never come to coordinate and accommodate to these tasks. And yet, once acquired, seasoned drivers, as with my own experience, will travel for miles negotiating traffic lights, stop signs and different speed limits while our conscious attention is mainly focused elsewhere, often listening to the radio or the incessant internal conversation that goes on in our heads with often only minimal recall of the journey, as this takes place at a very low level of conscious awareness. We may only become consciously aware of the journey, or indeed our driving, if something of note or unusual happens along the way. The reason is that we have practised these kinds of activities and corresponding actions so frequently that they have been neurologically and physically embodied such that they have become, in a sense, almost like walking or breathing. They become 'second nature' to us. While much of what I've described relates to what's referred to as motor memory, principally involving the basal ganglia and cerebellum, it seems reasonable to assume that our internalization and negotiation of the familiar aspects of social life operate much like this. This view was informed by my introduction to Gerald Edelman's Neural Darwinist perspective as an undergraduate: that significant and recurrent experiences are reflected in changes to the structure of the brain, with those most enduring and routinely activated forming resilient synaptic connections.[30] This perspective was also informed by Craik and Lockhart's observation that what becomes most enduringly engrained in memory is that which has been subjected to the deepest levels of processing.[31]

This allows us to conduct the ordinary business of daily living with less thought and attention so long as what goes on broadly meets with our expectations and fits with what is familiar; we hive off the basic, the routine and habitual to neural circuits that develop to a degree that they function semi-independently of executive control. As will be discussed later on, this raises a range of issues when we consider how we negotiate the demands of modern societies. However, before engaging with these issues directly, there is an important observation to be made here in terms of the emotional dimension to this process.

Our sense of feeling safe and in control rests on us being fairly confident that we can comfortably identify and deal with the demands that are presented to us at any given point. As was noted earlier, this applies to circumstances previously tagged as meaningful and important (positive and negative) as well as to new and unfamiliar experiences and situations, brought to our attention by the emotional arousal stimulated by the amygdala and associated structures. Given that our cognitive and emotional capacities, as noted previously, have developed in such a way that their primary purpose is to keep us safe and to identify opportunities and dangers, anything new or unexpected in relation to the map we've internalized could be either an unanticipated threat or a potentially missed opportunity.

What is critically important in all of this is that we're not presented with more than our limited capacity for conscious attention can handle at any given time, that we feel capable of dealing with important situations as they arise and at a relatively comfortable pace, and that we are able to identify and accommodate to the unexpected to a degree that we're not overwhelmed. This allows us to feel that life is under a degree of control and can be fairly safely negotiated; that we can largely rely on our well-practised responses to get us through.

By contrast, too many simultaneous demands on our attention readily present themselves as unmanageable threats or potentially missed opportunities, both of which are experienced as life not being under our control – an unpleasant experience almost regardless as to the nature of what is generating it. This is why psychologists have long recognized that too many novel experiences and life changes – sometimes positive as well as negative, albeit with the latter having greater impact – contribute to stress. This may be adaptive in the short term, but raises a wide range of issues where stress is severe and/or experienced on an ongoing basis. As we know, we also get stressed when we are presented with experiences that are ambiguous, incoherent and which generally conflict with our internalized expectations, when we feel unsure of our ground and how to proceed.

The individual and The Social Map

A further critical aspect of the processes described here is the relationship between our internalized worldview and our view of who we are as individuals, our sense of self. This is evidently an immense topic of itself that has spawned a vast range of writings and perspectives, some of which will be engaged with throughout this book, and here we can only address key points. However, what is important to point out is that our understanding of who we are is very evidently bound up with our understanding of the world; of what's out there. *The Social Map* is relational, where our self-perception and worldview develop in tandem; it is indeed embedded.

Individual self-identity evidently develops from what a person knows about the world, and how they apply meaning and understandings from their culture and environment to construct a view of themselves, and how they relate to their environment and to the other people they encounter. In turn, how other people react to us, and the ideas they express, can evidently either reinforce or challenge our thoughts about our world and ourselves.[32] The strong investment in the coherence and continuity of these internalized constructs means that this has to be managed as we go about our day to day business, as *we have a deep-seated desire to have both our worldview and presentation of who we think we are generally accepted*. Significant challenges produce the negative emotional arousal described previously, introducing uncertainty about who we are, whether our judgements as to how things will play out in a range of situations are reasonably sound and, therefore, whether we should feel confident or apprehensive regarding how we manage future social situations.

Belonging to the tribe

On the issue of acceptance, as well as being taken to be an affirmation of who we are and what we think, this may also hark back to very deep-seated anxieties about being ignored, rejected or excluded. We are social creatures, whose evolution and survival was largely reliant on the solidarity, support and collective action of the group. This is also a critical part of our constitution, as the evolution of our complex verbal and nonverbal communication and highly developed capacity for facial expression is testament to the importance that social interaction has played in our development. Reflecting on this, our ancestors would have had a very strong interest in being accepted and even admired, and having their understanding of their world confirmed, as the former would have enhanced the likelihood of survival (access to food and potential mates), while the latter would have conferred confidence in their capacity to survive. While conditions have substantially changed, in modern societies it's now social and economic 'survival' and prosperity that depends on these factors, but, crucially, with a broadly similar emotional impact.

An important outcome of all of this is that, in general and as identified by numerous writers, we exhibit a preference for routine, habit, coherence, relative predictability and order, entailing that the world makes sense to us – that we can readily identify, relate to and deal with what we encounter, including other people, with reasonable ease and sense of safety.[33] It is perhaps not difficult to see why this would be a deep-seated and adaptive orientation. The more our experiences match with what we know, the less we're going to be faced with having to work out what's going on, how to proceed, or to go through the task of reframing our view of ourselves and our world.

It has been suggested that most human beings find comfort and even meaning and satisfaction in habit and routine, while this is also associated with belonging and conformity to a similar group where we can experience a sense of coherence, safety and community. All of this also reduces *cognitive load*, where we feel that we can connect with, understand and trust those around us, as their broad similarity and conformity entails that we feel that we can comprehend their behaviour and anticipate their actions, and they ours. This is evidently a further deep-seated feature of the processes described here that applies to interpersonal relations. I have described this tendency towards conformity being imposed and sustained (this will be discussed in more depth later on) in terms of *reciprocal restraint* and *reciprocal reinforcement*, where we make demands on each other through, respectively, negative and positive sanctions and rewards.[34] The need to do this can also be clearly appreciated if one considers a scenario where we imagined that the full gamut of potentially unchecked human behaviour might be encountered at any time. Everyday life would be very precarious indeed. Any sense of stability in human relations is only possible because this is not generally the case, as for the most part we present recognizable performances to each other, in line with mutually understood social meanings, characteristics and scripts, reducing the potential complexity of social life and our engagement with it.[35]

In a sense, we are all stereotypes and for social life to function smoothly we have to be. Stereotyping in one sense can, of course, be prejudicial, but in a more general sense readily identifiable appearances and role play are demanded of us in societies of strangers if we want to be accepted and to meet with others' approval. One of the first questions I regularly ask the hundreds of first-year students at the beginning of each academic year is to stand up 'if they're an individual'. Invariably, given the cultural emphasis on individualism in many contemporary societies (as is particularly prevalent in Anglo-American culture), most do, only to be asked to sit down as 'they're going to find out why they can't be'!

Diversity, values and morality

Following on from the preceding discussion, it seems to logically follow that our desire for coherence, consistency and manageable change would lead us to wanting to limit engagement with people who either don't appear to support our ideas and presented characteristics (instigating uncomfortable *map challenges*) and, conversely, to seek out and establish relationships with those who do. This certainly appears to be the case to an extent. We're also likely to trust people if they appear to be like us. This is something that is well understood by many sales organizations who may advise their salespeople to subtly mimic the body language, accents and, even for some, elements of the interests and back story of those with whom their doing business:[36]

> Humans are helpful or hurtful toward others based on perceived similarity to themselves. As adults, this like-me psychology manifests itself as in-group favoritism across a variety of contexts and cultures (Mullen et al. 1992). This favoritism results in a high degree of tolerance toward in-group members that facilitates unique forms of collaboration and conformity (Burton-Chellew & West 2012, Kurzban et al. 2015). In contrast, ostracism and lethal aggression among hunter gatherers primarily targets nonconformist or out-group members (Boehm et al. 1993, Wrangham 1999). This type of antisocial or agonistic response is facilitated by the readiness of humans to dehumanize out-group members or those that dehumanize their own in-group (Hodson et al. 2014, Kteily et al. 2016).[37]

All of this arises in the modern urban setting as we need to be able to feel relatively secure that we can infer what other people are like and, crucially, that we can anticipate how they're likely to behave. This is a key element of Erving Goffman's famous works on social interaction, *The Presentation of Self in Everyday Life*[38] and *Stigma: Notes on the Management of Spoiled Identity*[39] and *Relations in Public*.[40] Goffman places emphasis on describing the importance of predictable appearances, in terms of social presentation, performance and interaction, as the bedrocks of social order, a scenario which my own model seeks to explain more fully in relation to our neurology and biology. In those terms, as suggested previously, we engage with the routines of social life mainly at a relatively low level of consciousness, alerted by the activation of the amygdala and related areas when aroused by the matching of an occurrence with a previously significant or, indeed, when encountering a novel experience. Otherwise, to avoid cognitive load, we tend to screen out the presence of others, employing what Goffman called 'civil inattention' or what the early urban sociologist Georg Simmel called the 'blasé attitude'.[41] A good demonstration of this is where we have to be in close proximity to others we don't know, such as in a lift or on a crowded tube – there is a tacit prohibition on eye contact and talking unless we're subtly invited to engage or where we share the experience of something out of the ordinary occurring that provides us with a common cause to break the ice. Otherwise, ignoring strangers is a device employed to keep the overloading of our attentional capacities at bay, particularly as we have come to inhabit potentially overwhelming modern urban environments. This phenomenon has also been documented in a wide range of works and is supported by evidence indicating that those raised and living in urban environments are prone to greater amygdala activity than inhabitants of more peaceful and less populous rural settings.[42] Cognitive load is also associated with sensory load, where the latter, by definition, relates to being overwhelmed by sensory stimuli, while both excess task demands and sensory overload are potentially prevalent in modern and particularly urban settings.

This is something to which I will return towards the end of this chapter and throughout the later chapters, but the preceding point also has a bearing on the broader tacit rules that govern modern living, which in many ways intensify some of the processes described thus far. For example, in traditional small-scale settlements, social values and norms of conduct were commonly shared and fairly well understood within communities who may have known each other since birth and perhaps over generations. Such communities would also tend to accept and adhere to various aspects of a broadly shared *map*, given the lesser exposure to people and ideas who might fundamentally challenge their own. In such a scenario, people could rely on informal rules of conduct and, as there were unlikely to be many encounters with individuals from outside the community, as such, there would be less chance of being presented with unsettling map challenges. By contrast, large and densely populated settlements have the potential to regularly test our capacities. Moreover, the impact of shifting life events which evidently become more prevalent in dynamic, populous societies further compounds the burden of dealing with the preceding discussion. More recently, the advent of the web and social media, as will be addressed in Chapter 8, has also added a new and disconcerting burden in this regard.

Achieving balance and control

The preceding discussion may seem a fairly logical and simple outcome of our biosocial proclivities. Given our limited tolerance to complexity and change, if we could only ditch or evade much of the variation, the vague, the disconcerting and the unpredictable, then lives of ease and tranquility would presumably be achievable. To some extent, this would appear an attractive prospect for many harried modern citizens and, as suggested, most of us in the main exhibit a preference for predictability and a significant element of routine in our experiences. But it is important to note that this is only the case up to a point and is by no means the whole story.

There is evidently another side to this equation, where too much routine and lack of variation generates its own problematic issues. It would not be a revelation to point out that where we are consistently greeted with similarity, stultifying routine and a general lack of stimulation, we may in the short term feel a sense of calm and peace. However, where this persists, sooner or later we are likely to experience a variety of negative feelings ranging from mild boredom to deeper feelings of emptiness and frustration. This is because just as we can feel unnerved by more stimulation and experiences than we feel we can accommodate, we nonetheless require a certain level of stimulation and variation to render life meaningful and interesting. Creativity and personal growth also depend on us at least encountering new ideas and experiences that might be novel or challenging to an extent.

Given that emotional stimulation is involved in drawing our attention to variation in our environment and experiences, helping us to identify and recall the contours of our world, a lack of stimulation and experience can actually be as unnerving as overstimulation. Referring to the spatial roots of memory formation described earlier, without difference we simply don't know where we are. If we think of the confusion that presents us when we enter undifferentiated urban landscapes, the inability to find our bearings can leave us feeling at a loss as to how to proceed, which is no less bewildering than when we encounter chaotic settings. It is argued here that similar emotions may be elicited by invariant routine, as we're removed from the ebb and flow required to feel alive and engaged with the world around us. As such, being pushed too far out of our comfort zone towards either of these polarities, and feeling that we lack the capacity and autonomy to find a way out, is a fundamentally anxiety-producing experience. It's also the case that these feelings are compounded when we feel little sense of *control* over our circumstances – that is, having a sense of perceived control provides a crucial prop to our emotional wellbeing, which has a clear bearing on how we experience a range of experiential challenges.[43]

It might also be noted here that, at the other end of this spectrum, when thinking about 'risk takers', life's 'adrenaline junkies', a key element of this conduct appears to rest on their perception that they retain an element of predictability and control regarding the risks they confront. This is a critical observation with respect to the arguments set out in the succeeding chapters, in that a lack of control, clarity and consistency in terms of our engagement with the world and each other, and the pervasive effects of an unstable, unjust and unpredictable socioeconomic environment appears to be at the root of many of our current social ills and wider collective malaise. By contrast, we are also impacted by the negative emotional experience of significant and persistent underarousal when consigned to unremitting organizational routinization, social isolation and invariant routines, while an optimal state seems to be between these two polarities, with some individual differences coming into play as to where this optimum level sits for each of us. This balancing act was broadly characterized by Csikszentmihalyi in his analysis of 'flow'– what we might colloquially refer to being 'in the zone', where we feel a sense of security together with controlled and comfortable stimulation.[44] However, it is when we feel that life seems out of control and the swings and roundabouts buffet us to the edges of anxiety (and at times ennui) that trouble ensues, particularly where such experiences persist, that we begin to experience profound problems in coping and adjusting, accompanied by chronic levels of negative emotional arousal, and with a range of personal and social consequences. Overall, what is important is that we can approach life's challenges from a relatively stable standpoint, and at a manageable pace, that we can accommodate to experience without being overwhelmed and without too much unnerving dissonance, and that we can find a comfort zone between angst and stultifying despair.

Why this matters

So far, the reader might be excused for wondering what all of the preceding discussion has to do with the diverse range of topics covered in this book, from work and markets to climate change, consumerism, social media, politics and so on. However, what is critical here is that the aim is to offer a fuller understanding of the social, economic and political conditions we've created and how we're affected by them at the deepest level. A central argument here is that we have created a world, particularly since the neoliberal turn, that for many of us fails to meet, and in fact critically undermines, the very fundamental basic human needs outlined here, destabilizing and overloading us. Evidently, of course, some would go to great lengths to argue that it is through confronting challenges and adversity that we grow, as individuals and as a species, while as was noted earlier, there is some truth in that. However, the consistent mantra of the neoliberal right tends to overemphasize one side of this equation while ignoring the critical importance of the other.

In the first instance, longstanding evidence suggests that we are more likely to engage in moderate, calculated risk taking and creative activity when we do so from a position of relative security; as John Bowlby once described it, from a 'secure base'.[45] As to significant and precarious exposure to risks – social, economic and otherwise – as suggested in the Introduction, those who make the most of espousing and dispensing this 'medicine', advocating its benefits for others, often go to very great lengths to avoid either experiencing it for themselves or administering it to their offspring. This is reflected in the resistance to real competition, progressive income, and the wealth and inheritance taxes that might reduce the increasing insulation around those at the top of the socioeconomic pile as inequalities have widened. The argument presented here is that with the current return to societies increasingly divided between have and have nots, where those at the top have become ever more detached from an insecure and anxious mass, we are currently in a period where we are increasingly losing our way and need to understand how we arrived here, how we are affected by the conditions we've created, and how we might learn from the experience and find a better way forward. However, as is argued in the subsequent chapters, human history is a story of alternating periods of progress, stasis and regression, with shifts often taking place quite radically and abruptly, where periods of stasis and reversal endure until they are widely recognized as such and where remedial action is developed to move us onwards onto a better track.

As well as the widely observed relationship between insecurity, inequality and negative individual and social outcomes, two key further issues of fundamental significance will be addressed in the following chapters that have not been identified thus far. I want to discuss each of these areas in turn as a means of pointing towards their origins and effects, as these disrupt our present and threaten to disfigure our future. The first is a concept that I have advanced and entitled *primalization*.[iii,46]

Primalization

Through the concept of *primalization*, I aim to offer some deeper understanding of the current trend towards seemingly emotionally driven, angry, fearful, fatalistic and broadly irrational conduct that has become a growing phenomenon across our societies. This is evidenced in a wide range of social ills, from angry interpersonal conflict (both online and offline), personal angst across a wide range of issues, substance abuse and engagement with bizarre ideas and conspiracy theories to the embracing of radically problematic political agendas. This is by no means an exhaustive list. The process I describe here may be regarded as a source of the political instability and even the growing geopolitical tensions that have pierced the bubble of longstanding assumptions that we might be moving towards a more stable politically and economically integrated world order. While the more detailed causes and precise consequences of this growing malaise are teased out in the following chapters, these effects are underpinned by the way in which a societally induced state of negative emotional arousal is impacting not just on many people's emotions and wellbeing, but also on their capacity for reasoned thought and action.[47]

It has been widely observed that stress narrows the focus of our attention.[48] This makes immediate sense if we consider that it's adaptive for us to focus and screen out extraneous details when faced with a stressful or, indeed, dangerous situation, and potentially some that appear positive but are perceived as being particularly important. Stripped of the few props that once enabled people to reasonably negotiate complex modern living with a modicum of control and comfort – stable secure jobs, relatively accessible, secure and affordable housing, and a residual if fragile sense of community and solidarity – in the

---

iii   This term has been employed elsewhere, but in a different context and with a fundamentally different meaning from its employment here. See Gilbertson, R. (2012) *A Free-Range Human in a Caged World: From Primalization into Civilization*, Finagle Watcher.

neoliberal era many have been confronted with conditions that are consistently emotionally draining and overwhelming, while simultaneously being affected in these largely unrecognized ways that further impair their capacity to cope. Map challenges, where our tolerances are exceeded and expectations are regularly contradicted by experience are manifest, and where this regularly arises our ability to confidently rely on our internalized worldview is eroded. Under these kinds of conditions, fear, anger and frustration are never far from the surface. Moreover, as will be discussed later on, these feelings are increasingly amplified and exploited by media and social media corporations that often appeal to peoples' worst fears and enmities (as well as desires) as a means of monetizing their attention, while also become ripe for manipulation by unscrupulous corporations and a rising crop of populist authoritarian politicians. In short, the myriad stressors to which we are exposed in contemporary societies makes it more difficult to approach everyday life in a measured, reasonable and emotionally balanced state, while rendering us more susceptible to manipulation via a range of influences that may appear to offer relief or release in terms of negative feelings.

Further support for this position can be gleaned from Arnsten's work on the negative impact of stress on the functioning of the PFC and its potential to disrupt our higher-level and reflective thought processes and actions, producing a tendency towards more impulsive and emotionally driven thought and action:

> [S]tress impairs higher-order PFC abilities such as working memory and attention regulation. Thus, attention regulation switches from thoughtful 'top-down' control by the PFC that is based on what is most relevant to the task at hand to 'bottom-up' control by the sensory cortices, whereby the salience of the stimulus (for example, whether it is brightly coloured, loud or moving) captures our attention ... Thus, during stress, orchestration of the brain's response patterns switches from slow, thoughtful PFC regulation to the reflexive and rapid emotional responses of the amygdala and related subcortical structures.[49]

In sum, *primalization*, as its name implies, refers to the disruption of our higher-order thought process via the proliferating stressors to which many contemporary publics are exposed, promoting an increasing tendency towards less considered, reflective and more fearful and angry engagement with the world and each other.

Unpredictability and *experiential overload*

As was noted earlier, a central concern in coming to understanding who we are and how we engage with the world is the way in which its complexity, demands, unpredictability and insecurities can readily overwhelm us, largely due to our attentional limitations, with deleterious consequences. This, of course, has been previously recognized and described in a number of ways with a variety of connotations by a wide range of writers, particularly since the advent of modern industrial society and urbanization. Aside from the aforementioned concept of cognitive load, there is the notion of *nervous exhaustion* coined by Georg Simmel in relation to the bewildering experience of early industrial city dwellers,[50] to Émile Durkheim's concept of *anomie*,[51] as a condition of normlessness, and being overwhelmed by societal change and the fragmentation of social connections. These ideas are testament to the fact that these 19th-century writers were very aware of this broad phenomenon, if not its wider and deeper ramifications. More recently, the social psychologist Kenneth Gergen employed the term *multiphrenia* in relation to the proliferating demands of modern living.[52] Sociologist Anthony Giddens also referred to the angst experienced by modern citizens in relation to the concept of *ontological security*, as the psychological need for a sense of continuity in terms of both one's sense of self and the lived environment.[53] In a similar vein, Atchley's *Continuity Theory* describes a condition where 'middle-aged and older adults attempt to preserve and maintain existing internal and external structures; and they prefer to accomplish this objective by using strategies tied to their past experiences of themselves and their social world'.[54]

Allostatic load

A related concept advanced by US neuroscientist Bruce McEwen is especially useful in capturing the impact of complexity and flux over time, where consistent exposure to taxing life events accumulates to impose what he referred to as *allostatic load*.[55] Allostatic load is effectively another way of capturing what I have previously described in terms of chronic cognitive overload, as an inability to manage the persistent demands and negative experiences that destabilize the balance between underarousal and overarousal.[56]

Allostasis refers to our ability to sustain a sense of equilibrium as we adapt to experience, whereas allostatic load (or overload) refers to the testing of our capacity to deal with the variety and cumulative volume of challenges that confront us over time.[57] McEwen suggested that a moderate level of time-limited stress induced by everyday living can be beneficial, providing the stimulation, motivation and capacity to successfully adapt to new experiences in a healthy manner. However, while the latter is consistent with the prior discussion of the need for a balanced state of emotional arousal, more serious and enduring allostatic load impairs not only our capacity to adaptively respond, but may also have epigenetic effects that impact on brain function, mental and, indeed, physical health from childhood and throughout our life course (see Figure 1.2).[58]

Figure 1.2: Social structure, social supports, adversity, toxic stress and brain/body development in childhood

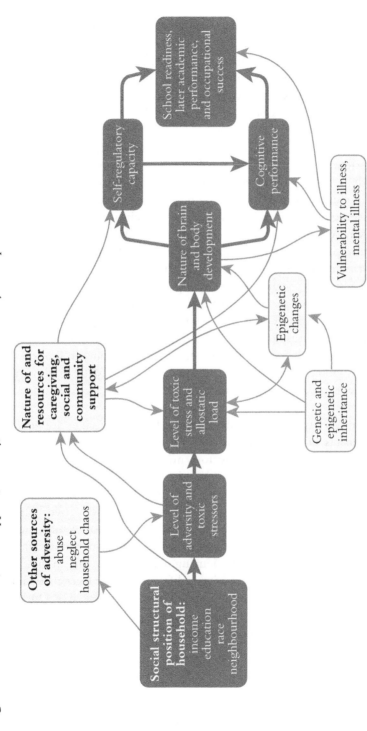

Source: McEwen, C.A. and McEwen, B.S. (2017) 'Social structure, adversity, toxic stress, and intergenerational poverty: an early Childhood Model', *Annual Review of Sociology*, 43: 445–472.

In short, if cognitive overload represents the acute and immediate experience of being overwhelmed by the demands, dangers, insecurities, dissonances and uncertainties of living, then the concept of allostatic load helps to illustrate the difficulties in adjusting to chronic and prolonged stress with life challenges over the longer term, including their cumulative effects for our health and wellbeing when our capacity to adapt and engage is exceeded, while the concept also extends to include some of the damaging means by which we attempt to cope:

> The definition of allostatic load ... reflects the cumulative effect of experiences in daily life that involve ordinary events (subtle and long-standing life situations) as well as major challenges (life events), and also includes the physiological consequences of the resulting health damaging behaviors, such as poor sleep and circadian disruption, lack of exercise, smoking, alcohol consumption and unhealthy diet. When environmental challenges exceed the individual ability to cope, then allostatic overload ensues ... as a transition to an extreme state where stress response systems are repeatedly activated and buffering factors are not adequate ... Situations that may lead to the development of allostatic load/overload are: (a) exposure to frequent stressors that may determine a status of chronic stress and repeated physiological arousal; (b) lack of adaptation to repeated stressors; (c) inability to shut off the stress response after a stressor is terminated; (d) allostatic response not sufficient to deal with the stressor ...[59]

Given the variety of ways of describing what, in my view, are effectively various facets of overwhelming and unbalanced stimulus, for reasons of clarity and simplification going forward, I employ the term *experiential overload* as a shorthand for capturing the multidimensional and temporal aspects of this broad cognitive and emotional phenomenon, encompassing the immediate experience of cognitive and sensory overload (and *nervous exhaustion*), including that now imposed via social media and the web.[60] This also recognizes the longer-term and wider neurological and epigenetic ramifications of experiencing ongoing stress due to difficulty in accommodating to taxing and adverse life events over time that McEwen describes, as well as the 'normlessness' and fugue represented by Durkheim's 'anomie', where the ability to make sense of and negotiate society and to control and constrain one's conduct is also compromised.[61]

Social epigenetics

In terms of the epigenetic ramifications of this critical aspect of the human condition, as Figure 1.2 indicates, our biological and neurological response to experience goes beyond neural plasticity to affect our genetic constitution through epigenetic effects on the brain and body. Originally associated with the biologist Conrad Waddington, who advanced the concept in the 1950s, epigenetics refers to biological changes that affect gene expression in response to experience, both prenatally and throughout life, without altering the genetic sequence (DNA).[62] This has been an area of growing interest that's now no longer confined to biologists and neuroscientists due to the implications for our understanding of some of the deeper issues involved in our engagement with society. As such, a small band of philosophers and political and social scientists have begun to take an interest here.[63] This is one of the important ways in which the environment impacts on people's biological constitution in a bidirectional process where we, both individually and collectively, shape the social and physical environment through our activities, while simultaneously being moulded by our experiences. Hence, what happens to us over time not only impacts on neural plasticity, but also on the way in which our DNA is 'played' and replicated in our cells throughout our lifetimes. An important caveat here, however, is that while this seems in line with the less radical variants of social constructionism, it does not imply the sort of more radical, strong social constructionism mentioned earlier. We are by no means wholly malleable. Waddington proposed that epigenetic changes were *canalized*, such that there could be a range of environmentally influenced changes to an organism's gene expression while still producing a recognizable phenotype, in this case a human being with the usual general attributes. More fundamental alteration of the phenotype occurs only when the impact of an environmental influence is so profound that it has a serious and obvious effect on an organism in terms of birth defects or developmental abnormalities.[64]

Waddington's perspective broadly informs the view proposed here: that our biology is shaped by experience, but within limits defined by our evolutionary inheritance and the general morphological structures associated with our species. In short, through neural plasticity and epigenetics, we shape ourselves as we construct our social environment in that, as we produce an increasingly human-manufactured environment, both physically and culturally, we may be effectively contributing to our own evolution in very small steps. Reciprocally, the way in which we shape our world, and our interaction within it, is also a reflection of limitations and propensities imposed by our biological inheritance. This notion also has some broad resonances with Norbert Elias' concepts of sociogenesis and psychogenesis, where we construct social relations and institutions that feed back to impact on our thinking and emotions and are then expressed through our actions.[65]

This depiction of our relationship with the lived environment has more recently been referred to as *evolutionary niche construction* and can be seen to apply to all creatures that have a significant impact on their environments. For us, the implication is that how we arrange society may well have consequences that go far further than most people, including our political leaders, currently imagine.[66] This is critical in terms of what's been flagged up so far and for what will be discussed through the succeeding chapters, as the stressful conditions we've generated impose changes that go deep. The main mechanisms are suggested to be 'histone modifications, DNA methylation and small RNA (sRNA) inheritance, prions or microbiota'.[67] As Figure 1.2 suggests, these socially induced epigenetic changes not only impact on our mental health, but also on our physical health. Over time, exposure to adverse circumstances, life events and resulting stress can increase our vulnerability to disease and accelerated ageing, an issue to which I will return more explicitly in Chapter 12.[68] In short, many of the observed differences in health and life expectancy that are apparent within and across societies can, at least in part, be associated with the stressors associated with living in increasingly unequal and unforgiving neoliberal societies. However, despite the seriousness of this observation, it still fails to fully capture the extent of these effects. New understandings of intergenerational inheritance also have further highly significant implications, in that epigenetic changes can also confer disadvantage across generations, passing on adverse reactions to inhospitable conditions and negative life experiences, such as those associated with trauma and chronic stress.[69]

On a more positive note, epigenetic changes can often be reversible if conditions change significantly. Nonetheless, it has to be borne in mind that continuing exposure to adverse social conditions may have an impact on individuals and, if widespread enough, potentially even on our species over the longer term.[70] While this is contentious, its implications are so important that it is surely something with which we must engage and explore, and so critical are these developments that they have begun to call into question how the very process of human evolution itself has been understood.

The Extended Evolutionary Synthesis?

Consistent with these recent understandings regarding plasticity, niche construction and epigenetics described earlier, an interesting revisionist understanding of evolutionary processes, a new thesis termed the *Extended Evolutionary Synthesis* (EES) has challenged both the randomness and timeframes associated with the long-accepted account of human evolution; the Modern Synthesis (MS). On this first point, the EES critiques the notion that evolution is a process where wholly random genetic mutations increase the fitness of members of a species in particular environments, making it more likely that those gene carriers will survive, prosper and pass on those genes to subsequent generations. By contrast, EES takes account of the niche construction and epigenetic processes described previously – that many species (and not just humans) have an impact on their environments to a degree that suggests a co-evolutionary process where each shapes the other over time. In addition, in this view, evolutionary process can be directional, with epigenetic modifications arising within individual lifetimes being passed on to succeeding generations. In this view, evolutionary adaptations can be more rapid. Moreover, the EES model presents these more rapid adaptations as being potentially positive for a species in relation to their environmental niche.[71] However, if the preceding point is accepted, the implications are profound in terms of the shaping of our own evolutionary trajectory. In light of what has been argued previously, under the influence of neoliberalism's regressive impact on the social, economic and indeed physical environment, we can be seen to be shaping our own evolutionary niche in a direction that may well be highly negative for the health, wellbeing and fitness not just of current generations, but also of future generations and, if this persists for long enough, perhaps even for humanity more broadly and over the longer term.

On a final note, pulling many of the themes discussed earlier together: as suggested, key drivers of human conduct, at the individual, interpersonal and wider collective levels, can be understood by the need to make sense of, simplify, classify, routinize and achieve a sense of balance and control in terms of our engagement with the world. At the root of this process is the desire to avoid the negative feelings that result from our limits being tested and the world failing to meet with our expectations, together with an aversion to conditions where we fail to find meaning and a sense of our own significance. The drive to understand what confronts us, to control others, to impose sanctions on members of the community who challenge our internalized 'maps' and even the desire to exclude, conquer or expunge those who do not share and support our worldview and everyday norms, ideals and practices can be understood through this lens, as can a great deal of our historical development, including many of our current troubles. This includes the way in which we are motivated, if not driven, to persuade or at times impose our worldview on others, and particularly those who individually and collectively challenge our deeply engrained attitudes, norms, values, beliefs and cultural practices. In effect, while subject to interpretation, the *will to power* that Nietzsche famously cited as a key force driving force behind human conduct can be understood in terms of the need for control, relative order and predictability, together with resistance to unsettling complexity and map challenges in line with the biosocial processes set out earlier, as we attempt to sustain a relatively comfortable state in terms of experiential load in an environment that fits with our own (and our social groups') socially learned preferences.[72]

Notes

1   Allen, G.E. (1999) 'Modern biological determinism', in M. Fortun and E. Mendelsohn (eds), *The Practices of Human Genetics: Sociology of the Sciences*, vol. 21, Dordrecht: Springer.

2   Burr, V. (2015) *Social Constructionism*, Abingdon: Routledge.

3   Graves Jr., J.L. (2015) 'Great is their sin: biological determinism in the age of genomics', *Annals of the American Academy of Political and Social Science*, 661(1): 24–50.

4   L. Birke, *Women, Feminism and Biology: The Feminist Challenge*, Brighton: Wheatsheaf, p x.

5   Van Krieken, R. (2003) 'Beyond the "parsonian problem of order": Elias, habit and contemporary sociology or Hobbes was right', invited paper delivered at the 'How Is Society Possible' Workshop: Department of Sociology and Centre for Research in Social Inclusion, Macquarie University, 30 June.

6   Renwick, C. (2012) *British Sociology's Lost Biological Roots: A History of Futures Past*, Basingstoke: Palgrave Macmillan.

7   Van Krieken, R. (2003) 'Beyond the "parsonian problem of order": Elias, habit and contemporary sociology or Hobbes was right', invited paper delivered at the 'How Is Society Possible' Workshop: Department of Sociology and Centre for Research in Social Inclusion, Macquarie University, 30 June.

8   Elias, N. (1939) *The Civilising Process*, Oxford: Blackwell; Goffman, E. (1973) *Relations in Public*, Harmondsworth: Penguin; Giddens, A. (1991) *Modernity and Self-Identity*, Cambridge: Polity.

9   Meloni, M., Williams, S. and Martin, P. (eds) (2016) 'Biosocial matters: rethinking sociology-biology relations in the twenty-first century', *Sociological Review*, 64: 1–6.

10   Goldinger, S., Papesh, M. and Barnhart, A. 2016 'The poverty of embodied cognition', *Psychonomic Bulletin Review*, 23: 959–978.

11   Foster, J.A., Rinaman, L. and Cryan, J.F. (2017) 'Stress & the gut-brain axis: regulation by the microbiome', *Neurobiology of Stress*, 7: 124–136.

12   Carpenter, S. (2012) 'That gut feeling', *Monitor on Psychology*, 43(8), http://www.apa.org/monitor/2012/09/gut-feeling

13   Foster, J.A., Rinaman, L. and Cryan, J.F. (2017) 'Stress & the gut-brain axis: regulation by the microbiome', *Neurobiology of Stress*, 7: 124–136.

14   Goldinger, S., Papesh, M. and Barnhart, A. 2016 'The poverty of embodied cognition', *Psychonomic Bulletin Review*, 23: 959–978.

15   Clark, A. and Chalmers, D. (1998) 'The extended mind', *Analysis*, 58(1): 7–19.

16   Fodor, J. (2009) ' "Where is my mind?" Review of Clark 2008', *London Review of Books*, 38(3): 13–15; Waddington, C.H. (1957) *The Strategy of the Genes*, London: Allen & Unwin.

17   https://www.youtube.com/watch?v=kc-TdMjuJRU

18   LeDoux, J. (1998) *The Emotional Brain*, New York: Phoenix.

19   Capitanio, J. (2017, January) 'Animal studies in psychology', *Psychology Student Network*, http://www.apa.org/ed/precollege/psn/2017/01/animal-studies

20   Menzel, R. et al. (2005) 'Honey bees navigate according to a map-like spatial memory', *Proceedings of the National Academy of Sciences (USA)*, 102: 3040–3045.

21   O'Keefe, J. and Nadel, L. (1979) 'Précis of O'Keefe & Nadel's *The Hippocampus as a Cognitive Map*', *Behavioral and Brain Sciences*, 2(4): 487–494; Roxo, M.R., Franceschini, P.R., Zubaran, C., Kleber, F.D. and Sander, J.W. (2011) 'The limbic system conception and its historical evolution', *Scientific World Journal*, 11: 2428–2441.

22   Epstein, R.A., Patai, E.Z., Julian, J.B. and Spiers, H.J. (2017) 'The cognitive map in humans: spatial navigation and beyond', *Nature Neuroscience*, 20(11): 1504–1513; Tavares, R.M., Mendelsohn, A., Grossman, Y., Williams, C.H., Shapiro, M., Trope, Y. and Schiller, D. (2015) 'A map for social navigation in the human brain', *Neuron*, 87(1): 231–243.

23 Sander, D., Grafman, J. and Zalla, T. (2003) 'The human amygdala: an evolved system for relevance detection', *Reviews in the Neurosciences*, 14(4): 303–316.

24 Hamann, S., Ely, T., Grafton, S. and Kilts, C. (1999) 'Amygdala activity related to enhanced memory for pleasant and aversive stimuli', *Nature Neuroscience*, 2: 289–294.

25 LeDoux, J. (1998) *The Emotional Brain*, New York: Phoenix.

26 McElree, B. (2001) 'Working memory and focal attention', *Journal of Experimental Psychology: Learning, Memory, and Cognition*, 27(3): 817–835.

27 Miller, G. (1956) 'The magical number seven, plus or minus two: some limits on our capacity for processing information', *Psychological Review*, 63: 81–97.

28 Halford, G.S., Cowan, N., & Andrews, G. (2007) Separating cognitive capacity from knowledge: a new hypothesis. *Trends in Cognitive Sciences*, 11(6): 236–242.

29 Sweller, J (1988) 'Cognitive load during problem solving: effects on learning', *Cognitive Science*, 12(2): 257–285.

30 Edelman, G. (1992) *Bright Air, Brilliant Fire*, vol. 114, New York: Basic Books.

31 Craik, F.I. and Lockhart, R.S. (1972) 'Levels of processing: a framework for memory research', *Journal of Verbal Learning and Verbal Behavior*, 11(6): 671–684.

32 Cooley, C.H. (1902) 'Looking-glass self: the production of reality', *Essays and Readings on Social Interaction*, 6: 126–128.

33 Heintzelman, S.J. and King, L.A. (2019) 'Routines and meaning in life', *Personality and Social Psychology Bulletin*, 45(5): 688–699.

34 Bone, J. (2005) 'The social map & the problem of order: a re-evaluation of "homo sociologicus"', *Theory & Science*, 6(1): 1–20.

35 Goffman, E. (1959) *The Presentation of Self in Everyday Life*, Harmondsworth: Penguin.

36 Bone, J. (2006) *The Hard Sell: An Ethnographic Study of the Direct Selling Industry*, Aldershot: Ashgate.

37 Hare, B. (2017) 'Survival of the friendliest: homo sapiens evolved via selection for prosociality', *Annual Review of Psychology*, 68(1): 155–186, at 170.

38 Goffman, E. (1959) *The Presentation of Self in Everyday Life*, Harmondsworth: Penguin.

39 Goffman, E. (1963) *Stigma: Notes on the Management of Spoiled Identity*, Harmondsworth: Penguin.

40 Goffman, E. (2009) *Relations in Public*, Piscataway, NJ: Transaction Publishers.

41 Goffman, E. (1963) *Behavior in Public Places: Notes on the Social Organization of Gatherings*, New York: Free Press; Simmel, G. (2012) 'The metropolis and mental life', in J. Lin and C. Mele (eds), *The Urban Sociology Reader*, Abingdon: Routledge, pp 37–45.

42 Lederbogen, F., Kirsch, P., Haddad, L., Streit, F., Tost, H., Schuch, P., Wust, S., Pruessner, J.C., Rietschel, M., Deuschle, M. and Meyer-Lindenberg, A. (2011) 'City living and urban upbringing impact neural social stress processing in humans', *Nature*, 474: 498–501.

43 Mirowsky, J., and Ross, C. (1990) 'Control or defense? Depression and the sense of control over good and bad outcomes', *Journal of Health and Social Behavior*, 31(1): 71–86.

44 Csikzentmihalyi, M. (1990) *Flow: The Psychology of Optimal Experience*, New York: Harper & Row.

45 Bowlby, J. (2012) *A Secure Base*, Abingdon: Routledge.

46 Bone, J. (2021) 'Neoliberal precarity and primalization: a biosocial perspective on the age of insecurity, injustice, and unreason', *British Journal of Sociology*, 72(4): 1030–1045.

47 Bone, J. (2010) 'Irrational capitalism: the social map, neoliberalism and the demodernization of the West', *Critical Sociology*, 36(5): 717–740.

48 Kowalski-Trakofler, K.M., Vaught, C. and Scharf, T. (2003) 'Judgment and decision making under stress: an overview for emergency managers', *International Journal of Emergency Management*, 1(3): 278–289.

[49] Arnsten, A.F. (2009) 'Stress signalling pathways that impair prefrontal cortex structure and function', *Neuroscience*, 10(6): 410–422, at 410.

[50] Simmel, G. (2012) 'The metropolis and mental life', in J. Lin and C. Mele (eds), *The Urban Sociology Reader*, Abingdon: Routledge, pp 37–45.

[51] Durkheim, E. (1964) *The Division of Labour in Society*, New York: Free Press.

[52] Gergen, K.J. (1991) *The Saturated Self: Dilemmas of Identity in Contemporary Life*, New York: Basic Books.

[53] Giddens, A. (1991) *Modernity and Self-Identity*, Cambridge: Polity.

[54] Atchley, R.C. (1989) 'A continuity theory of normal aging', *The Gerontologist*, 29(2): 183–190, at 183.

[55] McEwen, B.S. (1998) 'Stress, adaptation, and disease: allostasis and allostatic load', *Annals of the New York Academy of Sciences*, 840(1): 33–44.

[56] Bone, J. (2005) 'The social map & the problem of order: a re-evaluation of "homo sociologicus"', *Theory & Science*, 6(1): 1–20; Bone, J. (2010) 'Irrational capitalism: the social map, neoliberalism and the demodernization of the West', *Critical Sociology*, 36(5): 717–740.

[57] McEwen, B.S. (1998) 'Stress, adaptation, and disease: allostasis and allostatic load', *Annals of the New York Academy of Sciences*, 840(1): 33–44.

[58] McEwen, B.S. (2004) 'Protection and damage from acute and chronic stress: allostasis and allostatic overload and relevance to the pathophysiology of psychiatric disorders', *Annals of the New York Academy of Sciences*, 1032(1): 1–7.

[59] Guidi, J., Lucente, M., Sonino, N. and Fava, G.A. (2021) 'Allostatic load and its impact on health: a systematic review', *Psychotherapy and Psychosomatics*, 90(1): 11–27.

[60] Bone, J. (2010) 'Irrational capitalism: the social map, neoliberalism and the demodernization of the West', *Critical Sociology*, 36(5): 717–740; Simmel, G. (2012) 'The metropolis and mental life', in J. Lin and C. Mele (eds), *The Urban Sociology Reader*, Abingdon: Routledge, pp 37–45.

[61] McEwen, B.S. (1998) 'Stress, adaptation, and disease: allostasis and allostatic load', *Annals of the New York Academy of Sciences*, 840(1): 33–44; Durkheim, E. (1964) *The Division of Labour in Society*, New York: Free Press.

[62] Waddington, C.H. (1957) *The Strategy of the Genes*, London: Allen & Unwin.

[63] Meloni, M. (2014) 'The social brain meets the reactive genome: neuroscience, epigenetics and the new social biology', *Frontiers in Human Neuroscience*, 8: 309.

[64] Waddington, C.H. (1957) *The Strategy of the Genes*, London: Allen & Unwin.

[65] Elias, N. (1939) *The Civilising Process*, Oxford: Blackwell.

[66] Odling-Smee, F., Laland, K. and Feldman, M. (2003) *Niche Construction: The Neglected Process in Evolution*, Princeton: Princeton University Press.

[67] Rothi, M.H. and Greer, E. . (2022) 'From correlation to causation: the new frontier of transgenerational epigenetic inheritance', *BioEssays*, 2200118. P.1.

[68] Horvath, S. and Raj, K. (2018) 'DNA methylation-based biomarkers and the epigenetic clock theory of ageing', *Nature Reviews Genetics*, 19(6): 371–384.

[69] Lacal, I. and Ventura, R. (2018) 'Epigenetic inheritance: concepts, mechanisms and perspectives', *Frontiers in Molecular Neuroscience*, 292.

[70] Meloni, M. (2014) 'The social brain meets the reactive genome: neuroscience, epigenetics and the new social biology', *Frontiers in Human Neuroscience*, 8: 309; Bonduriansky, R. and Day, T. (2009) 'Nongenetic inheritance and its evolutionary implications', *Annual Review of Ecology, Evolution, and Systematics*, 40: 103–125.

[71] Laland, K.N. et al. (2015) 'The extended evolutionary synthesis: its structure, assumptions and predictions', *Proceedings of the Royal Society B: Biological Sciences*, 282(1813): 20151019.

[72] Nietzsche, F. (2017) *The Will to Power*, Harmondsworth: Penguin.

2

The Long Road to Modernity

Building from the basic conceptual foundations of Chapter 1, I want to move the narrative forward to begin to outline how these foundations can start to illuminate some of the conditions of the present, but firstly by beginning to outline the story of the present within the context of a whistlestop excursion through the past. This is in recognition of the fact that our current circumstances, and the processes that might inform our understanding, have been long in the making and might be best appreciated as part of a wider narrative. While a broad number of writers have engaged with issues relating to the problems generated by contemporary social organization, many have taken an approach that deals with the evolution of political, economic and social developments, but with little attention paid to the deeper and more fundamental currents that have shaped these events. With apologies for the lengthy outlining of the various works and ideas that informed my own approach in the previous chapter, I think it is clear that this is not the form or scope of what's being engaged with here, and hence a range of issues needed to be discussed to provide context for what follows. This is necessary given that, as indicated in the Introduction, the intention is to approach the questions and challenges of the present from a historical and even an evolutionary scale to some extent. There are also some crucial issues, like those identified towards the end of Chapter 1, that to the best of my understanding have not been applied as broadly previously. Overall, the point is to try to gain a deeper understanding of where we are by offering an exploration and explanation of contemporary social, economic and political arrangements that can be understood within the context of what we know about the evolving story of our species and its biosocial development over the *longue durée*.

From the Holocene

Perhaps one of the most interesting factors in our development is just how recently in our evolution we started to move beyond a hunter-gatherer existence, leading to questions relating to what aspects of who we are were set in train during those times and how far we have actually come since then. While estimates vary and are keenly debated among palaeontologists, evolutionary anthropologists and so on, it is suggested that our species, *homo sapiens*, emerged in Africa around 300,000 years ago, which, in evolutionary terms, is itself the blink of an eye. The story of what follows is also contested, but recent thinking suggests that we emerged from Africa around 50,000– 60,000 years ago and we became the sole human species around 40,000 years ago. Much of our evolution to this point had been driven by adaptation to shifting climatic conditions that had favoured the emergence of the creative and social primates that we became, and it was climatic change that was central to the surge in our development that propelled us from a nomadic, small-scale existence towards the complex civilizations of the ancient to modern eras.[1]

For most of our history until around 10,000–12,000 years ago, we had a nomadic existence in a world often subject to inhospitable climactic conditions. As will be addressed in Chapter 9, this may be a salutary lesson for the present as we confront what may be the self-induced ending of a long period of relatively stable climate, the *Holocene*. It was after the last ice age as the climate started to settle that our ancestors were able to begin setting down firmer roots and generate larger-scale sources of food that allowed for the growth and development of more complex and more formally organized social groups.[2] Some interesting facts present themselves here that have a bearing on the more contemporary debates that appear later on in this book.

From small-scale to large-scale societies and the production of social order

The move from our long history of living in small to medium-sized hunter-gatherer bands towards the complex populous societies we subsequently produced is attributed to two 'revolutions': the *Neolithic* and then the *Urban*. The former was marked by the emergence of fixed settlements and farming in numerous regions simultaneously as the climate became more temperate, paving the way for the eventual emergence of urban settlements, together with rapid population growth, beginning in the Middle East, the Indus Valley and expanding elsewhere.[3]

Understanding of this stage of human development has been greatly influenced by the works of the celebrated archaeologist V. Gordon Childe. The model of social, technological, economic and cultural evolution he outlined has been the subject of vast debate since his works were published in the early to mid-20th century, albeit that much of what he proposed continues to inform our understanding of the evolution of human societies. The transformations that Childe charted, firstly towards ever larger agrarian and then urban settlements, marked the beginnings of human civilization, and he identifies that it was the capacity to generate a consistent surplus of food by increasingly efficient means that allowed this to take place, as decreasing numbers needed to be involved in food procurement on a hand-to-mouth basis. Social complexity soon followed with larger settlements, a military to defend them and the land that sustained them, together with a broad range of other specialisms that could be pursued by people no longer focused simply on gaining enough food to make it through the day:

1. 'In point of size the first cities must have been more extensive and more densely populated than any previous settlements' (p 9).
2. 'In composition and function the urban population already differed from that of any village ... full-time specialist craftsmen, transport workers, merchants, officials and priests' (p 11).
3. 'Each primary producer paid over the tiny surplus he could wring from the soil with his still very limited technical equipment as tithe or tax to an imaginary deity or a divine king who thus concentrated the surplus' (p 11).
4. 'Truly monumental public buildings not only distinguish each known city from any village but also symbolise the concentration of the social surplus' (p 12).
5. 'But naturally priests, civil and military leaders and officials absorbed a major share of the concentrated surplus and thus formed a "ruling class"' (pp 12–13).
6. 'Writing' (p 14).
7. 'The elaboration of exact and predictive sciences – arithmetic, geometry and astronomy' (p 14).
8. 'Conceptualised and sophisticated styles [of art]' (p 15).[4]

It seems clear that in our ancestors had to adapt over a fairly short period of time to occupying these larger and more complex societies equipped with a brain that, while very highly developed in relation to other animals, nonetheless exhibited the cognitive limitations outlined in Chapter 1 in terms of its highly constrained capacity to deal with multiple conscious tasks simultaneously. For the argument presented here, this is critical, as it is key to understanding a range of important phenomena that have been observable throughout our history and that can also help us better comprehend some of the travails of the present that are outlined in this and the subsequent chapters.

Firstly, it has been proposed that these cognitive limitations may be related to the fact that the neocortex of the human brain developed in relation to both social complexity and group size through the greater part of our evolutionary development.[5] However, the pace at which we have had to adapt to living in much larger settlements after spending the vast majority of our history in relatively small groups, as argued earlier, is at the root of some of the difficulties we observe in relating to life in larger-scale societies and in particular modern living, including some of the particular difficulties of the present. Also, and of great significance, the innate cognitive limitations that we carried forward from our earlier development can be seen have shaped the structure of our societies over time. When applying this perspective to the changes that arose following the emergence of cities in the ancient world, many of the hallmarks of the trajectory of our historical development become more explicable. In support of the argument that our biology and, more specifically, our neurological functioning play an important role in shaping our societies, it has been recognized that urban civilizations past and present and over time, and even those which emerged in places without contact between them, appear to exhibit remarkable similarities in terms of social structures, interaction, configuration and architecture. Hence, despite differences of appearance and particular aspects of culture, these seem to develop within 'limited parameters', suggesting that our species responded similarly to the increasing dynamic density of settlements regardless of where and when these emerged.[6]

When we think about city-scale living, it is evident that various factors come into play that substantially change the way in which we relate to each other. In the first instance, we begin to encounter strangers and, as such, must embark on a process of making inferences about them on the basis of their appearance, manner, expression and so on to try to consider what they are like. Are they likely to be friendly and cooperative or do they represent a threat? Overall, we become more concerned as to how we appear to others as we no longer live in a world where most people we routinely engage with are those with whom we likely have a deep and long-lasting acquaintance and familiarity. This shift of itself is mentally taxing and so we began to develop strategies to simplify aspects of social life and habituate to others in line with the processes described in Chapter 1.

In large part, this involves the previously addressed fundamental aspects of classification and routinization of experience and action. We want to be able to clearly identify things, to avoid uncertainty and to develop practical strategies for dealing with regularly encountered experiences and situations. Underlying this is the alarm that we experience when we cannot readily make sense of and respond to what is presented to us. The fact that this is so deep-seated and ubiquitous is illustrated by the fact that the fear of complexity and the unknown was represented by chaos deities in pretty much all ancient cultures.[7] Of course, these traits would have been part of our makeup from earlier in human history as we adapted to a broader range of demands, including those associated with dealing with different environments and climatic conditions, as well as the exigencies of sustaining close human relations within our groups. However, all of this now comes much more extensively into play as our social environment becomes significantly more complex.

In line with this, in more populous social settings we begin to classify people more in terms of outward appearance and conduct. Modes of dress and social statuses become very important in identifying who's who within urban communities and how we might relate to each other. As will be discussed later on, this becomes an important role of fashion and consumerism in modern industrial cities and is more significant in relation to human conduct than most people realize, as the latter helps reduce the complexity of a visually oriented culture.[8] Meanings are also applied to different settings with different expectations guiding the appropriate, dress, behaviours and activities. However, rather than being a wholly modern urban phenomenon, the roots of this type of emerging sensibility, including a nascent conspicuous consumerism, were apparent in the larger cities of the Roman world and elsewhere.[9]

The ability to identify others is also related in various ways to the specialization that takes place in cities. As Childe observed, the capacity of significant numbers in cities to engage in specialist activities other than food production also differentiates us from each other and creates the potential for a much broader variety of occupations and roles, with the latter also often accompanied by identifiable modes of dress and so on, which helped guide people's impressions of each other.

Of course, the act of specialization in and of itself emerges from the same limitations described earlier – quite simply, as the range of possible activities expands, clearly individuals cannot acquire the necessary skills to be masters of all, in contrast to the hunter gatherer past, where many basic skills were likely to be shared across the whole group. In the city we can engage in specific activities in much greater depth. However, once again, this also has the effect of making us more differentiated from each other; we become relative strangers who do different things, have different experiences and, to a much greater extent than previously, chart different life courses. The fact that in a society of specialists and strangers we inevitably see the world differently, at least to some degree, also provides a further basis for potential conflict and hence, for all of these reasons, as we move into more complex societies, social life becomes more of a contest for position in an attempt for some to reach a level where they can impose their preferred conditions and worldview on the rest. This is something that, as we know, hasn't changed very markedly throughout our history and across civilizations; in other words, we seem to be consensual up to a point in small-scale, relatively homogeneous settings, while this breaks down as the scale and complexity of societies increase. Specialization also leads to further issues relating to social status, the allocation of resources and critically how societies are organized at a larger scale. Again, the biosocial imperative is integral here, as our emotionally driven concern for the world to make sense to us is key to understanding how this plays out. Applied to urban living, this entails that we internalize the ever more complex and widely shared rules and guidelines that govern expanding societies and, as we are inclined towards reducing experiential overload wherever possible, we tend to develop new means of establishing a sense of order, consolidating these, while accepting ideas and practices imposed by those more powerful than ourselves unless we have a compelling reason to do otherwise. As will be discussed later on, often both the obvious physical and lesser-understood psychological costs of disruption regularly outweigh those of compliance, or even grudging resignation, unless we find ourselves in a position where the status quo has become untenable.

Marx's famous observation that human history is a story of oppressors and oppressed appears relevant here as, beyond the adoption of a fairly sophisticated and enlightened mindset among a populace, our history so far would suggest that this seems almost inevitable. As a species we don't seem very well disposed towards egalitarianism, albeit that we often express utopian imaginings of such a world in the future. However, as we are very well aware, when the opportunity arises, people are often inclined to pursue a Nietzschean path towards high status positions with greater access to influence and resources, often leading them into conflict with others as to who wins out and gets to set the rules and what they define. Of all of the things that Marx got right, paradoxically, this was the trait that seemingly undermined the implementation of the communist systems he imagined wherever they were introduced, as initial euphoria of replacing often despotic systems of governance led to some 'comrades' having designs on being 'more equal' than others. Exploiting the opportunity provided by revolutionary social breakdown to seize power, the winners have often eventually simply produced equally despotic systems under the new regime, as with the scenario that Orwell succinctly depicted in *Animal Farm*.[10]

As will be discussed in later chapters, while imperfect and often fragile, for evident reasons it is usually only systems of authority where positions of power are genuinely provisional and insecure – that is, genuine, well-functioning and highly responsive democratic systems – that seem capable of producing a modicum of equity and social justice. This is clearly a situation that was in scarce supply historically, improving only gradually through the middle of the last century, only to whither precipitously over recent decades.

There may also be a further related reason as to why all large-scale human societies, and indeed organizations, appear to be highly hierarchically organized, which also relates to the cognitive limitations and emotional imperative described thus far. Very simply, in order for large-scale organization to function, given our limitations, this can only happen at increasing levels of abstraction. Hence, while those conducting specialist tasks at the lower levels may have in-depth specialist knowledge, at each successive stage going up the line the capacity to handle the span of that knowledge or skill reduces, so that those leading and coordinating activity will often only know enough to oversee the activities of their subordinates but not enough to carry out specific tasks themselves. This is something that will also be discussed further on, as it has often arisen as an issue in power struggles over work extending well into the modern era.

Crystallization and decrystallization and the dialectic of order and disorder

Once a particular social order is established, as we know, it tends to settle for periods of time when a ruling group manages to gain control, advancing and sustaining an associated set of prevailing ideas, with greater or lesser degrees of consensus. The resultant organization of society, and the ideas on which it is based, then becomes broadly understood and internalized by the population to the extent that the main rules and arrangements that govern everyday life become habitual, operating beyond fully conscious reflection by dint of the neurological processes described previously, engrained within the collective *maps* of the populace, to the extent that the imagining of different worlds often seems implausible, impractical and even potentially threatening to various degrees. This is what arises when sets of practices, ideas and values become *crystallized*, persisting over time and being passed on from generation to generation. Experiences that correspond with habituated norms pass with little reflection, while *map challenges* that represent significant perceived deviations from the internalized worldview raise the type of emotional alarm mentioned earlier. In large-scale societies this is evidently likely to occur much more often, hence the aforementioned tendency towards 'screening out' of strangers in public space to reduce experiential overload.

In milder forms, breaches in our expectations can be a source of humour, mild discomfort or even entertainment, where something that surprises strays not so far from the familiar that there is serious emotional discomfiture. This is one of the fundamental processes that structures social life as we generate a sense of order by imposing constraints on each other over time, a process I have previously described in terms of *reciprocal constraint* and *reciprocal reinforcement*, alluding to, respectively, the negative and positive means by which we routinely temper and shape each other's everyday conduct to sustain a sense of order and continuity.[11]

However, more significant breaches of people's normative expectations have long been subject to sanction ranging from mild rebuke to exclusion and, in the extreme, even the most horrifying of physical punishments and death. The latter, of course, are often imposed by those with the greatest power and position, and who are also those with the most at stake in sustaining particular social arrangements and the set of ideas that govern them. As we know, social life is self-evidently a contested terrain, where clashes between groups who have different worldviews and interests will seek domination by means up to and including open conflict. All of this, as the reader may be thinking, is blatantly obvious and so routinely observed to appear banal. However, as I argue throughout this work, the innate impulses that drive these processes, as being founded on fundamental aspects of the structure and function of biological imperatives in the manner outlined here, as well as the wider implications that follow from this, are not well understood or appreciated.

Perceiving order

All of this raises a further equally well-recognized aspect of human organization and history that can also be more readily understood. Given the aforementioned need for sense making and security, the desire to maintain a sense of control even extends to the tendency to see logic or patterns in unknown or random occurrences and events, referred to as *apophenia*, accompanied by the closely related phenomenon of *pareidolia*, which refers to the tendency for humans to discern recognizable shapes and patterns from random images; seeing faces and shapes in clouds being a notable example.[12] Once thought to be a symptom of pathological delusion, in its milder form, this is a common aspect of human thinking and perception driven by our drive towards neutralizing the unknown, while the consequences are manifold. From gamblers who imagine that they can discern a *system*, to the credibility of fortune tellers, psychics and perhaps some economic forecasters, all may be to a degree bound up with this tendency. Somewhat more contentiously, the phenomenon has also been applied to understanding religious and other forms of supernatural belief that bridge the gap between the known and unknown.[13] While the latter are all considered to be regular manifestations of the phenomenon, in its more extreme form it is regarded as the basis of conspiracy theories and also some of the bizarre beliefs associated with serious mental illness which will be addressed in later chapters.

However, in terms of religion, and indeed other similar widely held belief systems applied to explaining phenomena that seem beyond our immediate grasp or ability to control, the broadly accepted ideas explaining why the world is the way it is, as once more Marx observed, are usually fashioned and tailored in such a way that supports the legitimacy of the elites who have won out in the contest of ideas, resources and, often, simply naked power. By one means or another, a legitimating story will be presented as to why they are rightfully in charge and why often inequitable social arrangements are the way they are.

Overall, as argued, in various ways our aforementioned innate predispositions may render us more vulnerable to accepting these narratives than has been appreciated while, as noted earlier, those who might for one reason or another challenge prevailing ideas are regularly subject to sanction, from ridicule to much worse.

Order, governmentality and crises

While force might be employed to deal with the recalcitrant in some social circumstances, unless there are very good grounds and opportunities to do otherwise, this isn't often required as the biosocial mechanisms described often mean that as described, the ruled are often highly complicit in their own domination, much as Michel Foucault observed in relation to his concept of governmentality; in effect, where people tend to govern themselves in line with the norms, values and prescriptions that they have internalized and that are often imposed from above.[14] Having habituated to the worldview, values and norms that are prevalent within our social group, engrained in our neural connections, we rely on these to make sense of and engage with the world, with our sense of safety and stability being dependent on the perceived efficacy and rectitude of our internalized map. As suggested, while mild and positively perceived (usually familiar) departures can be stimulating, we experience negative emotional arousal when others significantly challenge this framework, while this can also readily arise even where we do this ourselves, both externally and internally. Just as we react to experiences that are novel or those previously deemed significant with an emotional jolt to alert us that something beyond our normal expectations has arisen, which needs our attention and potential action, this clearly also occurs where we act and think in ways that significantly depart from the tracks of our internalized worldview. This is the mechanism that guilt and conscience are founded upon. In short, as proposed, the neurologically engrained lifeworld of the individual is relied upon and defended as external or internal contradiction is inclined to trigger the amygdala and other subcortical regions, and in turn the autonomic nervous system, as an experience we find discomfiting and would rather avoid. As will be discussed in later chapters, the 'tightness' or otherwise of cultural norms and values, together with individual emotional sensitivity, also plays a role here in terms of the degree to which this is experienced. However, in most instances, as was described earlier, significant challenges to our worldview are staunchly resisted, both individually and collectively. As such, it is usually only where we experience and justify to ourselves that something is wrong with the status quo, where we are presented with contradictions or seemingly compelling new ideas, often with input and support from others and in a state where the emotional and other costs of acquiescence or defence appear to outweigh the costs of reframing our worldview, that we may be inclined to revise our position. In terms of very profound or fundamental change, it usually takes some form of internal or external crisis and culmination of disaffection or incongruity in relation to our experience to shake us sufficiently to offer the possibility of such a significant shift. In essence, this is the process that has driven our history and it is worth pausing to clearly address it here as it further contextualizes some of what follows.

In line with the view that history develops via a sequence of contests between oppositional forces succeeding or accommodating each other over time, Marx argued that historical development was driven by changes to material conditions; in other words, technological and economic developments that brought successive elites to the fore who controlled the production and allocation of resources and who dominated through the imposition of ideas and regulations that maintained the system and their power and position. Marx developed these ideas in opposition to the philosopher Georg Hegel's thesis that successive epochs emerged as prevailing *ideas* were found wanting, questioned and subsequently challenged, producing a shift or accommodation within a new set of prevailing ideas that operated as the dominant worldview in each phase of development, once more often accompanied by the rise of those who had won out in the contest of ideas. What I propose here is broadly consistent with both of these notions that society evolves via ongoing oppositions, but where order and unnerving complexity are key elements. To clarify, human history does appear as a sequence of stages where order and organization is imposed by successive elites on the potential chaos that accompanies the increasing scale, differentiation and population density of society, with change occurring at critical points. Periods of disorder can be driven by challenging ideas and/or developments in technology and economy, and also by warfare and natural events such as disease, famine and climactic shifts. What is important here is that both human activity and natural events can lead to a scenario where the grip of a prevailing system of authority and the props supporting a dominant worldview may begin to weaken or fracture, providing a window of opportunity for large-scale societal shifts and a contest over whose new order wins out. In short, throughout human history, crises of a broad nature, human-made or otherwise, can break the mould, leading to periods of relative disorder and uncertainty, creating the motivation for order of some kind to be re-established in order to avert ongoing existential angst. Successive forms of social order will normally be of a kind that meets the needs and ambitions of an elite (new or pre-existing) and, to a lesser extent, a sufficient number of the subordinated populace who are co-opted in the belief that they also have a stake in the game. Those even further below are kept in check through the re-establishment of a minimal level of manageable continuity and a sliver of vain hope that they might also advance over time, together with fear instilled by the actual or implicit threat of chaos, rejection, destitution or various forms of punishment to achieve a degree of compliance.

Given people's fundamental need for at least a minimal degree of order, these tendencies can also be exploited by elites to sustain and reinforce ideas and societal conditions that fail to meet the needs of the majority, established in conditions of cognitive and emotional turmoil, but which are consolidated and sustained through consistent reinforcement and subsequent resistance to revision once the new conditions are substantially established. In the current era – and a point to which I will return – this is what I would argue underpins the process that Naomi Klein described in *The Shock Doctrine*.[15] Through these tendencies, we can regularly be complicit in our own subjugation where we have internalized and become resigned to an unjust social order, through both emotionally charged redirection and inertia, even where the latter might leave many of us in a chronic state of negative affect and fatalism, as evidenced across numerous societies past and present. In this way the historical crystallization and decrystallization of societal arrangements is underpinned by our deepest biopsychosocial tendencies.

Towards the early modern world

Returning to the substantive history of Western modernity, this is evidently a massive topic that has spawned an enormous body of work. However, it forms only a small (if important) part of what's presented here and, as such, only a brief overview of specific events that have direct bearing on the issues at hand is necessary or – indeed, as noted – possible. At this point, it is also important to note that, as suggested at the outset, it is fully recognized that world history is about much more than the story of the West, while European and North American scholars have been, quite rightly, challenged for the sidelining of other histories. In fact, it must be recognized that, while enjoying a period of economic and cultural dominance of late, and one that may well be about to be eclipsed, Western development came fairly late in the story of human civilization, a fact often forgotten via the lens of our colonialist, Eurocentric and revisionist history.[16]

However, the aim of this book is to chart key aspects of the rise and, in particular, the fall of the West, its socioeconomic development, and its impact on the present and possible future. This is also in recognition of the fact that the trajectory of Western development, while, as suggested, merely one short phase of the human story, has nonetheless been pivotal in shaping the conditions of the recent past and present. As such, in terms of what is possible within the scope of the book and what is relevant to the specific issues here, and with apologies for not being able to include more, what follows in this and the succeeding couple of chapters is a brief excursion towards where we are now, while setting out the way in which key developments in that journey fit within the theoretical framework that informs this work as a whole.

The rise of the West

As we moved from the ancient world of city states which reached its zenith with Rome, the West had experienced a period of longstanding continuity, albeit that the hegemony of the Roman Empire was continually tested on its borders. As we know, the dominance of Rome and its continuing legacy in terms of Western thought, language, architecture, laws, social structures and so on was only one of a wide range of possibilities, given that the city's rise to prominence was only achieved by its winning out in a long sequence of struggles with other city states, other emerging societies across the European mainland and the Mediterranean, and notably the long contest (the Punic Wars) fought against its arch-rival, the Carthaginian Empire. While Rome had the upper hand, certainly after the first of three major conflagrations spanning 264–146 BCE, had Carthage won out early in this contest, as was conceivable, then the history of European and world development would have evidently followed a substantially different trajectory.

Rome's dominance and the extension of its social organization, culture and practices, as we know, lasted until its long decline between around 150 and 476 CE, via internal weakening and divisions, corruption and, of course, the eventual onslaught from invading 'barbarians'. It might also be noted that both changing climactic conditions, which rendered food production more problematic, and disease (the Antonine Plague of 165–180 CE) were also contributory factors. This latter point is significant, given that climate change, as already noted, has been so important in invoking large-scale social change, while disease has also played an important role, all of which has resonance not only with other historical bends in the road, but also for us at the present time. As suggested earlier, such occurrences, in profoundly shaking the foundations of the societal status quo in the manner described earlier, have often contributed to historical inflection points.

Feudal Christendom

The Europe that emerged during the long period between the end of the Western Roman Empire and the Renaissance is often viewed in the public imagination as a period of decline. The period was marked by a retrenchment of urbanization across Europe, where Roman cities were abandoned or greatly reduced in scale – a return to agrarian localism amidst a landscape interspersed with small villages, towns and the remnants of depleted cities – not recovering until the middle of the following millennium.

As to the societal developments that arose throughout the Middle Ages, once more, a few key developments are pertinent. In line with the preceding argument, Europe for much of this era, again as we know, was dominated by a particular and enduring social structure held in place by a raft of competing monarchs, across the various territories that had been formed from the fragmentation of the Roman Empire, and critically by the dominance of the Catholic Church and its popes. The church claimed supremacy and dominion over European kings and their aristocratic supporters and subjects, while legitimating rulers' positions in return for their allegiance to the papacy. This was of course at times an uneasy alliance, and was subject to dispute as the church asserted its supremacy over powerful kings by virtue of divine authority.

As such, the social structure of the times was dominated by the feudal oligarchy of the clerical and aristocratic elite who held sway over the mass of a peasantry, where the latter worked the land and paid rents and a tithe to their lords and clergy, in return for 'protection' and religious ministry respectively. Such is the power of narrative that modern images of the period often comprise an odd amalgam of savagery and chivalry; horrific tales of warfare and ill-treatment countered by romanticized depictions of medieval nobility derived from folk tales and popular culture, some of which continue to inform perceptions of our remaining royalty and aristocracy. However, from a more objective standpoint, as proposed earlier the system of social, political and economic organization bears more than a passing resemblance to a medieval 'mafia' employing a combination of extreme violence or its threat, and the elaborate apophenic storytelling of opportunistic mystics, to control territory and the resources produced by its subjugated inhabitants.

As is widely acknowledged, in securing its dominance, the medieval church maintained a very tight control over ideas until well into the 16th century, a scenario dramatically depicted in Umberto Eco's novel *The Name of the Rose*.[17] As such, much of the learning from the ancient world, and new ideas emerging later, were strictly proscribed, particularly where they might come into conflict with church doctrine. This was a 'map' supporting aristocratic and clerical dominance and a worldview that was strictly and violently imposed. The heresy trials of Galileo, Copernicus and the activities of the Inquisition being notable examples of the assertion of church power, with the former two cases being pressed as its dominance had been challenged by the Renaissance and the Reformation (this will be discussed in more detail later on). It might also be noted that, in contrast to some popular imaginings of world development, Europe in the Middle Ages had fallen significantly behind many other of the great world civilizations such as China and the Islamic world, and did not recover until the grip of the medieval church and the feudal order began to weaken, which was a lengthy and painful process.

War and (Black) Death

As noted earlier, for most of the Middle Ages in Europe, the Catholic Church's grip on ideas was virtually unassailable. This is in keeping with the argument set out here as, in communities presented with a body of unchallenged ideas, it's clear that these will tend to become deeply engrained. Shared beliefs also tend to further strengthen when external challenge comes from those identified as 'other'. The long-running contest between Christendom and Islam, marked by the sequence of crusades from 1096 to 1270, was a notable example of what we have come to refer to as the clash of civilizations, which as we know reverberates into the present, and provided an 'enemy' that bolstered the church's Western hegemony.

However, the influence of ongoing warfare, famine and, critically, the emergence of what is regarded as the greatest pandemic in human history, the Black Death, were key factors that would set in train a sequence of events that gradually eroded the struts supporting this enduring feudal era. The first wave of the pandemic in Europe spanning 1347 to 1352 was responsible for the deaths of somewhere between 30 and 60 per cent of the European population (up to around 50 million).[18] This was compounded by the Hundred Years' War that lasted from 1337 to 1453, while both of these events followed in the wake of famine that had ravaged Europe between 1315 and 1317 (whose likely cause was due to the climactic effects of a volcanic eruption occurring in New Zealand). Given all of this, the 14th century was perhaps not an ideal time to live out what could well be a very short and uncomfortable stay on our planet. This sequence of events was sufficiently destabilizing to shake the foundations of the social, economic, political and cultural arrangements that had prevailed through the early Middle Ages, creating conditions that allowed for the emergence of the Renaissance, the Reformation and, eventually, the Enlightenment and transition to the modern era. Some other developments that precipitated this transition had begun to emerge earlier, around the turn of the millennium, with an expansion of trade and commerce and the partial revival of cities and larger towns. Merchants, trade and craftspeople began to congregate in slowly expanding urban settlements, while the promise of bounty from trade had also seen an expansion of seafaring, commerce and banking largely centred around Southern Italy, with the famous Venetian trading families, and the Northern European trading group the Hanseatic League, both of which flourished through the late Middle Ages and the Renaissance and that began the expansion of capitalism that would displace the feudal system and, eventually, undermine the dominance of the church.

The Black Death, in and of itself, also loosened the structural bonds of feudalism as the decimation of a plentiful pre-pandemic labour force declined to render labour a scarcer commodity. Many serfs and poorly rewarded artisans saw this as an opportunity for advancement and left their lords and traditional settlements in search of higher wages. In England, the indignation of the feudal authorities towards these practices saw the introduction of the Statute of Labourers in 1351, making the practice of leaving one's feudal lord and asking for higher pay as well as voluntary idleness among the able-bodied illegal. This was a power struggle that would be repeated in its broadest sense over the coming centuries. However, the efforts of the ruling classes to sustain the old system ultimately proved unsuccessful. The Peasants' Revolt of 1381 in England was a noticeable instance of an emerging conflict between the old order and the fledgling roots of something new, while similar power struggles emerged across the European mainland. This was a power struggle that would be repeated in its broadest sense across much of the globe over the coming centuries. Yet, growing disaffection with the prevailing order was not confined to the labouring classes; as will be discussed later on, it would also emerge as a schism between an increasingly economically powerful rising commercial class and the old elite, as the former saw their social advancement and status ambitions impeded by the traditional, rules, values and identities of medieval feudalism.[19]

While the Middle Ages was marred by conflict and violence, from the interpersonal level through to large-scale warfare, contrary to popular imaginings, this did not diminish during the 'golden age' of the Renaissance that followed, but notably increased. This underscores one of the key arguments of the book: that rapid social change, insecurity and inequality, due to their impact on our fundamental biosocial constitution, produce a more febrile state that renders unruly and emotionally driven conduct and upheaval more likely, as well as a drive to reassert a renewed sense of control, even by force. It was the latter, in the midst of a growing climate of uncertainty, that would drive the next steps towards the modern world.

Notes

[1] 'An evolutionary timeline of homo sapiens', *Smithsonian Magazine*, 2 February 2021, https://www.smithsonianmag.com/science-nature/essential-timeline-understanding-evolution-homo-sapiens-180976807/

[2] Mithen, S. (2011) *After the Ice: A Global Human History, 20,000–5000 BC*, London: Weidenfeld & Nicolson.

[3] Bocquet-Appel, J.P. (2011) 'When the world's population took off: the springboard of the Neolithic demographic transition', *Science*, 333(6042): 560–561.

[4] Childe, V.G. (1950), as cited in Smith, M. (2009) 'V. Gordon Childe and the urban revolution: a historical perspective on a revolution in urban studies', *Town Planning Review*, 80(1): 3–29.

[5] Dunbar, R.I.M. (2009) 'The social brain hypothesis and its implications for social evolution', *Annals of Human Biology*, 36(5): 562–572.

[6] Smith, M.L. (ed) (2013) *The Social Construction of Ancient Cities*, Washington DC: Smithsonian Institution.

7   Höfele, A., Levin, C., Müller, R. and Quiring, B. (eds) (2020) *Chaos from the Ancient World to Early Modernity: Formations of the Formless*, Berlin: De Gruyter.

8   Simmel, G. (1957) 'Fashion', *American Journal of Sociology*, 62(6): 541–558.

9   Robertson, R. and Inglis, D. (2004) 'The global animus: in the tracks of world consciousness', *Globalizations*, 1(1): 38–49.

10   Orwell, G. (2021) *Animal Farm*, Oxford: Oxford University Press.

11   Goffman, E. (2009) *Stigma: Notes on the Management of Spoiled Identity*, Harmondsworth: Penguin; Bone, J. (2005) 'The social map and the problem of order: a re-evaluation of "homo sociologicus"', *Theory & Science*, 6(1): 1–20.

12   Whitson, J. and Galinsky, A. (2008) 'Lacking control increases illusory pattern perception', *Science*, 3: 115–117.

13   Wolpert, L. (2006) *Six Impossible Things before Breakfast: The Evolutionary Origins of Belief*, London: Faber & Faber.

14   Foucault, M. (1991) 'Governmentality', in G. Burchell, C. Gordon and P. Miller (eds), *The Foucault Effect: Studies in Governmentality*, Hemel Hempstead: Harvester Wheatsheaf.

15   Klein, N. (2007) *The Shock Doctrine: The Rise of Disaster Capitalism*, New York: Macmillan.

16   Hobson, J.M. and Hobson, J.M. (2004) *The Eastern Origins of Western Civilisation*, Cambridge: Cambridge University Press.

17   Eco, U. (2004) *The Name of the Rose*, New York: Random House.

18   Gottfried, R.S. (2010) *Black Death*, New York: Simon & Schuster.

19   Aberth, J. (2009) *From the Brink of the Apocalypse: Confronting Famine, War, Plague and Death in the Later Middle Ages*, Abingdon: Routledge.

3

From Golden Age to Golden Age?

In this chapter, as with the last, the intention is evidently not to attempt anything more than a brief overview of the timeframe in question to contextualize what follows and tell the story at hand. I say this to avoid the very obvious objection that the historical accounts presented here may be very one-sided and partial, as it's clear that they must be given the vast swathe of history they cover and the various ideas and perspectives that numerous writers have exhaustively debated in relation to this historical arc. Given that disclaimer, I want to move on to discuss some of the significant events that have bearing on the themes I want to address.

The Renaissance

The previous chapter concluded with the observation that the Renaissance, often understood as a postmedieval reawakening of ideas, an era of great progress and the route to the Enlightenment and modern Western society, may have been a period of more equivocal progress than is commonly understood. To put it succinctly, the Dark Ages may have been a little less dark and the new age a little less 'golden' than is popularly imagined.

Firstly, as will be discussed in what follows, while this period did represent a sea change on the road to modernity, it might be regarded as being the stage when an incipient evolving transition began to become apparent rather than as an abrupt disruption in human affairs. It is also the case that while discovery, art and literature all advanced from the late 14th century onwards, the implication that lives blighted by the tribulations of the medieval era were somehow substantially improved is more questionable. Beyond the small coterie of rising economic and cultural elites, for many people Renaissance living was just as arduous and dangerous as the assumedly dark era that preceded it, particularly when one considers that the devastation wrought by the Black Death became an endemic feature of the era. Nonetheless, of course this era moved Europe forward from the period of relative scientific and cultural stagnation that had emerged with the fall of Rome.

As with most large-scale transitions, however, once more the driving factors were multidimensional.

After a long period where scholarship had been dominated by the church, the revival of classical knowledge and ideas that had been marginalized were rediscovered, largely due to the arrival in late medieval Europe of classical scholars and philosophers from the Byzantine Empire. Central to the ideas that emerged was the notion that the world was human-centred and that people should actively engage with knowledge, art and ideas for the betterment of humanity. It is important to note that this Renaissance *humanism* was distinctive from its later and more secular form. Its early advocates were avowedly Christian, albeit that the enquiring attitude, orientation towards learning and discovery, ideas and practices they set in motion would come into conflict and undermine church doctrine, beginning a long process that loosened the intellectual grip of the church, drove the Reformation and splintering of Christendom, and ultimately set the path towards greater secularism.

Added to this heady mix was the questioning of religious faith given the plague, warfare and famine that had dogged the late medieval era. What is critical about this period is that the certainties once provided by the church, which claimed to explain everything as an expression of God's will, began to lose their explanatory and psychological power. Schisms between feudal lords and the church as well as those within the church itself also evidently impacted on its hold over the medieval world. We began to move into a more human-centred world that needed to be understood, explored and ultimately ordered to render it explicable and negotiable for a more sceptical and questioning segment of the populace who sought clarity from this ferment.

Discovery and change

In terms of what was set in train following the waning of medieval Christendom, what is important is the fact that a world of relative simplicity and homogeneity had begun to give way to one of more evident flux and uncertainty. Of course, as noted earlier, medieval life was marked by very low life expectancy by modern standards, violence, disease and other dangers. Nonetheless, in many ways this was a simpler world, one of greater homogeneity, where people knew where they fitted in and where the lived environment for most was the village or small town. Beyond the aforementioned perils, people largely knew what to expect and what was expected of them as they lived under the gaze of the community, governed by a collection of religiously defined social norms and values. The big questions of existence were also answered by the church. As such, there was little for most people to do but to follow the roles assigned to them while sustaining a relatively fatalistic perspective on life's travails, as these were simply God's will. By contrast, the long journey from the Middle Ages to the modern world as we know it led to numerous advances in technology, understanding of the world and, for many, a greater contribution to shaping their own lives and environment, but which also placed a greater psychological burden on individuals. From the Renaissance onwards, a dialectical process of uncertainty and control was set in motion with, at times, akin to what Beck described in relation to a much later period of modernity, where attempts to understand and generate order, organization and security from uncertainty and flux ended up simply producing more of the latter.[1] So, for example, the great voyages of discovery from this period onwards, while providing greater knowledge, also called into question or overturned long-held assumptions about the world, which had to be reflected upon and people's ideas reappraised and replaced by more plausible explanation as to how things were. In addition to these existential concerns and the decline in religious authority, there were questions as to how people would fit into a world where the legitimacy of an aristocratic ruling class was being challenged by the rise of an increasingly powerful bourgeois class of traders, merchants and makers. Hence, the economic impact of growing trade and commerce, while greatly expanding and formalizing the economy, simultaneously began to displace the power relations between nobility, clergy and commoners that had endured through the feudal era.

While calling into question many of the taken-for-granted assumptions and relations that had prevailed for hundreds of years, the Renaissance and, by the 16th century, the Reformation had begun to change the way in which people thought about themselves, with a fundamental impact on the trajectory of society. The Protestant notion that individuals were directly responsible to God over their whole lives – with salvation being dependent on their conduct throughout with no recourse to periodic absolution via an interceding priesthood – made people more anxious, self-conscious and reflective as to how they managed their life trajectories. Again, this underlines the need for control – both self-control and knowledge of and influence over the conditions in which one's life is played out.[2]

Further contributing to these increasing complexities of the age, the re-urbanization of Europe, where the rise of trade and commerce had created new economic centres that began to reverse the decline since the fall of Rome, also rendered everyday life more potentially complex, given the implications of routinely engaging with larger numbers of strangers.[3]

Rationalization, revolution and romanticism

For all of the reasons identified, as well as knowing more about their world, people became ever more focused on simplifying their experiences within it, with reason and rationalization emerging as key orientations coming to the fore in the early modern era and expanding through the Enlightenment. As has been widely observed, this emerging mindset informed the economic, political, scientific, cultural and social revolutions that we associate with the advent of the modern world. For many writers, particularly in the social sciences, this great transition occurs simply as the unintended outcome of a confluence of various factors, notably without any particular reference to how we're made. Of course, the precise developments that emerge through the centuries that follow the Renaissance era *are* often haphazard and dependent on the particular unfolding of events. Nonetheless, the broader logic of these developments can be more fully understood with reference to the deeper processes described thus far and, specifically, the interplay between, on the one hand, the limitations of our capacity to deal with uncertainty and simultaneous demands, and, on the other hand, the negative emotional experience when this capacity is exceeded, including our tendency towards defensive or aggressive conduct when we feel significantly overwhelmed or under threat.[4] The complexities of early modern urban living produced such conditions, stimulating an emotionally driven impetus for people to identify those around them, to anticipate their likely behaviour and to reduce the complexity of what was presented to them. In short, people had a growing interest in being able to go about their business without meeting with too many unusual situations among people they couldn't classify and, hence, anticipate their likely behaviour, including those they might want to avoid!

The consequence of all this from this period of re-urbanization onwards was reflected in a drive to institute greater formal social organization and instil social norms of appearance and conduct that reduced the complexity and uncertainties of everyday life. Corroborating this perspective, as noted in Chapter 1, work by Lederbogen et al found that those raised in cities exhibited greater sensitivity in the amygdala associated with vulnerability to stress.[5] This phenomenon is also implicit in psychologist Michelle Gelfland's work where she identifies a strong tendency towards cultural *tightening* in terms of socially imposed normative conformity in societies under threat or, significantly in terms of what is argued here, that are densely populated.[6]

Given this, as we moved from the small settlement world of closely associated individuals, whose conformity was directly imposed by the group and by religion, to a more populous environment where unpredictability appeared inherent, the re-establishment of a sense of control and order was imposed by more codified and formal standards of appearance and conduct, in tandem with the routines and more formal organization that needed to be applied to enable larger-scale settlements to function. Shifts in organizational and social rationalization processes can be understood in this way, the latter qualifying the famous work by the sociologist Norbert Elias that a rationalization of conduct emerged in European court society as a fashionable attempt to replace violence with cultivated etiquette and manners, or at least constrain and codify interpersonal violence as a vehicle for achieving and sustaining one's position. Elias describes this as rendering life safer for early modern monarchs and as a cultural development that began to spread through European populations via emulation down through the social classes over time.[7] However, while the courtly elite may well have played a pivotal role in driving this process, it is perhaps no coincidence that this phenomenon appears at a point consistent with the re-expansion of European cities, perhaps as a reaction to the social complexities inherent in living in a society of strangers and as a function of the aforementioned *reciprocal restraint* and *reciprocal reinforcement*. This interpretation is arguably supported by the example of societies like Japan, where a historically high population density was accompanied by its own form of highly codified and 'tightened' social organization, manners and interactional rules, including those governing violence.[8]

In Europe, the rationalization of conduct may be regarded to some extent as an interactional counterpart to the desire to banish the unknown through global exploration and scientific discovery to fill the void in understanding of the world left vacant by the waning influence of religion. Of course, the development of Western society's ongoing march of social, organizational and scientific rationalization was not a unidirectional or linear process, as the rationalization process itself threw up its own paradoxical contradictions. As was suggested earlier, rationalization has been somewhat of a dialectical process, where efforts to categorize, comprehend and organize activity and experience have often produced new categories and contradictions and further challenges. As is also apparent, 'progressive' rationalization, where societies began to develop in directions that enhanced the lives of populations, have, at times, created complexities that have become cognitively unwieldy, reflecting Tainter's argument regarding the *Collapse of Complex Societies*.[9]

The tensions and competition that emerged for the future of this reconstituting social order, as the foundations of the old feudal society crumbled, saw revolt and revolution becoming a recurrent phenomenon marking the growing pains of a new form of society. Political revolution, from the Glorious Revolution to the French Revolution, accelerated the dismantling of absolutist monarchy and aristocracy as an enduring and unopposed system of governance across Europe. While in the public imagination revolutionary activity has long been associated with the lower orders, the mob, a great deal of such action and, indeed, other less dramatic challenges to the old traditional European order engaged an emerging bourgeois middle class – the rising middle class of capitalist traders, merchants and financial interests, together with a small professional class and lower landholding class, who considered that the social and political structures of early modern Europe were anachronistic and did not take account of their beliefs, values and growing economic and social influence. While there is a good deal of academic debate on the particular role of the rising middle class in driving political change, it is generally regarded that they were its beneficiaries. However, for the poor and the masses, their co-option in such political and social adventures, then as now, invariably failed to deliver significant advancement.

What did emerge from the political upheavals on the road to modern society was a demand for 'rational' governance based on progressive ideals, to match the emphasis on human reason as the route to societal progress, even if these were embryonic or distorted and far from being realized at the time. Rationality was also applied to an expansion in bureaucratic organization and capitalist enterprise,[10] as well as to the modes of enquiry and discovery that characterized the Enlightenment and the century or so that followed, the latter producing the groundwork for revolutions in agriculture, science and industrialization that marked this era, while generating the conditions for the further rapid expansion of urbanization across Europe and beyond.

All of these changes taken together, as argued previously, while being driven by the need to know and the desire for control, were simultaneously generating a potentially bewildering juggernaut of rapid change. However, this emerging modern world was one where, aside from politically progressive ideas, the application of new technologies, mechanistic organization and 'cold reason' was, as was suggested earlier, countered by the production of inherent unpredictability.

Moreover, disaffection with the emerging zeitgeist of the rational, industrial world emerged, was marked in the late 18th and early to mid-19th centuries with the rise of a Romantic movement within the Western nations themselves, as a set of ideas and collective that considered the world being created by modern rationalism to have distorted both the human condition and debased the environment.

The Romantics opposed the calculating and unemotional orientation that was deemed to characterize the modern rational mindset, while distaste for the latter was aligned with dismay regarding the sprawling, dirty and smoke-filled industrial landscapes that they considered it to have spawned. Romanticism bemoaned the loss of nature, the countryside, tradition and, critically, leisure, emotion and imagination. There was a sense of nostalgia for an imagined past, while these tropes would also come to inform the imagery that would inspire a rising tide of nationalism through the 19th and early 20th centuries. Again, the need for continuity, predictability and control, an aversion to experiential overload, played out as a desire to re-establish the simplicities of traditional agrarian society, nature and older forms of social order. As will be addressed later on, this is a recurrent tendency in times of uncertainty that is also central to the tropes and imagery of populist movements at the present time.

However, what the Romantic movement shared with the key ideas of rational modernity was an emphasis on the individual, further advancing an enduring core element of modern consciousness that had become ever more pronounced since the Renaissance and the Reformation. In addition, as will be identified in some of the following chapters, the seemingly oppositional themes of rationalism and romanticism were eventually reconciled to an extent, fusing as dualistic aspects of the modern psyche and modern culture, represented in the modern workplace, in contemporary consumerism, in art and culture, and reflected in aspects of the modern built environment. In a sense, rationalization and romanticism can be regarded as extensions of key elements of the human 'homeostatic' characteristics identified in Chapter 1, where the need for order, routine, control and knowing is counterbalanced by a desire for sufficient stimulation, variation and 'arousal', so long as the latter is perceived to be pleasurable, manageable and controllable.[11]

Towards 'high' modernity

As this new social order began to extend through the 19th century amid rapid economic and industrial expansion, to a great extent it generated an element of confidence and even hubris among an expanding middle and upper class in Western nations. As we know, technological advances followed earlier voyages of discovery and advanced competitive military expansion among what were now becoming modern nation states. Britain and the other major European nations increasingly vied for imperial domination and colonial expansion over non-European territories and populations, exploiting their labour power to the point of enslavement while also appropriating natural resources in various ways that marked, and enduringly scarred, this assertedly 'progressive' historical era.

Colonialism and imperialism

As we know, the development and expansion of what became a Western-dominated global order was far from positive for many of the legions of peoples who were subjugated and exploited in the pursuit of profit, power and socioeconomic and cultural hegemony that accompanied the emergence of Western modernity. Once more, this is a huge issue that has rightly been, and continues to be, the focus of a great deal of writings and debate such that, once again, only a very brief aspect of this can be engaged with here as it relates to the particular issues and themes being addressed.

At the heart of the colonial and imperial expansion of the West from the 16th century onwards, in addition to new ideas and technology, was the rapid expansion of capitalism that provided the wherewithal and much of the motivation that enabled the modern Western ascendancy. In short, the lure of riches likely played a greater role in spurring European 'voyages of discovery' than are depicted in more loftier accounts of Western expansion. However, then as now, while expanding Western capitalism aligned with scientific and technological advances enabled a range of positive developments, inventions and innovations, the growing power and capacities that these developments conferred was, as has been suggested earlier, significantly founded on the subjugation and exploitation of people and resources. The most iniquitous example of the latter of course, which was integral to the early expansion of Western capitalism, was the North Atlantic Slave Trade, the scars from which continue to balefully resonate to the present day. Slavery, of course, has been a feature of conflict and power relations between social groups since at least the advent of the civilizations of the ancient world, and was by no means confined to the activities of Western regions in the early modern era. However, from the late 1500s until the mid-1800s, they became the most prolific practitioners, with Spain, France, the Netherlands and Denmark heavily involved, and Britain and Portugal being at the forefront of this activity. Perhaps what set the North Atlantic Slave Trade apart was not only its scale but also the way in which it involved rationalized processes of capital accumulation, together with the moral and ideological contortions that were involved in justifying its practice. It continues to serve as a stark exemplar of the potential excesses, amorality and dehumanizing features of underregulated and amoral capitalist accumulation. A key element of this phenomenon at its height was the Middle Passage trade route, a feature of the triangular conveyor of shipping lanes across the Atlantic carrying enslaved Africans to the West Indies and the Americas. Manufactured and other goods were transported to Africa in payment to local rulers for providing slaves from among their own and conquered peoples, In turn, the proceeds from the sale of slaves in the West Indies and Americas facilitated the purchase of raw materials and other commodities (cotton, sugar, coffee, furs, tobacco and so on) which were then shipped to Britain and the other European nations involved in this 'trade', all of which occurred in an ongoing cycle.

As is widely acknowledged, those enslaved were subject to the most extreme levels of unimaginable torment and dehumanization. One of the most infamous examples of this, and an event that spurred on efforts towards the abolition of slavery, involved the particularly abhorrent events that occurred on board the British-owned slave ship *Zong* in 1781:

> On 29 November 1781, the master of the merchant vessel Zong made the decision to jettison a portion of his cargo into the Caribbean. The Zong was a slave ship and the jettisoned cargo comprised 132 living men, women and children, yet despite their deaths, and the two court hearings of 1783 ... no criminal prosecution would ever result from the Zong incident.[12]

As well as the tragic loss of freedom, right to life and any sense of control over any aspect of existence for those consigned to this fate, what this particular incident made explicit was the degree to which racialization and extreme prejudice were accepted by segments of the British authorities of the times. The court hearings referred to previously, rather than addressing the plight of the human casualties, focused on a legal dispute between the ship owners and their insurers over recompense for the loss of valuable 'cargo'. This latter definition of the deceased slaves was horrifically applied in a subsequent attempt to bring about a charge of murder, which, as shown in what follows, was dismissed on these grounds by Justice John Lee, British Solicitor General: 'What is this claim that human people have been thrown overboard? This is a case of chattels or goods ... it is madness to accuse these well-serving honourable men of murder.'[13]

While this was not an uncommon attitude advanced in support of the slave trade, it was also the case that it was not universally held in 18th-century Britain, with many believing that ownership of another human being was unacceptable, particularly on British soil. It was the growing abhorrence to such attitudes and the gross violations of this period that, among more enlightened figures, began to galvanize movements that would eventually lead to the abolition of slavery across Europe and the Americas by the mid-19th century.[14]

As has been noted previously, slavery, of course, was an extreme feature of the wider process of imperialist domination, discrimination and exploitation that emerged from around the 16th to the 19th centuries. Driven by the dual and interrelated imperatives of power and profit, as we know, Britain and other European powers scrambled to compete for land, resources and dominion across the globe. Much of this was advanced under the arrangements we refer to as mercantilism, where state-backed large-scale enterprises like the British East India Company conquered territories for profit to the benefit of both the company and the crown and under the latter's patronage. This conflation of capital and state was common across Europe, with nations and their aristocratic and economic elites competing with each other to establish colonies in the Americas, Africa, India, the Middle East and the Far East. In a sense it marked an important stage in the process by which the economic sphere and interests came to dominate the business of national statehood.

The legacy of imperialism

Of course, the imperial and colonial era, despite the gradual dissolution of much of Western formal rule in the 20th century, has continued to exert a huge influence over the trajectory of development of colonized nations. Firstly, there is the issue of *dependency*, prominently highlighted by Immanuel

Wallerstein in his works on world-systems theory, where he charted the rise of Western political and economic dominance from early overseas ventures through the mercantilist to the postcolonial era. Again these are broad issues, but the argument asserts that the Western powers, due to their removal of talent, control and raw materials, constrained the self-development of colonized nations and, when formal political control was relinquished, this was supplanted by economic dependency and control exerted via Western transnational corporations (TNCs), global financial institutions and also Western-controlled authorities such as the World Bank and the International Monetary Fund. Moreover, control by and indebtedness to the latter, as will be discussed later on, also left these nations vulnerable to accepting the neoliberal policies of the West and opening up their markets, utilities and services to Western companies.[15]

These more large-scale legacies of imperialism and colonialism aside, the trajectory of Western-led development has also greatly impacted on the identities, self-worth and wellbeing of dominated peoples as the political and cultural hegemony of the Western-advanced notion of a hierarchy of peoples with, unsurprisingly, white Europeans at the top and others defined by a variety of negative stereotypes. The experience and the lasting discrimination that the latter instilled can be seen to have exerted an ongoing influence on the psyche of non-White peoples and their descendants that persists to the present day. The plight of Black Americans, for example, following enslavement and the ongoing discrimination, oppression and differential treatment that followed, was characterized by classic US sociologist W.E.B. Dubois, as creating a 'double consciousness'. Here Dubois observed that black Americans experienced an ongoing burden in terms of the capacity to build and sustain a coherent, and workable sense of identity, ostensibly as the self had to be constructed within the context of a society where the individual was constantly aware of being negatively evaluated, of never being whole:

> From the double life every American Negro [sic] must live, as a Negro [sic] and as an American, as swept on by the current of the nineteenth while yet struggling in the eddies of the fifteenth century – from this must arise a painful self-consciousness, an almost morbid sense of personality, and a moral hesitancy which is fatal to self-confidence. The worlds within and without the Veil of Color are changing, and changing rapidly, but not at the same rate, not in the same way; and this must produce a peculiar wrenching of the soul, a peculiar sense of doubt and bewilderment. Such a double life, with double thoughts, double duties, and double social classes, must give rise to double words and double ideals, and tempt the mind to pretence or revolt, to hypocrisy or radicalism.[16]

Broadly similar sentiments were expressed by Franz Fanon, a French Caribbean colonial-born psychiatrist, philosopher and social thinker of note. Fanon, in his most influential work, referred to Black people as constantly adopting a shell or mask of whiteness in their efforts to fit in and sustain some sense of dignity and self-worth in a society that treated them as inferiors.[17]

This idea of being the bearer of a damaged identity in this way has evident resonances with Erving Goffman's work on stigma, and can be seen to be the case here and indeed in relation to all of the ethnic and cultural groups devalued by Western discourses of White superiority.[18] To some extent, there were also gradations applied to those who were ostensibly White but who were also deemed inferior, a condition applied to the Irish under British rule both in Ireland and the early Americas. In such conditions, people must constantly negotiate and be hyperconscious of their engagement with others, at least those beyond their own social group, in the effort to sustain some form of positive self-worth. In terms of the understanding of identity processes set out in Chapter 1, living under such conditions constitutes a denial of the capacity to maintain a positive worldview and biography, and the easy adoption and expression of norms of interaction that will support social acceptance. All of the latter are integral to maintaining a workable 'social map' and, hence, an ongoing semblance of cognitive and emotional ease.

Internal divisions

The drive by Western elites for dominance and control at the global scale was, of course, replicated within European nations themselves. The concern of elites to sustain their expanding wealth, status and unbalanced property rights and privileges saw them expend considerable effort to both control and protect themselves from what they regarded as the subordinate and potentially 'dangerous classes' within their own borders, those whose short and hard lives were given over to creating the wealth that their betters enjoyed. It is with these developments that we begin to move on from outlining the antecedents of the themes addressed in the book and start to embark upon the main thrust of the argument, as the die began to be cast in terms of the ideas and social arrangements that continue to influence the darker aspects of our own times that, while challenged and assuaged for a short time, as will be identified subsequently, were determinedly re-established when the opportunity arose.

Returning to the burgeoning industrial cities of the 19th century, it can be argued that social divisions were ostensibly as wide as they had been in the feudal era, while, given the great expansion in economic activity, financial divisions were even wider. In cities like London, New York, Berlin and Paris, the municipal boundaries incorporated two worlds. Wealthier urbanites had begun to establish themselves in leafy areas and expanding suburbs, largely beyond sight of the factory chimneys and dilapidated and overcrowded slums that housed the poor. As an interesting if sad aside, it is notable that in British cities, for example, the poorer areas tended to be located in the north and east, and the better areas in the south and west. This is not coincidental as, while not always the case, the prevailing wind more often than not tended to blow the noxious factory smoke across the poorer areas in the north and east and away from the middle and upper-class areas: 'In Manchester ... prevailing and strongest winds [blow] from the South West. This meant that when the dense sulphurous smoke left Manchester's tall chimneys it usually moved North East, and this was to have a marked effect on the shaping of the city.'[19]

This phenomenon resulted in a good deal of respiratory disease that added to the list of factors bearing down on working-class mortality; compounding low wages, arduous and dangerous working conditions, inadequate food and nutrition, little access to healthcare, squalid and overcrowded living conditions, as well as the less visible scars of endemic insecurity and inequality that will be addressed in later chapters. When contemporary political pundits demonize mention of the work of Marx and Engels, due to its association with failed attempts to establish successful communist societies, regularly highlighting the significant brutalities that have often accompanied past attempts, what is often forgotten is that their work was forged as a reaction to the gross iniquities they observed in 19th-century England.[20] As such, their ideas were devised in understandable circumstances and with the best of intentions, only to fall foul of very human characteristics – as was noted earlier – that blighted the lives of those they sought to help as competition, greed and the desire to dominate were no less prevalent in the societies established in their name. This was also the world of Charles Dickens, Charles Booth and, across the Atlantic, Jacob Riis, where a rising leisure class dominated a mass of the disenfranchised, dispossessed and needy who often led miserable lives while driving the engine of economic expansion.

Keeping this system in place, while being enforced physically where necessary, the highly divided industrial societies of the West were forging a revised legitimating story. By the latter part of the 1900s, religious legitimation continued to play a residual role in underscoring the righteousness of the social order, appealing to notions of the meek and poor being rewarded in the afterlife while the wealthy made hay in the present. However, in a society where belief based on observable evidence had become more prevalent and a tide of secularization was lapping at the margins, the supernatural ordaining of social and economic injustice began to cut less ice. As such, legitimating religious stories began to be supplanted by an emerging complementary doctrine, by further misapplication of Darwinism and, to some extent, by cherrypicking of Adam Smith's now well-established arguments regarding the *invisible hand* of self-regulating markets as complementary themes that continue to support inequalities into our own times.

Thus, so the story goes, people are stationed in life in accordance with innate talent and effort in an economic environment that rewards these *abilities* largely without fear or favour. The notion of a secular meritocracy began to take shape. Such ideas of course were (and still are to a very significant extent) heartily embraced by the comfortably off. However, aside from a very few of the wealthy who emerged from humble origins – and where even among those their initiative and industry was regularly accompanied by fortunate timing, conditions and a strong element of luck – there was little acknowledgement by many of the elite that much of their good fortune was a simple accident of birth and sustaining their advantageous position required little effort.[21] Nonetheless, these ideas permeated 19th-century society and were advanced among the working classes via approved activities sponsored by elites and via popular literature that emphasized individual self-improvement and the possibility of going from rags to riches through individual effort.

The 'kailyard' stories offered by a range of Scottish authors and, more importantly, the inspirational 'rags to riches' stories of the writer Horatio Alger (the latter associated with the 'American Dream') weaved an enduring mythology that reinforced notions of being 'self-made' and the inherent virtues of the successful. In fact, with reference to the influence of serendipity mentioned previously, the perspective among both the wider public, and to a significant extent those who have 'made it', is attributable to some extent to the aforementioned processes of apophenia, where random and chance events are falsely attributed to logical patterns or *intentional* developments, as a form of post hoc rationalization that some individuals were inevitably destined for success.[22] This way of thinking also tends to support the belief that 'making it' is more readily achievable than is actually the case, as it often fails to account for unacknowledged support and, critically, the vast legions of the similarly talented and aspirational on whom fortune does not smile. These are issues I return to more explicitly and in more detail in Chapter 10, as it is a discourse that has continued to inform public perceptions of contemporary inequality.

However, throughout the 19th century, a combination of this type of ideological belief, tight social norms and, where these failed, punitive sanctions meted out to the lower orders kept this system of widening structural inequality in place. Yet, this was a society where those at the top retained a keen awareness that sustaining control over this unbalanced society required vigilance.

As well as the cultural exemplars described earlier, a variety of other related strategies were employed to neutralize the perceived threat from below.

The introduction of mass basic education, for example, was equally aimed at the training and socialization of compliant citizens/workers as it was in its manifest function of advancing learning. Other strategies for containing the potentially unruly lower orders on both sides of the Atlantic included temperance movements and advocacy for *rational recreation* as devices for distracting the working classes from less morally upstanding pursuits.[23] In a sense, the reformist zeal of the urban bourgeoisie reflected the legacy of Reformation self-denial and asceticism turned towards a strong moral impetus for social control, including the advancing of a code of strict social norms and etiquette, publicly endorsed in the angst-inducing setting of the expanding and unruly industrial city and held out as an ideal for the working classes to aspire to, even where this could often be disregarded by at least some of the rising middle classes in private who might on occasion resort to aping the lifestyles of their more hedonistic aristocratic associates. Evidently, this was also a highly class-conscious society where people wanted to identify their social status in the public realm, along the lines discussed previously, played out in the form of nascent consumer practices, fashion and elaborate displays and manners and etiquette that were emerging among the urban elite and the expanding middle class.

In qualification, it should be noted that by no means were all Victorian reformers wholly motivated by a self-interested desire to contain the unruly working classes, as many were equally driven by a general desire for the betterment of society, including working-class lives and conditions. Religious and utilitarian ideas on generating social improvement also spurred these developments. Nonetheless, the overall drive to constrain behavioural excess in increasingly populous and potentially unruly urban settings can be seen as a move to neutralize its potentially unnerving complexity, unpredictability and inherent dangers, in line with the fundamental tendencies described in Chapter 1. This evidently accords with the need to confront and neutralize experiential overload while having clear resonances with Gelfland's cultural tightening and Elias's civilizing process identified earlier.[24]

In spite of such efforts, the 1800s was a period of considerable turbulence as well as unwieldy change both within and across nations. Clashes between rich and poor in the form of successive revolts, particularly in 1848 and 1870, trade union organization and demands for higher wages, calls for better and more affordable housing, civil rights and political representation for all had stimulated a groundswell of activity that regularly unnerved authorities and leaders of the business community during the period. While advances for the poor were slow and gains were hard won, by the time of the outbreak of World War 1, developments were underway that would begin to move things forward, albeit in a stuttering fashion, towards some improvement in the mid-20th century. In part this was driven by a morphing of Victorian reformism into the progressive movements of the very late 19th and early

20th centuries, which drove forward an 'enlightened' programme to generate social improvements entering the new century.[25]

It is fair to say that, as well as the reforming movements and politicians that instituted social advances, some positive changes were equivocal and came from more ambiguous sources and developments. Of particular importance, changes to production and labour arrangements associated with Henry Ford during this period would have an enduring legacy throughout a large part of the 20th century. Ford's aims were neither liberal nor progressive, as the latter were really unintended consequences of his real aim, which was to improve efficiency and secure control over the production process. Ford had embraced F.W. Taylor's scientific management techniques, which broke down complex procedures into smaller tasks that could be performed with minimal training by interchangeable workers and standardized 'tools, parts and rules', minimizing the need for bespoke manufacturing and special skill or oversight among the general labour force. All of this gave management more control over industrial production and made it more efficient, less prone to interruption, and with less sway and knowledge left in the hands of an artisan workforce. To this, Ford famously added the conveyor belt-style assembly line that gave management control over the pace of production, further enhancing productivity. The resultant jobs involved simple, repetitive, highly routinized tasks being conducted at a pace dictated by the speed on the line. However, the downside of working in the resultant tedious and relentless conditions led to a very high turnover of workers that Ford wanted to resolve as, even though the need for training had been reduced, this still reduced the effectiveness of Ford's strategy. By means of resolution, Ford raised wages for his workforce significantly, reducing working hours as a trade-off for fatigue and tedium, while encouraging other industrial magnates to follow suit. However, there was also a strong element of social control here, as part of the Ford workforce contract extended into his workers' personal lives, with prohibitions on drinking, gambling and working wives, very much imposing bourgeois morality and traditional patriarchal norms on his workers. In this, the legacy of Victorian reformist zeal appeared very much alive.

However, one further consequence of this development affected the economic sphere more broadly, resonating into the current era. While this will be discussed explicitly in Chapter 8, the combination of increased earnings for a segment of the working classes, and hence an expansion of disposable income across a section of the population who had previously just gotten by, together with the expansion of the capacity to produce goods associated with 'Fordist' mass production techniques, created a seemingly beneficial partnership, as better-off workers began to become consumers of the expanded capacity they generated, engaging in an activity that had previously been the strict preserve of the leisure classes and wealthier members of the workforce. In short, mass production began to meet with mass consumption, only to be interrupted by war, economic crisis and then war once more within the space of less than half a century.

Clearly, the first of these devastating events arrived with the First World War of 1914–18, born out of the dying embers of the old European multinational dynastic kingdoms of Austria-Hungary and the Ottoman Empire, and a united Germany's moves towards territorial expansion and challenge to Britain's imperial dominance as the foremost global power. By the end of the war, the world order had changed radically, but with neither of the main protagonists coming out on top. Germany was, of course, humiliated in defeat, as had France been to an extent on the opposite side, while Britain's global prominence was terminally eclipsed by the entry of America into the war as an event marking a change of world leadership in the new century, while Russia had embarked upon its decades-long communist experiment.

The aftermath of the war did not see the relief that many must have hoped for, with the devastating Spanish flu pandemic killing millions, including significant numbers of those who had been fortunate enough to survive the war. However, the short hiatus between these events and the economic crisis that was to engulf the US and the world economy from 1929 was interspersed by a short period of significant hope and transition.

The industrial economy and consumerism began to expand rapidly in the 1920s, building many of the foundations of the form of consumer culture that we know today, aided in a variety of ways by expanded disposable income and the arrival of cinema as a mass pursuit that will be unpacked in later chapters. With the rise and popularity of cinema and an extended print media, a mass culture was emerging across more predominantly urban societies in the West, and prominently in the emerging global economic and cultural powerhouse of the US. It might be argued that this is the point where traditional identities and means of making sense of the world began to be supplanted by the mass-mediated culture of the high modern era, and where consumerist images from entertainment and advertising really began to shape people's image of themselves and others, providing a commercialized template for making sense of the urban landscape and those encountered within it. This was also the period where traditional gender roles had begun to change, with more women in the workplace, a demand for greater autonomy and freedom, at least among better-off young women, as a trend that was both caught up with and amplified by advertisers who considered women's emancipation as a theme that might be exploited to sell consumer goods.[26]

While this was a period of relative optimism, there was no less anxiety among the urban bourgeoisie in relation to overwhelming change, increasing social complexity and, indeed, the potential unpredictability and unruly conduct of the masses, compounded by concerns over the bewildering social and cultural change and rapid urban expansion to which they were exposed. The consequent need for control perhaps expressed itself most notably with the introduction of prohibition in the US, banning all alcoholic drinks of over 0.5 per cent volume, that is, a level that we now associate with being close to alcohol-free. There were also moves to stem the flow of the immigration that had created the modern US, and continuing high levels of discrimination towards Black Americans, numbers of whom were moving north from the former confederate states to escape harsher ongoing discrimination, prejudicial Jim Crow laws and the nefarious and hate-fuelled activities of a highly active Ku Klux Klan.[27] As noted earlier, and as will also be discussed later on, 'othering' is an important element of the process of primalization identified in Chapter 1, where the stresses produced by conditions of insecurity and inequality can lead to a reduction in measured reflective thinking and an associated tendency towards impulsive, emotionally driven thought and conduct.

The Great Crash

Of course, this short period of rapid growth experienced during the 1920s came to an abrupt end with the Great Crash of 1929 and its aftermath in the 'hungry thirties', generating the conditions for the Second World War. The crash itself will be discussed in more detail in Chapters 4 and 5. Briefly, however, economic management continued to be informed by liberal economic nostrums that markets were self-regulating entities best left to operate without significant intervention. In short, the market mechanism was hailed as the best way to ensure efficiency and to freely and fairly allocate resources, while it is no surprise that such ideas had persisted since the 19th century in spite of regular economic crises leading up to this one. In the years running up to the crash, particularly in the US, there was a tide of optimism around people's prospects for getting rich amid a period of expansion. As well as directly engaging with productive businesses, a lack of control over investment and finance, and the perceived profits that might easily 'earned' in this way, led to more and more people investing in property and crucially the stock market in the hope of making quick and easy gains. As is in all speculative economic bubbles, this initially seemed to pay off, as early investors saw their holdings increase in value as more people piled into the market.

It is not difficult to see the motivation here, given that this was arising in a fledgling consumer society, where status was increasingly defined by conspicuous consumption. As such, the prospect, no matter how distant, of joining the ranks of the urban wealthy, and in some small way emulating the lifestyles depicted in the movies and advertising, had a seductive pull. Equally motivating in such circumstances is the fear of missing out – a powerful emotional drive regularly exploited by consumer and advertising organizations.

Inevitably, as has been widely documented, the top was reached after stratospheric rises in the value of stocks, well beyond their assumed fundamental value, with a surge occurring over a relatively brief period of a year or so leading up to the collapse, when speculative fever had set in and the working and middle classes had joined the fray. When the collapse came, as we know, it produced shock waves in the US and across the globe as investors, large and small, private and institutional, watched gains rapidly evaporate and losses mount. While tales of bankers throwing themselves from buildings, according to the great economist J.K. Galbraith, one of the documenters of these notable events, were largely fictional, nonetheless, the social and economic fallout from the Great Crash was, as we know, cataclysmic and sent ripples of economic and social turmoil across the globe. As well as the direct damage to banking and financial institutions, the fledgling consumer economy was critically impacted. In no small part, this was due to the fact that 1920s societies across Europe and the Anglosphere remained highly unequal, despite limited advances for the working classes and, hence, while they had emerged as a consumer group, demand in the economy was still skewed towards the spending power of the better off. The traditional investing classes had lost a great deal in the crisis and, given that much of their spending tends to be discretionary, as opposed to the more predominantly essential spending undertaken by those on modest incomes, demand in the economy was hit hard as the consuming classes pulled back, leading to the downward spiral towards depression, a destination accelerated by unwise austerity policies imposed at the same time.[28]

As has also been extensively debated, responses to what became a prodigious and lengthy global slump helped shape the political and social and economic agenda in a new more progressive direction. The combination of job security, full employment policies, welfare and other social protections, together with state intervention to regulate and temper the unruly 'animal spirits' that had governed pre-Crash markets, began to stabilize demand and recharge the consumer economy in the late 1930s, only for this transition to be dramatically interrupted by the Second World War only twenty years after the end of the presumed 'war to end all wars'. Again, the causes of the war are too complex and extensively charted to be dealt with here, and to attempt to do so would go beyond the scope of what is required. Of note, however, is the fact that the sociopsychological impact of defeat in Germany, together with the economic conditions endured by its citizens, where punitive war reparations compounded the impact of the economic crisis, created fertile conditions for political turbulence and extremism. As has been argued elsewhere, and as can be applied to a good deal of what's happening in our own times (and with similar roots), populism and political unrest feed on *primalization*, providing an entrée for opportunistic leaders who can, as was suggested earlier, offer disenchanted and insecure people an illusory sense of hope and security based on simplistic and often romanticized discourses, a positive collective identity, origin story and destiny, almost no matter how distorted, together with convenient targets for pent-up ire.[29]

Keynes, welfare capitalism and the New Deal

Following the well-charted horrors of the war, the collective experience had, nonetheless, provided further impetus for consolidating the fledgling aspects of a more equal, progressive and rational social order, ushered in by the New Deal and welfarist social democratic trends that had begun to take shape in the late 1930s. The shock of crises and war had once again shaken habitualized worldviews. Shared traumatic experience and common purpose had ameliorated prewar class divisions and antagonisms to an extent, making concessions to the working classes more likely, while this solidarity was also expressed via increasingly powerful labour organizations. The tight management of the economy, society and industrial production during the war had also provided a template for a more state-directed economy, supporting Keynesian interventions on behalf of states to embed the economy within society, privileging the latter in relation to the former in a way that had been unprecedented before the war. Business and finance were also persuaded that they must give in to higher taxation, better wages, working conditions and job security, where profits should be gained more from expansion and growth rather than exploitation. As was noted earlier, all of this is well observed.

However, perhaps a less widely vaunted rationale for these postwar social and economic concessions can be understood in terms of the inherent dangers of returning a generation of battle-hardened, mostly young men to idleness, deprivation, poor housing and hungry children, given that the relationship between despair and insurrection was well understood, and while Western nations also wanted to ensure that life under a more managed capitalism seemed significantly more attractive than the communist alternative. From all of this, a new era began to emerge, still very far from perfect and scarred by continuing inequities of class, race, ethnicity and gender, as well as sporadic proxy wars and confrontations and stand-offs between two competing global superpowers, but where lives and standards of living were nonetheless generally improving and there was a strong drive to challenge remaining injustices. Consumerism, security, better housing, a burst of technical and artistic creativity, and, overall, a measure of hope began to generate a confidence that the future would be better than the past. It seemed at least that a form of society had emerged that was beginning to, and promised in future, to more readily meet the material and psychological needs of a greater number of citizens.

Importantly, while there was still a great deal to be done, the fundamental human need to balance a sense of security and order with controlled stimulation began to be addressed. Leisure and pleasure also became a social and political aim to a hitherto unprecedented degree, albeit that the tight normative climate of the 1950s had fomented a degree of hedonistic rebellion among the young who found some conditions too prescriptive and constraining. However, with a number of exceptions, and while observing that the Vietnam War had also generated very significant social tensions and disaffection, much antipathy towards the 'system' was expressed through popular protest and the arts rather than via violent uprisings, creating the impression that further progressive change was a highly popular cause, but towards a destination that did not dispense with the most fundamental securities and opportunities of the times. Notable exceptions were the Paris riots of 1968, where hopes of sparking revolutionary change were fatefully dashed, and the tragically ill-fated student protest at Kent State University. For the most part, however, it can be argued that the young of the 1950s, 1960s and early 1970s wanted to dispense with the bathwater, but to keep the baby.

However, as we know, while the incumbents of the postwar social democratic era thought that the harsher aspects of the modern economy and society had been consigned to the past, this at least qualified progressive societal trajectory was not to last, as those who imagined a quite different vision of the future were already setting out the rationale for the return of something more reminiscent of what had gone before.

Notes

[1]   Beck, U. (1992) *Risk Society: Towards a New Modernity*, London: Sage.

[2]   Dumont, L. (1982) 'A modified view of our origins: the Christian beginnings of modern individualism', *Religion*, 12(1): 1–27.

[3]   Mumford, L. (1961) *The City in History*, New York: Harcourt, Brace, & World; Friedrichs, C.R. (1995) *The Early Modern City, 1450–1750*, New York: Longman.

[4]   Bone, J. (2005) 'The social map & the problem of order: a re-evaluation of "homo sociologicus"', *Theory & Science*, 6(1): 1–20; Bone, J. (2010) 'Irrational capitalism: the social map, neoliberalism and the demodernization of the West', *Critical Sociology*, 36(5): 717–740.

[5]   Lederbogen, F., Kirsch, P., Haddad, L. et al (2011) 'City living and urban upbringing affect neural social stress processing in humans', *Nature*, 474: 498–501.

[6]   Gelfand, M.J., Raver, J.L., Nishii, L., Leslie, L.M., Lun, J., Lim, B.C., Duan, L., Almaliach, A., Ang, S., Arnadottir, J. and Aycan, Z. (2011) 'Differences between tight and loose cultures: a 33-nation study', *Science*, 332(6033): 1100–1104.

[7]   Elias, N. (1978) *The Civilizing Process: The History of Manners*, New York: Pantheon Books.

[8]   Chan, D.K.S. (1996) 'Tightness-looseness revisited: some preliminary analyses in Japan and the United States', *International Journal of Psychology*, 31(1): 1–12.

[9]   Tainter, J. (1988) *The Collapse of Complex Societies*, Cambridge: Cambridge University Press.

10. Weber, M. (and Kalberg, S.) (2013 [1930]) *The Protestant Ethic and the Spirit of Capitalism*, Abingdon: Routledge.
11. Bone, J. (2010) 'Irrational capitalism: the social map, neoliberalism and the demodernization of the West', *Critical Sociology*, 36(5): 717–740.
12. Webster, J. (2007) 'The Zong in the context of the eighteenth-century slave trade', *Journal of Legal History*, 28(3): 285–298, at 285
13. https://www.blackpast.org/global-african-history/zong-massacre-1781/
14. Kaifala, J. (2017) 'Granville Sharp's fight to free the slaves', in *Free Slaves, Freetown, and the Sierra Leonean Civil War*, London: Palgrave Macmillan, pp 33–58.
15. Wallerstein, I. (1974) 'The rise and future demise of the world capitalist system: concepts for comparative analysis', *Contemporary Studies in Society and History*, 16 (4): 387-415.
16. Du Bois, W.E.B. (2008) *The Souls of Black Folk*, Oxford: Oxford University Press, p 157.
17. Fanon, F. (2016) 'Black skin, white masks', in W. Longhofer and D. Winchester (eds), *Social Theory Re-wired*, Abingdon: Routledge, pp 394–401.
18. Goffman, E. (1963) *Stigma: Notes on the Management of Spoiled Identity*, Harmondsworth: Penguin.
19. Mosley, S. (2013) *The Chimney of the World: A History of Smoke Pollution in Victorian and Edwardian Manchester*, Abingdon: Routledge.
20. Engels, F. (2005) 'The condition of the working class in England', in D. Bsnks and M. Pyrdy (eds), *The Sociology and Politics of Health*, London: Routledge, pp 22–27.
21. Veblen, T. and Mills, C.W. 2017. *The Theory of the Leisure Class*. Abingdon: Routledge.
22. Taleb, N. (2005) *Fooled by Randomness: The Hidden Role of Chance in Life and in the Markets*, vol. 1, New York: Random House.
23. Thompson, F.M.L. (1981) 'Social control in Victorian Britain', *Economic History Review*, 34(2): 189–208.
24. Gelfand, M.J., Raver, J.L., Nishii, L., Leslie, L.M., Lun, J., Lim, B.C., Duan, L., Almaliach, A., Ang, S., Arnadottir, J. and Aycan, Z. (2011) 'Differences between tight and loose cultures: a 33-nation study', *Science*, 332(6033): 1100–1104; Elias, N. (1978) *The Civilizing Process: The History of Manners*, New York: Pantheon Books.
25. Gutzke, D.W. (2008) 'Progressivism in Britain and abroad', in D.W. Gutzke (ed.), *Britain and Transnational Progressivism*, New York: Palgrave Macmillan.
26. Rabinovitch-Fox, E. (2016) 'Baby, you can drive my car: advertising women's freedom in 1920s America', *American Journalism*, 33(4): 372–400.
27. Parrish, M. (1992) *Anxious Decades: America in Prosperity and Depression, 1920–1941*, New York: Norton.
28. Galbraith, J.K. (2021 [1961]) *The Great Crash 1929*, Harmondsworth: Penguin.
29. Bone, J. (2021) 'Neoliberal precarity and primalization: a biosocial perspective on the age of insecurity, injustice, and unreason', *British Journal of Sociology*, 72: 1030–1045.

PART II

Derailing the Modern Project

4

The Neoliberal 'Dawn': Mont Pelerin, Fear of Socialism and the Backlash of Privilege

As was noted in the last chapter, the progressive social democratic experiment of the postwar era produced many, if far from complete, advances for the numerous citizens of Western societies. The policies advanced in the US, the UK and across mainland Europe accorded the working classes a modicum of security and control over their lives. This inevitably involved constraining the power and privileges and 'freedoms' of the landed, financial and corporate elites that had formerly been able to deploy their economic and political power with a degree of impunity, exercising a strong element of control over the lives of the general public. The revised social contract of the New Deal/welfare state era had involved curbing elite power together with a slightly more equitable distribution of the rewards and risks of the capitalist economy. The tendency for the market power of the elite to enable them to capture an ever-higher share of economic growth was constrained by greater regulation, labour organization (trade unions), workplace protections, housing policies that removed a degree of rent extraction from the poor, and progressive taxation that had begun to tentatively challenge the unequal distribution of reward that unbalanced power had permitted. In short, the rich and powerful were no longer so readily allowed to retain their property and other rights while, simultaneously, remaining as free to employ coercive power over the majority or ignore their obligation to the people who generated much of their income and wealth. However, it doesn't take much of a leap of imagination to understand that many of the elite desired that things were otherwise and had never (or only very grudgingly) accepted the constraints of New Deal/welfare capitalist arrangements.

What had arisen during this period once more raised the perennial issue as to who controls society, in whose interests it operates and, critically by this time, issues relating to the proper relationship between the economic and the wider social imperatives and needs within societies – that is, should the economy operate to meet the needs of society and the majority its people or, alternatively, should the needs of the latter be subordinate to the needs of the economy and the aims of elite business owners, landlords and financial interests? This debate was notably set out by Karl Polanyi in his 1944 book *The Great Transformation*, which charted the rise of market capitalism.[1] A central concept in the book relates to what Polanyi calls the 'double movement', referring to the tension noted earlier between the economy and society. In a 2008 article on Polanyi's work, Block describes this as follows:

> On one side is the movement of laissez faire – the efforts by a variety of groups to expand the scope and influence of self-regulating markets. On the other side has been the movement of protection – the initiatives, again by a wide range of social actors, to insulate the fabric of social life from the destructive impact of market pressures. What we think of as market societies or 'capitalism' is the product of both of these movements; it is an uneasy and fluid hybrid that reflects the shifting balance of power between these contending forces.[2]

This is central to the argument presented here, recognizing the basic need for people to have a sense of control over their circumstances within a reasonably understandable, orderly and predictable environment that allows them to negotiate everyday life with relative ease and a sense of security. As was discussed in the previous chapters, until this point the ordering of the mass of individual lives had invariably come from above and reflected the interests of society's elites, while what was predictable for those further down the pecking order came in the form of bowing to the norms, values and rules set out for them and largely enduring whatever was imposed, albeit with breakouts of resistance or revolt at critical points. More regularly, the reality of everyday life for the majority entailed fatalistic acceptance of one's lot under the influence of an ideological 'story' that asserted that one's subjugation was only right and proper. As was identified earlier, this was very much the case under feudalism and, under different 'management', had also been very much the case throughout the 18th and 19th centuries as the economic imperative advanced by the rising bourgeois elite was privileged over the needs of the mass of people. The limited progress achieved in the postwar era not only constrained the economic and political sway of the powerful to a degree that had never happened previously, but also came in a form much as Polanyi described where the economy became more embedded in society, slightly more as a partner than master and with much greater attention paid to the wellbeing of society as a whole.[3]

In addition to the economic gains made by the labouring classes under this revised socioeconomic contract, which will be discussed in more detail in the following chapters, the dominance of elite culture was also challenged and upended, at least for a time, reflecting the challenge to the old order and an accompanying upsurge in progressive social mobility in terms of culture as well as the economy. There was an explosion of working-class culture in theatre, film, popular music and the arts in general that had once been dominated by the upper classes. The class backgrounds of leading film and stage actors shifted dramatically, albeit that this was perhaps more obvious in Britain than in the US, given that the US's odd juxtaposing of high economic inequality with a widely asserted claim to social classlessness entailed that it had never experienced quite the concentration of elite status depicted in the popular arts. Certainly, there were lots of early Hollywood films where the actors sounded as though they were from the upper echelons, interestingly sounding almost like a variant of the English upper classes. However, US popular movies had always had a broad range of 'voices', in contrast to the pre-1950s and, particularly, pre-1960s situation in Britain where the 'cut glass', received pronunciation of the upper and aspiring middle classes had been the norm, at least for leading roles. These developments not only reflected but also changed the way in which the social order was perceived to a great extent. This was a period where it became 'cool' to be young and working class, and slightly less so to be 'posh', with the latter lampooned by figures like John Lennon with jocular irreverence. Such was the shift that many well-heeled youths of the time took to downplaying rather than flaunting their elite backgrounds.

While the focus of this chapter is largely on the economic arrangements that changed with the eclipsing of the postwar 'settlement', the cultural aspects of this era were of critical significance, while this is also taken up again in later chapters, as the cultural zeitgeist evidently reflects and confers power and control as an integral companion to economic resources in shaping the internalized 'maps' that define our social reality.

Returning to the central argument, as was noted earlier, the upending of the longstanding status quo over the few decades after the war turned out not to be the permanent change of direction that many at the time assumed, as a revised economic credo was emerging almost before the ink was dry on the social democratic contract, which would shift the societal trajectory back towards its familiar pathway in the neoliberal era that persists into the present.

Enter neoliberalism

As argued in the Introduction, whenever neoliberalism is mentioned, particularly in academic circles, it regularly inspires debate regarding what the term means and so on. This tendency towards arguing over definitions is a familiar preoccupation of many academics who, in my view, while not always but largely for lack of original or insightful ideas, fill the void by pedantically and forensically debating the meaning of terms that are fairly well understood, along the lines of angels dancing on the head of a pin. As to neoliberalism, as also noted, I would argue that its key tenets are not mysterious or complex, while in my view Bob Jessop's broad definition succinctly covers the key points:

1. Liberalization: promote free competition.
2. Deregulation: reduce the role of law and the state.
3. Privatization: sell off the public sector.
4. Market proxies in the residual public sector.
5. Internationalization: free inward and outward flows.
6. Lower direct taxes: increase consumer choice.[4]

As suggested earlier, the neoliberal standpoint is consistent with a belief in the virtues of a small state, privatization and private property, deregulation, and the lauding of individual responsibility and self interest in capitalist markets as the best means of organizing the economy and society. In keeping with this, it is also characterized by an antipathy towards all forms of socialism, collectivism and anything beyond minimal taxation and state provision of services and welfare. In a milder form it can present as a belief in markets whose roughest edges might be slightly tempered for the public good, as with the so-called Third Way or German Ordoliberalism, while in its more outré form, its adherents lionize a form of Randian hyperindividualism and libertarianism, as advanced by the misanthropic Russian-American philosopher Ayn Rand. Rand's views are in a sense diametrically opposed to those advanced in this book; however, some understanding of their roots can be gleaned from acknowledging that, at the age of twelve, Rand and her family had experienced some of the negative excesses of the Russian Revolution and its aftermath.[5]

In the West, paradoxically given its lionizing of individual 'freedom' and 'free' markets, exponents of neoliberalism have also been associated with a leaning towards authoritarianism and social conservatism, in some ways echoing the mores of the Victorian bourgeoisie, and with a similar perspective towards the 'losers' within the market society. As will be discussed later on, neoliberal freedom is of a particular flavour and is as unequally distributed as income and wealth under this form of capitalism, as the degree of freedom (or 'licence') granted to those at the top is regularly at the expense of increasing constraint, as well as risk and insecurity, being imposed on the rest.[6] As to neoliberalism's value system, the late (and great) liberal Canadian economist J.K. Galbraith pithily characterized the overall credo of neoliberal conservatism (referred to here simply as conservatism) as follows:

The modern conservative is engaged in one of man's oldest exercises in moral philosophy, that is the search for a superior moral justification for selfishness. It is an exercise which always involves a certain number of internal contradictions and even a few absurdities. The conspicuously wealthy turn up urging the character-building value of privation for the poor.[7]

In qualification, there is little doubt that many of the early architects of neoliberalism advanced the credo earnestly and with a view that they were contributing to the greater good. For example, the Austrian classical liberal economist ('liberal' in the European rather than North American sense) Friedrich Hayek was largely concerned that the embracing of Keynesian approaches to economic organization in the 1930s, and the emphasis on state intervention in the economy, distorted the normal and efficient operation of markets. However, also driving this perspective was an anxiety that an interventionist 'big state', even in the form of mixed economy that had emerged in the capitalist economies of the West, might represent a step towards the form of totalitarianism that had emerged in the Soviet Union under Stalin:

> The central values of civilization are in danger. Over large stretches of the earth's surface the essential conditions of human dignity and freedom have already disappeared. In others they are under constant menace from the development of current tendencies of policy. The position of the individual and the voluntary group are progressively undermined by extensions of arbitrary power. Even that most precious possession of Western Man, freedom of thought and expression, is threatened by the spread of creeds which, claiming the privilege of tolerance when in the position of a minority, seek only to establish a position of power in which they can suppress and obliterate all views but their own.[8]

The intellectual roots of neoliberalism were forged by Hayek together with a number of other notable figures, such as Karl Popper, Milton Friedman, Frank Knight, Ludwig von Mises and George Stigler, as well as a range of other voices from academia and business.[9] Collectively, this group was known as the Mont Pelerin Society after the location in the Swiss Alps where they had convened in 1947. Over the next almost thirty years, their ideas were advanced and proliferated via various think tanks, the latter backed by 'elite' wealth and a predominantly right-wing press. However, during the height of the 1950s and 1960s postwar boom, their ideas were regarded as being marginal, and even a bit odd, given that they seemed to fundamentally contradict the received wisdom and zeitgeist of the times:

In 1945 or 1950, if you had seriously proposed any of the ideas and policies in today's standard neoliberal toolkit, you would have been laughed off the stage at or sent off to the insane asylum. At least in the Western countries, at that time, everyone was a Keynesian, a social democrat or social-Christian democrat or some shade of Marxist. The idea that the market should be allowed to make major social and political decisions; the idea that the State should voluntarily reduce its role in the economy, or that corporations should be given total freedom, that trade unions should be curbed and citizens given much less rather than more social protection – such ideas were utterly foreign to the spirit of the time. Even if someone actually agreed with these ideas, he or she would have hesitated to take such a position in public and would have had a hard time finding an audience.[10]

However, as was noted earlier, the neoliberal cause was backed by powerful forces: a network of business and financial, academic, media, think tanks and lobby groups, and an emerging group of politicians on both sides of the Atlantic, comprising a force ready to be unleashed when the opportunity arose. For much of the postwar era, despite some disaffection among the young, there seemed little appetite for fundamental change among a significant majority of the public, and particularly for those who had experienced the contrast between prewar and postwar conditions. However, by the early 1970s, this began to change as a series of economic crises once more destabilized the socioeconomic order, while there was also some impetus for change that, in a sense, could be seen to arise from sheer restlessness and from the fact that social advancement was breaking down some old allegiances.

Restlessness, 'freedom' and aspiration

The corporatism that had characterized the governance of the economy and society in the postwar era – a tripartite arrangement bringing together state, business and labour – that broadly followed the logic of the collective alliance that had been forged in support of the war effort, of collective engagement in pursuit of common goals, began to falter as the regular divisions between capital and organized labour began to reassert themselves. Business began to experience shrinking profits and rising costs, while the growing power of trade unions in the latter stages of the postwar era had begun to tarnish their image with the perception of growing militancy, a scenario widely amplified by the right-wing press.

As was noted earlier, during the 1960s there was also a growing anti-establishment sentiment among the young, as a central core of an expanded youth culture (itself a product of the postwar boom), that was in no small part influenced by the aforementioned antipathy toward the Vietnam War in the US and, more generally, by a desire to be free of the world created by 'the man'. The latter was advanced, as well as via street demonstrations, through the popular music and artistic expression of the era. Interestingly, however, while the youth culture at this time was largely left-leaning and seemingly oriented towards socialism or even more outré forms of collectivism, it has been argued that it contained a strong current of 'romantic' individualism that had some subtle resonances with the discourse that would later be advanced by neoliberal politicians. The implication here was that this aspect of the youth culture might have provided a conduit for persuading at least some of the young to embrace neoliberalism as the postwar settlement began to founder. It is also the case that the measured upward social mobility experienced by many of the working classes during this period may also have played a role in supporting a shift in allegiances, as some of the more aspiring working classes began to align themselves with the bourgeois middle classes.

Economic crises

While the preceding factors began to provide nascent conditions for the rolling back of the postwar settlement, this would have been unlikely to have been sufficient grounds for the fundamental shift in the political status quo that emerged from the late 1970s onwards. Rather, a developing sense that the postwar boom had run out of road amid a developing climate of economic crisis during the 1970s can be seen to have been the main catalyst for change. Crucial to this was the decision by the Organization of the Petroleum Exporting Countries (OPEC) to introduce an oil embargo in 1973 in response to the Arab-Israeli War, leading to a financial crisis and a rapid rise in inflation across the globe as oil prices quadrupled. The impact of inflation in eroding real incomes was also involved in the upsurge in trade union activity and strikes, as the labour movement tried to secure pay increases that kept up with rising prices. Of course, this in itself led to 'cost push inflation' as employers who conceded to higher wage demands raised their prices to compensate, stoking an inflationary spiral, while further squeezing corporate profits. Against this background, in terms of the economy itself, the 1970s was a period of recurring economic crises that also broke apart global arrangements, such as the Bretton Woods system for managing exchange rates, which had added to the wider stabilities of the wider postwar economy. The emergence of Japan and Germany, having recovered from wartime defeat and destruction, to enter the fray as important competitors in manufacturing industries also placed pressure on previously dominant Western economies like Britain and America. As the crisis of the 1970s evolved, the combination of companies attempting to retain profitability where they could led to an increase in unemployment, which had been historically low throughout the postwar era, as well as recurrent stand-offs over wages and conditions. Governments were hence struggling with increasing economic turbulence while attempting to manage a rising undercurrent of social unease, albeit that perceptions of socioeconomic troubles were amplified by right-wing commentators who saw an opportunity for a political reset.[11] Overall, it seemed clear that this was an opening for a challenge to the postwar settlement that might offer scope for rolling it back, while political figures who had embraced neoliberal ideas were waiting in the wings for just such an opportunity. On this point, and as noted earlier in relation to the processes Naomi Klein notably identified in *The Shock Doctrine*, these conditions provided scope for a further turning point in human affairs and societal arrangements. The advocates for neoliberal policies have remained highly aware of this tendency to the extent that, from the early 1970s, they have tended to exploit opportunities presented by a sequence of crises (often of their own creation) to further advance and entrench neoliberal policies.[12]

The political shift

Prior to the move to advance neoliberalism in the US and the UK, an infamous 'controlled experiment' had already taken place in the early 1970s, as the model was imposed as a central feature of a right-wing coup to overthrow the democratically elected, but, for the US authorities, unacceptably leftist Chilean government of Salvador Allende. In the midst of the Cold War era, in addition to its activities in Asia and elsewhere, the US was particularly concerned that a successful socialist government in Latin America might provide a model for others in the region, triggering a 'domino effect', leading to an exponential expansion of the communist threat on its doorstep that extended beyond Castro's Cuba. The response was a campaign to undermine the Chilean economy and its government from within, where the Central Intelligence Agency (CIA) supported right wingers among the upper echelons of the Chilean army to stage a coup d'etat, led by General Augusto Pinochet. The coup, as has been well documented, was extremely brutal and installed Pinochet as the head of an unelected military junta which engaged in violent repression and subjugation of any opposition. However, what is relevant here is that economic policy was overseen the 'Chicago Boys'; Latin American economists who had been trained by neoliberal guru Milton Friedman at the University of Chicago (with the department receiving funding from the Ford and Rockefeller Foundations) and whose ideas were implemented to restructure the Chilean economy. While this experiment was hailed as an economic 'miracle' by neoliberals in the 1980s, all was not quite as it was presented, as Chile's economic performance had been comparatively weak and crisis-prone during the unfettered neoliberal period from the mid-1970s until a banking crisis of 1982, while it has been argued that it was only when the state began to engage in significant intervention after this crisis that Chile's economy really started to improve – that is, in spite of rather than because of neoliberal policies.[13] Nonetheless, as will be discussed in Chapter 5 with respect to the financial crisis of 2007/2008, for the true believers revisionism is the regular response to even the most dramatic evidence of neoliberalism's deficiencies.

As was noted earlier, the Chilean experiment aside, the economic problems impacting on Western economies in the early 1970s provided the rationale for a push to overturn the postwar model and apply the neoliberal 'medicine' asserted to be the cure. As we know, the chief standard bearers were the Conservative Thatcher administration in the UK and the Republican Reagan administration in the US. From this point, the credo was promoted as the pragmatic solution to the economic travails of the times and was eventually adopted, to greater or lesser degree, across the globe via a reconfiguration of international institutions such as the World Bank and the International Monetary Fund, where what was once marginal and seemed to have significant resonances with discredited laissez-faire policies emerged as the new economic and, to no small extent, social common sense.[14]

The revolution

In the UK, prior to the Thatcher administration, it has been suggested that the Conservative Party regarded itself at least as the nonideological alternative to a socialist Labour Party. The Conservatives, while still being seen as the party of business, finance and the better off, had largely accepted the postwar settlement, however reluctantly, and policy didn't seem to vary dramatically between the two major parties from the late 1950s up to the early 1970s. However, the Thatcher 'revolution' changed the complexion of her party as well as the nation she led.

The story of Margaret Thatcher's ascendancy begins with her tenure as Education Secretary in the Edward Heath administration of 1970–1974, a period that coincided with the aforementioned OPEC crisis and as the UK's faltering economy worsened with high inflation and industrial unrest. Heath lost the subsequent election to a Labour government led by Harold Wilson, but despite the latter's attempts to bring capital, labour and government together to curb inflation and stabilize the economy, the sense of ongoing instability continued. Wilson resigned in 1976, to be replaced by Jim Callaghan who continued to lead a minority government supported by the Liberals and, for a time, the Scottish Nationalists. Callaghan attempted to curb union wage demands amid high inflation, but these efforts fell apart with the infamous Winter of Discontent of 1978–1979 and led to defeat in the general election of that year by the Conservatives, now led by

Margaret Thatcher, having claimed the leadership from Heath during the period of opposition.

Thatcher, supported by arch-neoliberal ideologue allies such as Keith Joseph, proceeded to refashion British Conservatism as she also began to reshape the UK as a neoliberal nation. However, the radical policies that were introduced actually deepened Britain's economic and social woes. In line with the Friedmanite monetarist prescription for inflation, interest rates were raised to 17 per cent to squeeze inflation out of the system. This was partially successful, but in many ways it has been suggested that the medicine, and the way in which it was implemented, was worse than the disease. Evidently, mortgage costs rocketed, putting a squeeze on family finances. Yet, adding to this burden was a precipitous rise in unemployment. Ironically, as has been widely acknowledged, the Thatcher administration gained power in part due to perceived instability in the wider economy, but, also more specifically, due to its charge that the Labour Party had overseen a rise in unemployment to over one million in the UK, an emotional milestone that had dented the postwar full employment scenario. This formed a key part of the election platform with a poster and slogan declaring that 'Labour Isn't Working', and featuring a line of the presumably unemployed, all of which hit a particular chord with a public that had come to take the relative security of employment as being central to the postwar social contract. By contrast, the policies pursued by the Thatcher government pushed unemployment ever upwards, placing downward pressure on inflation. Her policies also generated a contraction of so-called 'lame duck' companies that hollowed out the UK's once-dominant manufacturing sector, while there was a turn to services, consumerism and, importantly, finance as the key engines of economic growth and employment.

One byproduct of this was that lower-paying and less secure work supplanted secure and relatively high wage manufacturing jobs. Taxation was also revised with a move to increase more regressive taxes like Value Added Tax, paid on the purchase of goods and services, together with a reduction in income tax for higher rate – that is, wealthier taxpayers. These measures taken together contributed to a precipitous increase in inequality that began to reverse the levelling measures taken after the Second World War. In retrospect it has been somewhat forgotten just how unpopular the new administration became in the early 1980s amid increasing insecurity, division and austerity – so much so that it has been argued that, but for the popularity-boosting impact of the 1982 Falklands War and the papering-over of some of the economic cracks as North Sea Oil revenues came on stream, the Conservatives may well have lost a general election and the Thatcherite experiment might well have drawn to a swift conclusion, perhaps in a broadly similar vein to the more contemporary 'Trussonomics' debacle.[15]

However, as we know, this was not to be the case, while the neoliberal agenda would also be shortly advanced even more powerfully across the Atlantic with the election of Ronald Reagan as the 40th US President in January 1981. Reaganomics, the new president's variant of neoliberal policy, was the US counterpart to Thatcherism in the UK, while the embracing of neoliberalism by both the senior and junior partners of this *special relationship* began the process of institutionalizing this credo on the world stage, while the World Bank and the International Monetary Fund imposed structural adjustment programmes that would institute free market principles of open markets, privatization (including of public utilities and services) and austerity policies, particularly in developing economies, as a quid pro quo for financial assistance.

The Reagan administration was no less determined in overturning postwar norms than its UK partner. In fact, one of the hallmarks of neoliberal administrations that have led to the installation, advancing and sustaining of the credo in the late 20th and early 21st centuries has been the tendency for neoliberals when elected to 'hit the ground running' with a relatively radical policy agenda, while more left-of-centre administrations, where they have been successful at the ballot box, have tended to be more tentative, accepting the key tenets of neoliberalism with an, at times, apologetic programme aimed at simply ameliorating its most negative social consequences. The Clinton and Blair 'Third Way' administrations formally recognized this accommodation, as they triangulated between a largely neoliberal approach to economic affairs while applying some measures to address the more extreme privations and insecurities experienced by neoliberalism's casualties. In their failure to challenge the legacy of their predecessors, in many ways, Clinton and Blair may even be regarded as consolidators of the Thatcher/Reagan revolution, as they operated within its normative framework, while prosocial policies were muted and differences tended to be rhetorical and cultural rather than economic. In effect, what they did in adopting a 'third way' platform was to dash the hopes of those who yearned for a real challenge and reversal of policy direction, while removing the possibility of substantial democratic choice from their electorates, who could now only effectively choose between neoliberalism and neoliberalism lite with a sprinkling of tentative prosocial intervention. Despite the hopes raised by the later Obama administration and the popularity of a more progressive politics among the young, the political ground moved rightwards to an extent that would have placed many in the postwar right-wing conservative parties of the UK and US to the left of many of their later counterparts in contemporary, assertedly 'left-of-centre' parties.

However, as was noted earlier, where there became little to choose from between the major political parties in the key neoliberal states in terms of economic policy, differences came to be expressed via presentation and, more specifically, between social conservatism and social liberalism as safer ground that supplanted the requirement for any substantial departure from the new economic status quo. This scenario led political theorist Sheldon Wolin to argue that contemporary politics had given way to a scenario where choices in nations like the UK and the US were largely illusory and where democracy was 'managed', in that voters merely had an option of choosing between slightly different flavours and of the same policy agenda, but with little prospect of fundamental change, at least in a leftward direction. This is a set of issues to which I will return in Chapter 11: 'Democracy and hegemony are coupled by means of managed democracy, where the elections are free and fair but the people lack the actual ability to change the policies, motives and goals of the state.'[16]

Culture warriors: free markets and social conservatism

As was argued earlier, the distinctions between the key political parties and leading politicians have tended to shift towards identity and cultural areas rather than anything that might frighten the economic and political elite who have greatly benefited from these policies, just as many poor and 'average' citizens have become relatively poorer. At least in part, this was also a consequence of the new vision of society that Thatcher and Reagan advanced.

Allied to Thatcher's embracing of economic freedom was a strident petit bourgeois social conservatism. In addition to her antipathy towards social democracy, 1960s 'permissiveness' was anathema to Thatcher, who seemed to want to return to the social mores of the 1930s to the 1950s that she'd grown up with. This was also allied to a Presbyterian attitude to work, which informed her strident approach to the labour market and welfare policy. In many ways, the echo of 19th-century laissez-faire in her approach to economic affairs was accompanied by a neo-Victorian asceticism. While of a slightly different complexion, Reagan's economic liberalism was similarly aligned to social conservatism. In his case, the ideal was the America of the late 1940s and 1950s, a vision of a nation associated with the traditional nuclear family and gender roles; a homespun small-town and suburban America of tidy streets, white picket fences and God-fearing, conscientious and aspirational individuals. Paradoxically, as will be discussed more fully in Chapter 11, social conservatism also has appeal to many of the dispossessed working classes. Working-class culture has long contained a significant element of social conservatism. Indeed, nationalism, religion and traditional roles and values are often embraced as a defence in response to the experiential overload and angst imposed by economic insecurity. The emotionally driven need for simplicity, clarity and a sense of community, no matter how illusory or distorted, has a strong appeal to the atomized, insecure and bewildered in unforgiving societies. This is a condition that has long been exploited by populist politicians, including Thatcher and Reagan, as well as earlier and, indeed, more recent figures in their cultivation of the contemporary 'culture wars' that are highly prevalent in the UK, the US and elsewhere.

Freedom, risk and insulation

As was discussed earlier, another of neoliberalism's key selling points has been its appeal to notions of individual freedom and self-reliance, which, in practice, is of a very particular form. What has happened in deregulated neoliberal societies like the US and the UK has been the alleviating of constraints for those at the top of society in terms of curbs on economic power and influence, obligations to society via taxation and regulation, as well as exposure to the risks inherent in modern living. As Ulrich Beck once suggested, many of the risks of modern society were largely democratic in the contemporary era, examples being environmental degradation and climate change. However, as will be addressed more specifically in Chapter 10, as well as many of the other key risks affecting us, there are reasons to seriously question how far Beck's analysis holds.[17] Again, one of the key effects of the neoliberal turn is that it has reversed the (albeit moderate) trend towards greater equality that emerged after the war and led to a restoration of levels of inequality more akin to those prevalent in the late 19th and early 20th centuries.

One of the key benefits that wealth confers is precisely the ability to insulate oneself and one's dependants from the risks inherent in everyday living. With few exceptions, self-evidently, great wealth enables people to buy their way out of, or at least mitigate, many of the hazards confronting those further down the economic hierarchy. Climate change can be more readily evaded (at least so long as its manifestations remain fairly localized), health can be improved and illnesses, while far from being avoidable, have the prospect of better outcomes with access to routine screening and the best care and treatments available. And, of course, many routine stressors – overwork, housing costs, managing one's finances, status anxiety, and being consistently at others' beck and call – can be more or less avoided. By contrast, and while this is not a zero-sum game, burgeoning elite wealth confers the capacity to influence politics and exercise relatively unimpeded control over deregulated businesses and their workers, as well as the ability to corral scarce commodities and necessities like housing. All of this entails that there is a corresponding deficit of freedom, autonomy and capacity to exercise control for those less fortunate. As will be discussed in subsequent chapters, the growing power of finance, the dilution of workplace protections, benefits and trade union power, as well as developments in terms of the 'offshoring', the casualization and automation of work, and the erosion of welfare have all combined to greatly reduce worker autonomy and security. In housing markets, the purchasing power of wealthier families, and developments in market organization and finance have reduced options, raised housing costs and in many cases left renters more exposed to the whims and diktats of landlords as housing has, once again, become a key investment vehicle and source of income for the better off. All of these features of the neoliberal era, plus a few others that will also be explored more fully later on, combined to shake the foundations of what had become the key pillars of postwar security, while those with the wherewithal have been able to stay above the fray of the anxious world they have generated.

A VUCA world?

On a final aside, the evolution of neoliberal society since its inception in the late 1970s and 1980s, when considered together with the technological, political, financial and social developments that have arisen of late, has produced a form of society that is potentially more overwhelming and bewildering than anything that has gone before – so much so, in fact, that I have argued elsewhere that previous attempts to characterize the late modern era, such as Beck's and colleagues 'reflexive modernization' and 'risk society' as well as Bauman's 'liquid modernity'[18], have been superseded by the sheer pace and multiplicity of demands and incongruities that confront contemporary citizens. As such, an alternative depiction that I encountered seem to me to better capture the conditions of the present milieu. This is the VUCA concept, which was first developed in the US military and was taken up by business organizations as a means of characterizing the nature of an ephemeral contemporary world. The concept, as outlined below, seems to go beyond earlier characterisations of contemporary precarity and flux while providing a useful starting point for exploring the pressures imposed on individuals and communities under neoliberalism as it has advanced into the digital age:

V = Volatility: the nature and dynamics of change.
U = Uncertainty: the lack of predictability and prospects for surprise.
C = Complexity: the multiplex of forces and confounding of issues and cause and effect.
A = Ambiguity: the haziness of reality, the potential for misreading cues, and the capacity to discern fact from fiction.[19]

I would suggest that it takes little imagination to see how this would fit with numerous aspects of contemporary experience. When the inherent complexities of late modernity are compounded by the disorientating effects of marketized deregulation, ever more capricious labour markets and organizations, insecure housing, increasingly threadbare social safety nets, as well as the complexities and ambiguities unleashed by new technologies, information overload and inconsistency (as a multitude of vociferous voices presenting diametrically opposed opinions and values), this scenario is easy to comprehend as describing current conditions. Lastly, with the failure of leadership under neoliberalism, as will be discussed later on, and a rise in opportunistic and unscrupulous populism, mendacity and post-truth rhetoric, the conditions for a level of *experiential overload* that is toxic to human wellbeing are ever present. As will be set out in more detail in the subsequent chapters, these and other aspects of the world that neoliberalism has delivered represent a fundamental challenge to the biological imperatives that govern our essential needs.

Notes

1   Polanyi, K. (2001) *The Great Transformation: The Political and Economic Origins of Our Time*, Boston: Beacon Press.

2   Block, F. (2008) 'Polanyi's double movement and the reconstruction of critical theory', *Interventions Économiques*, 10.4000/interventionseconomiques.274.1

3   Harvey, D. (2005) *A Brief History of Neoliberalism*, Oxford: Oxford University Press.

4   Jessop, B. (2002) 'Liberalism, neoliberalism, and urban governance: a state–theoretical perspective', *Antipode*, 34: 452–472.

5   Duggan, L. (2019) *Mean Girl: Ayn Rand and the Culture of Greed*, vol. 8, Berkeley: University of California Press.

6   Wacquant, L. (2009) *Punishing the Poor: The Neoliberal Government of Social Insecurity*, Durham, NC: Duke University Press.

7   *Toronto Globe and Mail* (6 July 2002).

8   https://www.montpelerin.org/event/429dba23-fc64-4838-ab847011022a4/websiteP age:6950c74b-5d9b-41cc-8da1-3e1991c14ac5

9   Mirowski, P. and Plehwe, D. (eds) (2009) *The Road to Mont Pèlerin: The Making of the Neoliberal Thought Collective*, Cambridge, MA: Harvard University Press.

10 George, S. (1999) 'A short history of neoliberalism'. Presented at the Conference on Economic Sovereignty in a Globalising World, Bangkok, 24–26 March.

11 Harvey, D. (2007) 'Neoliberalism as creative destruction', *Annals of the American Academy of Political and Social Science*, 610(1): 21–44.

12 Klein, N. (2007) *The Shock Doctrine: The Rise of Disaster Capitalism*, New York: Macmillan.

13 Solimano, A. (2012) *Chile and the Neoliberal Trap: The Post-Pinochet Era*, Cambridge: Cambridge University Press.

14 Harvey, D. (2007) 'Neoliberalism as creative destruction', *Annals of the American Academy of Political and Social Science*, 610(1): 21–44.

15 Norpoth, H. (1991) 'The popularity of the Thatcher government: a matter of war and economy', *Economics and Politics: The Calculus of Support*, 141–160.

16 Wolin, S.S. (2008) *Democracy Incorporated: Managed Democracy and the Specter of Inverted Totalitarianism*, Princeton: Princeton University Press, p 47.

17 Beck, U. (1992) *Risk Society: Towards a New Modernity*, London: Sage.

18 Bauman, Z. (2000) *Liquid Modernity*, Cambridge: Polity Press.

19 This definition is adapted from Evans, C.J. (2020) 'Thinking strategically', in A. Viera and R. Karmer (eds), *Management and Leadership Skills for Medical Faculty and Healthcare Executives: A Practical Handbook*, Dordrecht: Springer, pp 229–230.

5

Financial Alchemy and Economic Crises

When approaching an exploration of the transition from the mid-20th-century Keynesian model of state intervention and regulation to the current era of 'free' markets and deregulation, a central feature has been the loosening of many of the controls that were imposed on the financial sector after the Great Crash. Two key observations are relevant from the outset here in terms of addressing the relationship between the growth of finance and the advancing of the neoliberal model itself. Firstly, it is no surprise that the deregulatory model advanced by Hayek, Friedman and others was underwritten and heavily promoted by powerful financial interests, in concert with big business as a whole, who had much to gain from the loosening of the shackles of postwar regulation, and who greatly resented the constraints that were imposed from the 1930s. Secondly, the fact that the world's largest financial centres are in London and New York, in the nations long associated with laissez-faire capitalism, makes it fully understandable why neoliberalism was so readily embraced and championed in the UK and the US. In effect, this was as much a restoration as it was a revolution in these nations.

Evidently, the capitalist zeitgeist runs deep within Anglo-Saxon societies, given their longstanding mercantile and commercial prominence, and it has been argued that a particular leaning towards finance and commerce over industry has also been an important feature of the form of capitalism that emerged, particularly in the UK and to an extent in the US, for reasons that are as much cultural as they are economic. This relates to the social context in which the capitalist economy had evolved, particularly in England, that would later influence the economic culture of its colonies. While the Industrial Revolution in England had brought great wealth to new factory owners and merchants, the English class system continued to place the old landed gentry at the pinnacle of a highly class-conscious societal hierarchy. One of the key social attitudes and practices by which 'old money' distinguished itself was by asserting that working was for the lower orders and 'new money', while living from inherited family fortunes, investments and land ownership was what set the 'better' class apart. This was, in a sense, an extension of the longstanding division between the old aristocratic ruling class and the rising bourgeoisie. There was a great deal of snobbery aimed at the nouveau riche who had gained their wealth from industry. Nonetheless, there was also little hesitation for aristocrats of modest means to offer a socially advantageous marriage to the son or daughter of a very rich industrialist to secure the family's future economic fortunes in exchange for some social cachet. In this climate, given the social prestige associated with being labour-free, many of the newly risen were attracted to the notion of stepping back from the day-to-day running of their enterprises, joining the socialite elite and turning to investment as a way of expanding their fortunes. In this way, as UK economist Will Hutton has observed, a tendency to view finance, business and commerce as vehicles for leisurely capital accumulation and 'passive income', and as being somehow superior, goes some way towards explaining the emphasis on finance and commerce as opposed to engineering and industry that has come to dominate the UK and, albeit to a lesser extent, the US economies, particularly in the neoliberal era.[1]

What does finance do?

For the majority of people, the financial sector remains a mysterious and remote zone of economic activity, at least beyond the periodic crises that draw particular attention to the sector. As I argue here, the effects of financial sector organization and activity make a pivotal contribution to many of the 'negatives' experienced by ordinary citizens in contemporary neoliberal societies, undermining the fundamental needs and conditions outlined in Chapter 1. In short, a larger and less controlled financial sector, aligned with other aspects of the neoliberal 'settlement', has returned to playing a central destabilizing and polarizing role, while also being associated with a form of 'wealth creation' where questionable activity and rewards have vastly enriched a largely unproductive minority to the considerable detriment of those engaged in the nuts and bolts of the real economy and to societies as a whole:

> Once the belief that money is wealth is implanted firmly in the mind, it is easy to accept the idea that money is a storehouse of value rather than simply a storehouse of expectations, and that 'making money' is the equivalent of 'creating wealth'. Because Wall Street makes money in breathtaking quantities, we have allowed it to assume control of the whole economy – and therein lies the source of our problem. Financial collapse pulled away the curtain on the Wall Street alchemists to reveal an illusion factory that paid its managers outrageous sums for

creating phantom wealth unrelated to the production of anything of real value. They were merely creating claims on the real wealth created by others – a form of theft.[2]

The occupants of Wall Street, the City of London and other financial centres have become the high priests of neoliberal capitalism, inhabiting a seemingly mystical world and a way of life that appears detached from that of ordinary mortals, with incomes and wealth to match. In fact, in no small part, the mystique surrounding financial dealings was a central feature of the failure to anticipate the causes of the 2007/2008 financial crisis which threatened to bring the global economy to its knees.[3] Moreover, the power wielded by the sector saw a shifting of focus regarding culpability from the banks onto the state, notably in the UK and to some extent in the US and elsewhere (for more on this, see later on in the chapter), while the 'big state' was called upon to shore up a banking and financial sector whose practitioners largely escaped the consequences of their activities unscathed and have continued largely free of significant reform.[4] In fact, the problems encountered with Credit Suisse and other banks in 2023 clearly illustrated that the genie had by no means been put back in the bottle. How then did we get to this point?

As was noted in Chapter 3, modern banking came of age from the 17th to the 19th centuries with the expansion of global capitalism, aligned with the financial centres and practices that we recognize today, and where Britain and then the US became its key exponents. As we know, a basic function of banking is to store deposits and channel these savings as loans for the further expansion of commerce and industry, while this is largely how it is perceived in the public imagination. In addition to commercial lending, its other main functions are to provide a secure means of conducting everyday financial transactions and to offer a source of lending for purchasing larger items, particularly housing, as well as cars and so on. The financial sector also operates to underwrite the financial risk of doing business as well as the hazards of everyday living through, respectively, insuring a range of business assets and activities, as well as a range of potential risks related to homes, transport, health, wellbeing and pension savings for retirement. In short, and in terms of all of these longstanding and commonly understood purposes, finance is considered to be a central adjunct to the functioning of commercial and everyday activity in capitalist societies, providing investment funds for new commercial ideas and ventures, enabling people to manage their money and make critical purchases and to provide a financial safety net when things go wrong. So far so good. However, as will be argued later on, with the advent of neoliberalism, the financial sector once again strayed significantly from its key supporting role in economic life to play an increasingly dominant role in both the economy and society, while many of its activities have become ever more arcane and detached from its assumed role in a number of ways that have undermined 'real' industry and commerce as well as the wider needs of society.

The problem of 'big finance'

Finance as a sector in the UK, the US and other developed economies had been growing ever larger in relation to the wider economy until the aftermath of the Great Crash, when it contracted precipitously. After a partial rebound until the 1960s and into the 1970s, it grew exponentially from the 1980s onwards, enabled by neoliberal deregulation. In each instance the growth of finance would bring about a period of questionable activity and economic instability. Also, this relative growth of finance has led to its increasing power and influence in relation to the economy and society as a whole, as the needs of economy became increasingly subordinate to financial imperatives and the interest of its institutions and beneficiaries: a process referred to as *financialization*.

Recognition of the tendency for finance to outgrow its scale and function and stray from the letter and substance of its core activities was, of course, recognized by Keynes in his response to the fallout from the Great Crash, as described earlier, that had led to bank runs, bankruptcies and ushered in the Great Depression. As Keynes maintained, this was an apt demonstration that markets, including financial markets, did not necessarily enhance economic and societal wellbeing if their operations were not managed in the interests of the wider economy and society, an idea that was anathema to previous generations of economists schooled in laissez-faire economics. The vigour with which Keynes and a growing number of politicians challenged these ideas rested on observing unregulated finance's potential to impact on social stability as well as the economy. This was, and still is, often a consequence of the inclination of underregulated finance to generate economic bubbles and busts where it steps too far across the line where rational investment gives way to irrational gambling. As Keynes observed:

> [S]peculators may do no harm as bubbles on a steady stream of enterprise. But the position is serious when enterprise becomes the bubble on a whirlpool of speculation. When the capital development of a country becomes a by-product of the activities of a casino, the job is likely to be ill-done.[5]

Keynes was referring here to the tendency for investors to focus less on the future real earnings likely to flow from the real activity, profitability and growth of an enterprise, the textbook rationale for investing, in favour of simply aiming to buy and hopefully sell shares and other assets to capitalize on fluctuations in their short-term value, paying more attention to what others are buying and selling than engaging in long-term investment based on careful analysis of the viability of an organization or its product.

Debates over the irrationality and emotionally charged nature of market speculation and the bubbles it generates have often cited the infamous case of the Dutch Tulip Bubble Mania of 1663/1667, where tulip bulbs changed hands for sums well beyond their intrinsic value, as people bought in on the promise of quick and substantial gains by simply following the herd.[6] Of course, many of the details of the events surrounding 'Tulipomania' have been disputed and, in fact, some of the retelling may well have been overblown to an extent. Nonetheless, this is not to say that the tulip bubble was in any way fictional, but perhaps simply that some of the ramifications were overstated. However, it's also the case that there has been a tendency for neoliberally inclined writers to attempt to debunk evidence of such free market irrationality with the intention of defending and/or rescuing the notion that markets are inherently efficient, rational and self-regulating – the *efficient market hypothesis*.[7] This has been an increasingly regular preoccupation of those who cling to the neoliberal mantra that free markets offer the only practicable means of organizing the economy, and for the most part society (the primary justification for deregulation and 'rolling back the state'), as they stand guard to dissemble and distract whenever it becomes apparent, as is regularly the case, that such a position flies in the face of the available evidence. That irrational exuberance, or 'animal spirits' and regular crises, as Keynes suggested,[8] are routine features of capitalist markets that get out of control without firm governance and state control is a fact of life.

All of this is important to set out as, in line with the pithy aphorism attributed to Mark Twain, 'history doesn't repeat itself but it does rhyme'. This observation points towards the fact that there are certain social and economic phenomena that seem to recur, tending to reproduce recognizable parallels with broadly similar historical scenarios. This is also in line with the view that there are some invariant attributes of being human that entail that history is not as open-ended a process as some commentators, including many social scientists, would like to believe. In terms of finance and markets, from 'Tulipmania', the South Sea Bubble and the Great Crash to more contemporary economic crises, historical parallels are difficult to ignore; the activities of finance have regularly given rise to the more recent period of social, political and geopolitical instability as well as individual privations. As was described earlier, the Great Crash had represented the zenith of a period of financial instability where throughout the 19th and early 20th centuries there had been recurrent economic crises. The Great Crash, however, had invoked social instabilities so profound as to have created the conditions for a more febrile politics in many areas across the world. As was the case then, so it is now, with widespread and often unacknowledged consequences, including the ushering in of the economic and social turmoil that, as already noted, was seen to be a key contributor to the conditions leading to the Second World War and which, I have argued, has brought about similar conditions in the present.[9]

Financial fictions and the 'little people'

Increasing bank reliance on complex financial innovations is a hallmark of the recent turn towards financialization (Bryan and Rafferty 2006; van der Zwan 2014; Cetorelli et al. 2012). Prior to the 1980s, US banks made most of their money from traditional banking activities, like accepting deposits, making loans to consumers and businesses, or investing in low-risk government securities. But with the turn towards financialization, banks became more dependent on revenue from two financial innovations in particular: asset securitization and new financial derivatives. We can see evidence of this turn towards non-traditional activities in changing sources of bank income.[10]

As the preceding quote notes, there are numerous ways in which the deregulation of finance in the recent era has had negative consequences for wider society. One of the issues here is that as the financial sector expands, its practitioners tend to invent new ways of making money for their clients and for themselves, often involving complex schemes and 'investments' that are ever more disconnected from 'real' economic activity. The collapse of the postwar Bretton Woods system that had helped stabilize currencies, and hence national economies to an extent, opened up new opportunities for currency speculation that, conversely, undermined that stability. There has also been the development of new forms of securities and financial instruments derived from the real economy – derivatives – that have created another layer of financial 'assets' and activity. This is what is benignly referred to as financial innovation. Financial innovation has destabilized economies generally, much as it did in the past, a fact that was evidently experienced most starkly with the financial crash of 2007/2008. As a huge range of books have been devoted to discussing the events surrounding this most recent financial crisis and, given the layers and extent of debate, I don't intend to engage in a forensic discussion as it is beyond both the scope of what's required here. Rather, I want to point to particular consequences that relate to the argument at hand – in other words, that 'unearned' fortunes were effectively secured at the expense of the stability of the lives of the 'little people'.

In the first instance, there has been a significant impact on housing, as a fundamental pillar of everyday security that has become more costly, inaccessible and insecure due to the influence of banking and finance. This will be explored more fully in Chapter 7, but some key points need to be flagged up at this point. Fundamentally, the ability for deregulated finance to create credit with little restriction, particularly in the digital age, has transformed bank lending. A key point relating to this is that, as previously noted, commercial banks don't rely directly on recirculating deposits to make loans as many of the public believe, as such constraints have been continually eroded over time.

> One common misconception is that banks act simply as intermediaries, lending out the deposits that savers place with them. In this view deposits are typically 'created' by the saving decisions of households, and banks then 'lend out' those existing deposits to borrowers, for example to companies looking to finance investment or individuals wanting to purchase houses ... in reality in the modern economy, commercial banks are the creators of deposit money ... rather than banks lending out deposits that are placed with them, the act of lending creates deposits – the reverse of the sequence typically described in textbooks.[11]

This type of scenario is typical of deregulated banking systems which became turbocharged with the advent of digitalization. Money became little more than a digital entry on a screen, created as a loan and becoming a deposit. The erosion of the amount that banks held on reserve, together with relatively low interest rates and increased competition in mortgage markets, meant that more and more credit was issued, adding to both public indebtedness and fuelling a house price spiral. The latter was also gradually turbocharged by the expansion of another banking 'innovation', securitization. Put simply (and the arrangements could be quite complex), this involved the bundling of mortgage loans into securities such as Mortgage-Backed Securities (MBSs) and compilations of the latter known as Collateralized Debt Obligations (CDOs). These complex financial derivatives bundled loans into tranches of varying risk, with returns to investors being commensurate with that level of risk. Ironically, a key rationale of securitization was that the bundling together of loans into these packages would reduce risk in the mortgage market as there would be safety in numbers and only a small proportion of loans within a CDO would be likely to default, providing confidence for investors in these asset-backed securities. This was also the view of the key ratings agencies that tended to give these securities a cleaner bill of health than appeared wise in retrospect, and also the view of other institutions who offered a form of insurance against default – the Credit Default Swap (CDS) – that was purchased by holders of these securities and, subsequently, others who were effectively betting against such confidence.[12]

Housing derivatives were also just one feature of the practice where financial institutions and high net-worth individuals attempt to ameliorate their risk in a range of markets by setting up contracts with others who have a different view as to whether the price of an asset, commodity or currency will rise or fall in future. In a sense, as with securitization and a range of other forms of financial sector activity, this practice was also based on a reasonable assumption that these derivatives help some investors and companies hedge risk if they feel that their business or portfolio might be badly affected if the price of a commodity or asset were to breach a certain level, either too high or too low. For example, the price of oil, food products, a particular currency and so on could be hedged to compensate one of the parties to a contract depending on whether the price exceeded an agreed ceiling or floor. In that sense, derivatives contracts are a form of insurance. However, here we begin to encounter the law of unintended consequences. While all of this might sound a little arcane, these are merely the headline aspects of what are some fairly complex processes, so much so in fact that the financial regulators on both sides of the Atlantic – as the neoliberal-steeped US and UK financial sectors spearheaded what became a global phenomenon to a significant degree – didn't really appreciate the myriad problems that were being incubated, as these practices began to build towards a crisis in 2007/2008 that would echo its major predecessor of 1929.

Returning to housing, low interest rates, looser lending practices and securitization began to contribute to a prodigious house price bubble. For some time, this produced a feelgood factor, at least among those who owned property. As asset prices rose and interest rates remained low, homeowners began to remortgage at highly competitive rates, using their homes as ATMs and fuelling a consumerist splurge. While household debt expanded, it appeared manageable and the short-term proceeds provided a sticking plaster for wages that had been stagnating for some time (for more on this, see later on in the chapter), while this expansion of credit bolstered aggregate demand. Again, the historical echoes are not coincidental.

As with the stock bubble of the 1920s, the seemingly ever-rising value of real estate began to be seen by growing numbers of the public as a 'get rich quick' investment vehicle, while there was increasingly easy access to credit for those who fancied themselves as budding landlords or how merely wanted to flip houses, buying one day and selling shortly afterwards for a quick capital gain at seemingly minimal risk. Early casualties of this scenario were those who watched prices get away from them, often first-time buyers or those on low incomes, who became the renters served by the new legion of landlords whose activities had been at least partially responsible for driving prices ever higher. However, securitization also provided additional opportunities for first-time and low-income entrants to the market who were willing to assume a financial risk themselves, and this is where some of the fault lines in this burgeoning edifice began to appear.

Enter sub-prime

The fact that securitization entailed a separation of the credit risk between the originator and holder of mortgage loans, as these were effectively bundled and sold on, introduced a significant element of moral hazard into the process. Put simply, if you are selling on the risk of loans that you've issued, then you have much less interest in the ability of borrowers to pay them back, as you won't be the person or institution liable to take the financial hit. Given this, and the appetite for mortgage securities from investors, more and more loans were advanced to people who could barely afford them, often on interest-only arrangements and/or with low entry repayments that would step up a few years into the loan. Sensing a bonanza of profits and commissions, there was an expansion of mortgage brokers and sellers offering these and other loans. It is also significant that the finance and housing boom was particularly prevalent in the Anglo-Saxon economies of the UK, the US and Australia, all of which experienced credit and housing booms.

It is no surprise that the outcome of all of this lending and activity produced a seemingly inexorable rise in housing markets, with ever-rising prices in these countries building further confidence as well as the collateral for further loans and opportunistic investment in both housing and the derivatives related to the market. Much as had occurred in the 1920s boom, growing numbers saw a rentier income as being preferable to salaried toil, while others, often middle-aged workers, sought to augment retirement income in the face of reduced workplace pension benefits.

This seemingly unstoppable engine of debt-fuelled expansion contributed to consumption and growth, while a combination of weak unions, stagnant wages and cheap imports from offshored production (for more on this, see Chapter 6) kept inflation in check. Given this overtly benign scenario, governments and authorities continued to hold to the view that, through the economic management of the neoliberal era, they remained in an era of 'Great Moderation' or 'Goldilocks' economy.[13]

Of course, this hubris was misplaced and the bubble inevitably burst in 2007/2008 as many more 'homeowners' than anticipated started to default on their loans, triggering panic regarding the value of housing derivatives and the insurance contracts (CDSs) that were about to be triggered by these defaults. The fact that these contracts had also been treated as 'assets' and had themselves been traded among high net-worth individual and financial institutions also meant that it became almost impossible to identify who actually held particular liabilities. The upshot was that, rather than mitigating risk and producing an era of global financial stability, the unanticipated risks of underregulated debt-fuelled expansion and associated financial engineering had lined some silk pockets with considerable 'earnings', but of questionable foundation and source at the expense of economies and societies globally.[14]

Financialization and phantom wealth

Phantom wealth refers to financial assets that appear or disappear as if by magic as a result of accounting entries and the inflation of asset bubbles unrelated to the creation of anything of real value or utility. The high-tech-stock and housing bubbles are examples. Phantom wealth also includes financial assets created by debt pyramids by which financial institutions engage in complex trading and lending schemes using fictitious or overvalued assets as collateral for loans in order to feed and inflate asset bubbles to create more phantom collateral to support more borrowing to further feed the bubble to justify outsized management fees.[15]

With a general collapse in confidence in the viability of financial institutions, homes were foreclosed (or 'repossessed' as it is termed in the UK), businesses folded through lack of access to credit, and jobs were lost as global economic foundations shook.

However, while society at large suffered, this was not to be the fate of many of the protagonists. Numerous avowedly 'small state' neoliberals, normally averse to any state interference, not least in their 'freedom' to generate profits in the 'good times' and opposed to taxation and state welfare and other forms of collective state intervention, immediately turned to 'big states' in order to restore the financial stability of their institutions and the wider economy. This is in line with the aforementioned tendency towards, at times, dissembling and mendacious revisionism whenever the neoliberal model is seen to fail.

There was also no recouping of the large bonuses earned during the bogus bonanza. Rather, those who caused the crisis tended to remain largely unscathed, despite suggestions of fraudulent as well as simply reckless activity, as many states (including the UK and the US) were called upon to bail out their financial sectors to restore stability.[16] In the US, the Troubled Asset Relief Program (TARP) injected billions of taxpayer-funded dollars into the financial system, as did the financial authorities in the UK and to a lesser extent elsewhere. Not content, however, to run for cover and retain what had already been 'earned', bonuses continued to be paid to these financial alchemists even from the taxpayer largesse that had secured their livelihoods. Shame or even responsibility did not appear to be in the financial sector lexicon.[17]

Aside from this epochal event, the ripples from the crisis continued. Due to intense lobbying, governments and financial authorities provided ongoing liquidity and purchasing of the 'toxic assets' of financial institutions, keeping the practitioners and beneficiaries of these arrangements in the style to which they'd become accustomed, as intervention boosted asset prices, securing and enhancing the wealth of bankers and their well-heeled clients, while the wider public paid the price. In fact, state-underwritten 'wealth' for those at the top has grown exponentially since the crash, also benefiting from state support during the COVID-19 pandemic, while wages and conditions have stagnated or deteriorated for the rest.

However, by a deeply ironic sleight of hand, the seeds of neoliberalism's destruction, rather than heralding its displacement as its key justifications were undermined by these events, were turned against the very state intervention of which big finance had availed itself, at least in terms of taxation and public spending that didn't benefit the financial and corporate sectors. The story that was woven to rescue and, to some degree, further extend the neoliberal model entailed an attempt to pin responsibility for the debacle largely on the state. In the US, the argument ran that it was state backing and support for the extension of mortgage lending to low-income and often minority households that had sown the seeds of the housing and, hence, the economic crisis. In the UK, much was also made of government spending and debt, which had been rising before the crisis, but which had taken a huge hit from the need to bail out the financial sector. This led to a cunning shifting of focus, where spending and debt, particular on public sector jobs and welfare (the 'big state'), were outrageously and successfully tagged as the key causes of the crisis, as opposed to the unencumbered greed and profit seeking and the subsequent financial and corporate welfare that was deemed 'essential' to stabilizing the economy. Before moving on, it might be argued on this particular point that the 'real economy' of retail depositors and sources of finance for productive businesses might have been supported at a much lower cost to public funds, while the fictions generated by the alchemists of Wall Street, the City of London and other financial centres, could have been dismissed with only marginal economic impact; state recovery banks dealing with retail and commercial banking could have been supported and genuine economic activity recovered and sustained. However, this would have meant that a powerful, wealthy and entitled elite would have had to tighten its belts and, of course, belt tightening is a condition that can only be 'economically' justified where it is meted out to the lower orders.

Some of these issues will be returned to in more detail in the following chapters. Prior to this, however, it is worth revisiting and expanding upon a few further important issues at this point in terms of the key themes being presented here.

Regulation, security, insecurity and the conscience of capitalism

In the aftermath of the financial crisis, in spite of (or perhaps because of) the bailout, much was made of the reckless, irresponsible and, at times, amoral behaviour in some sectors of finance that had been responsible for this epochal financial meltdown. Aside from the practical implications for the wider public, which will be discussed later on, this also leads to some observations as to how this resonates with key themes and ideas informing this work as a whole.

As was set out in Chapter 1, a key feature of the human condition is that circumstances and experiences that seem to conflict with our internalized model of the world, and how we feel it should be, trigger an emotional alarm indicating that something is unusual, wrong or potentially threatening (or its inverse if we perceive the departure from the norm as something reasonably familiar and positive). Regardless, the initial emotional response narrows our focus of attention and prepares us for action, while alerting us that there is something that at least warrants our attention and possible action. As was noted earlier, *this equally applies when our own personal conduct or even inner thoughts transgress the norms, rules and expectations that we have internalised.* This is the biosocial foundation of moral conduct and conscience and (as will be outlined in more detail later on) is a key element in understanding the undermining of both rational and ethical conduct in sectors of contemporary neoliberal societies. What I am suggesting here is that where rules and norms are dismissed, are lacking or become more conditional – for example, in settings where loose regulation and malleable ethics become normalized – the internal injunctions that invoke the fear system to place constraints on our thinking and conduct become less effective. In short, we no longer feel the jolt from the brain and the central nervous system reminding us that something is amiss, or at least that it lacks sufficient intensity.[18] There are of course individual variations in terms of emotional sensitivity that come into play here. For some people, a lack of clear rules and boundaries may be highly disconcerting, even among those who might take advantage of a level of moral anarchy. Conversely, a small minority of individuals with low emotional sensitivity will consistently seek advantage by subverting internalized rules and norms with impunity, imposing them on others for personal advantage while disregarding them themselves. Big finance has played a central role in both reflecting these processes and advancing them in contemporary society. The incessant push for ever more capital accumulation and political influence reflects the ever-greater need to insulate oneself from the potential insecurities and the abyss of poverty in an increasingly unequal, competitive, insecure and unforgiving society. This also feeds both the capacity to act without constraint and the dilution of the moral compass that makes this possible and acceptable, where the ends increasingly justify the means in a post-truth, postprobity, rigged economy and society. It also the case that the financial and political clout of elites has become ever more self-reinforcing as wealth provides the means of gaining further control over the system, policy makers and institutions that allow its accumulation. *Deregulation, in effect, does not just dilute the rules but also the conscience of those who should be subject to those rules.* In a real sense, this echoes Émile Durkheim's concept of anomie, where normlessness was described as being at the root of a range of social ills.[19]

As a consequence of financial activity in underregulated markets, wealth and influence become ever more concentrated with insufficient checks and balances to rein it in. Aside from the reckless conduct that brought about the financial crisis and the influence that was brought to bear in protecting and supporting the protagonists, perhaps the most concerning aspect of these developments can be understood in the way in which the loosening of constraints, and the increasing distance that characterizes the lives of the neoliberal elite and the rest, has advanced the aforementioned culture of impunity. As will be discussed in the subsequent chapters, the latter and its influence on aligned senior corporate managers and a generation of mainstream politicians, a trend particularly evident in the increasingly cavalier business and political culture of the UK and the US, have produced a scenario where the needs of the economy and society, and of ordinary citizens, become collateral damage in the unethical and uncaring pursuit of wealth and power, where social 'goods' flow upwards and social 'bads' flow down.

On a final point here, in terms of the consequences of financial sector activity that spill over to have detrimental effects on everyday lives, perhaps one of the most damaging issues recognized of late relates to speculation and profiteering in essential commodities like food and energy. A number of commentators have pointed to the impact that speculative investment has had on the latter, particularly in the aftermath of the financial crisis and the incidence of the global pandemic and international conflict, in each case exacerbating the impact of these events for the public at large.[20]

Runaway price increases in essentials due to market speculation is just part of a chain of capitalist sleight of hand that appears to have used genuine input price increases as a smokescreen for price gouging – what has become known as 'greedflation'. Within a context of increasing demands from financial markets and shareholders, companies were accused of exploiting public perceptions that commodity prices were rising as cover for driving these as far as could be attained, and significantly beyond that justified by additional costs and supply chain issues, as a means of increasing profit margins. This also arises in markets where there is insufficient competition, or even tacit collusion, among the big players. This is a view that has been supported by work in the UK and the US exploring the relationship between increased business costs and the huge increases in prices for goods and services that have been imposed on the public at large.[21] Robert Reich, an economic commentator and former adviser to Bill Clinton, also raised the point that a lack of real competition enabled corporations to use this situation as cover for profiteering, raising their prices (and hence profits), including the household energy costs that rose exponentially.[22]

Overall, among the various effects of financialization, that are further discussed in the following chapters, including poor work, stagnating wages and high accommodation costs, the general 'cost of living crisis' can in no small part be traced back to the operations of big finance and the way in which its activities have affected economy and society in a general sense under neoliberal governance. Given all of this, the need for greater oversight of finance and the re-establishment of stricter controls is clear. In short, as in the aftermath of the Great Crash, the financial genie needs to be put back in the bottle.

Notes

[1] Hutton, W. (1996) *The State We're in*, New York: Random House.

[2] https://davidkorten.org/new-economy-part-i/

[3] Elliott, L. and Atkinson, D. (2008) *The Gods That Failed: How Blind Faith in Markets Has Cost Us Our Future*, New York: Random House.

[4] Stiglitz, J. (2010) 'Moral bankruptcy: why are we letting Wall Street off so easy?', *Mother Jones* (January/February), http://motherjones.com/politics/2010/01/joseph-stiglitz-wall-street-morals

[5] Keynes, J. (1936) *The General Theory of Employment, Interest and Money*, London: Macmillan.

[6] Dash, M. (1999) *Tulipomania: The Story of the World's Most Coveted Flower and the Extraordinary Passions It Aroused*, New York: Crown Publishers.

[7] Garber, P.M. (2000) *Famous First Bubbles: The Fundamentals of Early Manias*, Cambridge, MA: MIT Press

[8] Keynes, J.M. (1936) *The General Theory of Employment, Interest and Money*, London: Macmillan.

[9] Doerr, S., Gissler, S., Peydró, J.L., & Voth, H.J. (2022) Financial crises and political radicalization: 'How failing banks paved Hitler's path to power', *The Journal of Finance*, 77(6): 3339–3372; Bone, J. (2010) 'Irrational capitalism: the social map, neoliberalism and the demodernization of the West', *Critical Sociology*, 36(5): 717–740.

[10] Pernell, K. (2020) 'Market governance, financial innovation, and financial instability: lessons from banks' adoption of shareholder value management', *Theory and Society*, 49: 277–278.

[11] McLeay, M., Radia, A. and Thomas, R. (2014) 'Money creation in the modern economy', *Bank of England Quarterly Bulletin*, Q1, https://www.bankofengland.co.uk/-/media/boe/files/quarterly-bulletin/2014/money-creation-in-the-modern-economy#:~:text=Money%20creation%20in%20practice%20differs,create%20new%20loans%20and%20deposits

[12] Tett, G. (2009) *Fool's Gold: How Unrestrained Greed Corrupted a Dream, Shattered Global Markets and Unleashed a Catastrophe*, London: Little Brown; Elliott, L. and Atkinson, D. (2008) *The Gods That Failed: How Blind Faith in Markets Has Cost Us Our Future*, New York: Random House.

[13] Bernanke, B. (2004) *The Great Moderation*. Washington DC.

[14] Tett, G. (2009) *Fool's Gold: How Unrestrained Greed Corrupted a Dream, Shattered Global Markets and Unleashed a Catastrophe*, London: Hachette UK.

[15] Korten, D. (2009) *Agenda for a New Economy: From Phantom Wealth to Real Wealth*, San Francisco: Berrett-Koehler.

[16] Fligstein, N. and Roehrkasse, A.F. (2016) 'The causes of fraud in the financial crisis of 2007 to 2009: evidence from the mortgage-backed securities industry', *American Sociological Review*, 81(4): 617–643.

[17] Atkinson, D. and Elliott, L. (2008) *The Gods That Failed: How Blind Faith in Markets Has Cost Us Our Future*, London: Bodley Head.

[18] Bone, J. (2012) 'The deregulation ethic and the conscience of capitalism: how the neoliberal "free market" model undermines rationality and moral conduct', *Globalizations*, 9(5): 651–665.

[19] Durkheim, E. (1964) *The Division of Labour in Society*, New York: Free Press.

[20] 'Curbing commodity-market speculation', *Project Syndicate*, 10 August 2022, https://www.project-syndicate.org/commentary/financial-traders-commodity-market-speculation-by-jayati-ghosh-2022-08

[21] 'Companies are using the pain of inflation as an opportunity to boost profit and line shareholder pockets, report shows', https://www.marketwatch.com/story/companies-are-using-the-pain-of-inflation-as-an-opportunity-to-boost-profit-and-line-shareholder-pockets-report-shows-11651159317

[22] 'The hidden link between corporate greed and inflation', https://robertreich.org/post/679072770118877184

6

Globalization, the 'New' Labour Market, AI and the 4th Industrial Revolution

Following on from the previous chapter, one of the key effects of neoliberal financialization, together with the impact of globalization, has been its influence on labour markets, workplaces and working conditions. Overall, as is widely recognized, the neoliberal era has seen a continuous decline in the security and benefits available to much of the workforce in nations like the UK and the US, as with many nations elsewhere, particularly for those at the expanding lower end of the labour market. In his highly regarded outlining of the changes that have arisen in terms of work quality and security, Guy Standing refers to the emergence of a *precariat* – an expanding segment of the workforce subjected to conditions of stagnant and low pay, chronic insecurity and diminishing benefits.[1] This is a scenario also predicted by writers such as Ulrich Beck, who as far back as the turn of the millennium charted the development of a 'brave new world of work' where risk was increasingly being passed from business owners and investors to the workforce in developed economies, rendering them vulnerable to the forms of punitive work experience and low reward that had long prevailed in developing market economies. As Beck noted:

We are eyewitness to a historic turnaround in the work society. The first modernity was characterized by a standardization of work; the second modernity is marked by the opposite principle of the individualization of work. The new potential of information technology – and we are certainly only at the beginning of an ongoing revolution – plays an important role by making possible both the decentralization of work tasks and their real-time coordination in interactive networks, whether across continents or across corridors … the revolution is signalled by a new set of enigmatic terms developed in the social laboratory of management ... lean production, subcontracting, outsourcing, offshoring, downsizing, customizing, to name but a few.[2]

What Beck, Standing and a range of others observed was the logical evolving of the deregulatory ethos of neoliberalism as it impacted on working lives, and an eclipsing of the social contract that had prevailed in the major industrial nations since the postwar era. The growth of finance in relation to the wider economy and society has been an integral driver of these developments. With respect to the central argument at hand, as was noted earlier, a key outcome has been a decline in the capacity of many workers to sustain a sense of control in terms of their incomes and, hence, related major aspects of their lives. Also, this is not simply a condition that is confined to those on the lower rungs of the career ladder, assuming that we still recognize that notion with relation to the experience of those in entry-level jobs. This change can also be seen to have shaken the confidence and security of those further up the workforce hierarchy, who remain aware that a collapse in their status and income may only be a redundancy or downsizing away.

Shareholder value and the privileging of the rentier

A key process by which the financial sector implemented the ethos of neoliberalism – underscoring its impact on the contemporary workplace – has been related to the way in which markets and investors have imposed demands for ever-greater returns from firms in the 'real economy' with an increasing emphasis on short-term profits and *shareholder value* over longer-term growth. To some extent, this arose from the 1970s onwards as a response to the squeeze on profits experienced during that period and was consistent with the promoting of a more strident approach to management in response to reduced margins and increasing demands from labour, and particularly from unionized labour. In effect, as was noted earlier, the inflationary spiral generated by the oil crisis of the early 1970s, and the associated economic problems, saw capital become less sanguine in the face of labour's wage demands and historically higher postwar 'share'. This saw governments, finance and corporations alike begin to challenge the more conciliatory postwar status quo and, as was identified earlier, embrace what was in many respects a return to a form of capital and labour relations more reminiscent of the late 19th and early 20th centuries.[3]

The growing scale and power of an increasingly deregulated and *hungry* finance helped drive this process in a number of important ways. Firstly, more financial activity was directed towards mergers and acquisitions; where firms could be bought and sold, fees could be earned, ailing companies could be folded and their assets often sold off at a profit. In these undertakings, and with the new mindset that the business should be focused on profitability above all other considerations, there was no longer a view of the firm as being answerable to a wide range of stakeholders. Customers and communities were no longer important beyond their contribution to the bottom line, and workers became increasingly viewed as simply commodities and costs that must be minimized as far as possible to sustain short-term profits. The latter was critical for sustaining increasingly footloose and capricious investment as well as share prices, which had to be sustained as a defence against unwelcome and potentially predatory takeover. Given this demand for maximizing profitability in shorter timeframes over other considerations, the key means of achieving this was for staffing to be as 'flexible' and cheap as possible.[4]

This scenario also entailed a shift in senior managerial focus, culture and organization, away from seeing the firm as a broadly based collective, aiming for long-term growth and with a range of obligations, as was suggested previously. Businesses became entities where the singular goal of profitability should be achieved by almost whatever means necessary that were permissible under the law, and sometimes at its margins. This was a view famously expounded by Milton Friedman, who underscored the neoliberal business ethic:

> When I hear businessmen speak eloquently about the 'social responsibilities of business in a free-enterprise system', I am reminded of the wonderful line about the Frenchman who discovered at the age of 70 that he had been speaking prose all his life. The businessmen believe that they are defending free enterprise when they declaim that business is not concerned 'merely' with profit but also with promoting desirable 'social' ends; that business has a 'social conscience' and takes seriously its responsibilities for providing employment, eliminating discrimination, avoiding pollution and whatever else may be the catchwords of the contemporary crop of reformers. In fact they are – or would be if they or anyone else took them seriously – preaching pure and unadulterated socialism. Businessmen who talk this way are unwitting puppets of the intellectual forces that have been undermining the basis of a free society these past decades ... In a free-enterprise, private-property system, a corporate executive is an employee of the owners of the business. He has direct responsibility to his employers. That responsibility is to conduct the business in accordance with their desires, which generally will be to make as much money as possible while conforming to the basic rules of the society, both those embodied in law and those embodied in ethical custom.[5]

Aligning senior managers' priorities with this new colder logic was readily achieved as hard cash was the motivation, where rewards began to greatly exceed previous norms, paid as bonuses based on profits and share price; a golden 'carrot' that ensured the demise of what remained of postwar paternalist management in favour of those more willing to adopt a more 'on message', detached and, at times, ruthless attitude to their employees. The so-called 'job for life' was an early casualty, as ever more contingent forms of employment relationship, once viewed as a historical anachronism, an image of Dickensian precarity and servitude, were gradually normalized. It might be argued that the key difference was the cleaner and, for the most part, safer workplaces that still remained, together with a superficial gloss of noblesse oblige that has often seemed more about managerial and HR ideology than constituting any genuine form of reciprocal obligation. Some other issues related to this will be returned to later on.

However, this new climate within business organizations both reflected and supported a general extension and rationalizing of neoliberal rhetoric, once again particularly in the US and the UK by the Reagan and Thatcher administrations and their media and corporate cheerleaders. The narrative maintained that workers had become lazy and self-indulgent, trade unions had become overly greedy and disruptive, and that while there would be some pain in getting our house in order, in the end everyone would benefit from a more stable, efficient, go-getting entrepreneurial economy. This would be a positive new world where workers became more self-sufficient, flexible, diligent and adaptable, and where managers were less 'hogtied' by restrictive legislation, the so-called 'red tape' that constrained their right to manage. By implementing these changes, it was claimed that profits from leaner and more vibrant businesses would inevitably raise general standards of living. Through the fabled neoliberal mechanism of *trickle down*, all boats would rise, while those at the top should be rewarded without limit and with minimal taxation, as it was only logical that their investment and spending guided by the wisdom of the market could only be of benefit to everyone over time.[6] As was noted in the previous chapter, this move was consistent with the logic of neoliberalism that entailed a move away from focusing on industry, workers and societal wellbeing to one that more directly favoured the interests of investors and rentiers above all else.

Globalizing labour

As the process of reducing wages, conditions and security began to be normalized, the move towards a more globalized economy, better communications and transportation systems allowed the efficiency of labour and, hence, firms to undergo a process of further 'enhancement'. Jobs were to be 'offshored', as the globalizing economy and global finance were to be logically followed by a redistribution of work, wherever possible, to locations with the cheapest labour and the lowest regulatory 'burdens'. When this process started to get underway, it was largely associated with the global outsourcing of repetitive manufacturing functions to workers in developing economies. However, one consequence was that a good deal of the displaced workforce in Europe and the US had relied on solid blue-collar work of this nature as their bread and butter. These were the Fordist-era jobs that had partnered the postwar consumer boom. The question was how they would be replaced, while the fallout from this shift continues to be a point of political contention along with social discontent that persists, with a variety of ongoing consequences.

Government reaction to these developments on both sides of the Atlantic was relatively sanguine. Industrial job losses were deemed to be of little importance, given that overall employment levels would be balanced by growth in the burgeoning service sector. In this optimistic vision, jobs lost in industry, which could often entail demanding and repetitive physical work, would be replaced by more fulfilling, creative and less arduous employment opportunities.[7] Boosterish politicians have often cited an emerging 'knowledge economy', and upskilled nirvana, as the potential outcome of this tectonic shift. However, as we now know, in spite of the emergence of high-reward, high-autonomy and high-tech jobs for a minority (at least for a time), for growing numbers the outcome has been precisely the opposite.

On this point, and something I want to stress, is that we can see the impact of offshoring as a remnant of the early 2000s and earlier, and, in fact, there may be signs of a limited move towards reshoring of some activities more recently, given global supply problems, reduced cost advantages and geopolitical tensions.[8] However, it seems clear – and as I will set out in more detail later on – that a good deal of current social and political upheaval, and its manifestation in populist and authoritarian politics, has its roots in these changes (and the legacy of financialized capitalism more generally). This includes the suspicion and antipathy towards 'foreigners' and 'others', cultivated by opportunistic politicians and others that pervades our societies as it did in insecure societies in the past. What is also important is that, as we stand on the cusp of a potential change to working lives and labour market organization, precipitated by artificial intelligence (AI) and automation, that threatens to eclipse by some magnitude what has already been experienced, the fact that we still haven't been reconciled to such longstanding changes is cause for trepidation.

Offshoring itself was a logical step in the globalizing of the market where the worldwide production of trade and services was accompanied by the movement of jobs, if not workers, to far-flung regions of the world. Workers were forced into competition over ever-extended distances, threatening a race to the bottom in terms of wages and conditions that was hailed in some quarters as being essential to producing greater economic dynamism (for more on this, see later on in the chapter). For the workforce displaced by this movement of jobs in developed economies, as above the alternative was less secure and, potentially, less well-paid work in the expanding service sector. Many would be employed in call centres, as expanding sales and services 'factories', with a large contingent of the workforce finding work in the retail, hospitality and leisure sectors.[9] This was also a set of developments that brought more women into the workplace, where flexible employment was welcomed by some as a means of juggling work and family responsibilities, which as we know continue to be unevenly managed. Regarding the issue of more women entering the workforce, what was once regarded as an overdue move towards greater gender equality and a means for families to raise their standard of living, which it was for some, did not play out for very long for many, as more families began to need two incomes simply to meet everyday costs, expanded debt repayments and burgeoning housing costs (this will be addressed in the next chapter). These developments, taken together, particularly in the UK, resulted in a transformation of the economy to become more reliant on financial services and the consumption and the debt-fuelled expansion discussed in the previous chapter, albeit that manufacturing continued to play a larger role in the US and mainland Europe.

Viewing the ideological platform that had legitimated and advanced these changes with unabashed gusto since the 1980s from the standpoint of the present, as was noted earlier, it's a tune that has continued to be played with considerable enthusiasm. However, I think it's fair to say that it is a melody line that may have less of a confident ring to it of late. Decades of yawning inequality, the return of Gatsby-esque excess and perceived questionable ethics at the top, destroyed careers and lives further down the hierarchy, and the return of levels of poverty that were thought to have been distant memories, have tended to undermine the brash confidence with which this doctrine was introduced. Nonetheless, multitude pages have expounded this narrative, as was noted in Chapter 4, which emerged from the right-leaning media, neoliberal think tanks, academic institutes and assorted political pundits via the mainstream and social media. This will be addressed in more detail in Chapters 8 and 11.

This mindset, and the neoliberal vision for the future of work in the UK, was notably advanced in the 2012 publication of a book and prospective manifesto, *Britannia Unchained*, written by a cast including a future Conservative government minister – a short-lived Prime Minister – together with an equally transient Chancellor. The book was singled out for its derogatory depiction of 'lazy' British workers, its arguing for a furthering of already intense marketization and its antipathy towards what had become a much-withered 'nanny' state.[10]

In line with the central thesis presented here, the principal impact as well as economic inequality and impoverishment has been in terms of the emotional and psychological effects of the move towards this more precarious variant of working life. This has also been recognized by a range of commentators. Richard Sennett's *The Corrosion of Character*[11] and Mark Fisher, in his brief but insightful book *Capitalist Realism*,[12] which eloquently describes and analyses the travails of the present, as well as previously mentioned works from Standing, Beck, Bauman and a host of others too numerous to mention have all charted in various ways the negative impact of the neoliberal settlement on working lives and hence the wellbeing of those exposed to its depredations.[i] As Fisher and others observed, the response has been a well-documented increase in depression and anxiety as an epidemic of our age. As I argue here, this is also associated with the anger and disaffection described in relation to the biosocial processes I have discussed in relation to *experiential overload* and *primalization*, while increasing understanding of the physical and wider societal consequences is developed in the subsequent chapters.

Repression, emotional labour and toxic positivity

However, one further associated development in the neoliberal transformation of work, in addition to its inherent insecurities, has been manifested in terms of the increasing cognitive and emotional burden that has been placed on individuals in the new service economy. Work in the Fordist manufacturing economy, and its associated commercial and service sector, was demanding, but it can be argued that it allowed something of a divide between people's work role and self-identity. Yet, work in services, particularly since the advance of the neoliberal era, has been seen to demand an increasingly greater element of personal presentation, investment and performance, from finance, business, sales, customer services and routine retail occupations. As such, it has entailed that a greater aspect of the *soul* and identity of workers has been captured in the service of their employers.

This aspect of employment was notably identified by the US writer Arlie Hochschild in her work on emotional labour[13] at a point where the service economy was expanding. Hochschild focused on various ways in which service workers are required to fabricate and sustain particular displays of emotion consistent with their occupational role.[14] Her discussion notably described the experience of flight attendants in the 1970s, who were called upon to maintain a veneer of friendly competence and unflappability as a means of both welcoming and reducing the anxieties of travellers in what

---

[i] While differing in approach and focus, there are some very broad resonances here, largely in terms of engagement with the psychosocial and biological factors associated with stress producing working arrangements, as outlined by Wainwright, D. and Calnan, M. (2002) *Work Stress. The Making of a Modern Epidemic*, Buckingham: Open University Press.

for many people remains a slightly unnerving mode of transport.[15] While the work focuses on specific occupations. this is a phenomenon that has been recognized as becoming more generalized and intense as neoliberal service work has expanded. Ritzer, in his McDonaldization thesis,[16] highlights a complementary set of performance demands in the fast-food restaurant, charting the way in which lower-level service workers have been subjected to increasingly demanding forms of regimented interaction to sustain a 'standardized' customer experience that mirrors that of the product itself. This is the perception of the sector that gave rise to the term 'McJobs', a form of employment that has clear parallels with Standing's *precariat*, as workers are subjected to intense systems of control while having little control over their working or, to a great degree, private lives, given their dependency on unpredictable and often capricious management diktat.

In terms of control, workers under these conditions must accede to a tight regimen of procedures and practices. In a sense, this is akin to the form of control exercised over inmates in total institutions. This may perhaps sound like hyperbole, taking an analogy to its extremes, but certain synergies can be considered. Examples include the way in which work is organized according to very strict timetables and standards, and the way in which contemporary workers are subjected to constant systems of surveillance and evaluation. There is also tight prescription over uniforms and appearance, particularly for front-facing service workers, and control as to where workers are allowed to go within the workplace and when they are permitted to do so. While this can be taken too far, as workers can go home at the end of the day (for more on this, see later on in the chapter), but the resonances are nonetheless apparent.[17]

One workplace that has come under particular scrutiny in recent years for its purportedly strict and pervasive regimen of control has been Amazon, the powerhouse company that became even more of a mainstay for global shoppers during the COVID-19 pandemic:

> '[P]ickers', push trolleys around and pick out customers' orders from the aisles. Amazon's software calculates the most efficient walking route to collect all the items to fill a trolley, and then simply directs the worker from one shelf space to the next via instructions on the screen of the handheld satnav device. Even with these efficient routes, there's a lot of walking. One of the new Rugeley 'pickers' lost almost half a stone in his first three shifts. 'You're sort of like a robot, but in human form', said the Amazon manager. 'It's human automation, if you like.'[18]

Amazon has been cited specifically due to what has been described as its almost machine-like system of control and its suggested dehumanizing effect on its workforce, where digital technologies appeared to have become the master rather than the servant of the contemporary worker.[19] Of course, something approaching these conditions was described in relation to the 'Fordist' workplaces since the early 20th century. As Harry Braverman notably outlined, these were work environments where Taylorist Scientific Management techniques radically increase the division of labour, coupled with the assembly line that extended mass production, producing pervasive systems of control and de-skilling. However, it is in terms of the increased *intensity* of such conditions enabled by further technological advances to extend close monitoring and control the extent that one local bar owner in an English community where Amazon had installed itself noted that 'the feedback we're getting is it's like being in a slave camp'.[20] This is in keeping with a general concern regarding the stresses generated by ever-increasing workloads and stifling surveillance that has been a hallmark of the neoliberalization of work, and a situation further 'enhanced' with the advent of new 'supervisory' technologies and AI. The broader implications of the latter are discussed later on in this chapter.

The other major departure from Fordist working arrangements is of course in terms of the Fordist 'bargain' of relatively good wages, benefits and job security as features of the trade-off that motivated workers to accept alienating and tedious work.[21] However, while the downsides have increased, the quid quo pro of this type of arrangement has effectively been withdrawn in the neoliberal, 'flexible' workplace. Much of this has been discussed in relation to frontline workers in the lower echelons of the new labour market, but these exigencies have their correlates with what's happening to many white-collar, lower and middle management employees in current workplace organizations. While having a nominal degree of autonomy in relation to 'front liners' and a slightly greater latitude over time, which (as will be discussed later on) exerts its own particular burdens, many of this echelon of the workforce are also subject to endemic insecurity and control through often rigid bureaucratic demands and, not least, often unrealistic and pervasive assessment via targets and other performance indicators. In effect, the limited autonomy accorded to this group within scheduled working hours and settings is often heavily counterbalanced by poorly defined boundaries between work and home, as well as the psychological pressure imposed by ongoing personal tasks and targets. Fisher's concept and discussion of what he calls 'Market Stalinism' neatly captures many of the key aspects of this phenomenon.[22]

It might be suggested that the preceding discussion departs from the issues concerning emotional labour and self-expression flagged up at the beginning of this section, but there is a strong thread of connection here. Such regimes of simultaneous tight control and insecurity deny the worker autonomy and, hence, a sense of self-control, while they also require the tight suppression of the negative feelings provoked by the experience of domination, management caprice, uncertainty, endless tedium, routine, scrutiny and exhaustion. In essence, such workplace arrangements entail ongoing suppression of the self and one's real feelings. Returning to the issue of emotional labour, in the contemporary neoliberal workplace, this can take a less obvious but no less insidious and damaging form. This relates to the culture of positivity, angst-ridden chutzpah and devotion to the firm/ job that is demanded of many workers even from middle management to the lowliest level, and insecure areas of the workforce:

> In Smile or Die, Barbara Ehrenreich (2009) attacked the modern cult of positive thinking. She recalled how in the United States in the 1860s two quacks (Phineas Quimby and Mary Eddy) set up the New Thought Movement, based on Calvinism and the view that belief in God and positive thinking would lead to positive outcomes in life. Ehrenreich traced this through into modern business and finance. She described how motivational conferences had speakers telling short-term contract workers who had been made redundant to be good team players, defined as 'a positive person' who 'smiles frequently, does not complain and gratefully submits to whatever the boss demands'.[23]

This orientation to work arguably emerged in the US as an extension of the 'go-getting' attitude and 'hyperindividualism' of American culture and psyche, but which has arguably been hijacked and intensified with the neoliberal turn, complemented in the UK by an echo of its own Victorian hard work ethic as it embraced the neoliberal model. While this form of contemporary asceticism has had some influence elsewhere in Europe to varying extents, it has not chimed so easily, particularly with longstanding attitudes to work/life culture in France as well as some other Mediterranean nations. In fact, it has been suggested that the notable public anger and resistance in 2023 to the raising of the state pension age in France was motivated by concern that this was emblematic of challenging the French approach to welfare and work more generally, and a move towards the less generous, insecure and more punishing US and UK model.

The ideal UK and US worker is expected to accept an orientation of being a constantly 'on', indefatigable and spirited individual who is also a committed 'team player'. All of these traits, including the latter, are harnessed in the interests of contemporary employers and to the detriment of their staff. Moreover, a key issue here relates to the aforementioned notion of *toxic positivity*, which, together with the sublimated sense of injustice necessary to accede to many forms of current employment arrangements, compounds the constraints and insecurities that lead to psychological damage.

This is an issue that will be taken up in Chapter 12 as part of a more rounded critique of the role of our therapy culture in sustaining and, in many instances, potentially exacerbating some of the negative psychological effects of living and working in neoliberal societies. However, I want to briefly make the point that the demand for 'a positive mental attitude' and so on can in and of itself be psychologically and, as I will argue, later even physically damaging. In fact, it's beginning to be understood that presenting false emotions, and particularly engaging in what Hochschild terms 'surface acting', trying to present with a façade of positive emotions regardless of circumstances can, in and of itself, be a source of emotional and psychological problems.[24] This is consistent with what a relatively new form of psychological therapy, Acceptance and Commitment Therapy (ACT), refers to as 'experiential avoidance'.[25]

Without labouring the point, contrary to received wisdom that has long prevailed within clinical psychology and psychiatry, ACT asserts that viewing 'real' emotions negatively, as 'symptoms' or attempting to overly control inner emotional states, rather than letting them be as they are and possibly confronting the real circumstances that generate them, may be at the root of a range of mental health issues.[26] If this is indeed the case, its implications for contemporary service work and the neoliberal mindset more generally seem fairly obvious, as employers' demands for people to constantly suppress and manage their real emotional states, and fabricate positive alternatives, may well compound already-manifest toxic psychological pressures.

Unshared obligation

As was noted earlier, a hallmark of many business cultures is to demand allegiance to the firm, to exhibit strong 'interpersonal skills' and to exude enthusiastic commitment to the company management and work culture. One of the paradoxes of the neoliberal workplace is that such demands are met not with the paternalistic sense of mutual obligation that pertained in many postwar organizations, but by its opposite. Employees must run their lives in accordance with the demands of the organization, with little guarantee of reciprocity in terms of reward or security.[27] Denying the real nature of this relationship, a sense of inclusivity and positivity is sustained in many contemporary firms through small rituals of allegiance, the 'Walmart Cheer' being a notable example, where employees gather every morning and evening to enthusiastically sing the company song:

> But the absolute worst thing about working there had to be the Walmart cheer. In case you've never been fortunate enough to witness the daily Walmart pep rally, it basically consists of all the available 'Associates' gathering in a big circle to hear about how much money 'our' store had brought in the previous day and how we all needed to work even harder so 'our' store would bring in more money than all

the other Walmarts nearby tomorrow. And to seal the deal we would all take part in the Walmart cheer, a ritual that simultaneously drains you of all hope for the future while at the same time somehow numbing you to the point of lethargic resignation to your lot in life.[28]

This resonates with what *The Guardian* journalist Madeline Bunting explored in her 2004 book *Willing Slaves*, charting the way in which many contemporary organizations engage in workplace rituals of this nature, as well as dress-up days, company-organized outings and so on, all aimed at further aligning the employee's identity and commitment to the company and its 'values'.[29] 'Colleagues' are often referred to as though they are members of a tightly bonded collective, a family, and/or are given impressive titles in contradiction to their actual status, compensation, benefits and marginal position – what Standing has referred to as 'uptitling', where 'prestige' supplants real autonomy, pay and benefits.[30] As was noted earlier, this compounds the chronic stress inherent in much contemporary work as, particularly for those who recognize the disconnect, there is a sense of dissonance, cynicism, distrust and alienation in having to 'perform' as though this sham reflects reality, and a degree of shame as a result of being in the position of having to accede to it. However, the damage may well be exacerbated for those employees who have more heartily embraced the company line, who have fallen for the HR narrative and become emotionally and psychologically attached to the company and their role within it. While this may make the everyday experience of working in such conditions less jarring in the short term, it can be seen to render the relatively common experience of 'performance management', downsizing and redundancy more psychologically damaging, in being cast out from the 'family' who no longer require your happy and enthusiastic presence.

Going home

Following on from the preceding discussion, and as a very evident and well-observed point, as well as the pressure to exhibit psychological and emotional attachment to workplace organizations, recent technological developments have clearly made it infinitely more difficult to retain any form of distance, a factor that was turbocharged by the onset of the global COVID-19 pandemic. This effectively consolidated and extended a range of practices already in motion that most of us are familiar with in terms of the way in which mobile technology has left us ever more exposed to being on call and 'at work'. Workers in the past could legitimately avoid an inconveniently timed phone call from work, a last-minute request for overtime or a change of work schedule, or a late demand for data or a 'rush job' for those further up the organizational ladder. Now this distance has been effectively eradicated. Combined with the aforementioned targets, and competition between employees, there is the incessant pressure to allow work to blur the boundaries and intrude into one's personal time. As noted, this advanced significantly with the emergence of COVID-19, as working from home became more normalized and the development of technology to facilitate it accelerated faster than would likely otherwise have occurred; where some had once used Skype or Zoom on the odd occasion, the latter and Teams have now become routinely integrated into everyday work schedules. This has also intensified work for many, as meetings can be more numerous and the downtime of travel and small talk between them has contracted. Working from home for 'white-collar' employees is of course a double-edged sword, offering some conveniences, but greater isolation and less human contact, including the building of workplace solidarities and support that might assuage some of its increased demands and stresses.

For those in more routine occupations, the motivating factors driving flexibilization may vary, but the intrusion into personal time may not. The financial pressure to be on call for shifts at the store and in hospitality or other settings where flexibility is a job requirement may be profound, with the threat of being placed at the back of the queue for those who are consistently unavailable. This also raises the issue of the much-discussed gig economy, platform working and the zero-hours contract that have become a pervasive feature of the labour market at its most precarious in the neoliberal era, as this has been turbocharged by digitalization. The nature of this 'new' type of employment relationship is often presented by employers, right-wing politicians and other advocates in Panglossian and, one might even say, Orwellian terms. As with debates on flexibility more generally, rather than the much-vaunted 'freedom' and autonomy asserted to be enjoyed by the employee, flexibility is often clearly at the gift and whim of the employer. Where there is no pay without work and no obligation for it to be provided, workers' autonomy, time and sometimes dignity are wholly subjugated to the demands of the business. At best, this often provides insecure, top-up incomes for some students and others who might happily work under this kind of arrangement for short periods. However, for people wholly reliant on or trying to build a life around this type of employment over longer periods, gig work is inherently exploitative, the contemporary e-variant of lining up at the dock gates in the 19th century.

It might be noted that this has also been the longer-term experience of the commission-only salesperson. I conducted a study in this area more than twenty years ago, suggesting that this might become an exemplar of the neoliberal workplace if flexibility was driven to its logical conclusion, which is effectively where we are now. Salespeople were required to be available at almost any time when an appointment might become available. This meant effectively being always on and having little time for family or a social life, as sales appointments were normally more numerous when most potential customers weren't working, during evenings and at weekends. As such, salespeople inhabited a twilight world of insular socializing at odd hours and in unpredictable breaks when appointments were scarce. Successful salespeople could generate relatively high if insecure incomes, albeit at a cost. For those who failed to show enthusiasm or success, the result would tend to be far fewer and lower-quality appointments; as managers' income was drawn from their sales teams' earnings, more numerous and better-quality appointments went to those with a better track record, becoming to some extent a self-fulfilling scenario. Moreover, success was overwhelmingly dependent on emotional labour and presentational skills. In this instance, however, the psychological pressures were partially assuaged by reimagining the work as a form of competitive game, and by the gallows humour and relatively high level of camaraderie within the insular insider culture.[31]

It can be argued that the various developments associated with the neoliberalization of work outlined earlier – largely implemented to satisfy the short-term acquisitiveness of corporations, investors and financial institutions – have been legitimated by the ideology of neoliberalism to the detriment of many of those who have accepted this narrative. The rhetoric around 'hard work', 'self-reliance' and 'positivity' as social 'goods' have been distorted to become an alibi for exploitation and insecurity. In a similar vein, and again an issue I will return to in later chapters, the mantra of meritocracy as a legitimator of widening inequality, that workplace reward simply reflects talent and effort, contrasts with what many observe and experience, creating its own dissonances and disaffections. Moreover, this can also be seen to represent a distortion of 'the calling' that Max Weber set out in *The Protestant Ethic and the Spirit of Capitalism*,[32] where he cited the turn to expressing godliness and piety through devotion and diligence to everyday tasks, duties, work and business among early Protestants as a development that evolved over time to emerge as the modern work ethic. As was noted earlier, neoliberal ideology echoes rhetoric around the work ethic of the Industrial Revolution - as a set of values with which to 'educate' and control the working masses – and is now often employed as a legitimating discourse by those who have benefited most but shared little in terms of 'honest toil'. However, the one factor that continues to resonate with Weber's account is the fusing of occupational and personal identity, and the extension of the workplace into the soul and being of contemporary workers. Yet, paradoxically, this may be arising at the very point where the centrality of paid work and occupational identities in everyday life that has persisted since the Industrial Revolution, and not least the capacity of people to sustain themselves at all in this way, is itself being called into question. This, it has been argued, may be presenting us with the nothing less than the prospect of a fundamental reorientation of the way in which we work and live, a shifting of the tectonic plates, of a magnitude last experienced by those confronted with the huge changes that accompanied the last Industrial Revolution.

Automation, artificial intelligence and the future of work

We can now begin to see how the age of labour is likely to end. As time goes on, machines continue to be more capable, taking on tasks that once fell to human beings. The harmful substituting force displaces workers in the familiar way. For a time, the helpful complementing force continues to raise the demand for those displaced workers elsewhere. But as task encroachment goes on, and more and more tasks fall to machines, that helpful force is weakened as well. Human beings find themselves complemented in an ever-shrinking range of tasks. And there is no reason to think the demand for those particular tasks will be large enough to keep everyone employed. The world of work comes to an end not with a bang, but with the withering – a withering in the demand for the work of human beings.[33]

The preceding quote encapsulates the growing concern that the work that is central to sustaining current economic arrangements and, not least, the livelihoods of contemporary individuals and their families may be fundamentally under threat from advances in new technology. This is a refrain that emerged in the mid-2000s and that's even been recognized by the global elites of the World Economic Forum, with discussion of the 4th Industrial Revolution being advanced in a book of that title by none other than its founder and executive chairman, Klaus Schwab.[34] However, it is a view that has also been contested by a wide range of economists, politicians, sundry pundits and detractors, who critique such notions with reference to the *Luddite fallacy*, associated with workers who feared efficiency-enhancing mechanization during the Industrial Revolution. This counterargument to asserting that our relationship with work as we know it will come to an end, or be greatly diminished, argues that new jobs always emerge from old, that all new technologies in the past have generated such unfounded fears, and that new technology will usher in a new world of high-level well-paid work. Yet, as the various proponents of the post-work model maintain, things are likely to be different this time.[35]

The technological developments of the past were usually confined to displacing aspects of mostly highly routinized activity. It is also the case that many prior workplace innovations arose when there was very significant scope for the expansion of commerce, consumption and leisure that could provide alternative forms of employment for displaced agricultural and then factory workers. However, not only are many economies now more developed, and those that aren't are financially constrained, but the key issue is that AI and robotics are advancing to such an extent that they are gaining the capacity to displace a vast range of functions in previously unimagined ways. Hence, the notion that job displacement is usually at the lower end of the job market no longer holds as it once did, as many of the jobs that are now becoming vulnerable to technological displacement, either wholly or in part, include some we have regarded as being highly skilled and which have been thus far well rewarded. Jobs in areas like law, medicine, education, accountancy and so on require a good deal of knowledge, but many of the functions are nonetheless often routinized, providing the prospect of displacement.[36] It's perhaps only the aspects of these types of roles that require considerable critical reflection and analysis at a higher level that will survive, while many of the day-to-day tasks will be delegated to AI. This is certainly the view of many of the writers cited here.

At the lower end of the job market, of course, the impact is liable to be profound, at least once the cost of automation undercuts the wages of lower-paid workers. These workers will now find themselves in competition not only with each other and with cheaper labour across the globe, but also with machines that need no remuneration, breaks, holidays, sick pay or much in the way of management. These new 'workers' will only require maintenance and replacement presumably after reasonably lengthy service and may even be self-sustaining. It might readily be argued that in contemporary neoliberal labour markets, we're already seeing evidence of these developments. The rise of flexible and gig work, in and of itself, is at least in part a symptom of increasing automation where workers are only employed where they are relatively cheap and more will presumably be replaced as these technologies advance, much as Daniel Susskind has proposed.[37] It's also very much the case – as will be discussed later on – that, if not yet translating to higher unemployment, this is currently being manifested in the expansion of the working poor.

From an everyday perspective, we can see this every time we visit a supermarket or other major store, where staffing levels appear to be very visibly contracting and more of the service is delivered with little or no human involvement. As was noted earlier, it must also be the recalled that retailing was one of the key sectors intended to replace manufacturing when a significant proportion of this was offshored. While, as will be discussed later on, online shopping has led to a precipitous contraction of retail outlets, AI and automation also threaten the jobs of those still employed in the sector. Similarly, the same process can be observed in call centres, as noted, once regarded as the new 'factories' of the service sector, and in hospitality. With respect to the latter, this is a process already well underway at McDonald's, where automation and technology has been a major aspect of a parcel of developments that has seen employment worldwide fall by more than half over the decade since 2012.[38] This was underlined in December 2022 when the company opened an almost fully automated restaurant in Texas.[39] At present, customer services rather than sales are where most of us encounter the frustrating experience of trying to have something relatively complex solved by a 'bot' with a limited range of responses. Nonetheless, these machines are getting better to the extent that I've even found myself lately taking a number of seconds to recognize that I wasn't actually speaking to a human being, and this will evidently continue to develop apace. The release of Open AI's ChatGPT in November 2022 went viral and also led to discussion that we are crossing the Rubicon in terms of these developments, belying the adherents of the Luddite fallacy. This and similar technology associated with generative AI already has prodigious capacity and is expected to advance exponentially, raising the prospect of even occupations that we now consider require a significant degree of high-level skill and creativity being potentially displaced in media, art, communication, administration and even computer coding among other areas. This was the view expressed by Microsoft CEO Satya Nadella in an interview with the *Wall Street Journal* at the World Economic Forum at Davos in 2023, while Microsoft has invested several billion dollars in Open AI with a view to integrating AI functionality with its software packages. It might also be noted that many large tech companies have begun to shed jobs rather than prove to offer new avenues for much-vaunted upskilled employment: 'It's a bit terrifying. Knowledge workers, I've heard it already here at Davos this week already anxious in some ways about their future jobs and what it means when you see technology spread on that scale.'[40]

Such arguments and concerns around the potential impact of AI on work have grown ever more insistent where, for example, the International Monetary Fund notably entered the debate at the opening of the subsequent 2024 Davos meeting, with new analysis echoing the view that AI would likely deepen inequality, particularly in advanced economies, while leading to widespread global job displacement and the need for an expansion of 'social safety nets' as well as retraining.[41]

Nonetheless, the mantra that 'hard work' is an indispensable feature underpinning economic and social life remains a core tenet of the neoliberal mindset, most vigorously expounded wherever issues of poverty, inequality and welfare are addressed, despite the growing awareness that employment prospects may potentially diminish for significant numbers. As UK Prime Minister Rishi Sunak noted in November 2023: 'We believe in the inherent dignity of a good job. And we believe that work – not welfare – is the best route out of poverty.'[42]

Even among those who accept the prospect of large-scale change, the belief that the AI revolution will somehow lead to higher-skilled and better-paid work in future remains, with little focus on exactly where those high-skill jobs will come from or how many people will be needed, even if some do succeed in new occupations. While, as was noted earlier, what are currently considered to be skilled, professional jobs are far from being immune to displacement, there is also the obvious question as to what happens to the legions of people without much-vaunted 'high skills'. There is a clear risk that work will become ever more insecure and poorly rewarded, particularly at the lower end of the labour market and, quite simply, there may be not of enough of it to go around across the board. The question then is how we sustain the economy, our way of life, social stability and wellbeing in such a scenario? Of course, as was suggested earlier, global supply chain issues and other political pressures and concerns have raised the prospect of some manufacturing and other services being *reshored*, perhaps mitigating some of the fallout from rapid automation at least for a time. However, it is difficult to see how this would provide anything more than a brief hiatus in the decline of work, as AI and robotics become more advanced and increasingly cheaper than human labour.[43] This is a particular concern in already unequal atomized and fracturing societies, and marks a point where what was once one of the key pillars of personal and social stability and identity in modern societies is eroding. As I will address in the Conclusion, there are evidently ways in which these developments could clearly be beneficial, removing people from drudgery and providing them with time for friends, family, leisure and work that provides a strong element of self-satisfaction and, potentially, social good and greater wellbeing. There may even be scope for some new lines of work that have a more communitarian, creative, caring and social focus. All of this is positive and possible. This, however, would entail a fundamental revision to the current individualistic, profit-led, privatized and competitive approach to work and the economy as a whole, including a less avaricious business culture. However, if we continue to allow the majority of economic gains from these developments to flow upward to a small, gilded minority, while casting the majority towards an insecure world fraught with endemic experiential overload, the outlook is not looking good. In line with the discussion in Chapter 1, the prospect of an ever more insecure and economically deprived and primalized populace, with little hope for the future, may see a further turn in the breakdown of civil society, leading to the wealthy seceding from the public realm into the secure private space, and where life for many becomes more anarchic, dangerous or subject to increasing authoritarian control via the very technologies employed by those who have imposed these conditions.

This latter point raises a further issue of debate concerning the emergence of generative AI and automation in that, as while as threatening people's incomes and way of life in the economic sphere, it is feared that this technology may present us with more existential risks. Here a wide range of professionals, pundits and politicians from across the mainstream political spectrum have raised concerns over the way in which AI may increase the capacity of individuals, collectives and hostile governments to apply this technology to do harm, from the cheap and efficient building of biological and other weapons with devastating potential, to the further extension of disinformation via social media, including the use of deepfake technology, sowing ever more social and political instability.

> History has shown in the absence of regulation and strong government oversight, some technology companies choose to prioritise profit over the wellbeing of their customers, the security of our communities and the stability of our democracies ... One important way to address these challenges – in addition to the work we have already done – is through legislation. Legislation that strengthens AI safety without stifling innovation.[44]

The concern here is real, and not simply the stuff of science fiction, particularly given the potential for this to develop within the context of further demoralized, disenfranchised and, possibly, destitute populations. It is also clear that the governance of technologies with such potential cannot simply follow the neoliberal playbook and be left to the market.

Notes

[1] Standing, G. (2011) *The Precariat: The New Dangerous Class*, London: Bloomsbury.
[2] Beck, U. (2000) *The Brave New World of Work*, Cambridge: Polity Press, pp 55–56.
[3] Harvey, D. (2005) *A Brief History of Neoliberalism*, Oxford: Oxford University Press.
[4] Lapavitsas, C. (2009) 'Financialisation, or the search for profits in circulation', *Economiaz*, 72(3): 98–119.
[5] Friedman, M. (2007) 'The social responsibility of business is to increase its profits', in W.C. Zimmerli, M. Holzinger and K. Richter (eds), *Corporate Ethics and Corporate Governance*, Berlin: Springer.
[6] Friedman, M. (2007) 'The social responsibility of business is to increase its profits', in W.C. Zimmerli, M. Holzinger and K. Richter (eds), *Corporate Ethics and Corporate Governance*, Berlin: Springer.
[7] Atkinson, R. (2004) 'Understanding the offshoring challenge', Progressive Policy Institute.
[8] Vanchan, V., Mulhall, R. and Bryson, J. (2018) 'Repatriation or reshoring of manufacturing to the US and UK: dynamics and global production networks or from here to there and back again', *Growth and Change*, 49(1): 97–121.
[9] Standing, G. (2011) *The Precariat: The New Dangerous Class*, London: Bloomsbury.
[10] Kwarteng, K., Patel, P., Raab, D., Skidmore, C. and Truss, E. (2012) *Britannia Unchained*, London: Palgrave Macmillan.
[11] Sennett, R. (1998) *The Corrosion of Character: The Personal Consequences of Work in the New Capitalism*, New York: Norton.
[12] Fisher, M. (2009) *Capitalist Realism: Is There No Alternative?*, New York: Zero Books.
[13] Hochschild, A. (1983) *The Managed Heart: The Commercialization of Human Feeling*, Berkeley: University of California Press.
[14] Wainright, D. and Calnan, M. (2002) *Work Stress: The Making of a Modern Epidemic*, Buckingham: Open University Press.

15 Wainright, D. and Calnan, M. (2002) *Work Stress: The Making of a Modern Epidemic*, Buckingham: Open University Press.
16 Ritzer, G. (1993) *The McDonaldization of Society*, London: Sage.
17 Goffman, E. (1961) *Asylums: Essays on the Social Situation of Mental Patients and Other Inmates*, United States: Anchor, Doubleday.
18 O'Connor, S. (2013) 'Amazon unpacked', *Financial Times*, 8 February.
19 Guendelsberger, E. (2019) 'I worked at an Amazon fulfillment center; they treat workers like robots', *Time Magazine*, 18 July.
20 Guendelsberger, E. (2019) 'I worked at an Amazon fulfillment center; they treat workers like robots', *Time Magazine*, 18 July.
21 Grint, K. (2005) *The Sociology of Work*. Cambridge: Polity Press.
22 Fisher, M. (2009) *Capitalist Realism: Is There No Alternative?*, New York: Zero Books.
23 Standing, G. (2011) *The Precariat: The New Dangerous Class*, London: Bloomsbury, p 21
24 Hochschild, A. (1983) *The Managed Heart: The Commercialization of Human Feeling*, Berkeley: University of California Press.
25 Gloster, A.T., Walder, N., Levin, M.E., Twohig, M.P. and Karekla, M. (2020) 'The empirical status of acceptance and commitment therapy: a review of meta-analyses', *Journal of Contextual Behavioral Science*, 18: 181–192; Blackledge, J. and Hayes, S. (2001) 'Emotion regulation in acceptance and commitment therapy', *Journal of Clinical Psychology*, 57(2): 243–255.
26 Blackledge, J. and Hayes, S. (2001) 'Emotion regulation in acceptance and commitment therapy', *Journal of Clinical Psychology*, 57(2): 243–255.
27 Standing, G. (2011) *The Precariat: The New Dangerous Class*, London: Bloomsbury.
28 'America circa 2013 in a nutshell: the "Wal-Mart cheer" is the most depressing thing you'll ever see', https://dangerousminds.net/comments/america_circa_2013_in_a_nutshell_the_wal_mart_cheer_is_the_most_depressing
29 Bunting, M. (2004) *Willing Slaves: How the Overwork Culture Is Ruling Our Lives*, London: HarperCollins.
30 Standing, G. (2011) *The Precariat: The New Dangerous Class*, London: Bloomsbury.
31 Bone, J. (2017) *The Hard Sell: An Ethnographic Study of the Direct Selling Industry*, Abingdon: Routledge.
32 Weber, M. (2001 [1930]) *The Protestant Ethic and the Spirit of Capitalism*, London: Routledge.
33 Susskind, D. (2020) *A World without Work: Technology, Automation and How We Should Respond*, Harmondsworth: Penguin.
34 Schwab, K. (2017) *The Fourth Industrial Revolution*, Cologny: World Economic Forum.
35 Brynjolfsson, E. and McAfee, A. (2011) *Race against the Machine: How the Digital Revolution Is Accelerating Innovation, Driving Productivity, and Irreversibly Transforming Employment and the Economy*, Digital Frontier (electronic); Frey, C. and Osborne, M. (2013) 'The future of employment: how susceptible are jobs to computerisation?', http://www.oxfordmartin.ox.ac.uk/downloads/academic/The_Future_of_Employment.pdf; Schwab, K. (2017) *The Fourth Industrial Revolution*, Cologny: World Economic Forum.
36 Felten, E., Raj, M. and Seamans, R. (2023) 'How will language modelers like ChatGPT affect occupations and industries?', arXiv preprint arXiv:2303.01157.
37 Susskind, D. (2020) *A World without Work: Technology, Automation and How We Should Respond*, Harmondsworth: Penguin.
38 'Number of McDonald's employees worldwide from 2012 to 2022', https://www.statista.com/statistics/819966/mcdonald-s-number-of-employees/
39 Do Couto, C. (2022), 'Burgers, fries and robots: McDonald's opens 1st mostly automated location in Texas', https://globalnews.ca/news/9370313/mcdonalds-robots-automated-restaurant-texas/
40 'Satya Nadella: Microsoft's products will soon access Open AI tools like ChatGPT', https://www.youtube.com/watch?v=UNbyT7wPwk4

41 Cazzaniga, M., Jaumotte, F., Li, L., Melina, G., Panton, A.J., Pizzinelli, C., ... & Tavares, M.M. (2024) Gen-AI: Artificial Intelligence and the Future of Work. Staff Discussion Notes, 2024(001).
    https://www.imf.org/en/Publications/Staff-Discussion-Notes/Issues/2024/01/14/Gen-AI-Artificial-Intelligence-and-the-Future-of-Work-542379?cid=bl-com-SDNEA2024001
42 UK Prime Minister Rishi Sunak, 20 November 2023, https://www.gov.uk/government/speeches/pms-speech-on-the-economy-20-november-2023
43 Brynjolfsson, E. and McAfee, A. (2011) *Race against the Machine: How the Digital Revolution Is Accelerating Innovation, Driving Productivity, and Irreversibly Transforming Employment and the Economy*, Digital Frontier (electronic).
44 'Kamala Harris to call for urgent action on AI threat to democracy and privacy', *The Guardian*, 1 November 2023, https://www.theguardian.com/technology/2023/nov/01/kamala-harris-to-call-for-urgent-action-on-ai-threat-to-democracy-and-privacy

7

Marketized Housing: An Insecure Base

As was argued in the last chapter, stable and decently paid work offers people some certainty over financial decisions while allowing them to plan for the future with a degree of confidence. The social contract, workplace regulations, trade union engagement and full employment policies of the mid-20th century began to provide this for growing numbers, as well as the prospect of a reasonably decent retirement. This was central to progressive measures that improved many people's lives health and happiness, at least to a degree at that time. Critically aligned with this, secure and affordable housing also clearly has a bearing on our ability build a solid foundation, sense of identity and wellbeing.[1] A decent secure home evidently anchors people in the community and provides a place of refuge from the stresses of everyday life in modern societies, once more offering stability in a potentially insecure and complex environment. Together with the 'job for life', stable, secure and affordable housing provided the other pillar of continuity and predictability that had begun to serve as a bulwark against experiential overload for growing numbers, prior to being derailed with the onset of the neoliberal era and which has been eroding since that point for all but the securely insulated.

Such is the importance of these critical props of modern life that, as we know, they have long been fought over and have been central to political skirmishes, actions, protests and, at times, large-scale insurrection. This chapter continues from where the previous one left off, to consider the way in which housing in the neoliberal era, as with work, has been subject to this kind of turning back of the clock that has meant that having a decent place to live has once again become a source of profound economic and social insecurity for many, and particularly the young who failed to gain a foothold on the so-called property ladder at the right time, while imposing poor mental and physical health outcomes for growing numbers.

The uneven development of urban housing

The unregulated and exploitative housing arrangements of the early modern industrial cities is something that many people recognize, often through novels and films depicting those times, as being associated with overcrowding, squalor and terrible conditions for the masses of the poor. Reflecting the deep inequalities of those times, this imagery is counterposed by the opulence and grandeur of the homes occupied by the minority of the urban rich. Numerous novelists, social commentators and activists, some of whom have been mentioned previously, have described the poor conditions in early industrial cities as backdrops to crime and deviance, and, on occasion, to provide a dramatic starting point for more optimistic rags-to-riches stories. Celebrated writers such as Dickens and Jacob Riis in the US provided literary excursions into such settings and lifestyles that were often beyond the gaze of polite society. In *How the Other Half Lives*,[2] a phrase that entered everyday parlance, Riis described conditions that seemed nothing short of barbaric in the way in which many poorer inhabitants of rapidly industrialized cities like New York were forced to live. Early academic or at least learned studies of housing at the time came from eminent figures like Charles Booth, who in the course of exploring the occupations and housing conditions in Victorian London noted the dire conditions imposed on the poor as well as the need for both philanthropic and municipal intervention.[3] Similar observations were also made in Roberts' *The Classic Slum*, in which he charted the class divisions and housing conditions of early 20th-century Salford, near Manchester.[4]

In addition to illustrating the depredations of overcrowding and squalid accommodation, these works pointed to the fact that two key factors were critical to this scenario. Firstly, housing was very loosely regulated and privately owned, but with ownership restricted to a small detached financial elite. Rather than providing decent affordable homes, housing in the industrialized cities operated as a commodity for investment, a store of wealth and a vehicle for the accumulation of passive rentier income for the better off, with its functioning as a very poor-quality source of shelter being secondary to those priorities. Given this situation, it's perhaps no surprise that, alongside the rise of trade unionism and Chartism that aimed to give the lower orders more of a say and a better deal in terms of industrial society's rewards, strife over housing conditions was part of this mix, the main target of which was the perceived exploitation by the wealthy (rentier) landlord class:

> The ordinary progress of a society which increases in wealth, is at all times tending to augment the incomes of landlords; to give them both a greater amount and a greater proportion of the wealth of the community, independently of any trouble or outlay incurred

by themselves. They grow richer, as it were in their sleep, without working, risking, or economizing. What claim have they, on the general principle of social justice, to this accession of riches? In what would they have been wronged if society had, from the beginning, reserved the right of taxing the spontaneous increase of rent, to the highest amount required by financial exigencies?[5]

In Britain, as the foremost industrialized economy of the 19th century, around 90 per cent of the population were renters.[6] In a very real sense the urban workforce were not only exploited by factory owners and other members of the economic elite at work, but a large portion of their meagre earnings was subsequently captured as rent for, as was noted earlier, often very poor-quality accommodation. The social tensions produced, in addition to workplace strikes and wider social and political unrest, were represented by rent strikes at times when the burden and injustice of housing arrangements and conditions became intolerable.

A notable instance of this occurred in Glasgow, Scotland, the city of my birth and one of the leading industrial cities of the British imperial era. Glasgow in the 19th and early 20th centuries was a city of dark factories, shipbuilders, heavy engineering and dockside trading warehouses, reflecting its geographical position as one of the key British ports. It was also infamous for the squalid tenement housing occupied by the lower classes and the social problems therein, a reputation that persisted until the 1960s and 1970s when the city undertook a massive redevelopment programme, some aspects of which were successful and others less so (for more on this, see later on in the chapter).

By the turn of the 20th century, some efforts had been made to improve health and sanitation among the slums of Glasgow, as with other UK cities, given concerns over the health of the urban public as a whole. That aside, however, low pay and onerous working arrangements were compounded by poor living conditions among the highest-density housing in Britain at that time, providing tinder to be lit when the population's sense of insecurity and injustice reached breaking point. Rent strikes were sparked as landlords began to impose substantial rent increases at the beginning of the First World War, at a point where many 'family wage'[i] earners had joined the fight. Demand for housing had been boosted by workers coming to the city for employment

---

[i] The so-called family wage was one of the demands of trade unions in the late 19th century, where it was asserted that men's wages should be enough to sustain a nuclear family, without the need for the wife and children to work. This was bound up with the bourgeois ideal of the times, traditional gender roles and changing perceptions of childhood.

in munitions factories, contributing to a serious housing shortage. The fact that there were very few houses available for rent in working-class districts of Glasgow and the further intensity of overcrowding, together with landlords' moves to decant serving soldiers' families to smaller houses or to evict them, had exacerbated an already fraught situation. The wave of rent strikes started in 1914 and 1915, with action often mainly fronted by working-class women, with action against rent increases and conditions also emerging in the English industrial city of Leeds and to a lesser extent elsewhere. Action was also coordinated with key trade unions, with strikes among dockers, as well as shipyard and factory workers. In Glasgow, the tensions of this period came to a head with the so-called 'Battle of George Square' in January 1919, where fears of the triggering of a Bolshevik uprising in the city led to the calling in of the army to restore order.[7]

While Britain's attachment to deregulation, laissez-faire and its rigid and highly unequal class system drove serious social tensions, these were far from being isolated instances at the time, sparked by the twin concerns of work and housing. Having transported a strong element of its socioeconomic and political culture to the New World, albeit that it had developed some particular variations and similar inequities of its own by this point – scarred by the legacy of slavery and the continuing racism that had been employed to support it – similar social and political tensions around work and housing in the US were also clearly observed, including in the form of rent strikes:

> Tenant mobilization across the Americas during the early twentieth century reveals several common characteristics. From our survey of the most significant mobilizations during the first three decades of the twentieth century, we discuss collective action in New York City (1904), Buenos Aires (1907), Mexico City and Veracruz (1922), Santiago and Panama City (1925). In nearly every case, activist renters forged close connections with members of different labor and/or progressive organizations calling for social reform.[8]

While having its own variations, the ills of early capitalist urbanization were also clearly evident in France, as Udovic observed: 'the poor of Paris – its men and women, its elderly, its adolescents, its children, and its infants – all paid the comprehensive human costs of this industrialized and capitalistic "urban pathology"'.[9]

Some social reforms began to emerge in the late 19th and the early 20th centuries, spurred mainly by the authorities' fear of the threat from below, implemented in variable forms in different settings. However, this was often only grudgingly conceded and limited in scale.

In Britain, housing reform saw new regulation, as well as limits placed on rent increases, extended across Britain as a whole by Lloyd George's Liberal government in line with other limited liberal forms. On this point and on balance, it is also fair to say that there was also an element of reformist sentiment among a segment of the elite, as was noted earlier, that also fed into these changes. Moves to regulate and improve housing were also introduced in parts of the US and across various areas of mainland Europe. In all of these situations, work and housing both remained key battlegrounds over which the contest between basic human needs and profit extraction was fought.

Overall, the social unrest across industrializing nations into the early 20th century, as with numerous other historical uprisings and as if anyone needed reminding, provided myriad examples of the way in which people and societies inevitably reach breaking point when insecurities and inequalities are allowed to continue unchecked. As was noted in earlier chapters, the drivers at that time were the predations of laissez-faire capitalists, both industrialists and rentier landlords, allied to continuing appropriation by the remaining aristocratic landowning class, while the masses enjoyed little state protection as this was largely deployed to support and protect elite interests. While these are exhaustively observed issues, as is argued throughout this book, superficial description and understanding often fails to appreciate that such events are a manifestation of a much wider and deeper malaise imposed on individuals and communities, with consequences that are only beginning to be fully appreciated and understood, when socioeconomic and political arrangements become toxic. What is important is that when we chart these developments into the current era with its growing social and political pathologies, we can identify a return to many of the same causal factors under neoliberalism that threaten human health, wellbeing, dignity and the very fabric of modern life that many had come to take for granted. They may be less extreme, but the key facets are there, of increasingly precarious lives and even levels of hunger, poverty and squalor that were once thought to have been consigned to the past.

Housing policy and social reform

In the UK, as was noted earlier, Lloyd George's government (1916–1922) was associated with a range of reforms, with limited introduction of public housing being a critically important development. This was driven by a recognition that housing left to the free market was a source of ill health, as well as social malaise and strife, and so began a long process of intervention to improve and manage housing and to control its costs. This also underscores the fact that markets for limited and such fundamentally essential resources as housing readily become expensive, as people obviously can't easily opt out and generally have to accept what is on offer at whatever price they can afford. This is a really critical issue, as something that appears to be often overlooked in public discussion of social housing is that it does more than simply offer a very basic alternative to marketized housing. Rather, it helps to prevent exploitation, reduces the necessity to accept substandard accommodation and limits the capacity for private providers to enhance their profits by restricting supply to raise prices. While free market orthodoxy proposes that competition prevents housebuilders and landlords from driving up prices, as new entrants would presumably soon enter the market with cheaper alternatives, this has not been the experience in the past or in the neoliberal era. In essence, as was indicated in Chapter 5, house prices in the run-up to the 2007/2008 financial crisis, and indeed since, were largely only limited by what people could borrow when affordability criteria were stretched to the limit. As will be argued in more detail later on, this was largely due to the fact that the increased demand created by deregulated lending was not met with anything like an adequate increase in supply, as builders often focused on raising profit margins rather than volume. As one UK MP noted:[10] 'I think it is clear that the big developers are building at a rate to maximise their profits rather than addressing the country's housing need.'[11]

'Returning to the issue of early housing policy', (I think this is needed for continuity here). Mirroring the situation in the UK, housing developments in the US and across Europe were marked by a variety of interventions associated with variations in political culture, but with some general consistencies:

> From a European perspective, it would appear that housing policy over much of this century has been concerned with the legacy of the rapid urban growth of the nineteenth and early twentieth century. Issues of housing conditions and their impact upon health and the economy, subsequent slum clearance and, in some countries, the associated rise of social housing, the decline of private landlordism, the growth of individual home ownership and the development of contemporary financial mechanisms and institutions are all rooted in that period.[12]

In the US, housing policy was always more marketized by European standards, but followed a very broadly similar pattern of development in the first half of the 20th century. Particularly, public housing expanded during the New Deal era, together with controls on some private rents and moves to extend owner occupation, while US public housing was largely targeted at the urban poor and low paid as a means of alleviating public health and social issues in America's cities.[13]

Architectural trends, garden cities and 'brutalism'

Driven by all of the concerns around the issues outlined previously, more enlightened policy makers across industrial developed nations also began to address how they might reorder the urban landscape, improving the lot of the mass of citizens, while assuaging the wide variety of ills derived from poor housing. As with the US, while the aforementioned limited interventions had arisen in Europe, state intervention at scale only really began to develop more extensively in the 1930s, with further expansion after the Second World War.

One of the early concerns was to provide public housing that was very different from the cramped and often overcrowded tenement dwellings that housed the less well off. Room sizes and aesthetics were both considered important to improving life chances. As was noted earlier, some of the motivation was altruistic and some was a defence against the perceived unruly lower orders, while a further motivation can be understood in terms of the desire to sustain a reasonably fit and healthy workforce, which hadn't been the case in many 19th-century cities. In the UK, much of the 1930s new provision was inspired by the 'garden cities' design associated with Ebenezer Howard. Howard's vision was to reproduce the idyll of rural village life in suburban and greenfield sites, providing reasonably spacious family accommodation with gardens in pleasant surroundings with a good level of green space. Housing, based on this kind of approach, was not wholly the preserve of local authority and state-provided housing, as it was also adopted by a small number of philanthropic employers, often Quakers, whose religiously and morally inspired empathy and concern saw them introduce Howard-style settlements for their workers, Cadbury's Bourneville being a notable example. Here it seems that Peter Cadbury and Ebenezer Howard were an influence on each other, while Howard's subsequent work went on to shape the future of UK town planning.

Such paternalistic projects aside, Howard's ideas have continued to inform the layout and style of numerous private housing estates globally as a blueprint for the suburban idyll. In the UK this was also the model on which postwar new towns were created, decanting large cohorts of overcrowded city dwellers to new peripheral satellite towns, where living among cleaner air and open, green space was, for many, a novel experience. The latter were usually large-scale public projects, building on the Howard-style state housing model that had expanded in the 1930s, as a type of public housing in the UK that was highly successful, and much of is still associated with 'nice' areas and was the most sought-after form of social housing to be sold off with the Thatcherite turn to marketization in the 1980s. This type of housing continued to be popular into the postwar housing boom and beyond, but the need to build public housing more quickly, more abundantly and with a lower level of land use prompted planners to consider alternative models.

The main alternative form of housing and landscape design represented a significant departure from Howard's low-rise 'green villages'. This was in the form of the modernist or so-called 'brutalist' style notably associated with French designer Le Corbusier. Brutalism had become fashionable in modernist architectural circles in the early 20th century and became more prevalent across urban landscapes from the 1950s onwards. This had the advantage for city planners and housing authorities that they would be able to build more quickly and cheaply, while taking up much less space. This type of provision ranged from low-rise flats to the high-rise buildings that began to breach the skyline of many British cities, particularly in the 1960s. As well as its overt characteristics, a key factor that set this form of public housing apart was that, unlike the Howard-styled semi-detached housing on tree-lined streets, it was much less like private housing in style, setting public sector residents more clearly apart while often having fewer amenities. While popular with building aesthetes of the times (and since), consistent with its name, its often drab concrete and box-like exteriors, crammed together often offered unattractive and forbidding landscapes once the initial sheen began to wane.

In qualification, it's fair to say that early residents were often enthusiastic when moving into this style of housing due to much improved facilities and accommodation, inside toilets and bathrooms being a novelty for some, as an experience I shared as a young boy in Glasgow when moving from a cramped tenement in a poorer part of the city. However, as was noted earlier, the soulless landscapes and interiors of these concrete blocks soon deteriorated to become areas that were less than sought after. Recalling my own experience as a teenager from 'the flats' in an area dominated by large, quite grand and expensive private homes, my sense of being from a different class was much sharper than it had been in the poorer area I'd come from, where everyone had seemed of a broadly similar standing. I was also acutely aware that most of my new teenage friends came from the Howard-style tree-lined areas of 1930s neat semi-detached public housing with gardens in an area a mile or so away. Despite the fact that we were all council house kids (as public housing in the UK is referred to), whose parents had similar jobs, earnings and paid broadly similar rents, the feeling of being slightly ashamed of where I lived applied not only to my interactions with kids from the 'private houses' but also when compared with my better-housed council house pals, and was a feeling that they didn't seem to be similarly troubled by.

Brutalist high-density building was also replicated across Europe and the US, creating 'concrete jungles' that often ended up being the least desirable forms of housing and areas, riven with social problems. I mention this because the impact of housing and 'home' is evidently much more than economic, as it also relates to the way in which we respond to aesthetic and environmental quality and nature of the built environment itself.[14] From Yi-Fu Tuan's concepts of topophilia and topophobia and a range of associated perspectives on the impact of housing and neighbourhood design on wellbeing, it seems clear that, in spite of the enthusiasm of many architects and policy makers for, respectively, the aesthetics and practicalities of brutalist, high-density buildings, their impact and legacy has not been a particularly positive one.[15]

One issue regarding the preceding discussion that can be related to the way in which we respond to the built environment has resonances with *The Social Map* thesis set out in Chapter 1. Firstly, and as will be discussed in more detail later on, our physical environment may be much more important than has been previously appreciated. For example, it is already widely recognized that interaction with nature improves human wellbeing. In part this explains the appeal of Howard-style settlements. However, there may be subtler aspects to this that go beyond that kind of simple observation. While not always the case, there is also a tendency for developments generally based on Howard's design to exhibit a degree of environmental variation, that is, everything doesn't look precisely the same, and there are specific landmarks. Hence, it's not difficult to navigate these areas and to know where you are. This type of physical environment coincides with our fundamental preference for pleasant, even stimulating familiarity with variation, while also conferring a sense of order and control. By contrast, particularly run-down and importantly homogeneous areas of brutalist design can be bewildering, where it can become difficult find our bearings or feel in control, as well as presenting us with an aesthetic of unremitting and oppressive dystopian bleakness. This might go some way towards explaining why Howard-style council estates were the ones that were readily converted to private ownership with the implementation of a neoliberal housing policy in the UK, while the old brutalist estates, beyond the highest amenity locations, have tended to be those that remained in public hands, as residual remnants that have been used by neoliberal politicians to tarnish the image of public housing initiatives as a whole. On a more subjective point here, it is interesting to note that the Howard-style public housing once occupied by my teenage friends is still standing, is now privatized and continues to be of very good quality in pleasant surroundings. By contrast, the new block of flats where I lived at that time, built some decades later, was demolished some years ago.

Deregulation, housing finance and the return of the landlord

As was noted previously, the turn towards more mixed market housing and housing regulation in various guises in the post-Second World War period was also a prime area for deregulation and revision from the 1980s onwards with the turn to the belief that all aspects of society are improved by privatization and marketization. In the UK, the Thatcher government considered public housing to be a feature of the 'socialism' that had blighted the nation's economy, society and capacity for personal responsibility. For

Mrs Thatcher and her government, bringing about its demise was a moral as well as an ideological, economic and political project.

It should be noted that the proportion of the population living in public housing in my homeland of Scotland until the 1980s was one of the highest outside the communist Eastern Bloc, at around 60 per cent of homes. Given that this was the norm, there was no real stigma associated with not living in a 'bought house', with the latter considered to be the preserve of the relatively better off, while accessible for the aspiring working classes. As was suggested earlier, distinction often emerged between those living in different districts and types of housing design, as people will inevitably engage in various forms of status distinction wherever it's observed. Nonetheless, the generally more egalitarian housing landscape in Scotland, together with decent (secure) job opportunities and less overall economic inequality at that time, aided a level of social mobility and mixing that has not endured into the neoliberal era.

Nonetheless, it was considered that creating a nation of predominantly owner occupiers would enhance people's self-reliance and 'aspiration'; they would take greater pride in their homes and be more responsible upstanding citizens. The subtext to the latter was, of course, that it was assumed that creating new property owners would also make them more capitalistic in outlook, potentially extracting them from their Labour and trade-unionized ideological moorings and aligning them with the aspiring British middle classes, where they might switch political allegiance towards the Conservatives. As Britain had experienced a good deal of trade union strife, it was also the case that the UK government assumed that owner occupiers with mortgages might be less liable to take strike action as they no longer had the relatively low rents and firm security of tenure associated with the UK public housing at that time. Housing 'reform', the 'right to buy' policy of selling off the council house stock at large discounts to its fortunate incumbents, was a central feature of the Thatcherite transformation of the UK economy and society and its cultural and political compass.[16]

As was noted earlier, housing policy in the US had long adopted a less paternalistic model than the UK in the mid-20th century, with public housing and subsidies more narrowly targeted. However, this became even more so with the Reagan government's implementation of the neoliberal model, where public housing and assistance became more meagre and tightly targeted towards the 'needy'. These developments marked the move towards the residualization of public housing and the marketization and further commodification of housing as a whole under neoliberalism – in effect, a return to the market that would be supported by the deregulation of finance.[17]

Once more, the direction of movement in the major developed economies of the West, led by the UK and the US, was replicated to greater or lesser degree across Europe, with the Netherlands closely following the UK and US trajectory, albeit that this was patchier in France and Germany. In Germany, in particular, there has long been a tradition of private renting rather than homebuying extending up the social class structure, with security of tenure and cost being highly regulated, although this has begun to falter more recently.

As was identified in Chapter 5, the deregulation of finance played its part in turbocharging this transition as more lenders entered increasingly competitive mortgage markets, while the aforementioned capacity to create credit enabled by looser regulation saw an increase in mortgage funds flowing into housing markets. Turbulence in housing markets can be related to the increasing indebtedness of mortgage holders as prices rose significantly from long-term averages in relation to income, and as carriers of greater borrowing to income ratios became more vulnerable to the impact of interest rate rises. While in the postwar era, small interest rises might be an inconvenience and cause for belt tightening, larger swings, particularly in the early decades of the neoliberal transformation, could quickly lead to penury and foreclosure. Housing booms and busts became more extensive and frequent, while volatility in the housing market was also compounded by the increase in private property investment and easy access to finance as the banking sector sought expanded opportunities for lending.

Neoliberal converts: the small-scale rentier

The combination of rising house prices, constrained supply and easy credit saw housing return to something like its former status as an investment asset class for the accumulation of unearned income. Eager to extend credit in a market that was seen to provide a prime area for growth, mortgage lenders began to advance further loans to small-scale investors. In the run-up to the financial crisis, as noted in Chapter 5, this was a major factor propelling housing booms on both sides of the Atlantic as the house 'flipping' became popular (buying and selling in short order to make a quick profit) in much the same way as share purchases had appeared to small-scale investors in the 1920s.

From the 1980s, the impact of financialization on many housing markets was experienced mainly in terms of the shift away from public housing to private home ownership described earlier. However, from the late 1990s and early 2000s, with neoliberal governments' moves to dismantle some of the 'restrictive' protection and security for private tenants that had seen this sector residualized in the housing mix, financialization generated an expansion of lending supporting the growth of the sector. The UK was an exemplar of this phenomenon, where private renting had been eclipsed by the expansion of both public housing and more affordable home ownership into the 1990s. Until then, the private rented sector had largely become a temporary space housing students and other young people in transition, between education and adulthood, when purchasing a house would be the expected next step. Private landlords who were in the market at that time were normally medium to longer-term investors, lending criteria were restrictive and available only on commercial mortgages, while tenancy arrangements meant that these assets could not be liquidated very easily at short notice. Loosening of landlord obligations, including a marked reduction in security of tenure ushered in with the UK Housing Act of 1988, combined with new 'buy-to let' mortgage products introduced in 1996, made borrowing to buy and rent a much easier and accessible process. This led to a swift expansion of private renting from a small base to over a million homes by the mid-2000s, as many small investors saw this as an easy means of amassing wealth, with a whole industry of advisors and pundits emerged to advise (often at a price) on generating 'passive income' and getting rich from property investment. Small-scale amateur landlords were also attracted to property as a vehicle for supplementing pension income, given the declining generosity and reliability of workplace and private schemes respectively.[18]

The financialization of housing, while being most acute in neoliberal societies, has been a widespread phenomenon where financial institutional investors have also been highly active in acquiring large residential portfolios across the globe. Pension funds and other investors have entered the residential market in the UK, while private equity firms have been buying up foreclosed residential homes in the US. Even in Germany's once distinctively affordable and secure rented sector institutional investors have been engaged in large-scale buyouts of rented properties, leading to tensions over tenure, shortages and rising costs for new tenants.[19]

Overall, this broad transition towards the (re)marketization and financialization of housing has ensured that this has once again become a significant political issue across Western nations, and for historical reasons we can also include Australia among those, where increasing numbers of young people, and even those accessing relatively 'good jobs' in major cities, have found themselves being forced to take on historically eye-watering levels of credit in relation to income. This has been a particularly prevalent phenomenon in the UK, the US and Australia, as well as in a number of European nations such as the Netherlands, Spain and Ireland, particularly from the early to mid-2000s. Even in Communist China, in line with its strange hybrid fusing of 'communism' and turbocapitalism, a meteoric housing bubble was inflated with broadly similar causes and ramifications, generating societal and political problems.[20]

Across numerous developed economies, those able to become homebuyers have often been supported by more fortunate parents who benefited from spiralling house price inflation, while many others have remained in an increasingly high-cost, low-security private rented sector, with ownership becoming a pipedream. Rather than the benefits of relatively low interest rates that have been the norm over the last couple of decades flowing to budding homebuyers, this has merely fuelled price hikes as lenders eyed the opportunity to extend larger advances on the basis of improved 'affordability', effectively reducing the latter in the process.

Elite property investment has also grown apace. In some cases, this has led to developments where a large proportion of properties have remained empty, as assets where income and wealth can be parked by global high net-worth individuals and companies. Increased property investment has also been associated with a rise in properties being use as ultra-short-term lets, via Airbnb and similar platforms, in some cases creating friction between absent owners and longer-term residents who may be less than enamoured with regular partying or otherwise rowdy temporary occupants. From a wide range of these developments associated with the financialization of housing, the personal and societal consequences have been profound on a number of fronts and have become increasingly acute since the onset of inflation and interest rate rises since 2022.

Gentrification and ghettoization

In terms of social impact, one obvious consequence of divided and, for many, unaffordable housing markets has been an increasing segregation of housing haves and have nots, compounding and intrinsically bound up with the increasing labour market divisions discussed in the previous chapter, where those in the growing poorly paid and insecure sectors of labour markets have fallen further behind their more fortunate contemporaries in terms of their housing choices. This has extended and entrenched the rising inequality that has emerged since the neoliberal turn in the 1980s, which will be addressed directly in the Chapter 10. The housing divide, for evident reasons given the preceding discussion, has led to a starker geographical divide, with the wealthy increasingly occupying ever more exclusive and secluded enclaves, as the poor with fewer housing choices are stuck in less attractive, low-amenity locales. At its most extreme, this housing and socioeconomic divide has been evidenced by a move towards displacement of the poor and colonization of inner-city areas, as a form of socioeconomic cleansing.[21]

The shift from inner-city industrialization towards a service economy has also made city centres more attractive to well-heeled professionals who want to be close to work, amenities and cultural activities, leading to a so-called 'back to the city' movement among this group and the consequent pricing out of working-class families. This has been happening in major cities across the US, the UK, mainland Europe and elsewhere as the urban landscape has been transformed in some districts, seeing the opening of high-end restaurants, stores, bars, galleries and other commercial and cultural venues. By contrast, there has been a concentration of the poor in less salubrious areas or their decanting to more unattractive suburbs. At its most stark, something that might best be described as socioeconomic apartheid has been emerging in many major cities, and particularly those global cities housing prominent financial, commercial and new technology professionals, where there is both a yawning economic divide between high and decently paid professionals in these sectors and the poorly paid army of shop workers, security staff, cleaners and other workers who service their fundamental needs. Exacerbating this divide has been the tendency for property developers courting globally connected professionals to promote the asserted exclusivity and distinction associated with 'prestige' inner-city developments. This is occurring in global hotspots even where the fabric of buildings may not be particularly opulent, barring some internal flourishes and amenities. On that point, in London for example, there has been a longstanding arrangement that to gain planning permission for many new developments, there has had to be a provision for a proportion of units being 'affordable' or social rentals. This is often a contentious issue for developers whose sales pitch is precisely that their upmarket customers are buying into a distinctive locale and facilities that specifically exclude the less well off. To sustain this exclusivity, one of the most concerning solutions that developers have implemented is to design buildings with separate entrances, stairwells, corridors and outdoor areas, so-called 'poor doors', that segregate 'affordable'/social housing occupants from their 'betters' and the amenities they enjoy.[22] This has meant that families and their children have the stark everyday experience of exclusion and being identified as second-class citizens with this designation being purposely built in to contemporary housing design. It is also far from being a peculiar London phenomenon, as it has been in evidence in New York and other major US cities, as well as some other urban locations in Europe and elsewhere across the globe. The fact that this has arisen is a reflection of the decline of community, relative solidarity, empathy and trust that prevailed in the slightly more egalitarian mid-20th century, towards a segregation of classes and ethnicities more akin to that of the 19th century. This phenomenon was not only widely prevalent geographically but has also been just one facet of a wider process of segregation that has grown throughout the neoliberal era, with its other most serious incarnation commonly referred to as the gated community:

A 'gated community' is a residential development surrounded by walls, fences or earth banks covered with bushes and shrubs, with a secured entrance. In some cases, protection is provided by inaccessible land, such as a nature reserve, and in a few cases, by a guarded bridge

(Frantz 2000). The houses, streets, sidewalks and other amenities are physically enclosed by these barriers and entrance gates operated by a guard, key or electronic identity card. Inside the development there is often a neighbourhood watch organization or professional security personnel who patrol on foot and by automobile.[23]

Gated communities can be regarded as the suburban and rural counterparts of the segregated urban buildings described earlier and, while they also have their origins in the 19th century and the exclusive retirement and recreational (country club) communities of the 20th century, they have become more prevalent simply as secluded enclaves of the better off across the globe. A particular motivation for the establishment of these communities, in addition to exclusivity, is associated with the darker side of neoliberal division, founded on the 'othering' and stigmatization of the lower orders and people who are different that is a feature of unequal fractured societies. In line with the discussion in Chapter 1, much of this stems from the way in which the heightened stress and emotional temperature that pervades societies in the neoliberal area have rendered defensiveness, distrust and discrimination more prevalent and easily provoked. That is aside from the more threatening social settings that people often experience in highly unequal societies, where frustration, anger, insecurity and desperation create the conditions for social conflict and crime. In terms of 'fear of crime', a critical factor with respect to the expansion of gated living, this is also clearly related to inequality.[24] Again, in line with the perspective that informs this work, this can also be seen to be self-reinforcing to an extent, as the more segregated people become, the more likely they are to regard each other in terms of negative stereotypes, to distrust and to stigmatize, all of which further reinforces social divides and the impetus for entrenching them socially as well as in the built environment.

While gating is one of the more explicit forms of division, it seems clear that the process has been more widely replicated in less evident forms, where new housebuilding projects often have subtle boundaries of dividing green space, road layouts, railway lines and other infrastructure that, nonetheless, reflect the increasingly sharp division between neoliberalism's haves and have nots, and that visually reinforce the socioeconomic divisions that have become entrenched across numerous societies.[25] It might also be noted here that the COVID-19 pandemic, and the rise of working from home it precipitated, has led to some of the housing haves beginning to reverse the process of flocking to city centres described earlier to a degree, decanting from the city to more spacious homes in the suburbs or rural areas, or indeed purchasing second homes in pleasant rural surroundings, once again displacing and limiting the choices for the housing poor.

The psychosocial impact of housing inequality and insecurity

Picking up on housing's impact on more personal aspects of wellbeing, there are other issues (some widely acknowledged and others less so) that warrant discussion here. In the first instance, there is the obvious issue of the way in which housing costs have impacted on people's capacity to access and sustain secure accommodation. Previous work I conducted with Karen O'Reilly prior to the housing and financial crash of 2007/2008 focused on the impact on individuals and families caught up in the house price spiral and the proliferation of high-cost insecure renting.[26] With respect to very high-cost house purchase, as was noted earlier, this has led to a significant proportion of young adults being priced out of home ownership. Mirroring to an extent Ricardo's 'Iron Law of Wages', which in free markets wages would tend towards the subsistence level, in deregulated and financialized markets, housing costs will tend towards the maximum sustainable level given that a place to live is not a discretionary purchase.[27]

The combination of high-priced owner occupation and high-cost and insecure private renting as the main forms of contemporary housing has led to more young adults failing to leave their parental home, some even returning at times, and can also be seen to have played a part in delaying the traditional rites of passage towards adulthood and parenthood. While the circumstances are likely to be complex, including a drop in fertility perhaps associated with environmental factors, the declining birth rate in developed nations like the UK, the US and others may at the very least be partially attributable to neoliberal housing arrangements.[28] As house purchase now often requires two incomes, family pressures over childcare and the juggling of home and work have also taken their toll, with the ever-present possibility that the loss of one job can quickly produce financial crisis. For private renting households, the pressures can be intolerable. This as noted is most manageable for students and young singles who have lower requirements for security and stability. However, legal frameworks favouring the new rentier class of private landlords have generated a huge level of insecurity, particularly for families with children. Aside from the relatively poorer quality of housing in the private rented sector, families face the constant threat of upheaval at short notice should the landlord raise rents substantially or simply wish to sell the property. The situation of families being moved from place to place, and living with the constant threat of this arising, places huge pressures on relationships and serious issues in terms of the raising and education of children, given the disruption inherent in moving schools, having to make new friends and, critically, having a constant sense of rootlessness.[29] In terms of our human needs, this is a critical and thus far poorly understood issue. In the first instance there is a return to the chronic insecurity and lack of control over a fundamental aspect of people's lives, the critical importance of which was outlined in Chapter 1, that had begun to be addressed by postwar housing reform and policy. On this point, the argument presented here regarding the negative mental, physical and epigenetic effects of neoliberal insecurity and unpredictability related to housing has been supported by empirical evidence. In a 2023 paper, Clair et al identified accelerated biological ageing (associated with DNA methylation) among those exposed to housing insecurity, pollution, poor-quality accommodation and affordability issues. The effects were highly evident among private rented-sector tenants, as opposed to both owner occupiers and social/public housing renters.[30] However, as will be argued later on, there may also be other subtler detrimental effects of housing insecurity aside from those previously identified.

Aligned with our attachment to particular types of environment is the fact that there are potentially deep-seated processes of identity construction that may well be related to the places where we live. As was also indicated in Chapter 1, the hippocampus, a key area of the brain associated with the formation of the long-term episodic and semantic memories that form our perspective on the world and our place within it, is also the area that orientates us in physical space. This is why I have argued that we build on the foundations of our evolutionary ability to recall and negotiate our geographical environment to construct the complex worldview and anchor our sense of self that governs our activity in the social world, with the two being inexorably linked in subtle ways. In this way, our identities, and their consistency, might be linked as much to where we are as to what we experience while we're there. I have argued that this is likely to be the case – that is, the foundation of *The Social Map* is always constructed within the context of our geographical location. Perhaps this is why, as I and I'm sure many others have experienced, we tend to have a different *feel* for the world when we view it from different locations, particularly where this is more than a fleeting experience, while the episodes of our lives are often punctuated by moving between different places, as the references to my own youth given earlier allude. If we take this seriously, then it reasonably follows that frequent geographical relocation might place a considerable psychological burden on people, as they try to sustain a consistent worldview and self-narrative built on ever-shifting sands. This has been the experience of many of those living in private rented accommodation and may evidently be particularly acute for children attempting to forge a notion of who they are and their place in the world. One caveat here also relates to something I highlighted earlier, in that choice and control may be critical to understanding the effects of being on the move. For those who can move while readily choosing their place in the world, particularly between pleasant locations, regular relocation may not be a great problem if one can choose when to stop and where to be at any particular point – once again, a sense of control is key here. It may also be the case that for those who enjoy a wealthy globetrotting lifestyle, the world effectively becomes their psychological home as they flit from opulent place to place, mixing with their peers. For those less fortunate, pushed and pulled by the demands of employers, landlords and housing costs, this may be a more bewildering, disorientating and chronically stressful way of living, with unnerving, abrupt change and a lack of continuity contributing to experiential overload. This may go some way towards explaining why less wealthy groups on the move – that is, migrating from place to place – have often defensively congregated in new surroundings that replicate and emphasize their culture and community, supporting a sense of identity, continuity and security.[31]

For all of the reasons outlined previously, including those deep-seated issues just described, the home is much more than just a place to stay, as it also gives us a foothold and standpoint in the world. However, under neoliberalism, as with the secure job, this has been fatefully undermined for many adding to the cognitive and emotional burdens of negotiating modern living. Moreover, as will be discussed in Chapter 10, these effects are integral to the widening inequalities and injustices that pervade neoliberal societies with further unrecognized but serious consequences, as well as those that are already well understood.

'Outsiders'

During the late 1980s, rough sleeping (street homelessness) became visible in London in a way not seen since the Great Depression in the 1930s.[32] On a final point here, the rising cost of accommodation and the contraction of affordable public housing have also led to an inexorable rise in those who have no access to a home at all, something that developed societies were moving towards proactively moving towards consigning to the past. Across the UK, the US, Australia and other major developed nations, rough sleeping and living in trailers, tents, cars, doorways, and substandard and often overcrowded temporary accommodation has become a way of life, if we can really call it that, for increasing numbers, sadly again including families with children.

This obviously imposes an even higher psychological burden and long-term harm on all of those excluded in this way, in nations where multiple home ownership and investment has been prioritized over essential human needs. There is the ever-present stigma, shame and dejection of being effectively outcasts in status-obsessed societies and the internalization of society's view that you are somehow personally lacking, despite the fact that the inherent precarity of the contemporary labour market leaves many vulnerable to homelessness with a bit of bad luck, or a relationship breakdown, where the latter may very well also have been impacted by financial or some of the many other stresses of current living. Despite this, the blaming of the individual for society's failings is the preferred stance of the current crop of right-wing politicians in defence of the failed market model and in absolving them from its consequences. As with other aspects of welfare, the public is encouraged to see things in this way – homelessness as deficiency, degeneracy and quasi-criminality. This also subtly exploits the fear of the majority that, should they view the homeless as people like themselves, they might then have to contemplate the risk of experiencing this should they fall foul of flexible employment arrangements and threadbare welfare provision. In fact, and contrary to public perceptions, aside from the casualties of labour market precarity, many of those in this position are families who are in work, but have fallen between the cracks due to low and insecure wages and exorbitant housing costs. In 2018, Shelter England made clear the extent to which this was occurring:

> Our findings show that, in England, the majority of families who are currently homeless are in work. They also show that the proportion of working families who are homeless has been growing steadily across the last five years. The absolute number of working families has risen dramatically, from over 19,000 households in 2013 to over 33,000 in 2017. While this has coincided with a sharp increase in the total number of homeless families (43,750 in 2013 to 60,520 in 2017) the rates of change indicate that there is a problem specific to working families. Between 2013 and 2017 the number of working families in temporary accommodation rose by 73%, in comparison to the total population of families which grew by 38%. Underpinning this trend is the chronic lack of affordable housing.[33]

Homelessness is an even more widespread phenomenon in the US, where trailer-park living for the poor has long been normalized, together with the associated stigma, while 'villages' of the urban homeless, both working and workless, have grown across US cities. Once again, and contrary to public perceptions, many of the homeless across the UK are in work: 'a 2021 study from the University of Chicago estimates that 53% of people living in homeless shelters and 40% of unsheltered people were employed, either full or part-time, in the year that people were observed homeless between 2011–2018'.[34]

Perhaps one of the strongest indicators of the inherent cold heartedness of the neoliberal mindset, which damages even those who have internalized it, is the acceptance and even vilification of those who are excluded from something as basic as decent shelter in rich developed societies like the UK and the US. In the UK, devices such as spikes and anti-homeless lighting have been used to exclude rough sleepers from areas where the well heeled might have to encounter them.

A regrettable indication of the UK government's attitude to homelessness was captured by Conservative Home Secretary, Suella Braverman's controversial statement in November 2023 where she objected to charities providing tents to the needy, stating that 'we cannot allow our streets to be taken over by rows of tents occupied by people, many of them from abroad, living on the streets as a lifestyle choice'. This might be viewed as being in keeping with Braverman's previously observed stance on poverty issues, reflecting her position as a key figure among the increasingly strident right wing of her party, while her controversial comments in this case provoked a strong response from a range of anti-poverty and housing charities.

The US, of course, has long had a somewhat disparaging and punitive attitude towards the poor, including laws that effectively criminalize homelessness. This is an issue that also attracted the attention of Donald Trump, as he set out a plan for homelessness on his Truth Social platform in April 2023:

> To combat homelessness, which is driven first and foremost by high housing costs, Mr Trump is proposing opening large 'tent cities', or camps, where homeless people would be forced to live if they did not want to go to jail. 'We will then open up large parcels of inexpensive land, bring in doctors, psychiatrists, social workers, and drug rehab specialists and create tent cities where the homeless can be relocated and their problems identified', Mr Trump said in the video. 'But we'll open up our cities again, make them livable and make them beautiful.'[35]

Here Trump proposes something that appears superficially supportive, but which would effectively exclude the homeless from public space and public view, while subjecting them to further humiliation in a process that was described in an article even in the conservative and free market journal *Reason* as suggesting a form of 'mass incarceration'.[36]

Overall, when we consider the plight of the homeless and housing insecure along with the other profound negative developments associated with the neoliberal financialization and remarketization of housing, it's clear that we have come a very long way from the progressive interventions of the past.

Notes

1   Bowlby, J. (2012) *A Secure Base*, London: Routledge.
2   Riis, J. (1971 [1890]) *How the Other Half Lives*, Mineola, NY: Dover Publications.
3   Booth, C. (1902) *Life and Labour of the People in London*, London: Macmillan.
4   Roberts, R. (1990) *The Classic Slum: Salford Life in the First Quarter of the Century*, Harmondsworth: Penguin.

5   John Stuart Mill (1806–1873), in Principles of Political Economy with some of their Applications to Social Philosophy, 1848. found in Book V, Chapter II: On the General Principles of Taxation.

6   Hughes D. and Lowe, S. (2007) *The Private Rented Housing Market: Regulation or Deregulation?*, Aldershot: Ashgate.

7   McLean, I. (2022) *The Legend of Red Clydeside*, Edinburgh: Birlinn.

8   Wood, A., and Baer, J.A. (2006) 'Strength in numbers: urban rent strikes and political transformation in the Americas, 1904–1925', *Journal of Urban History*, 32(6): 862-884, at 862–863.

9   Udovic, E. (1993) ' "What about the poor?" Nineteenth-century Paris and the revival of Vincentian charity', *Vincentian Heritage Journal*, 14(1): 72.

10 Bone, J. (2014) 'Neoliberal nomads: housing insecurity and the revival of private renting in the UK', *Sociological Research Online*, 19(4): 1–14.

11 Labour MP Clive Betts, chair of the local government select committee, February 2016, https://www.theguardian.com/business/2016/mar/01/developers-restricting-supply-of-new-home-to-boost-profits

12 Forrest, R. and Williams, P. (2001) Housing in the Twentieth Century in *Handbook of Urban Studies*, 88–101, at 88.

13 Stoloff, J.A. (2004) 'A brief history of public housing'. In *Annual Meeting of the American Sociological Association*, San Francisco, CA.

14 Jones-Rounds, M.L., Evans, G.W. and Braubach, M. (2014) 'The interactive effects of housing and neighbourhood quality on psychological well-being', *Journal of Epidemiology and Community Health*, 68(2): 171–175.

15 Ruan, X. and Hogben, P. (eds) (2020) *Topophilia and Topophobia: Reflections on Twentieth-Century Human Habitat*, Abingdon: Routledge.

16 Riddell, P. (1985) *The Thatcher Government*, 2nd edn, Oxford: Basil Blackwell.

17 Roistacher, E.A. (1984) 'A tale of two conservatives: housing policy under Reagan and Thatcher', *Journal of the American Planning Association*, 50(4): 485–492.

18 Bone, J. (2014) 'Neoliberal nomads: housing insecurity and the revival of private renting in the UK', *Sociological Research Online*, 19(4): 1–14

19 Byrne, M. (2020) 'Generation rent and the financialization of housing: a comparative exploration of the growth of the private rental sector in Ireland, the UK and Spain', *Housing Studies*, 35(4): 743–765; Egner, B. and Grabietz, K.J. (2018) 'In search of determinants for quoted housing rents: empirical evidence from major German cities', *Urban Research & Practice*, 11(4): 460–477.

20 'China's housing market teeters between boom and bust', *Financial Times*, https://www.ft.com/content/b9f17616-3654-4a04-a778-e7fa66d8a898

21 Slater, T. (2011) 'Gentrification of the city'. *The New Blackwell Companion to the City*, 571–585.

22 Osborne, H. (2014) 'Poor doors: the segregation of London's inner-city flat dwellers', *The Guardian*, 25 July.

23 Low, S. (2008) 'Fortification of residential neighbourhoods and the new emotions of home', *Housing, Theory and Society*, 25(1): 47–65.

24 Kujala, P., Kallio, J. and Niemelä, M. (2019) 'Income inequality, poverty, and fear of crime in Europe', *Cross-Cultural Research*, 53(2): 163–185.

25 Otero, G., Méndez, M.L. and Link, F. (2021) 'Symbolic domination in the neoliberal city: space, class, and residential stigma', *Urban Geography*, 43: 1–27.

26 Bone, J. and O'Reilly, K. (2010) 'No place called home: the causes and social consequences of the UK housing "bubble"', *British Journal of Sociology*, 61(2): 231–255.

27 Stirati, A. (1994) *The Theory of Wages in Classical Economics: A Study of Adam Smith, David Ricardo, and Their Contemporaries*, Cheltenham: Edward Elgar.

28 Nargund, G. (2009) 'Declining birth rate in developed countries: a radical policy re-think is required', *Facts, Views & Vision in ObGyn*, 1(3): 191–193.

29 Bone, J. and O'Reilly, K. (2010) 'No place called home: the causes and social consequences of the UK housing "bubble"', *British Journal of Sociology*, 61(2): 231–255.

30 Clair, A., Baker, E. and Kumari, M. (2023) 'Are housing circumstances associated with faster epigenetic ageing?', *J Epidemiol Community Health*, 78(1): 40–46.

31 Bone, J. (2014) 'Neoliberal nomads: housing insecurity and the revival of private renting in the UK', *Sociological Research Online*, 19(4): 1–14.

32 O'Connell, M.E. (2003) 'Responding to homelessness: an overview of US and UK policy interventions', *Journal of Community & Applied Social Psychology*, 13(2): 158–170, at 161

33 'Briefing: Shelter research – in work, but out of a home', 19 July 2018, p 3, https://engl and.shelter.org.uk/professional_resources/policy_and_research/policy_library/working_ homelessness

34 'Employed and experiencing homelessness: what the numbers show', https://endhomel essness.org/blog/employed-and-experiencing-homelessness-what-the-numbers-show, p 1.

35 https://www.independent.co.uk/news/world/americas/us-politics/donald-trump-homel essness-policy-tent-cities-b2322102.html

36 'Trump advocates mass incarceration, "tent cities" to address homelessness', https://rea son.com/2023/04/20/trump-advocates-mass-incarceration-tent-cities-to-address-homel essness/

8

Consumerism, Community and Media

> The modern individual within consumer culture is made
> conscious that he speaks not only with his clothes, but with his
> home, furnishings, decoration, car and other activities [sic].[1]

While recognizing that the preceding comment by Featherstone had not
quite caught up with changing gender politics, this general observation
nonetheless identifies one of the key developments of modernity, which
generates both pleasure and angst, but which has become turbocharged
in the marketized neoliberal era to the extent that it challenges both
the direction of our development and the future of the planet. That is
consumerism.

For the peoples of the major developed economies, consumer culture has
become a central factor shaping our consciousness, our sense of who we
are and how we relate to others. In part, if we lump mass entertainment
and shopping together, they provide an element of colour to what for
many would be a life of fairly unremitting drudgery under current
arrangements. Less positively, consumerism prospers by also preying on
the status anxieties bound up with our labour market position and the
standing of where and how we live, as was discussed in the previous two
chapters. In our historically peculiar society, in addition to anxiety relating
to these pillars of subsistence, as Zygmunt Bauman observed, one of our
central preoccupations is that we are concerned to be successful rather than
'failed consumers', given that so much of our identity and personal value
depends upon what we own and what we display.[2] How did we get here,
and how can we reconcile our contemporary addiction to consumerism
with our identity needs and the threat that our hyperconsumption of
resources poses for the planet?

From citizens to consumers

For citizens of developed economies, a world without shopping and display of consumer goods seems peculiar, despite that fact that this didn't become a significant activity until the last 100–150 years or so. Of course, there is a long history of peoples, and particularly elites, distinguishing themselves publicly through their clothing, jewellery and possessions. However, the Industrial Revolution and expanded global trade, and the urbanization and economic arrangements that accompanied these developments, brought together a confluence of forces that can be seen to have made the emergence of consumerism as a mass phenomenon almost inevitable.

From the reurbanization of the early modern era, in line with what has been described thus far in terms of our fundamental needs and biologically mandated constitution, through the rapid expansion of the Industrial Revolution, the mass movement towards cities rendered a potentially bewildered and estranged populace vulnerable to confusion and overwhelming stimulation on the one hand and anonymous estrangement on the other. As such, not only was there was a need to be able to make sense of the urban environment as a whole and its physical characteristics, but people also had to find a way of accommodating to the numerous strangers they encountered; getting to know the ropes and finding where they might fit in.

Referring to some of the issues discussed in Chapter 3, once people no longer knew the majority of those that they regularly encountered, as had been more regularly the case during the pre-industrial era of small towns, villages and fairly static agricultural communities, in burgeoning cities deciding who to engage with or avoid, who seemed similar or different became both more defined by appearances and much more important to know. The previous discussion of the need to establish a sense order in the Victorian city through *reciprocal restraint* and *reciprocal reinforcement* refers to this, while in a society of strangers the visual becomes a primary element here. Reflecting this preoccupation, Lavater's *physiognomy*[3] and a wide range of other pseudoscientific schema depicted a relationship between outward appearance and character with reurbanization, reflecting the greater need to make inferences about others' conduct on the basis of appearances. Sustaining a positive sense of individuality and status became of concern to many city dwellers, generating a rise in self-consciousness. This is a preoccupation that, as will be noted later on, has become ever more sensitized and exploited by consumerist organizations, where our need for distinction, belonging and public approval in a potentially stultifying landscape provides a basis for the marketing of a wide range of consumer products as 'props' to enhance our personal presentation. In part, as well as the potential anonymity of the city, which appeared to offer some freedoms from the specific oversight and moral control once experienced in small traditional communities, our personal conduct nonetheless needs to be constrained and managed to meet the needs associated with predictability, order and social organization.

Again, given the need to organize and simplify human activity on a larger scale, people became caught up in a dilemma of needing the predictability offered by formal organization, while simultaneously being constrained and de-individualized by the rules and roles imposed by large-scale organizations. I have argued elsewhere that this tension between individualism and collectivism, freedom and constraint, and individual self-expression and conformity represent dualistic tendencies imposed by our need to sustain a balance of emotional arousal; too much uncontrolled freedom, stimulation, complexity and public scrutiny makes us uneasy, while, conversely, homogeneity, constraint, anonymity and a dearth of stimulation render us vulnerable to a sense of meaninglessness and lack of clarity in terms of how we relate to the world that contributes to cognitive and emotional distress almost as much as the bewildering conditions imposed by overwhelming insecurity and flux. While not expressed in those terms, largely as the neurobiological insights were not available at the time, this dualistic tension was clearly understood by modern social thinkers and, I would argue, particularly by Georg Simmel. Simmel, while being excluded from a central place among the key social scientific luminaries of the times, was especially prescient in terms of his understanding of the sensibilities of the modern city dweller, a fact that comes across clearly in his essay 'The metropolis and mental life'.[4] As was proposed in Chapter 1, this binary aspect of the human psyche can also be mapped onto the seemingly oppositional trends of romanticism (freedom, individualism, thrill and emotional excitation) and rationalization (classification, organization, routinization and conformity) that together became key elements in the formation of modern consciousness. A modicum of each can, respectively, provide a sense of wonder and even elation, or conversely security to mild boredom. A relatively middle ground between these polarities is where a sense of security and contentment lies for most people. A more extreme pull in either direction can begin to become unnerving, with angst, uncertainty, isolation and vulnerability at one extreme and boredom, bewilderment and meaninglessness at the other. As I have argued, these elements of what we are and how we relate to the conditions we've created have their roots in our neurological functioning.[5]

Early consumerism

Returning to the development of consumerism, this can be seen to have emerged against the backdrop of potential anonymity and estrangement presented by urban living, as mentioned previously, and also in the modern era by the alienating features of expanding rational bureaucratic organization. The latter, of course, as it was applied to commerce, production and capitalist organization, had by the 19th century also enabled a rapid expansion in the availability of manufactured and other goods in a rapidly expanding market, together with the wherewithal for their purchase, at least among the small contingent of the population who were the main beneficiaries of these developments.

As was noted earlier, during the early industrial period, any benefit from capitalist expansion was largely captured by capital: the upper and upper middle classes composed of a fusing of old aristocratic money and new industrial and commercial money. This emerging class at the apex of 19th-century social life began to coalesce around the adoption of the manners, affectations and approach to work that had long endured among the aristocracy. This was reflected in conspicuous displays of wealth, courtly manners and etiquette, and an aversion to personal industry, at least in the form engaged in by the lower orders, becoming an aspiration of the rising industrial classes whose growing wealth provided a passport to inclusion in the high society circles where these old and new elites would morph into Veblen's *leisure class*.[6]

By the middle of the 19th century, it was this group that was first initiated into what we now refer to as consumer culture, with the emergence of the department store. Until that point, buying goods had been confined to small specialist retailers who mainly sold goods on credit to an elite clientele. By contrast, the subsistence living masses bought only what was strictly needed from passing traders and markets. Department stores were first formed by combining small retailers, but began to grow larger and more exotic by the 1850s, producing a raft of opulent establishments across Europe and North America. These large emporia brought manufactured and other exclusive goods together in exclusive and often exotic settings, run on rationally organized lines with a veneer of romanticism appealing to the desire for predictability, ease, in terms of fixed, clearly displayed pricing and well-oiled organization amid entertaining diversion in often exotic surroundings for the leisure class. The new palaces of consumption provided another venue beyond the park, theatre and opera horse where the elite could see, be seen and mingle with their counterparts. There was also a gendered dimension to this, as many of these department stores specifically targeted the wives of those wealthy industrialists, financiers, businessmen and artisans who continued to work on their own account during the day. This saw the development of the gendered approach to marketing and advertising that identified women as the key consumers, and which persisted until around the 1960s when gender roles began to change substantially.[7]

Mass consumption

Consumerism largely remained a pursuit of the upper echelons through the early years of the 20th century, in line with the socioeconomic composition of society discussed earlier, with the mass of the lower orders continuing to devote most of their meagre incomes to the basics of food and housing. However, as we know, the developments around the early part of the century brought about substantial change. F.W. Taylor's application of intensive rational organization to production (discussed in Chapters 3 and 6) allied with Ford's assembly line had created the potential for the mass production of goods, far beyond that which could reasonably be purchased or used even by the most wasteful of the elite. Hence, the need for expanded markets that Ford identified could be achieved if wages were raised and greater leisure time granted as a means of squaring the circle between the need for more demand, and the industrial strife and rapid staff turnover that had arisen in response to Taylorism and Fordism's new workplace arrangements. As was also discussed previously, consumer credit became more widely available for those beyond the better off.

While some of this was also covered to an extent in earlier chapters, it is once again important to revisit some points, given the relevance of these issues here. One major development concerned the way in which the extension of consumerism required a major cultural shift among the masses that has shaped attitudes to consumption and important aspects of ourselves and our worldview up to the present day. As was suggested earlier, a culture of conspicuous consumption and of hedonistic self-indulgence and leisure had spread to the rising bourgeois industrial class, many of whom had once embraced the longstanding trope of the austere, diligent, thrifty and industrious work ethic of the aspirational capitalist that Max Weber notably identified, and that Dickens famously caricatured with *A Christmas Carol*'s Ebenezer Scrooge. However, the rising industrial and commercial classes, having divested themselves of a good deal of ascetic and arduous toil by the late 19th and early 20th centuries, had, nonetheless, continued to advocate this among their employees and the poor in general. As will be discussed in more detail in Chapter 10, the pious exhortation to abide by a strict self-denying and 'hard-working' moral code was an ethic assiduously advanced by the better off, and still is to an extent, in tandem with the increasingly questionable claim that the wealthy's success was achieved and sustained by being exemplars of this credo. This was certainly the moral framework that continued to be advanced by factory owners at this time, Ford included. However, there was a growing awareness that the workforce had to also be inculcated into at least a portion of the elite disposition towards self-indulgence, as a means of encouraging the desire for consumer products and services that could now be delivered via mass production. In effect, as Daniel

Bell neatly captured, the working classes were encouraged to adopt one ethos in the workplace and its opposite in their leisure time, as self-denying and diligent 'puritans by day' and self-indulgent, consuming and even wasteful 'playboys by night [sic]'.[8] In adopting this dual role, new 'consumers' were conditioned to meet the needs of a mass-producing and mass-consuming form of capitalism, as its further expansion now required the co-option of the masses beyond the economic elite.

This was the state of play for consumerism into the 1920s, when gradually better-off workers with more leisure time were targeted by a growing profession of advertisers, encouraging them to develop a consciousness where lifestyle and expressing taste and distinction through the ownership and display of a growing range of consumer goods was normalized. What also needed to be inculcated, from a social class long used to make do and mend, was a willingness to dispense with products not because they were no longer useful or fit for purpose, but when they were simply no longer the latest model, no longer fashionable and no longer served the identity needs with which they were associated. Increasingly, associating products with images of positive distinctiveness, attractiveness, popularity, belonging and success, rather than the functions they actually performed, became the method for achieving this mass psychological transition, supporting the emergence of the world's longstanding love affair with shopping and consumption. This was aided and abetted by the arrival of popular cinema and the cults of personality built around its new film stars. This rendered the visual and self-presentation even more central to people's sensitivities, while associating products with the stars of the big screen enhanced their desirability and appeal, the implicit message being that purchasing the product conferred a glimmer of the star appeal of its promoter.[9] As will be noted later, this is a familiar strategy that continues to be employed by the current era's ever proliferating Z list and would be celebrity influencers of contemporary social media. However, this 'positive' promotional strategy was only one feature of advertising's appeal to consume, as deeper desires and anxieties were and continue to be exploited in the service of creating demand. Allied to popularity, the prospect of gaining sex appeal through purchasing products began as an implicit association that became much more explicit in tandem with shifts in public morality, in which advertisers had a significant hand in shaping. Hence, the purchase of even the most tangentially related products could be associated with the promise of popularity and potential sexual gratification.

Conversely, as well as desire and aspiration, advertisers also became acutely aware of and adept at exploiting fear. Hence, consumer advertising also employed the fear of missing out (FOMO) in its repertoire – of being rejected, ignored, deemed unattractive and anonymous, operationalizing many of the deepest anxieties of modern city dwellers outlined earlier. In essence, advertisers targeted key elements of the binary of human desire and fear in modern societies, underpinned by the deep-seated fundamental needs described previously, exploiting this knowledge to generate a sense of insecurity and unbalance to be 'resolved' through the acquisition of consumer goods and the identity factors they promised to confer.

The expansion of consumerism followed the trajectory of economic development set out in earlier chapters, rising in the 1920s then faltering with the Great Crash, the subsequent 1930s Depression and the Second World War. It was largely in the postwar era, of course, that what we have come to regard as the mass-producing and mass-consuming society came of age, bringing about changes in the shaping of identity and community that persist, with some important modifications, to the present. The key factors in supporting these developments were the further extension of leisure time, higher pay, full employment policies and greater job security, welfare, and redistributive and more progressive taxation that accompanied the more egalitarian postwar social contract. As was noted in Chapter 3, this was by no means some lost utopian era, but merely a relatively more humane and optimistic period in comparison to what went on before and has since. Nonetheless, this measured but significant progress created a feelgood factor and greater time, confidence and wherewithal for citizens of key economies across Europe, North America and elsewhere. With postwar austerity over, publics from the late 1950s embarked on an unprecedented consumer splurge. This consumer boom of this period was also a jobs boom, aided by policy changes, strong trade unions and the fact that the conversion of wartime production facilities and techniques to consumer production had produced both more jobs as well as the capacity to produce more consumer goods.[10] Perhaps it is also no accident that greater postwar optimism, as well as growing job and housing quality and security, had also coincided with a baby boom, contributing to a growing population raised with the ethos of consumer society.[11]

The shop window at home: television, film and resocialization

The inculcation of consumer culture as a way of life was, of course, greatly aided by the arrival of television. This marked a critical stage in the relationship between community, identity, consumer culture and the media that has intensified over time. As cinema had begun to further catalyse modern citizens' sensitivity to appearances and the visual, as well as the linking of positive appearance, identities and consumer goods, by the 1950s and 1960s, television brought this directly into people's homes as TV became a prime leisure activity. Supported by advertising, public service broadcasting aside, one of the main effects of the advent of television was to extend advertising and, hence, to promote a consumerist outlook as a social norm across generations, as younger family members were to an extent socialized and provided with a pre-packaged worldview advanced by TV networks, advertisers and sponsors.[12]

In line with the theoretical model presented here, the image of the contemporary world and how people relate to it is in some ways an idealized image. In contemporary society much of this is based on advertisers' and programme makers' imaginings that via television began to be routinely communicated to succeeding generations, often with strong emotional overtones, shaping their view of themselves, others and the world around them. The implications of this perhaps go much further than has been currently imagined, given some of the issues raised in Chapter 1. Firstly, on an evident and widely recognized point, as advertising and consumer culture has long had a tendency to present unattainable standards of appearance, lifestyles and so on, the internalization of these standards and imagery would tend to create the conditions for persistent dissatisfaction, as most people, other than the most favoured, would find that their experience of the world and their relationships fell short. This also extends to narratives around personal intimate relationships, as people's love lives disconcertingly failed to live up to the 'happy ending' narratives presented in films and on television. While there are numerous reasons for relationship breakdown, and not least many of the financial and social pressures discussed thus far, unrealistic expectations based on fairytale or 'Rom-Com' endings might readily be added to the mix. In a similar fashion – and an issue I'll return to in more depth in Chapter 10 – the perennial socioeconomic, 'rags to riches' success stories promulgated in popular film and television might also be seen to add to the burden of failing in a world where the playing field has always been highly uneven and, in fact, has become much more so in the neoliberal era than it was when television first entered people's homes. While these are huge issues that will be returned to when discussing media in the digital era later on, and in some of the following chapters, the evolving impact of consumerism not just on individuals but also on the communities of the modern era also warrants discussion here.

Community, cities, television and consumer culture

When considering the impact of consumerism in this evolving modern society, it is important to recollect the key feature of the social context in which it emerged. As was noted earlier, since the onset of urbanization, this was less a society of communities than a society of strangers, where life had become more privatized and lived out among small groups of relations and acquaintances, in the workplace and neighbourhood, but where the central anchoring relationships were between nuclear family members. The latter had emerged as a key unit of social organization since the move to the cities precipitated by industrialization had seen the break-up of longstanding rural/ traditional communities and extended kinship groups. Of course, to sustain a sense of security, predictability, identity and continuity, some ethnic groups tended to band together in expanding cities with similar others, as was noted in the previous chapter, exercising a protective form of cultural defence – protecting their 'social maps' from potentially overwhelming dissonance in already inherently challenging environments. As we know, many of these districts still have a quasi-relationship with these ethnic identifiers, particularly in the US, although it might be argued that these are often now more symbolic and nostalgic markers rather than real representations of contemporary community.

This breakdown of community, in addition to the other cognitive and emotional travails of mass urbanization, was a major preoccupation of generations of social thinkers. As well as being consistent with Durkheim's previously mentioned concept of *anomie*,[13] this general concern around lost community in the city was also central to the work of Louis Wirth, a leading figure in the renowned Chicago School of Sociology who charted and explored the rapid expansion of Chicago as a model for understanding general processes of urbanization and the various ways in which individuals and communities adapted to the lived environment and each other. Wirth's analysis raised concerns over the way in which the dislocation and estrangement associated with urbanization could lead to 'social disorganization', which he argued was at the root of numerous social ills, including family breakdown, substance abuse, mental health issues and crime. The latter, advanced by Wirth and his colleagues, also provided the intellectual foundations that inform contemporary criminology. The sense of dysphoria depicted in Wirth's work also owes a considerable debt to Georg Simmel's aforementioned work on 'nervous exhaustion', while Simmel was a considerable influence on the Chicago School as whole.[14]

It seems clear how each of these visions of the effects of societal dislocation point towards a scenario where the need for sense making and predictability among populations affected by overwhelming complexity and rapid change, the key markers of experiential overload, create the motivation for the imposition of a variety of world-defining discourses, from the moral and regulatory and commercial to the political and ideological. As such, constant exposure to an assertedly taken-for-granted reality advanced by mass media, advertisers, film and television can be seen to readily fill the space vacated by traditional community and its religious and cultural reality-shaping narratives.

This latter point was recognized by Robert Bellah, who offered a vision of mid-20th-century quasi-community largely founded on a shallow allegiance to consumer tropes and lifestyles. What Bellah recognized was that the ties that bound modern citizens together were largely based on the fact that those with similar income levels and consumer habits and tastes tended to congregate in segmented 'lifestyle enclaves', where people were loosely bound together by having similar houses and cars, by the accoutrements that adorned their homes, and by the products they used and consumed. Bellah's world raises imagery of 1960s and 1970s suburbia, of neo-Howard-style housing estates where social class, tastes and identity, and a diaphanous shared culture is presented through the ownership and display of consumer practices and products.[15]

In essence, Bellah's 'lifestyle enclave' is reflective of the modern suburban ideal, where different strata of suburbanites, from the working classes/blue collar to the more solidly middle and upper middle classes congregated in their own particular areas and where loose communal ties would be enacted through the local parent–teacher association (PTA), the bar and the bowling alley for the working-class/blue-collar suburbanites, and the golf and country club for the better off, with each occupying their own lifestyle niche. For Bellah, these lifestyle collectives were not communities in the deeper sense, of people with a shared life and shared bonds, albeit that remnants of the latter might coexist, but were founded on loose affiliations of private families and individuals based on broadly similar socioeconomic standing among interchangeable inhabitants of suburban districts.[16]

If Bellah's characterization of modern communities represents a stage in the dissipation of traditional community, then Robert Putnam's *Bowling Alone*[17] depicts a further movement along this path. Putnam proposed that the growth of suburbia and its local institutions, clubs and so on enabled people to establish deeper connections, or *social capital* as he defines the latter. Nonetheless, for him, the affiliations of the suburban lifestyle were a preamble to charting their dissolution with the decline of the local institutions, local employers, clubs and recreational facilities that he identifies as bonding locations where people could establish and reinforce their ties to each other.

An important feature of Putnam's argument refers to the fact that people no longer in live and work in recognizable bounded districts. Here, we might think of *The Simpsons*, where Homer works at the local plant with a wide number of the inhabitants of Springfield. Putnam paints a picture where the plant has gone, where the workers travel throughout the region to a wide variety of occupations, and where the geography of the area itself has changed, as the boundaries that defined the community's locale have been blurred and even largely erased by urban sprawl. This latter point can also be related to the observation that the expansion of our cities has led to municipal areas as a whole, losing their geographical as well as social integrity, through the expansion and merging of their boundaries, emerging as multiple metropolitan areas.[18]

Given the previous argument over the significance of space for identity formation – that is, the relationship between episodic and semantic memory, biography and physical location – the disembedding of communally situated identity and affiliation from clear geographical moorings may also be seen to represent a further challenge to knowing who and where we are, and having a solid foundation on which to forge bonds, enduring or otherwise.[19]

Aspects of these processes might also be related to Anderson's seminal work on *Imagined Communities*.[20] Anderson turns to media as the source that binds the community, in this case his focus is national communities, where he presents a vision of collective affiliation based on access to national narratives, cultural norms and values gleaned from national print media. In contemporary society, however, television, film and now digital media have clearly eclipsed newspapers and magazines as the main medium shaping collective images of community, national and, indeed, consumer, class, ethnic, regional and political collective identifications.[21]

The above is also consistent to an extent with Hannah Arendt's observation in the late 1960s regarding the power of television to indoctrinate the masses, while this has come to the fore in the neoliberal era. In the US, the advocacy for neoliberalism and the market society has spawned a range of proselytising radio and TV stations, including the highly influential Fox News. The latter, in particular, has been charged with stimulating and exploiting fear and anger in its audience in the pursuit of market share and, not least, in extending the political influence and worldview of its founder, Rupert Murdoch:[22]

What Rupert Murdoch has achieved is the tabloidization of TV by successfully transferring tabloid elements from Murdoch's Sun in the United Kingdom and Australia's Daily Telegraph into American TV ... It is a sophisticated merger between a tabloidization of news featuring flashy pictures, shiny graphs, sensational videos and so on ... Fox's populist rhetoric defends the business class and the wealthy.[23]

Fox News is viewed as being at the mainstream forefront of a growing range of even more extreme right-wing media outlets fomenting division, conspiracy theories and the purveying of disinformation and Trump's cultish MAGA rhetoric.[24] On almost any issue – climate change, inequality, gun control, gender and race relations, state intervention, economic, tax and welfare policy – an increasingly powerful sector of the mass media and social media is unabashed in opposing almost anything that might be regarded as being empathic, egalitarian and inclusive (beyond the inciting of the mob) and, more broadly, rational or prosocial.

This is *primalization* media, appealing to the emotional, irate, disenchanted and disaffected, while further exploiting and entrenching this condition. Ironically, in the US, a range of right-wing channels also align themselves with the equally potent Christian lobby in the US, albeit that this is the form of Christian Evangelical Nationalism that is pro-private property, individualist and often disparaging of the poor.[25] The conflation of religion and right-wing neoliberal values can also be seen to be taken to its logical conclusion, as exemplified by the mediated funding calls that support the lavish lifestyles of so-called prosperity preachers.[26] What is particularly interesting here is that what appears to render people vulnerable to the overtures of charismatic preachers is highly consistent with the appeal of populist politicians and right-wing media: a promise of community, positive identity and salvation in a simplified and secure utopia, in this world or the next.

As was noted earlier, the UK, other European countries and Australia have their counterparts to the US-based right-wing media, albeit with a less religious flavour, purveyed by other arms of the Murdoch news empire and its fellow travellers. In the UK contemporary right-wing and neoliberal discourse is still communicated by via traditional newspapers like *The Sun*, the *Daily Mail*, the *Daily Express*, *The Telegraph* and a range of less prominent but often more virulent outlets, albeit that these are increasingly consumed online rather than in hard copy. As to recent entrant right-leaning TV channels in the UK, GB News and Talk TV have also joined the fray, albeit that they are constrained to some extent by UK laws regarding balance and veracity in terms of news output. While Fox News started broadcasting in the UK from 2001, it was pulled in 2017 apparently due to low viewing figures, although it has been suggested that it was subsequently deemed to have come into conflict with UK impartiality laws.[27]

Given what was discussed earlier regarding the role of television in shaping consumer culture, and the dominance of the latter in the construction of modern identity and community, it evidently follows that the further evolution and impact of visual and associated digital media towards the current era must be a key consideration when exploring a range of developments regarding the more recent trajectory of contemporary identity and community. However, as soon as one begins to consider this, as well as ideological manipulation, the issue of further atomization, fragmentation and dilution of communal ties becomes a very obvious and critical issue.

Towards the media 'multiverse'

As was argued earlier, television began as a kind of monolithic conveyor of images of individual and collective identities deeply imbued with the tropes of consumer culture, as well as national, political and other central aspects of identity formation. Indeed, where people were once exposed to a narrow range of content on a small number of channels, this may be seen to have provided the foundation for a semblance of a shared imagined community, a televisual basis for conversation and sense of mutual understanding and belonging, even if this was thin gruel in relation to previous forms of traditional deeply engrained identity and community.

However, if this is accepted, from the 1980s, the fragmentation and proliferation of TV channels and content, beginning with the emergence of cable and satellite television and video players, might be regarded as yet another leap in the direction of an increasingly all-encompassing but simultaneously less coherent and cohesive culture as people began to be exposed to a wider range of diverse content. While much of this was a consequence of technological developments, it has also been argued that the manner in which media and television governance developed was significantly impacted by neoliberal policy, reflecting the familiar trend towards deregulation and privatization from an ideological standpoint.[28] As such, public service and highly regulated networks have given way to a broad array of channels and content providers. This, of course, was just the beginning of the trajectory of massive expansion and diversification of content and media, which became turbocharged with the emergence of the internet and then social media. We have now become acutely aware that we are bombarded with a virtual tsunami of 24-hour entertainment, news, communication and myriad information sources at the touch of a screen, delivered through an increasingly interconnected and synced network of devices. It might be argued that this evolution of media in the digital age has not only transformed the scale and format of content provided, but has also impacted on contemporary individuals in numerous ways, driven by the technologies of themselves as well as the neoliberal cultural context in which they are offered and, indeed, which they have gone some considerable way towards further consolidating.

'Hyper' individuals

There has been a huge debate since the emergence of digital communication regarding its impact on our identities, communities, consumer behaviour and perspectives on a range of issues, including our political opinions as indicated above. Optimists have often argued, and did so enthusiastically in the early days, that the digital world was a potentially levelling and democratizing force, with the potential to provide a platform bringing people together in collective and free, open debate. This was seen to avoid the issues inherent in powerful governmental and commercial actors having a virtual monopoly over public communication and discourse. From this perspective, the internet, social media, the smartphone and so on might be regarded as tools of a potentially revitalized democratic public sphere. By contrast, others have argued that the experience has been somewhat different where, while pockets of progressive free speech still emerge, the experience of digital communication has been much more equivocal to say the least particularly as commercial and political interests have made significant strides in exerting control to advance their own interests.[29]

In the first instance, the prevalence of commercial and consumerist discourse has extended from the mainstream media into the digital realm. Following the neoliberal logic, the internet and social media have been subjected to a process of monetizing at every level and across every platform – from nonstop and ever-intrusive advertising to increasingly sophisticated harvesting of consumer activities, preferences and opinions, often demanded as the fee for accessing content, to the activities of the public themselves as the digital realm has become a marketplace in its own right. As we know, with particular respect to consumerism, this is now eclipsing the traditional, 'live' commercial outlets of the high street and the shopping centre that, as was noted earlier, once introduced consumerism to the masses. In many senses the ubiquity and penetration of marketization has led to a hypercommercialization of contemporary life where many people have become more atomized as competitive consumers and aspirational entrepreneurs both online and offline.[30]

As was suggested earlier, this process has been bound up with the proliferation of the neoliberal value system, instilling this ever more deeply in the public consciousness as the unequivocal common sense of the current era. Online, as legions of *influencers* promote myriad products to their online followers on social media, personality is traded in a self-promotional competition for hits and likes, together with product promotion, where popularity is monetized through payments from sponsors.[31] This has in a sense overcome an inherent problem for corporations regarding how they to continue reaching their target audiences with the proliferation and dispersal of media outlets. In this way, the promotion of big stars via mass media and television has been augmented by having the public generate their own celebrities and then co-opting them to sell products linked to the influencer's online persona, and is in many ways a microlevel extension of endorsement by the film stars of early cinema, now conducted by a dispersal of popularity among an army of small-scale 'celebrities' spread across numerous platforms and micromarkets.

It is evidently a huge understatement to argue that these developments taken together have had a profound impact on all of us, in often paradoxical ways (as will be discussed later on), and in some ways extending and intensifying some of the effects of media and consumer culture in urbanized societies discussed thus far.

For example, it is easy to see how this divides us ever more into target markets of dispersed and atomized individuals. Firstly, our atomization is well documented in terms of the rise of loneliness in our ironically heavily populated societies.[32] Of course, we want to be distinctive and sustain a clear sense of self in relation to the masses that are often around us, but simultaneously we crave the belonging and sense of warmth and security that comes from affiliation. I would argue that, in a sense, neoliberalism's turbocapitalism in the social media age destabilizes this quest for balance like never before.

In the 1980s, Michel Maffesoli suggested that there was a decline of individualism in mass-modern societies in favour of people being subsumed within a wide range of consumerist and other segmented groups, with varying degrees of attachment and commitment over time. As will be noted later on, there definitely seems to be something in this latter aspect of Maffesoli's analysis, although I remain sceptical that this implies a decline in individualism, or at least requires some consideration as to what we mean by individualism in the contemporary sense. It might be suggested that this viewpoint has captured one aspect of our dualistic identity while failing to recognize the contemporary guise of the other. For example, as was noted earlier, the growing incidence of loneliness and atomization, together with the aforementioned trend towards narcissistic and strident self-promotion, does not seem to suggest a decline in individualism. In addition, as will be argued in Chapter 12, the contemporary tendency towards therapy culture and focus on the self, mental health, emotion, soul searching and self-improvement appears highly individualistic. In some ways it may be argued that individualism has actually intensified in many respects in contemporary society. It is perhaps the way in which it is expressed that may have changed in that distinction appears to be pursued through allegiances and identifications to some extent along the lines that Maffesoli proposes, in a society where individuals seek varieties of belonging through the channels that are available, which are now even more intensively mediated, consumerist and segmented. While I'll return to the implications for contemporary community, this relationship between individualism and collective affiliation is now a central feature of our mediated consumer landscape, where cults of personality seem to span our commercial and, as will be argued later on, political realm with increasing prevalence.

As was briefly mentioned earlier, there is a rapidly expanding trend whereby individuals and groups are captured for short periods of time by varying degrees of attachment to carefully constructed online personalities. This world now proliferating across social media platforms also increasingly dovetails with mainstream media, where TV and film stars sit atop a hierarchy of celebrity, from 'A listers' and sundry ranks of the recognizable, through interchangeable and impermanent reality TV 'stars' down to those eking out a modest living via online followers (feeding a growing market for social media lighting, film kits and so on). Indeed, individual personality is now regarded by many as a road to riches or at least an exit route from penury from those not favoured by inheritance and/or unable to access lucrative positions in remaining decently paid professions.

In addition to the expansion of turbocapitalist logic, echoing the earlier discussion of media proliferation, within a relatively limited number of channels and other media outlets, mainstream advertising agencies could once confidently present their content to a significant portion of largely identifiable segments of the public, aligned with whatever programme was being broadcast in a particular slot or tailored to the readership of specific newspapers and other print media. With the audience now an amorphous mass punctuated by kaleidoscopic and sometimes intense interest groups and microcommunities, the problem becomes one of gaining attention among a public swamped with too many choices and a reducing attention span. This entails that the influencers of contemporary media at all levels have to become ever more 'larger than life' in order to stand out in an increasingly crowded marketplace. Here unabashed narcissism, sensationalism and self-promotion is the currency to be traded across platforms, where film, television (including critically reality television) and social media 'stars' exchange fame, or infamy, for fortune. In line with neoliberal ideology, the masses who fail are concealed or disappear from view, while many of those who succeed, particularly on reality programming, social media vlogging and so on, seem to have made it less by discernible talent than by a mix of luck and naked, unashamed ambition. This implies to many young people that a glittering life is readily accessible with sufficient drive, presentation and self-confidence, perpetuating notions of meritocracy where quick and easy success stories are readily realizable.

The impact of all of this appears to instil a form of desperate individualistic entrepreneurialism, further entrenching the neoliberal logic. As will be discussed in more detail in Chapter 10, everyday life appears as an unrelenting and unforgiving scramble for wealth and success, the rewards of which are a consistent feature of film, television and online presentation, as are the penalties for failure, communicated via content often referred to as 'poverty porn' where fake empathy often overlays a barely concealed contempt and disregard for those who have lost out in this race. The real winners, the uber-rich and those whose backgrounds allowed a relatively easy glide to the top table, are often concealed from public view aside from the odd drama or fawning documentary, offering the masses a glimpse of lifestyles that are presented as being theoretically accessible with talent and verve, but, realistically, remaining well beyond the reach of anyone beyond a tiny minority. Thomas Piketty's analysis of late capitalism, once more, illustrates the way in which, for most, access to the upper socioeconomic echelons is now becoming effectively closed off as accumulated wealth and inheritance, and the gains that can be made simply from the ownership of capital, go beyond what can be achieved from most people's work. In fact, as briefly noted in Chapter 4, and an issue I also return to in Chapter 10, such has been the re-establishment of the 'posh', particularly in the UK, that we are now seeing something of a return to the old status quo in popular culture, film, theatre, popular music and a range of other art forms. Where the working classes from the 1950s and 1060s to the late 20th century once challenged to old status quo in order to occupy a dominant cultural position, privilege appears to be making a comeback as being upper and solidly middle class, which was once an impediment to popular cultural fame, is now increasingly an entry requirement.

Contemporary community: simulacra and the viral village

In terms of experiencing a sense of belonging and collective affiliation within the current context, as was noted earlier, people will evidently try to access this by whatever means available, which now likely consists of a small number of intimate relations and a wider range of informal contacts; effectively for most, this may be a somewhat thinner variant of the relational norms that have predominated since the onset of modern urban society for the reasons outlined previously. In recompense we now have access to a multitude of online groups coalescing around a broad array of topics, fan sites, consumer, political and other movements where people can engage with the like-minded. With respect to the changing nature of contemporary community in our heavily mediated societies, the work of the French sociologist Jean Baudrillard, and particularly his concept of *simulacra*, seems to resonate with the discussion here.[33]

Baudrillard's simulacra refers to the way in which our concepts, perceptions and social contexts have become increasingly detached from any underlying reality, a notion that saw his work inspire the Wachowskis' 1999 epic *The Matrix*. In a sense it can be argued that the idea of community itself has now become largely simulacra, where consumerist-mediated affiliations and allegiances are formed between individuals who may not know each other very well or even at all. An example of this would be the way in which today's viral villagers, who occupy a wide variety of imagined communities around fan sites, celebrity culture and a range of other identifiers, often refer to the main characters in these networks with a sense of personal familiarity, by their first name and so on. A clear example of this relates to celebrities like the Kardashians, as reality TV stars and influencers at the very pinnacle of this phenomenon. The lead in the Kardashians' docudrama is, of course, Kim Kardashian, who gained global fame, wealth and unparalleled celebrity for reasons that often remain difficult to pin down. In effect, she is one of the new breed of celebrities created by social media and reality television who simply became famous because they are, for reasons that are not easy to identify. An important aspect of this appeal seems to be based on the way in which Kardashian and others like her manage to present themselves as being both charismatic celebrities and accessible and relatable companions, the latter via the way in which the audience is given access to a very carefully curated, 'intimate' back stage. As Ellis Cashmore succinctly observed, with the new breed of reality celebrities like Kim Kardashian, 'there is the feeling of intimacy with others who are, at once, proximate and remote'.[34]

In essence, the need for affiliation and having one's worldview (map) confirmed has moved to a significant extent from the real to the virtual community. Two key issues emerge from this. Firstly, the way in which social media has developed has evidently provided another means by which consumer culture has exploited deep features of human psychology in pursuit of sales and profit. Secondly, the technical operation of social media sites, in and of itself, has had wide-reaching effects on individuals and their relationships with each other. Some of this was discussed in relation to the narratives that influence how we see ourselves and the world around us in terms of the images and themes presented to us via a cacophony of mass media and now social-mediated content.

However, with respect to social media, its operation now has the capacity to identify, shape and intensify our association with an ever multiplying range of opinions, perspectives and narratives. As Eli Pariser notably observed, this has arisen as a consequence of what he refers to as the 'filter bubble'. As was noted earlier, initially enthusiasts (and current apologists) for the proliferation and impact of social media have argued that it creates spaces for open dialogue. The reality, however, is that in the quest to maximize profits, social media companies have two key aims: to harvest data regarding the profile, preferences and opinion of users to tailor adverts and sell products; and to keep them on their platforms for as long as possible in a crowded mediascape to maximize advertising revenue. This is all accomplished by ongoing profiling of users likes, opinions and perspectives, monitored continuously, to field adds and content that achieves these aims. The 'unintended' consequence is that individuals are bombarded with content and ads based on their profile and prior activity, which leads them to be fed more of the same, on the assumption that this will appeal to their interests, retaining their attention and engagement.[35]

As with other features of consumer culture, this further exploits fundamental human tendencies. Firstly, there is the need for the confirmation of one's worldview and connection to similar others who support this. Also, being part of an in-group associated with a particular narrative or trend, given that there are a multitude of these, promises to provide individuals with both a sense of security and belonging, but also distinction in relation to others who are not affiliated to that particular 'community'. So, paradoxically, association with a particular fan, fashion, lifestyle, cultural, religious, political or other affiliation becomes part of the identity presented to others in wider society as a mark of distinction as much as a mark of affiliation to one's tribe. However, a major issue is that the operation of social media algorithms, in feeding tailored content to individuals, evidently involves not only repetition but also emotion as groups discuss, at times, controversial or sensitive issues.

Given that repetition and emotion are key to long-term memory formation, shaping individual *maps*, this is how people may be led down particular pathways via filter bubbles, intensifying their beliefs and values along the way. What may have begun with loose affiliation or mild curiosity can, over time and with enough regular exposure and immersion with similar content and interaction with other 'recruits', lead to deep allegiance or even obsession. Moreover, subject to growing concern, there has been resistance by social media companies around any constraints on all but the most evidently dangerous pathways they facilitate. This is perhaps the ultimate exploitation of the atomized masses, while it takes little imagination to see the appeal for the disenchanted and the lonely as they are seduced and their needs are channelled for profit, for distraction and to mobilize sectors of the public in the service of narrow interests. However, these virtual allegiances appear less than satisfactory in terms of the need for real-world connections.

As we've seen, online communities may emerge as real-world movements, from the frivolous social media fashion or activity trend to more serious collective mobilization, spanning the progressive to the anti-democratic and potentially dangerous as people attempt to find a sense of meaning, purpose, identity and quasi-solidarity around emotionally charged events and narrow sectional or radical ideas. Hence, in terms of community, the 'rabbit holes' provided by filter bubbles can also generate deep divisions and polarization, extending the impact of partisan mainstream media, undermining mutual understanding and the shared sense of belonging to wider society on which 'real' community was founded.[36]

Overall, it might readily be argued that the social promise of digital technology, while having a great number of positive features, has been substantially undermined due to its marriage with a hyperconsumerism where profit comes before people. The mantra that 'we value your privacy' becomes an oxymoron when the whole project has been tailored towards the monetization of attention and personal information. Ultimately, data are harvested, and advertising is finely tuned and targeted, with consumption and profit being the goal at all levels. While the internet is a critical arm of this consumerist world, I would argue that it has become infinitely more corrosive with the advent of social media. Here, self-obsession, narcissism and fierce status competition exacerbate our anxieties, while algorithms distort our preferences and intensify our prejudices, no matter how damaging to ourselves and others, to keep us clicking and keep us buying.

On this latter point, however, the emergence of the internet and social media has been responsible for relocating consumer culture and consumer practice online, as the practice of shopping has moved from physical to virtual space. A major consequence of this shift has seen a contraction of the physical shops, the so-called 'retail apocalypse' that is leading to the decline in retail units and retail work mentioned earlier. One paradox here is that this shift may also lead to a contraction of consumerism itself, as shopping as an active leisure pursuit in the dedicated settings that spawned it declines.

Finally, returning to the issues of community and identity, in our atomized, hyperconsumerist society the need for real engagement evidently persists, while social media, and mediated connections in general, can actually distance us as they provide a very poor substitute for real human connection and community. One notable way in which this is regularly demonstrated is via the collective outpourings of emotion over celebratory or, more commonly, tragic public events (or even Trumpian political rallies) where these provide vehicles for at least a temporary sense of community and shared experience among disparate individuals and segmented groups where opportunities for regular expressions of 'communitas' have declined.[37]

Community is also routinely referred to by neoliberal governments, together with business, as an alternative source of social support and collective action that take up the space vacated by 'small state' governments, a notional and (as was argued earlier) mythical enabler of collective and restorative action. On this particular point, *community resilience* is increasingly cited as a potential resource as we confront the now-evident crisis posed by runaway climate change.[38] This is the subject of the next chapter. However, as was argued earlier, the very phenomenon on which that resilience is assumed to be founded is more an artefact of the past than an aspect of the current reality, its online derivatives aside, given that what remains of our collective identifiers has largely been co-opted, channelled and manipulated via new technologies within the logic of neoliberal hyperconsumerism, operating precisely to undermine the action that is needed to tackle many of our current problems including those posed by planetary warming.

Notes

1   Featherstone, M. (2007) *Consumer Culture and Postmodernism*, London: Sage, p 86.
2   Bauman, Z. (2007) 'Collateral casualties of consumerism', *Journal of Consumer Culture*, 7(1): 25–56.
3   Lavater, J.C. and Gessner, G. (1848) *Essays on Physiognomy: Designed to Promote the Knowledge and the Love of Mankind*. London: W. Tegg.
4   Simmel, G. (2012) 'The metropolis and mental life', in J. Lin and C. Mele (eds), *The Urban Sociology Reader*, Abindon: Routledge, pp 37–45.
5   Bone, J. (2010) 'Irrational capitalism: the social map, neoliberalism and the demodernization of the West', *Critical Sociology*, 36(5): 717–740.
6   Veblen, T. (with Mills, C.W.) (2017 [1899]) *The Theory of the Leisure Class*, Abingdon: Routledge.
7   Lancaster, B. (1995) *The Department Store: A Social History*, Leicester: Leicester University Press.
8   Bell, D. (1972) 'The cultural contradictions of capitalism', *Journal of Aesthetic Education*, 6(1/2): 11–38.
9   Ewen, S. (2008) *Captains of Consciousness Advertising and the Social Roots of the Consumer Culture*, New York: Basic Books.
10 Galbraith, J.K. (1998) *The Affluent Society*, Boston: Houghton Mifflin Harcourt.

11 Gauthier, F., Woodhead, L. and Martikainen, T. (2016) 'Introduction: consumerism as the ethos of consumer society', in Gauthier, F. (2016) *Religion in Consumer Society*, Abingdon: Routledge, pp 1–24.

12 Cashmore, E. (2002) *And There Was television*, London: Routledge.

13 Durkheim, E. (1964) *The Division of Labour in Society*, New York: Free Press

14 Wirth, L. (1938) 'Urbanism as a way of life', *American Journal of Sociology*, 44: 1–24.

15 Bellah, R.N., Madsen, R., Sullivan, W., Swidler, A. and Tipton, S. (1985) *Habits of the Heart: Middle America Observed*, London: Hutchinson.

16 Bellah, R.N., Madsen, R., Sullivan, W., Swidler, A. and Tipton, S. (1985) *Habits of the Heart: Middle America Observed*, London: Hutchinson.

17 Putnam, R. (2000) *Bowling Alone: The Collapse and Revival of American Community*, New York: Simon & Schuster.

18 Gottdiener, M., Hohle, R. and King, C. (2019) *The New Urban Sociology*, Abingdon: Routledge.

19 Bone, J. (2014) 'Neoliberal nomads: housing insecurity and the revival of private renting in the UK', *Sociological Research Online*, 19(4): 1–14.

20 Anderson, B. (1983) *Imagined Communities: Reflections on the Origin and Spread of Nationalism*, London: Verso.

21 Mi, J. (2005) 'The visual imagined communities: media state, virtual citizenship and television in Heshang (River Elegy)', *Quarterly Review of Film and Video*, 22(4): 327–340.

22 'Former Australian PM Malcolm Turnbull says Rupert Murdoch's "anger-tainment" damaged the democratic world', *The Guardian*, 22 September 2023, https://www.theguardian.com/media/2023/sep/22/former-australian-pm-malcolm-turnbull-comments-rupert-murdoch

23 Klikauer, T. (2020) 'The news that creates populism and polarizes, *European Journal of Communication*, 35(6): 629-633.

24 'What America could look like without Fox News', *Time Magazine*, 28 April 2023, https://time.com/6275452/america-without-fox-news/

25 Haynes, J. (2021) *Trump and the Politics of Neo-nationalism: The Christian Right and Secular Nationalism in America*, Abingdon: Taylor & Francis; 'So much for Christian charity: evangelicals blame the poor for poverty, which makes them a lot like other Republicans', *Salon*, 10 August 2017, https://www.salon.com/2017/08/10/so-much-for-christian-charity-evangelicals-blame-the-poor-for-poverty-which-makes-them-a-lot-like-other-republicans/

26 'A wealthy televangelist explains his fleet of private jets: "it's a biblical thing"', *Washington Post*, 3 June 2019, https://www.washingtonpost.com/religion/2019/06/04/wealthy-televangelist-explains-his-fleet-private-jets-its-biblical-thing/

27 'Fox News wasn't banned from UK, contrary to false claims online', *AP News*, 24 November 2021, https://apnews.com/article/fact-checking-010263624425

28 Jin, D.Y. (2007) 'Transformation of the world television system under neoliberal globalization, 1983 to 2003', *Television & New Media*, 8(3): 179–196.

29 Zhao, Y. (2014) 'New media and democracy: 3 competing visions from cyber-optimism and cyber-pessimism', *Journal of Political Sciences & Public Affairs*, 2(1): 114–118.

30 Zhao, Y. (2014) 'New media and democracy: 3 competing visions from cyber-optimism and cyber-pessimism', *Journal of Political Sciences & Public Affairs*, 2(1): 114–118.

31 Acerbi, A. (2016) 'A cultural evolution approach to digital media', *Frontiers in Human Neuroscience*, 10: 636.

32 Jeste, D.V., Lee, E.E. and Cacioppo, S. (2020) 'Battling the modern behavioral epidemic of loneliness: suggestions for research and interventions', *JAMA Psychiatry*, 77(6): 553–554.

33 Baudrillard, J. (1994) *Simulacra and Simulation*, Ann Arbor: University of Michigan Press.

34 Cashmore, E. (2019) *Kardashian Kulture: How Celebrities Changed Life in the 21st Century*, Bingley: Emerald Group Publishing.

35 Pariser, E. (2011) *The Filter Bubble: What the Internet Is Hiding from You*, Harmondsworth: Penguin.

36 Warner, B.R. and Neville-Shepard, R. (2011) 'The polarizing influence of fragmented media: lessons from Howard Dean', *Atlantic Journal of Communication*, 19(4): 201–215.

37 Turner, E. (2012) *Communitas: The Anthropology of Collective Joy*. Dordrecht: Springer.

38 Saavedra, C. and Budd, W.W. (2009) 'Climate change and environmental planning: working to build community resilience and adaptive capacity in Washington State, USA', *Habitat International*, 33(3): 246–252.

PART III

Permacrises

9

The Climate Emergency and Neoliberal Nihilism

Given a choice between an alarming abstraction (death) and the reassuring evidence of my senses (breakfast!), my mind prefers to focus on the latter. The planet, too, is still marvelously intact, still basically normal – seasons changing, another election year coming, new comedies on Netflix –and its impending collapse is even harder to wrap my mind around than death. Other kinds of apocalypse, whether religious or thermonuclear or asteroidal, at least have the binary neatness of dying: one moment the world is there, the next moment it's gone forever. Climate apocalypse, by contrast, is messy. It will take the form of increasingly severe crises compounding chaotically until civilization begins to fray. Things will get very bad, but maybe not too soon, and maybe not for everyone. Maybe not for me.[1]

As was suggested in Chapter 2, much of what most people have taken for granted regarding the earth's climate is imagined within a very short ecological timeframe. At least until recently, this has been reflected by a tendency to think about our climate as a given – as something that, beyond regular minor variation, is fundamentally locked in a state broadly consistent with what we have now. In keeping with the perspective presented here, this is understandable, as most people's view of history spans a very short timeframe, established by whatever they know about the conditions that have prevailed for the last few hundreds or even thousands of years, much of which likely comes from popular documentary or fictional media content. Moreover, in terms of the things that people worry about, timeframes are usually very much shorter than that, something that is becoming increasingly the case due to the stresses and the overwhelming stimuli encountered in contemporary societies. As suggested in Chapter 1, the latter greatly narrows the focus of attention and, of course, all of this has had significant implications for our capacity to deal with our growing climate emergency.

As was noted earlier, the relative climatic stability that developed after the last ice age, around 12,000 years ago, ushered in an era – the Holocene – that allowed our longstanding nomadic hunter–gatherer species to, quite literally, put down roots and develop the agricultural food production that supported larger fixed settlements, creating the conditions for the emergence of cities and the evolution of human civilization. Since that point, we humans have evidently had an increasing impact on our environment, and particularly so in the last 200 years, via industrialization, expanded mass urbanization and the hyperconsumerism discussed in the last chapter, all powered by the burning of fossil fuels that is the main contributor to the anthropogenic climate change scenario that now confronts us.[2] In observing these changes and their causes, many climate scientists and other commentators have begun to refer to the current era as the *Anthropocene*, a new epoch in the planet's climatic history as it responds to the increasing human impact on our ecosystem.[i]

Climate change: the evidence and impact

Climate change has brought into sharp focus the capability of contemporary human civilization to influence the environment at the scale of the Earth as a single, evolving planetary system. Following the discovery of the ozone hole over Antarctica, with its undeniably anthropogenic cause, the realization that the emission of large quantities of a colourless, odourless gas such as carbon dioxide (CO_2) can affect the energy balance at the Earth's surface has reinforced the concern that human activity can adversely affect the broad range of ecosystem services that support human (and other) life [1,2] and could eventually lead to a 'crisis in the biosphere' ([3], cited in Grinevald [4]). But climate change is only the tip of the iceberg. In addition to the carbon cycle, humans are: (i) significantly altering several other biogeochemical or element cycles, such as nitrogen, phosphorus and sulphur, that are fundamental to life on Earth; (ii) strongly modifying the terrestrial water cycle by intercepting river flow from uplands to the sea and, through land–cover change, altering the water vapour flow from the land to the atmosphere; and (iii) likely driving the sixth major extinction event in Earth history [5]. Taken together, these trends are strong evidence that humankind, our own species, has become so large and active that it now rivals some of the great forces of nature in its impact on the functioning of the Earth system.[3]

---

[i] Moreover, in terms of community, the 'rabbit holes' provided by filter bubbles can generate deep divisions, and social and political polarization, undermining the genuine mutual understanding and the shared sense of belonging to wider society on which traditional community was founded.

Greenhouse gas (GHG) emissions continue to rise and global warming above 3°C is increasingly likely this century (Raftery et al. 2017). There is emerging evidence of amplifying feedbacks accelerating (Natali 2019) and dampening feedbacks decelerating (Walker et al. 2019). These feedbacks exacerbate the possibility of runaway global warming (Steffen et al. 2018), estimated at 8°C or greater by 2100 (Schneider et al. 2019). Such temperature increases translate to a range of real dangers (The Center for Climate and Security 2020), shifting the narrow climate niche within which humans have resided for millennia (Xu et al. 2020).[4]

As was suggested by the preceding discussion, the impact of the warming climate has been manifold in terms of the threat it poses to a broad array of currently taken-for-granted human activities, lifestyles, settlements and our very survival, while this threat has been demonstrated by a range of evidence and impacts. However, a detailed exploration of these matters is not the key focus of this chapter, as this has evidently been exhaustively debated elsewhere by writers with much more specialist understanding of these issues. Rather, what I want to discuss here is our response to climate change, its psychosocial, socioeconomic and political implications, and, specifically, the way in which the neoliberal mindset, policy and practice has contributed to this scenario and is currently impeding its potential resolution or, at least, mitigation. That being said, some context is required to frame this discussion.

The Intergovernmental Panel on Climate Change (IPCC), the most widely acknowledged and authoritative UN body, which brings together scientists from across the globe to monitor the phenomenon, offers a broad scientific consensus view of the human impact on the climate and our ecosystems reflecting that indicated earlier, in that it regards this as being manifest and evidenced on a number of fronts with increasingly concerning implications. In terms of effects, these are clearly numerous and serious, as was outlined in an influential IPCC report released by the organization in 2021.[5] The extract from the IPCC's press release that follows sets out some of the key findings, summarizing some of the key effects the IPCC suggests that we currently confront and are likely to be presented with going forward:

For 1.5°C of global warming, there will be increasing heat waves, longer warm seasons and shorter cold seasons. At 2°C of global warming, heat extremes would more often reach critical tolerance thresholds for agriculture and health, the report shows ... Climate change is bringing multiple different changes in different regions – which will all increase with further warming. These include changes to wetness and dryness, to winds, snow and ice, coastal areas and oceans. For example:

- Climate change is intensifying the water cycle. This brings more intense rainfall and associated flooding, as well as more intense drought in many regions.
- Climate change is affecting rainfall patterns. In high latitudes, precipitation is likely to increase, while it is projected to decrease over large parts of the subtropics. Changes to monsoon precipitation are expected, which will vary by region.
- Coastal areas will see continued sea level rise throughout the 21st century, contributing to more frequent and severe coastal flooding in low-lying areas and coastal erosion. Extreme sea level events that previously occurred once in 100 years could happen every year by the end of this century.
- Further warming will amplify permafrost thawing, and the loss of seasonal snow cover, melting of glaciers and ice sheets, and loss of summer Arctic sea ice.
- Changes to the ocean, including warming, more frequent marine heatwaves, ocean acidification, and reduced oxygen levels have been clearly linked to human influence. These changes affect both ocean ecosystems and the people that rely on them, and they will continue throughout at least the rest of this century.
- For cities, some aspects of climate change may be amplified, including heat (since urban areas are usually warmer than their surroundings), flooding from heavy precipitation events and sea level rise in coastal cities.[6]

As well as the direct climatic effects set out by the IPCC, a wide range of other scientific positions point to the potential human cost of this phenomenon. Firstly, there is the issue of how we manage a world where the regional climate norms break down. There is some debate emerging as to how our ancient pre-Holocene ancestors lived. It has long been argued, as was noted in Chapter 2, that they were largely organized around relatively small, egalitarian and nomadic groups.[7] This prevalent view has been contested, to some extent, by a perspective suggesting that the situation is more complex and that some more populous, relatively sedentary collectives were also prevalent during this period, albeit that these will have been very much smaller than the large-scale urban settlements that would emerge in the Holocene's relatively stable climate.[8] However, there is little doubt that a large proportion of our ancient ancestors were moving regularly as the climate made certain areas more or less hospitable, and it appears that similar pressures are beginning to exert themselves as the impact on the local climate and agriculture renders some long-running human settlements unsustainable. The globally mobile wealthy will, of course, likely be able to insulate themselves from the worst effects at least for some time, barring widespread social, political and economic upheaval. However, many of the world's poor are already being badly affected by heat and flooding, with knock-on effects on food security, particularly in the poorer nations of the Global South, while the more vulnerable in the developed nations will undoubtedly be further affected should, as now seems likely, the climate becomes destabilized faster than our capacity to effectively respond.[9]

Climate, food production and security

In addition to the effects of flooding and wildfires, of course food security is, and will remain in the future, one of the most serious consequences of global warming. It has been suggested that roughly 2 billion of the world's over 7 billion population are currently food insecure. As well as the changes to rainfall, heat, flooding and so on that are impacting on communities' capacity for food production, environmental pollutants also impact on the ability to produce viable and safe foodstuffs. This is, of course, simply a major part of a wider and increasing problem with food security that is affecting not only those directly impacted by climate change in their own agri-economies, but also the less well off in developed economies. This is happening as a combination of shortages raise prices for everyone, exacerbated in no small part by the activities of financial markets, as was discussed in Chapter 5, through opportunistic speculation in commodities that can turn small shortages into larger price fluctuations, contributing to food price instability and inflation:[10]

> A broad set of risks needs to be considered, of which climate change is an increasingly important one, that can ripple out to destabilize food systems, resulting in high and volatile food prices that temporarily limit poor people's food consumption (70–73), financial and economic shocks that lead to job loss and credit constraints (74), and risks that political disruptions and failed political systems cause food insecurity (75). This complex system of risks can assume a variety of patterns that could potentially collide in catastrophic combinations.[11]

While this illustrates that this problem has been building for some time, this is now becoming so serious – particularly in light of COVID-19, geopolitical instability and global supply chain issues – that hunger, until quite recently thought to be largely a historical anachronism, is once more becoming a major issue for developed economies including in the UK and the US, underpinned by insecure, poorly paid work and increasingly threadbare social safety nets. In line with the argument presented here, the emotional impact and stressors associated with experiential overload, generated by having a lack of security and control over such fundamental needs, will undoubtedly only contribute to the primalizing processes I've outlined, creating the political conditions for further instability.[12]

There is also increasing concern not only in terms of how we produce enough food, but also in the way that our food production of itself can be seen to be contributing to warming the climate as cattle farming, and to lesser extent aspects of grain and vegetable production, contributes to rising methane in the atmosphere. At one point, much of the climate debate was around rising carbon dioxide levels, but methane is also being released from a number of sources, including agriculture, fossil fuel and biofuel emissions. Methane has much greater warming potential than carbon dioxide and this has led some of the most worried climate scientists (for more on this, see the discussion later on), to argue that global warming is in danger of becoming a self-reinforcing process, as temperature rises lead to thawing of arctic permafrost which, in turn, leads to the release of methane and a potential feedback loop. As well as food supplies, there is also the related issue of water shortages as a warming planet creates instability of supply. Firstly, a warmer planet will retain more moisture in the atmosphere. Flooding will also dump huge volumes over a short period that can contribute to contaminating water sources, exacerbated by heat, while rising sea levels will potentially introduce salt water into previously fresh water sources. All of this has the potential to reduce the availability of accessible, clean, fresh water suitable for drinking and agriculture.[13]

In response to these challenges, people may simply be driven to try and escape them by moving to more conducive environments, as did many of our pre-Holocene ancestors. However, the barriers they encountered would have been geographical, in terms of both knowledge and terrain, and technological in terms of transportation, whereas for modern people, the problems are largely related to financial resources and politics. As was suggested earlier, this will be a monumental problem for the world's poor, in terms of the financial ability to relocate and also as immigration, and a cultivated public resistance to it within developed economies has once more become a prominent feature of *dog whistle* right-wing politics, playing on the xenophobia associated with primalization. The prospective resistance to mobility for those badly affected by climate change, which is also underpinned by the selfish individualism that has also been cultivated in neoliberal societies, will likely become a bigger political and social source of instability in the future.

The climate debate

Given all of the clearly pressing issues presented by climate change, it has been widely asserted that the only solution or, rather, mitigation of the problem can be achieved by keeping the global rise in temperatures below

1.5°C. This has been advanced by the IPCC and widely accepted to be a ceiling that must be sustained in order to prevent further very significant harm to people and the planet. This targeting of temperature limits from governments around climate action really began to emerge with the Kyoto Agreement in 1992. This is now generally accepted by policy makers and has, since the international Paris Agreement on Climate Change of 2015, become the standard global target, replacing a previous 'acceptable' limit of 2°C, with the 1.5°C target also informing the basis for debate at the COP26 summit in 2021. However, it has been noted by the authoritative World Meteorological Organization that this limit is unlikely to be sustained and may be exceeded at some point by 2026.[14] Governments have also agreed to aim for net zero economies by 2050, a scenario where we are no longer adding to climate-changing emissions, with meeting this goal being related to capping global temperatures rises. However, at the time of writing, this target looks like unlikely to be realized, while even 2050 may be too far off as a point for achieving this if some of the worst effects of climate breakdown are to be avoided.

One of the key issues here, as has been widely argued, relates to the way that these intergovernmental accords tend to fail to produce action required to meet the set targets. Agreements are publicly announced to considerable fanfare and media debate, only for many of the signatory nations to return to pretty much business as usual, or the implementation of inadequate or piecemeal measures. Again, as I'm writing this, the UK government has just released a so-called 'Green Day energy security plan', sparking widespread criticism from environmental groups. The principal critique is that, rather than abandoning fossil fuels, the government seem set to rely on unproven carbon capture technology as a rationale for continuing or even ramping up oil and gas production, where other policy makers and international agencies like the IPCC have called for a cessation of fossil fuel activity as quickly as possible. This volte face was underlined in 2023 as the Conservatives gave the green light to the controversial Rosebank development west of Shetland. In part, this can be understood in terms of political expediency, as a weak Conservative leader bowed to the lobbying of the hard right within his party. It may also have been taken with an eye to securing the few Tory seats in the oil and gas region of Scotland's northeast, and as a feature of the culture wars upon which the party has become ever more reliant as an electoral strategy. In even more strident vein, Trump's declaration that he would drill from day one if re-elected plays to similar right wing political prejudices.[15]

This seeming tug of war between 'gradualists', those effectively promoting continuity, and those calling for swift action reflects that fact that this has, of course, long been feverishly contested terrain. Here, increasing calls for meaningful intervention from environmentalists and others concerned about the planet's future are met with the vigorous lobbying and influence of powerful vested interests who wish to sustain the status quo for as long as possible, retaining the energy sources, consumerism and related economic activity that is driving climate change. As well as influencing government, there has been the long-running campaign from both sides to capture public opinion.

Although, as was noted earlier, most climate scientists widely agree that anthropogenic global warming (AGW) poses a very serious risk to nature and humankind, as we know, there is nonetheless ongoing scientific dissent (albeit increasingly shrinking and losing plausibility) and continuing public debate questioning even the existence extent of climate change, whether it is in fact anthropogenic and not simply relatively normal long-term natural variation,[ii] and also how significant a problem it actually poses.

According to a systematic review conducted by Capstick et al,[16] public perceptions of climate change have evolved in a number of different directions since the issue became a phenomenon of wide mainstream interest in the 1980s. Initially, much of the debate was focused on depletion of the ozone layer and the implications for ultraviolet (UV) exposure. Gradually, the debate shifted to a focus on fossil fuels as the key driver of the climactic warming, moving up the list of concerns for many contemporary citizens. The climate debate evidently returns us to some of the issues raised in the previous chapter regarding the impact of mass media and now, in particular, social media, as people are increasingly exposed to conflicting, ambiguous and often directly misleading and distorted information that plays a critical role in shaping their opinions. As was noted earlier, this can lead people towards entrenched positions that become so deeply engrained in their internalized *maps* that they are staunchly defended, even when confronted with very compelling counterevidence.[17] However, there are also some more mundane reasons as to why concern over the climate is growing but still remains a sectional worry.

While, as was noted earlier, the speed at which climate change has emerged has been abrupt in broader historical terms, this has only really begun to register on much of the wider public's radar over the last few decades, and particularly since the turn of the century. It has also been argued that there has been an element of boiling frog syndrome associated with the phenomenon, as people's perceptions of changes in the weather, unless these are very dramatic, are perceived in relation to relatively short timescales (around two to eight years has been suggested) and tend to shift over time. The argument goes that this can establish a new baseline as to what is normal; hence, unless there is a sharp change or sequence of dramatic events, we are unlikely to experience a sense of significant unease

---

[ii] See Milankovitch cycle.

and consequent urgency in terms of the need to deal with potential threats of this nature.[18]

There is also the question that large-scale global problems, particularly when they seem to be ongoing rather than representing an imminent threat (as suggested in the opening quotation to this chapter), can present as being beyond people's capacity to meaningfully intervene and are, hence, often disregarded. Similarly, as will be discussed later on, a sense of futility, inevitability and the notion that the impact of climate change is something most likely to affect future generations rather than current cohorts, has often been seized upon by climate change deniers and sceptics as a means of confronting and downplaying calls for meaningful action. Nonetheless, this sense of distance from the impact of climate change has been diminishing significantly for a growing segment of the public. This has occurred, particularly since around 2010, where we have observed an evolving demonstration of the effects of the warming climate, with record temperatures being reached annually amid floods, wildfires, coastline erosion and other climate driven events. There has also been a growing incidence of 'freak' weather events, such as the unprecedented heatwave that affected parts of the US in June 2021 and the big chill in the winter of 2022, that brought this issue starkly into public view. Of course, the emergence of COVID-19, conflicts in Ukraine and the Middle East, and wider economic and political instability more generally have coalesced to vie with climate change for top-line media coverage. Nonetheless, public awareness was again jolted in 2023, with further incidences of wildfires, punishing heatwaves in previously temperate areas and flooding across major cities globally (with some occurring in normally arid areas), together with landslides and climate-induced disasters claiming numerous lives.

It is clear that climate change remains one of the major risks to the future of humanity and human civilization, alongside the raft of other self-imposed existential threats that neoliberal policy making has had a hand either in making or in obstructing meaningful intervention. In addition, despite the widening raft of concerns that seem to be expanding in the current era, as suggested, it is no longer viewed as quite so distant a threat by many, and particularly among the young who are likely to be most affected. Studies in the US and UK concluded that upwards of 70 per cent of people had been becoming more anxious about climate change, albeit that there are still significant pockets who remain unconcerned or dismissive of the threat.[19] Moreover, these positions tend to align with the stance of the main political parties in the UK and the US, reflecting an increasingly polarized right/left split that has reasserted itself across many societies in a variety of flavours and guises over recent decades, where climate denial alongside anti-vax, anti-mask wearing during the COVID-19 pandemic and being pro-gun in the US have become badges of right-wing allegiance.

Denial, doomism and distraction

Of course, there are also a variety of scientific perspectives on climate change regarding timescales and the severity of its impact, ranging from the relatively sanguine through the more measured to those that predict imminent apocalyptic upheaval. One of the most high-profile among the 'doomsayers' on climate change has been Emeritus Professor Guy McPherson of the University of Arizona. McPherson's perspective, which has been dramatically presented in the media and online over the past few years, is that we have gone beyond the point of no return in terms of global warming. According to this account, there is nothing now that can be done to prevent or effectively stabilize our march towards runaway global warming with catastrophic consequences – the best we can hope for is that our action avoids exacerbating this dire situation even further. As to those consequences, in this view they could not be more serious, entailing nothing less than the fairly imminent extinction of humanity alongside a mass loss of a wide range of other species.[20]

However, Professor McPherson's unnerving view is challenged by other leading climatologists like Professor Michael Mann, author of the famous 'hockey stick' graph that depicted relatively stable global temperatures suddenly taking off in an upward spiral, a model that continues to influence a good deal of the debate, including contributors to the IPCC. Mann regards the type of apocalyptic pronouncements of McPherson, and a number of others, as overblown and unhelpful 'doomism' that, while perhaps earnest in its conviction and intent, can paradoxically be employed by *opponents* of climate action. Simply, he asserts that such dire prognostications can evidently be used by vested interests opposed to climate action to advance a sense of fatalism, as evidence that remedial action is futile, and hence continuing with the status quo seems a reasonable option, much as was with the activities of the financial sector in the run-up to the 2007/2008 crisis.[21] If you can't do anything about some baleful event, this logic dictates, then you might as well indulge yourself as much as possible while you can. Recently, he has also taken aim at some of the other key tactics that have been employed to influence public opinion in this direction.[22]

In the early stages of the climate debate, according to Mann (and others), the major divide was between those who had begun to recognize the impact of human-generated climate change and environmental degradation, and those who claimed that climate change was either not really happening or was a natural variation, as was noted earlier, and who also sought to minimize perceptions of our other negative impacts on the planet. This position, however, has proved increasingly untenable in the public imagination as numerous indicators of global warming have become increasingly evident. Mann argues that this has now shifted to promoting what he terms 'inactivism', one tactic of which plays on the doomism and fatalism described previously. The promotion of 'inactivism' has been significantly driven by fossil fuel interests, neoliberal elites in the US, the UK and elsewhere who have formed think tanks and lobby organizations, in much the same way as they have advanced the neoliberal project more generally, to muddy the waters and present confusing and contradictory information on climate change:[23]

> The plutocrats who are tied to the fossil fuel industry are engaging in a new climate war – this time to prevent meaningful action. Over the past few years, you've seen a lot of conservative groups pulling their money out of the climate-change-denial industry and putting it instead into efforts by ALEC [the American Legislative Exchange Council, a conservative lobbying group], for example, to fund legislative efforts blocking clean-energy policies.[24]

As was argued in Chapter 4, this is a consistent hallmark of the Friedmanite neoliberal mindset, where short-term economic goals take priority over almost any other consideration. This consistent leaning towards profits before people and the planet was also demonstrated during the COVID-19 pandemic. This was evidenced in the right-wing stance favouring *herd immunity* and opposition to mask wearing and largely any other restrictions that might save lives if they impeded normal economic activity. Hence, the response to taking action on the climate and the environment that might mean moderating consumerism, fossil fuel burning and promoting energy transition and other protective measures has been similar and has been advanced by the same political constituency. The US organizations mentioned previously have their parallel collectives in the UK: oil-related companies, lobbyists, right-wing political groups, the media and think tanks, such as the Global Warming Policy Foundation and the Conservative Party's Net Zero Scrutiny Group. The latter have been associated with moves to sideline developments in renewable technologies in favour of expanding fossil fuel production, as well as other anti-environmental measures, with the argument being presented that the threat from climate change may be exaggerated and, critically, that we cannot economically accommodate the type of remedial action advocated by environmentalist groups, politicians and the climate concerned among the public. At least in part, the UK government's 2023 'Green Day' stance can be seen as a concession to this group and those it champions. Anti-climate action groups, often with ostensibly benign or official-sounding titles, tend to feature many of the same people whose aim is to advance the neoliberal agenda and deter any activity that threatens to derail or hinder unfettered capitalism wherever this arises:

Individuals and entities linked to climate denial, fossil fuels and high pollution industries donated more than £3.5 million to the Conservative Party last year, DeSmog can reveal. Electoral Commission records show that the party and its MPs received considerable sums from the highly polluting aviation and construction industries, mining and oil interests, and individuals linked to the Global Warming Policy Foundation, a think tank that denies climate science. This revelation comes on the government's supposed 'green day', when it has announced a long list of policies on energy and the transition to net zero. However, rather than strengthen the commitment to the government's legally binding climate targets, the policies are expected to entrench the role of fossil fuels in the UK's energy system. The government's updated measures include a plan to loosen restrictions on oil and gas extraction in the North Sea, in which it says "we remain absolutely committed to maximising the vital production of UK oil and gas as the North Sea basin declines.[25]

Returning to Michael Mann's work, he also cites the concept of the 'carbon footprint' as an ideological device, something that might surprise many moderate, environmentally concerned members of the public. However, this criticism is based on Mann's view that this notion is actually aimed at distracting the public from recognizing the key causes of the climate crisis and who is responsible, This, Mann claims, rather than being the pro-environmental concept that it first appears, was actually coined by the oil industry itself. What he points out, and what others have also observed, is that this tends to pass responsibility for climate change from corporations and fossil fuel corporations in particular, presenting this as an individual problem and responsibility. As will be argued specifically in Chapter 12, individualizing responsibility for the ills of neoliberal business and governance is a consistent gambit. In this case, the message is that if climate change is worsening, it's the public's fault for taking those flights, driving that car and using too much energy, deflecting attention from the much more important issue of governmental responsibility and the need for corporate and systemic change.[26]

Greenwashing

One of the most significant evasive strategies around climate action that has emerged in recent years has seen some corporations seemingly abandon opposition to the climate agenda and publicly declare their pro-environmental activities and credentials, including major fossil fuel companies and a host of other commercial organizations. Responding to growing public interest and concern, being green has become an important feature of corporate public relations presentations to their investors and the wider public. Linked to notions of corporate social responsibility (CSR), climate and environmentally friendly discourse has featured in a wide range of corporate promotional literature and advertising, often associated with images of unspoiled natural backgrounds, green colours and cute animals as well as more substantive commentary in annual company statements. However, this has been regarded by many commentators as being largely a further delaying tactic, serving as a backstop against fundamental change now that outright climate change denial has become increasingly untenable. While greenwashing can be found in a wide variety of forms, it has been argued that the rhetoric on such corporate green agendas has been to coalesce around a few key tactics and arguments.[27]

Firstly, in a paper addressing the latter, researchers Megura and Gunderson argue that many companies have advanced solutions to the climate crisis based on 'techno-optimism' where, rather than accepting the case for real change, technical changes to the efficiencies in the use of fossil fuels, technologies like carbon capture and storage, and some investment in renewables, it is argued, will allow for the continuation of business pretty much as usual without radical action. This is precisely what has been levelled at the UK government's 'green' agenda, as discussed earlier.

'Necessitarianism' is a second strategy that's highlighted, referring to the much-promulgated argument that the energy sources produced are essential to quality of life and wellbeing, and, hence, any real change would undermine that goal. This is the type of argument that came to the fore with the precipitous rise in fuel prices produced by the war in Ukraine and which was also advanced by some of the political groups mentioned previously, while this has been grasped as a rationale for postponing climate action on the premise that rising prices are hurting the poor and vulnerable. However, it might be suggested that the proposed resumption of fossil fuel exploration and production, given the often lengthy timescales involved, would do more to extend the fossil-fuelled turbocapitalist economy, while protecting and enhancing the future profits of fossil fuel and other major corporations and finance who are keen to sustain the status quo. Thirdly, there is 'compliance', where fossil fuel companies indicate that they are doing the right thing by following the law. However, there is also a question as to the influence these powerful actors, through lobbying and so on, exert to shape the inadequate legal frameworks to which they are subject. Finally, Megura and Gunderson discuss 'countermeasures'. These are activities that energy industry corporations often cite as being a key part of their good citizenship by taking action to involve themselves with, and invest in, environmental projects and organizations as an asserted recompense that offsets or at least mitigates any harm that they do. What these researchers and many others within this debate are arguing is that the key thing missing from this agenda is the need to radically challenge the way in which we consume energy and why we do it, that is, confronting the continuation of our hyperconsumerist and turbocapitalist lifestyles and replacing this with something more human-friendly, less energy-hungry and, hence, more sustainable for all of the world's peoples.[28]

A just transition

Of course, if we have to reshape our approach to mitigating climate change, while also supporting a sustainable planet more generally in terms of sustaining healthy ecosystems, then we also have to deal with the way in which this will impact on individuals and communities across a broad range of circumstances. Many of the current remonstrations against meaningful and radical climate intervention, as was indicated earlier, tend to rest on the argument that there would be too much disruption to employment, not only in the fossil fuel industry and in the regional economies and communities associated with the energy industry, but also in the wider economy and society more generally if we were to move to a more conservationist and less consumer-oriented way of life. Hence, the wider impact of effectively tempering climate change and supporting a sustainable environment would be too great to contemplate. In effect, this is a strategy that appeals to the deep-seated desire for consistency and predictability identified earlier, including public wariness of significant change. It is the prospect of the latter that also causes a great deal of concern for neoliberals as it entails nothing less than a wholesale reassessment of the world in which profits are gained and which maintains their positions at the upper end of the socioeconomic hierarchy in highly unequal societies; hence, significant change must be avoided at all costs.

However, as was noted previously, the need to address these issues and shift to a low carbon and more sustainable future has at least begun to gain increasing traction within and beyond environmentalist circles, including more enlightened governments. This has become associated with the notion of creating a 'just transition' as we reshape the economy to move away from fossil fuels. Integral to this notion is that change should be inclusive and equitable in supporting energy workers, communities, tacking inequalities and managing the environment in the interests of all who are affected rather than simply supporting sectional interests. A good deal of this focus has been on retaining the energy workforce for 'good jobs' in a new green energy sector that harnesses wind, solar and other forms of renewable energy, with the aim of smoothing out this transition to sustain impacted regional economies. Climate justice is also a key aspect of the notion that the move to clean energy should be considered in terms of the benefits to communities in terms of stabilising the climate and, not least, in reducing the environmental degradation endured in mining areas. With respect to the latter, this is of course not just about the climate, but also the way in which fossil fuel corporations, and others who now run former public utilities with environmental responsibilities such as water companies, regularly ignore aspects of their activities that create other forms of damage, largely in terms of polluted air, water and soil, with often serious consequences for communities that are exposed to the toxic byproducts of corporate profit maximization.[29]

Overall, there is an urgent need to produce a transformed energy landscape where people have access to clean energy a clean environment and good jobs, and where the 'goods' and 'bads' of the economy are more evenly distributed.[30] However, it can be argued that while the concept of just transition has been adopted by some policy makers, it remains the case that it is imagined that we can move from fossil fuels to green energy, shift the jobs and clean up the environment, while leaving everything else largely in place.

The circular economy

As was noted earlier, there appears to be little appetite for a radical shift in our lifestyles and economy. By contrast, many environmentalists have argued for a move to a 'circular economy' where we share, reuse, repair and recycle whatever we can, moving away from the economic model built on consumption and waste that now predominates. If we consider such a change, one that might really impact on planetary sustainability, this would evidently entail a fundamentally different socioeconomic model. Firstly, the transition from energy jobs and towards green energy would have to be approached within the context of the wider context of the impact of digitalization and automation on labour markets, as was discussed in Chapter 6. As was argued previously, there is little to reason to suspect that the energy industries of the future, whether clean or dirty, will require a workforce anything like as numerous as the one we have today, but will likely follow the same pattern as has been already happening across many other sectors, from retail, services and manufacturing, where far fewer are required to keep the wheels turning than was previously the case. It follows that this will lead to fewer secure employment opportunities and fewer well-paid jobs beyond the few sectors of labour markets where an element of human creativity is involved that cannot be replicated, at least thus far. It may even be the case that the reduction in incomes and job security imposes a form of circular economy for many, as they can no longer afford to engage in conspicuous consumption, returning us full circle to the form of limited elite consumer society of the leisure class versus the subsistence living conditions of the masses of the late 19th century. At present, as was also indicated in Chapter 6, the mantra from governments is that they are looking forward to more high-skilled, high-paying jobs in future, despite there being no clear idea of where these jobs would come from, and while this also seems contrary to current trends.[31] In short, the dual impact of climate transition and digitalization threatens to produce even more socially and economically polarized societies than is currently the case. These are issues that will be explored in the following chapter. However, there are a few final observations that are important to consider here regarding the deeper and wider ramification of what had been discussed with respect to the impact of climate change.

Climate change and wider implications

As was noted in the earlier chapters, we are greatly challenged in modern societies by cognitive overload – that is, being presented by more than we can cope with at any given time, leading to stress. This is a perspective that is also broadly consistent with previous references to experiential overload, referring to the level of simultaneous demands, information and ongoing social change that we can accommodate and to which we can adapt, while maintaining a level of relatively healthy and comfortable homeostasis. The fact that an excess of these demands can lead to chronic stress, mental and physical ill health also has a clear bearing on how we may be impacted by the potential transformations imposed by climate change should it – as is likely – develop broadly as described.[32] The wider health implications of this will be more fully discussed in Chapter 12. However, what is important to note is that the combination of climate change and wider socioeconomic pressures and dislocation undoubtedly threaten to place a heavy burden on individuals and communities exposed to these conditions, which, of course, will likely impact on all of us to greater or lesser degrees over time. In addition, this creates conditions for a vertiginous feedback loop, where economic insecurity and potential climate-induced forced migration and unpredictability in terms of access to work and basic resources intensifies the conditions for *primalization* discussed earlier, in terms of increasing angst, fear, rage and unreason, a consequence of which is vulnerability to political manipulation and further upheaval. Add to this regular flooding, wildfires and summer climate conditions that in many previously temperate areas across the globe are regularly reaching tolerable limits and we have a heady mix. This all sounds highly alarmist and depressing. However, I would argue that it is far from being an unrealistic assessment as to where we are now and where we are likely going in the medium term if we continue on our current course while allowing powerful actors to prevent remedial action and a real of change of direction. On a final point, at the time of writing, there is still an opportunity for us to take action to stave off the very worst effects of climate change. This requires that the political will is directed by public pressure as awareness grows in relation to the seriousness of the threat, countering the vigorous lobbying of the energy industry, corporations and the neoliberal right-wing ideologues and media moguls that support them. However, viewing the measured optimism of COP 26 give way to an almost fatalistic abandonment of targets and a failure to reach satisfactory agreement at COP 27 just one year later does not inspire any confidence that the fairly radical steps that are becoming necessary will be taken until climate events even more cataclysmic may be experienced. With apologies for contributing my own variant of doomism, the longer-term implications of climate breakdown may well be even more concerning for humanity as a whole when considered in the current context. As was noted in Chapter 1, there is the developing debate, fuelled by new evidence regarding the way in which our biology interacts with our environment, that the tarnishing of our evolutionary 'niche', via the effects of flood, famine and other effects of global warming, may interact with the impact of deleterious societal conditions to further degrade our 'fitness' over time.[33] All of this assumes, of course, that the more extreme doomists like McPherson don't prove to be right and the game is already up.

Notes

1   Franzen, J. (2019) 'What if we stopped pretending? The climate apocalypse is coming. To prepare for it, we need to admit that we can't prevent it', *New Yorker*, 8 September.

2   Childe, V.G. (1950) 'The urban revolution', *Town Planning Review*, 21(1): 3–17.

3   Steffen, W., Grinevald, J., Crutzen, P. and McNeill, J. (2011) 'The Anthropocene: conceptual and historical perspectives', *Philosophical Transactions of the Royal Society A: Mathematical, Physical and Engineering Sciences*, 369(1938): 842–867, at 842–843.

4   Richards, C.E., Lupton, R.C. and Allwood, J.M. (2021) 'Re-framing the threat of global warming: an empirical causal loop diagram of climate change, food insecurity and societal collapse', *Climatic Change*, 164(3): 1–19, at 2.

5   IPCC (2021) *Climate Change 2021: The Physical Science Basis*, Contribution of Working Group I to the Sixth Assessment Report of the Intergovernmental Panel on Climate Change, Cambridge: Cambridge University Press.

6   https://www.ipcc.ch/site/assets/uploads/2021/08/IPCC_WGI-AR6-Press-Release_en.pdf

7   Childe, V.G. (1950) 'The urban revolution', *Town Planning Review*, 21(1): 3–17.

8   Singh, M. and Glowacki, L. (2021) 'Human social organization during the Late Pleistocene: beyond the nomadic-egalitarian model', *EcoEvoRxiv*, 13 March.

9   Wheeler, T. and von Braun, J. (2013) 'Climate change impacts on global food security', *Science*, 341(6145): 508–513.

10 Wheeler, T. and von Braun, J. (2013) 'Climate change impacts on global food security', *Science*, 341(6145): 508–513.

11 Wheeler, T. and von Braun, J. (2013) 'Climate change impacts on global food security', *Science*, 341(6145): 508–513, at 512.

[12] Bone, J.D. (2010) 'Irrational capitalism: the social map, neoliberalism and the demodernization of the West', *Critical Sociology*, 36(5): 717–740.

[13] UNICEF (2020) 'Water and the global climate crisis: 10 things you should know', https://www.unicef.org/stories/water-and-climate-change-10-things-you-should-know

[14] 'WMO update: 50:50 chance of global temperature temporarily reaching 1.5°C threshold in next five years', https://wmo.int/news/media-centre/wmo-update-5050-chance-of-global-temperature-temporarily-reaching-15degc-threshold-next-five-years

[15] https://www.nbcnews.com/politics/donald-trump/trump-says-wont-dictator-elected-day-one-rcna128267

[16] Capstick, S., Whitmarsh, L., Poortinga, W., Pidgeon, N. and Upham, P. (2015) 'International trends in public perceptions of climate change over the past quarter century', *Wiley Interdisciplinary Reviews: Climate Change*, 6(1): 35–61.

[17] Dunlap, R.E. and Brulle, R.J. (2020) 'Sources and amplifiers of climate change denial', in D.C. Holmes and L.M. Richardson (eds), *Research Handbook on Communicating Climate Change*, Cheltenham and Camberley: Edward Elgar, pp 49–61.

[18] Moore, F.C., Obradovich, N., Lehner, F. and Baylis, P. (2019) 'Rapidly declining remarkability of temperature anomalies may obscure public perception of climate change', *Proceedings of the National Academy of Sciences*, 116(11): 4905–4910.

[19] Leiserowitz, A., Maibach, E., Roser-Renouf, C., Feinberg, G. and Rosenthal, S. (2015) 'Climate change in the American mind: March, 2015'. Yale Project on Climate Change Communication (Yale University and George Mason University, New Haven, CT).

[20] McPherson, G.R. (2020) 'Earth is in the midst of abrupt, irreversible climate change', *Journal of Earth and Environmental Science Research*, 2(2): 1–2.

[21] 'Michael Mann versus the "Doomists"', http://www.lajosbrons.net/blog/doomists/

[22] Mann, M.E. (2021) *The New Climate War: The Fight to Take Back Our Planet*, New York: Public Affairs.

[23] Schiffman, R. (2021) 'Climate deniers shift tactics to "inactivism"', *Scientific American*, 12 January.

[24] Schiffman, R. (2021) 'Climate deniers shift tactics to "inactivism"', *Scientific American*, 12 January.

[25] 'Conservatives received £3.5 million from polluters, fossil fuel interests and climate deniers in 2022', https://www.desmog.com/2023/03/30/conservatives-received-3-5-million-from-polluters-fossil-fuel-interests-and-climate-deniers-in-2022/

[26] Mann, M.E. (2021) *The New Climate War: The Fight to Take Back Our Planet*, New York: Public Affairs.

[27] Mann, M.E. (2021) *The New Climate War: The Fight to Take Back Our Planet*, New York: Public Affairs.

[28] Megura, M. and Gunderson, R. (2022) 'Better poison is the cure? Critically examining fossil fuel companies, climate change framing, and corporate sustainability reports', *Energy Research & Social Science*, 85: 102388.

[29] Sabah, J.T. (2021) 'Evaluation of genotoxic damage in buccal mucosa cytome assays in Iraqi school children exposed to air pollutants emanating from oil fields', *Mutation Research/Genetic Toxicology and Environmental Mutagenesis*, 863: 503304; Ukaogo, P.O., Ewuzie, U. and Onwuka, C.V. (2020) 'Environmental pollution: causes, effects, and the remedies', in P. Chowdhary, A. Raj, D. Verma and Y. Akhter (eds), *Microorganisms for Sustainable Environment and Health*, New York: Elsevier, pp 419–429.

[30] Newell, P. and Mulvaney, D. (2013) 'The political economy of the "just transition"', *Geographical Journal*, 179(2): 132–140.

[31] Edward, W. (2020) 'The Uberisation of work: the challenge of regulating platform capitalism. A commentary', *International Review of Applied Economics*, 34(4): 512–521.

32 McEwen, B.S. (1998) 'Stress, adaptation, and disease: allostasis and allostatic load', *Annals of the New York Academy of Sciences*, 840(1): 33–44.

33 Laland, K.N., Uller, T., Feldman, M.W., Sterelny, K., Müller, G.B., Moczek, A. and Odling-Smee, J. (2015) 'The extended evolutionary synthesis: its structure, assumptions and predictions', *Proceedings of the Royal Society B: Biological Sciences*, 282(1813): 20151019.

10

Inequality, Insecurity and Minding the Gap

It should be clear from what's been argued in the previous chapters that burgeoning inequality and its companion insecurity have greatly worsened with the advancing of neoliberal ideas and societal organization from the 1980s onwards. Numerous problems associated with the workplace, housing, finance, consumerism and, as will be discussed in the next two chapters, politics and health have reasserted themselves with renewed vigour since that time. As was argued in Chapter 3, these were issues that had been recognized and confronted with greater or lesser success during the postwar era, but have re-emerged with ever more damaging effects since that progressive agenda was upended.

While an imperfect measure of inequality, the *Gini coefficient* is the most widely recognized measure globally where a measure of 0 would reflect perfect equality of income (everyone gets the same) and 1 where a single individual secures all of a nation's income to the exclusion of everyone else. This measure rose precipitously in the UK, the US and to an extent in numerous other nations that have implemented neoliberal economic policies. In 2022, the US Gini coefficient reached 0.48, and while America has long been an unequal nation, this is the highest level on this measure for 50 years, placing the US among the most unequal developed economies in the world. While the measure was high throughout the 20th century, it fell to around the high 0.30–0.40 range in line with the general trend towards greater equality in the postwar era. However, it began to rise again from the 1980s and the coming to power of the Reagan government. For the UK, this measure is not as high as in the US, 0.35 in 2022, but has followed the same pattern, moving from a postwar level of around 0.25 to increase most significantly in the 1980s as the Thatcher government began to implement its broad range of pro-market economic reforms. As was noted previously, conservative administrations on both sides of the Atlantic would run out of steam in the 1990s, ushering in the Clinton and Blair assertedly centre-left administrations, largely due to growing dissatisfaction with the inequities and poor economic performance under neoliberalism. However, as was argued earlier, rather than overturning the neoliberal settlement, as many had hoped and expected, both Clinton and Blair merely set about tempering some of neoliberal policy's worst effects as opposed to substantially challenging the prevailing logic. This has ensured that both nations have remained among the most unequal in terms of income among 41 of the OECD's developed economies.[1]

One important caveat here is that some progress has continued with respect to forms of inequality in relation to race, gender, disability, age and so on. However, as will be discussed later on, much of this has involved politicians recognizing and offering a range of policies relating to *respect* and acceptance of different identity and diverse cultures, while paying less attention to economic divides. In fact, to a significant extent, neoliberal governments (and here, as was implied earlier, I include the New Labour and Democrat administrations in the UK and the US) have tended to focus more on equality with reference to culture and identity rather than economic factors, allowing them to sustain a façade of advancing progressive credentials while acceding to much of the dominant regressive economic agenda.

While I will return to some of these issues in more depth in the next chapter, in some ways an element of the left liberal constituency, while earnest and well meaning, has been charged with being at least partially complicit in allowing this reframing of inequality. This has led to it being suggested that it has offered straw targets while sewing division among its own ranks and failing to adequately engage with the concerns of the politically disenfranchised and economically marginalized. This line of argument proposes that this has provided opportunities for the exploitation of a divide on the left between those more focused on inequalities of identity and culture, and those more concerned with challenging injustices of class and the economy, allowing the right to paint the former elements of the left into an exclusive and detached corner of ignoring deep economic injustice in favour of the lofty concerns of the 'comfortable'. This is, of course, highly disingenuous and something that needs to be challenged, as it is the compounding of a variety of identity, cultural and socioeconomic inequalities that disadvantages people across these interlinked dimensions, so they have a common interest. Thus, in many societies, bound up with the personal damage associated with unequal identities and cultures, many of the profound injuries of intersectional inequalities are manifested and experienced in the economic sphere. To belong to a less valued or stigmatized group regularly entails poorer access to good jobs, decent housing, educational success and a broad range of the other pillars that support modern living and the 'opportunities' that nations like the UK and the US claim to offer. However, allowing the sleight of hand that denies these connections is what has enabled the co-opting of the poor by the real elite, such as the current coterie of right-wing populists, by directing their ire towards cultural and social controversies while distracting them from the real economic woes that blight their own lives and often those they vilify. As was suggested earlier, bad systems need complacency and misleading stories to keep them in place.

As more extreme forms of right-wing populism have entered the alleged centre ground, or as the latter has shifted ever rightward, as will be discussed in more detail in Chapter 11, an ever more regressive line on social and cultural politics has emerged among conservative parties. A resurgent form of populism has capitalized on the growing distress of the socially and economically marginalized, aided by social media, manipulating a segment of the disenchanted in support of a strident rightwing agenda. This tactic, I would argue, is what has allowed politicians largely of the privileged economic elite such as Donald Trump, Boris Johnson, Nigel Farage, Marine Le Pen, Giorgia Meloni, and a host of others who have risen to political prominence, albeit not in all cases actually gaining power, by presenting themselves as allies and supporters of 'the people' against the 'establishment'. Here, mendacity and philistinism are often presented as badges of honour, while familiar populist tropes of alleged solidarity with society's 'outsiders' are ranged against a common enemy in the shape of the so-called pretentious and 'woke' culture of educated 'elites'. The fact that many if not most of the latter are often very significantly less wealthy than the asserted champions of the common people is elided over amid the populist finger pointing and dog-whistle politicking that also singles out *other* 'outsiders' – anyone of a different ethnic background, gender identity, sexuality or religion – as a target for popular pillorying, fear and anger. That populists of this ilk often promote agendas in their own elite interests in this way and against those of their followers – who, one suspects, many privately view with a degree of disdain and contempt – is a fact that gets lost in the highly charged rhetoric, online debate and emotionally charged rallies.

As to the policies followed by many of these right-wing 'disruptors', this is where some of the previous arguments suggesting that the neoliberal era is over come in, as some commentators have argued that the rise of these populist politicians marks the end of neoliberalism.[2] It is conceded that, as was noted previously, many of these figures are nationalists rather than globalists who engage in prosocial rhetoric, if not action, in support of their followers. This change of political narrative, together with growing geopolitical enmities, may mark the end or at least a hiatus in terms of the global world of economically interconnected states that Fukuyama once hailed. However, this does not preclude the resilience of the neoliberal economic model. The international order may be changing, and it has, but this does not necessarily apply to economic management within nations or the ideology that continues to shape it. Rather, when it comes to the fundamentals of inequality, economic insecurity and injustice that have marred ordinary people's lives, it is difficult not to view the emergence of many populist figures as actually intensifying the neoliberal project, distracting their followers with ethnonationalist, ideological and cultural enmities, while it remains very much business as usual in terms of the neoliberal kleptocracy.[3] As Henri Giroux put it:

> A blend of neo-liberal orthodoxy, religious fundamentalism, educational repression and an accelerating militarism found its end point in the election of Donald Trump. Trump represents the transformation of politics into a Reality TV show and the belief that the worth of a candidate can be judged only in terms of a mixture of one's value as an entertainer and an advertisement for casino capitalism. Corporate money and the ideology of militarism define Trump's embrace of a war culture ... This is an upgraded version of neo-liberalism on steroids.[4]

As argued here, then, the voices, tone and hegemonic discourse may have evolved to an extent, but the basic foundations of the neoliberal zeitgeist remain, reflecting the mindset of much of the business and political order of contemporary nation states like the UK, the US and a host of others. Despite opposition from more socially concerned voices, economic and political impunity, injustice, insecurity, inequality amid a harsh grab-what-you-can culture remain the order of the day, regardless of the rhetoric of the people's 'champions'.

Inequality and 'efficient' markets

> While Britons have been living with low wages for the last 15 years, inequality has been a problem for more than twice as long. Having surged during the 1980s, and remained consistently high ever since, income inequality in the UK was higher than any other large European country in 2018.[5]

> ... tolerate the inequality as a way to achieve greater prosperity and opportunity for all ... Lord Brian Griffiths of Fforestfach and Goldman Sachs October, 2009.[6]

The preceding statement accredited to Lord Griffiths in many ways captures the mindset of the committed neoliberal approach to inequality, while advancing another strand of the disclaimer long offered to neutralize public unease around the burgeoning inequalities of wealth and income that have grown since the late 1970s. It's perhaps ironic, if not incendiary, that this statement came in the aftermath of the banking crisis, where the financial sector heavily supported by state bailouts, once again particularly in the UK and the US, was continuing to reward its top performers with eye-watering bonuses and pay packages. At the same time, as was also noted in Chapter 5, the public was subjected to austerity in terms of services and welfare provision in the interests of restabilizing state budgets impacted by financial sector recklessness. As such, this comment can be seen within the context of the broad defence of neoliberalism mentioned earlier, offered by its adherents as its obvious failings and inequities had been laid bare.

The sentiments expressed previously are also reminiscent of attitudes prevalent in the 19th and early 20th centuries, insisting that the economic wellbeing of societies as a whole is best served by celebrating personal economic gain, no matter how unequally this is distributed. Of course, a further defence of societies with high levels of inequality is often advanced with the proposition that the arrangements that permit this are nonetheless 'fair'. However, fairness here, as with the neoliberal understanding of freedom, is imagined within a very particular logic. As was noted earlier, neoliberal conceptions of freedom tend to be framed as individual or corporate freedom, with the capacity to do as you like socially and economically within the law, with little interference from the state. In unequal deregulated societies like the UK and the US, in practice, this has been experienced as the freedom to control and exploit others with minimal constraint in pursuit of economic gain, as the laws that govern such conduct have themselves been shaped by the powerful influence of the economic elite.[7] Nonetheless, economic success and failure is claimed to be wholly an outcome of individual ability, talent and industriousness in free market societies where opportunity is open to all. As we know, this is the mantra that has been taken for granted over the last 40 years or more, alongside presenting 'free' markets as the most efficient and fair way to organize the economy and society. This is still very much the narrative advanced by populist politicians. The state in any form other than of the radical right is presented as interfering and heavy handed in terms of interventions to constrain individual licence and impunity, notably in the US in relation to both the economy and the gun. Attempts to curb economic excess and impose taxes on the wealthy are somehow redefined as constraints on the aspirations of ordinary people, no matter how unlikely those ambitions are to be realized (rather than corporate and elite greed), while societies' problems are a consequence of 'others' – that is, competition from immigrants, dependent 'losers' and, of course, the shadowy and mythical deep state. However, an important caveat here is that exercising state power is deemed wholly appropriate where it comes to controlling 'unruly' segments of the poor, ethnic minorities, trade unions, and environmental and civil rights activism, given that right-wing populism and neoliberalism are part of a creed that is duplicitous to its core.

The validity and consequences of the widely accepted claims of the populist neoliberal right are discussed later on, but it is important to understand how they are instilled and sustained, often in the face of conflicting evidence and experience. For the reasons outlined earlier, people have a very strong tendency to protect their deeply held beliefs as a defence against experiential overload, cognitive dissonance and as a means of sustaining a sense of clarity and consistency. As such, they will be inclined to reject or rationalize away any countervailing evidence, almost regardless of how obvious or blatant this is, a tendency commonly referred to as *motivated reasoning*.[8] As was discussed previously, common-sense belief in ideas around 'free' markets, with life chances and success being defined by personal merit in open democratic societies, has been exhaustively promoted and installed via a longstanding, emotionally laden and repetitive discourse from right-wing politicians and media.

The system as 'common sense'

> Dictators realized that they could not sustain their behaviors and policies if they did not have at least some support from the masses. So instead of relying solely on force as a means of control, they attempted to get inside the minds of their citizens and indirectly control their thoughts and ideas so they would believe the government actually cares for them.[9]

Ideological 'indoctrination' in line with the above is a charge often aimed at the left by so-called 'freedom loving' right-wing politicians, pundits and academics. Rhetoric in this vein often cites George Orwell's *Nineteen Eighty-Four*, his famous allegorical tale of the potential soul-crushing aspects of state totalitarianism that was informed by his experience of Nazism, Spanish Fascism and, critically, his concerns around developments in Stalinist Russia. Of course, this is a sadly well-worn observation of what can happen in powerful anti-democratic states where human freedom is often an early casualty. Sometimes, however, as I will argue later on, pressure towards rigid conformity, ideological purity and so on can feature among some elements of the self-proclaimed enlightened and liberal left. As was noted at the outset, and as Nietzsche observed, it is an integral feature of the human condition that most people, given the opportunity, would prefer to control the world in their own image and interests, of whatever form, while co-opting others and challenging, undermining or expunging alternatives. This tends to make us feel safe, secure and in control. Challenges, depending on their magnitude, can be tolerated, easily or grudgingly, or subjected to resistance where they threaten our core worldview, norms, values and so on. Of course, we are all guilty of not seeing these traits in ourselves while levelling them at others. We are even-handed and objective, while 'they' are often prejudiced or deluded.

However, the right's insistence that its ideas come from and reflect the moderate and pragmatic political 'centre ground' denies the fact that neoliberal dogma is just as ideological, quasi-religious, cult-like and freedom-denying as the allegedly extreme 'leftist' doctrines that its exponents routinely rail against. In fact, as was noted in Chapter 4, neoliberalism has been the subject of one of the most assiduous programmes aimed at shifting public consciousness in modern history, backed by economic elites that have gone to great lengths to deny or justify its inequities and injustices. Suffice to say, as argued, belief in the naturalness and fairness of free markets has become an almost unquestionable 'common sense' for large numbers of the public and for our politicians, as the political centre of gravity has tended to incrementally move ever further to the right, extending from the Anglo-Saxon economies to span much of the globe. While the preceding chapters have charted the rise of neoliberalism and some its well-recognized consequences, this and the following chapters discuss some of the deeper and most profound and unsettling implications of this ideology that can be seen to have come to a head over the last decade or so, placing us at a precarious crossroads for the future of individuals, communities and, as I argue, humanity as a whole.

Mythic meritocracy

With the consolidation of this credo, much of the public absorbed the line that hard work and talent are the key drivers of economic success. Do the right thing, be industrious and eventually you'll make it. So deeply engrained is this belief that people often continue to believe it even when this is clearly at odds with their own experience and that of those around them. This position also allows for governments to refrain from tackling growing inequalities as solutions are seen to be in people's own hands, a view informing leading New Labour politician Peter Mandelson's (in)famous 1998 statement that Tony Blair's New Labour was less favourable towards redistribution than earlier Labour governments, with the suggestion that the government was 'intensely relaxed about people getting filthy rich as long as they pay their taxes'. In fact, a good deal of the 'gap' has arisen between those at the very top pulling away from the bottom and an increasingly hollowed-out middle, and with many 'good' secure jobs with benefits having been greatly eroded by the push for labour market 'flexibility' discussed in Chapter 6. As Ed West noted in *The Spectator*:

Today, however, we are witnessing the strange death of the middle class. In Britain, as in the United States, it isn't just being squeezed – it is actually shrinking and sinking. This is the most disturbing social change of our age and will probably dominate your children's lives. The lifestyle that the average earner had half a century ago – reasonably sized house, dependable healthcare, a decent education for the children and a reliable pension – is becoming the preserve of the rich.[10]

In a real sense, neoliberal policies have created a 'winner takes all' scenario where more and more of the resources, income and wealth gravitate towards the very top.[11] Much attention here has been focused on the stratospheric incomes enjoyed by the top 1 per cent or so in neoliberal economies, where this group inhabits a sphere vastly beyond the reach of the average person. Again, this is often ascribed to hard work and effort, that is, it's only fair reward for talent and diligence, while those pointing out the injustice inherent in this situation have long been dismissed on the ground that this is simply the 'politics of envy'. This plays to the notion that even the most exorbitant of gains are justified by claims that the winners are special or are wealth or 'job creators' whose rewards will inevitably *trickle down* to benefit everyone, as noted in Chapter 6.

In the first instance, increased gains at the very top can be traced more or less directly to the economic 'reforms' instituted by Thatcher and Reagan. As such, the changing of taxation laws, loose financial regulation and more flexible labour policies enabled businesses and individuals to extract and keep more and more of an economy's resources, taking us back towards levels of elite power, status and wealth that were prevalent in the late 19th century.

The 'self-made'

While I will deal specifically with the increasing role of wealth later on, as suggested earlier, justification for those at the top being awarded huge incomes in the first place is highly questionable. For the most part, when anyone questions this, the defenders of the system will swiftly cite a famous inventor, entrepreneur or other who has developed a new product or service, or an entertainer or sportsperson of note. As suggested, the claim is that such riches are conferred on unique abilities. This supports the aforementioned myth of the self-made, which many of the wealthy claim as the route to their success. Firstly, however, despite supporting an antipathy to taxes or any restraint on the building of their personal fortunes, the idea that anyone is self-made doesn't really pass muster. This was notably expressed by Barack Obama in his 'you didn't build that' speech while campaigning for the presidency in 2012. The point being made was that even the genuinely entrepreneurial were heavily supported by taxpayers, sometimes for research and development in the case of the internet, but also as their businesses could not exist without transport, laws and their legal enforcement, an educated workforce and so on, which were paid for by taxpayers. In terms of workers themselves, it is also the case that large corporations only operate with the coordinated activities of legions of people – not one or a few individuals. As such, most-cited examples justifying huge incomes don't stand up. However, looking beyond that, many of the 1 per cent are not drawn from the fabled ranks of buccaneering, risk-taking and inventive entrepreneurs. In fact, most corporate leaders are effectively administrators, accountants or lawyers, who have been fortunate or had the right connections to climb the greasy corporate pole. As was argued in Chapter 5, their fortunes have often been accumulated, assuming that they didn't start with one in the first instance, by the financializaton of the economy and the move to shareholder value, where CEOs' rewards and bonuses were linked to profits and share price. It has also been recognized that many of the 1 per cent gain their income through rents. This means that income is largely gained via the ownership of a variety of assets, including financial assets, land, property and stocks and shares, as well as lucrative government contracts that channel almost effortless income to individuals and companies who are well positioned and have the right contacts. This latter observation has led a number of leading economic figures to argue that we now inhabit an increasingly rentier economy. Of course, all of this tends to contradict the much-promulgated idea that income is related to personal merit and hard work. While, once again, Galbraith questioned the extent to which senior corporate executives engaged in what most people would regard as heavy toil, what's important about the rentier economy is that income is often captured with little or no effort on behalf of the beneficiaries. Despite this, successful people continue to assert that they are self-made.[12]

It seems clear that, in our society, most people who have been successful sustain some form of belief that their success was to some extent inevitable and down to their own efforts, as was briefly mentioned earlier, while this is presented as a badge of honour and a marker of personal worth in neoliberal societies like the UK and the US. Family background, social connections, inheritance and sheer dumb luck never seem to play much of a role in personal accounts. In fact, in line with the meritocratic narrative, the idea that equality of opportunity exists is taken for granted, despite all of the evidence to the contrary. This is often reflected in the back stories presented by aspiring political leaders on both sides of the Atlantic where the key contenders are usually assiduous in making this claim, often downplaying the role of private education, family wealth and the social status of the areas and schools where they were raised in their rise through the ranks. As was noted previously, this is a powerful idea that goes deep into the American psyche and one which has greatly influenced UK citizens since the 1980s. The rags to riches Horatio Alger myth and similar Scottish 'kailyard' tales, as mentioned in Chapter 3, underpin a longstanding narrative that we forge our own social and economic destiny.

Social mobility

What these success stories convey is the notion that social mobility is always accessible to those willing to try. As well as being expounded by conservatives on both sides of the Atlantic, this was also an aspect of the accommodation with neoliberalism by Blair's New Labour and Clinton's Democrats. In short, as suggested earlier, higher levels of inequality were deemed tolerable so long as open, free market economies allowed for a great deal of opportunity and advancement. However, once again, this has proved misleading. In the first instance, for reasons that will be explored in more detail later on, as well as being among the most unequal of the larger developed economies, the UK and the US are actually among the least mobile, with fewer people rising and falling than was the case for the generations that grew up in the more egalitarian postwar period. While there are a broad number of factors at play here, one of which relates to the burgeoning accumulation of wealth as well as income at the top, there has also been a focus on education as though this was the key or even the sole criterion determining life chances. However, this idea in and of itself is also highly questionable – as the French sociologist Pierre Bourdieu explained, the education system itself is very far from being an open field.

Bourdieu argues that our overall mental and physical attributes, knowledge, appearance and conduct, our *habitus*, is shaped by our socioeconomic background within social class systems in a manner that is valued or devalued depending on the extent to which these attributes align or otherwise with those valued by the dominant strata of society. The latter shapes our life chances in terms of the way we are evaluated by others and, as such, heavily influence the opportunities that are open to us, including within education systems. Aligned with habitus, Bourdieu refers to three forms of 'capital' (cultural, social and economic) that pupils bring into the education system that greatly influence success or failure. In terms of cultural capital, Bourdieu argued that children from well-off families are introduced to a much wider range of experiences than their poorer counterparts, in terms of access to books, the arts, travel and other cultural experiences. They are also likely to have the 'right' accent, linguistic register and demeanour. As such, they are less intimidated by educational settings, have more confidence and are likely viewed by their middle-class teachers as being 'bright'. In terms of the theory informing my own work, these pupils have internalized 'maps' that fit very well with the expectations in educational settings and, hence, there is little of the nervousness and uncertainty experienced by poorer children. Bourdieu recognized this in terms of pupils, and people generally, having a feel for the game that renders success more likely. While social capital – effectively social connections – does not play much of a role at school, it can play a very substantial role thereafter. Pupils who attend private schools and whose parents inhabit influential and well-heeled social circles can translate even moderate and assisted academic success into entry to the best universities and then top jobs. In fact, both attributes taken together are also critical in selection processes. Social capital ensures access to careers that are less open to poorer young people, while the 'polished' are often seen to have the right attributes for top jobs. There is also an issue of expectations here, as better-off children and their parents have an expectation of future success as well as a variety of means to make this happen, while poorer children have fewer realistic opportunities even if they 'aspire' to do so. Finally, economic capital (wealth) plays a huge role in potential success. As well as access to private schools and the best universities, well-off students are more likely to be free of the need to work while studying. Through parental help, they are also much more likely to have the wherewithal to live in major cities when undertaking the unpaid internships that are increasingly a route to top jobs.[13] In addition, for those who do decide to engage in genuine entrepreneurial activity, social connections and access to capital are evidently much enhanced for the children of the rich, while risk taking is much less of a concern if there is the cushion of family wealth to fall back on. And, of course, there is the issue that many of the assertedly self-made inherited their businesses in the first place. All of this undermines social mobility even before the issue of cumulative wealth is addressed.

Accumulating wealth

A key feature of the redistribution of wealth and power in the neoliberal era, of course, relates to the way in which wealth, as well as income, has become increasingly concentrated at the top. This has produced what some commentators have referred to as a new Gilded Age, where societies like the UK and the US are once more dominated by a dynastic plutocratic elite that have effectively appropriated – and continue to appropriate – power, resources, control, stability, security and justice from the mass of citizens.[14] As a range of writers such as Robert Reich, Thomas Piketty, Paul Krugman, Joseph Stiglitz and others have observed, neoliberalism has returned levels of wealth inequality not seen since the 1920s. Referring once more to the sort of claims made by Lord Griffiths, that inequality is the flipside of economic efficiency as those at top use their freedom and resources to generate more for all, just as in the 1920s the very opposite appears to be the case. As was discussed earlier, the concentration of income and wealth at the top reduces demand in an economy, as the rich minority can only purchase so much in terms of volume of goods, while removing spending power from the masses.

This leads to a contraction of demand which has to be resolved in some way. Then as now, the solution, at least in the short term, was the expansion of credit and the inflation of a credit bubble, filling in the gap between people's real earnings and their spending power. As we know, in the 1920s this ran out of road, as it did in the recent era in 2007/2008, producing banking crises and economic hardship. In the 1930s the solution was a New Deal and the introduction of state welfare and redistributive policies that led to the postwar boom and lower inequality across the major Western economies. In response to the 2007/2008 crisis, however, as free market policies continued to dominate, the solution was in the form of bailing out the banking sector and lowering interests to almost zero to restore a level of debt-fuelled spending, asset price inflation and anaemic economic growth. As was argued earlier, numerous liberal economists have long recognized that the inequalities generated in so-called free market economies are not just socially destructive but undermine the stability of the economy itself. Nonetheless, real solutions that might push us some way towards greater equity, such as higher real incomes further down the scale or any form of redistribution, remain inconceivable within the current logic. As such, and given the way in which the growth of wealth feeds on itself through the accumulation of rents and assets that generate ever-expanding returns, the divide between wealth holders and the rest continues to grow. This is particularly acute with respect to key assets like housing, where the buying power of the wealthy has driven up prices, as bricks and mortar remains a useful and solid place to park additional monies, in some cases regardless of the provenance of that money. As was noted in Chapter 7, this is having the effect of removing the prospect of home ownership from upcoming generations, while sequestering a large portion of their future incomes as rent. The prime means of wealth accumulation and generating a semblance of security for increasing numbers of those further down the line, at least without family financial help, has been appropriated by the already wealthy. As Piketty argued, all of this is taking us back to a form of society where social mobility dries up and life chances are largely founded on inheritance, further undermining the notions of freedom, opportunity and meritocracy discussed previously.[15] However, the notion of moving towards a level playing field by seriously applying estate and inheritance taxes that might temper and reverse this scenario has been successfully stigmatized to such an extent that 'death taxes' are hated even by those with no prospect of ever paying them: 'Inheritance tax is arguably the UK's most disliked tax. A recent YouGov poll found that just 20% of people deemed inheritance tax "fair"'.[16]

The suggestion is that ordinary people will be drawn into estate taxes through owning their own homes, grossly overstating the likelihood given the modest values of even the UK's and the US's overpriced houses against the hefty allowances allocated before inheritance taxes start. The argument is that estate taxes are also a grossly unfair tax on a lifetime's work and effectively theft of already-taxed monies, finessing the real situation that inherited wealth is actually unearned income being awarded via a simple accident of birth. It is also leading us towards a scenario where the very privileged may once more become a class who do not work from generation to generation, enjoying the greatest benefits from society while thwarting the life chances and opportunities of the less favoured.

Dream believers

In the UK, Prime Minister Theresa May proclaims that 'I want Britain to be the world's great meritocracy – a country where everyone has a fair chance to go as far as their talent and their hard work will allow' (May 2016). The former US president, Barack Obama, pronounced that 'we are true to our creed when a little girl born into the bleakest poverty knows that she has the same chance to succeed as anybody else'; the new US President Donald Trump argues that 'we must create a level playing field for American companies and workers' (Obama 2013, Trump 2017).[17]

In spite of the above, as was noted earlier, a large portion of the population of nations like the UK and the US continue to accept this scenario. Returning to the way in which our orientation to society operates, we become so reliant on our internalized maps that we are loathe to challenge them ourselves, even where a good deal of the content of what we have internalized has been ideologically imposed from above and our experience may leave us with a gnawing sense of anxious dissonance. It is often only where discrepancies became very obvious and/or intolerable, where the perceived emotional and physical benefits of challenging the system seem to outweigh the costs and, critically, where people are aligned with supportive others who are embarked on the same dissident journey that they are likely to demand real change.[18] However, in the contemporary UK and the US, and in many other developed neoliberal nations, there are numerous further factors working against such a likelihood.

Firstly, many people are deterred from dissenting from such an unequal and unjust system in the belief that they could 'reach the top', or at least that they are somehow aligned with those who are already there. In the first case, the anxieties presented by highly unequal societies often lead people towards fantasizing about success, as the prospect of perpetual subservience and struggle is too hard to contemplate. This is something that motivates both the aspirational and the already privileged. It also seems logical that where people inhabit highly insecure and unequal societies, there is an ever-greater impetus to seek the control and insulation that wealth provides.

Understandably, the greater the divide and the more uncomfortable the perceived 'abyss', the more people are likely to scramble competitively to secure a lifeboat in the form of excessive wealth, perpetuating the conditions that drive its accumulation.

Gross miscalculation regarding the likelihood of achieving overnight success also helps sustain the system, aided and abetted by many of the themes of our contemporary culture. Underscoring the aspirational narratives already discussed, there appears to be host of evidence on television and online that such a prospect is possible. In addition to lotteries that promise that 'it could be you', regardless of the overwhelming odds, people are constantly confronted by a range of others who do not appear to be vastly different from themselves, but who seem to have 'made it'. As was noted earlier, this arises often for little or no discernible reason other than 'personality' via game shows and reality television. It is no accident that in capitalist societies generally, and neoliberal societies in particular, we have highly publicized individual competitions of almost every conceivable nature from cookery, talent shows of various form and sports. The latter two are of course aligned with the entertainment, film, music and sports industries that, alongside the new breed of online influencers, appear to provide evidence that we inhabit meritocratic and socially mobile societies. These kinds of representations also imply that upward mobility is a fairly accessible trajectory rather than a conduit through which a tiny segment of the poor and very lucky are picked out of the crowd and move up, at least temporarily. They also further normalize the notion that excessive wealth, income and lifestyle are simply the reward for being uniquely endowed. This, of course, is also worthy of further scrutiny.

As above, and as was noted in Chapter 8, many new 'celebrities' appear to have been plucked from the crowd for reasons that are indiscernible. However, in terms of those who do appear to have significant talent in the arts, media and sports, the role of luck and timing in their journey to prominence is often overlooked, ignoring the legions of the similarly aspirational and closely talented who didn't make it through. There is also the question of the level of reward associated with achieving a prominent position in these areas where, as with the business and financial world, a huge divide appears to have opened up between those at the very top, who enjoy stratospheric incomes, and those in the lower divisions whose earnings are much more modest. The rewards for the 'anointed' in these areas have been greatly boosted by the increasing demands and effectiveness of entertainments and sports agents, and the huge salaries, sponsorship deals and other celebrity rewards captured on behalf of big names. In terms of those a little further down the pecking order, the rewards appear much more modest or even relatively meagre than they were in the past. In film and music, relative incomes have been greatly affected by the advent of online streaming, where the incomes of those beyond the elite have been significantly squeezed, while in sport, second rankers are unable to attract the huge premiums and endorsements accrued by those at the very top.

However, as was noted previously, as society has returned to historical levels of inequality, the most prestigious and favoured positions, including within culture and the arts, have increasingly been taken up by the children of the privileged themselves, as the 'funemployed' have squeezed out the upstart working classes in many of the more attractive spheres. In fact, it is often overlooked just how far many prominent positions in the arts and entertainment have been accessed by the offspring of the previous generation of the glitterati with the advent of the so-called 'nepo-baby' phenomenon, illustrating the increasingly powerful relationship between power, privilege and connections in enabling access to a seat at the top table. Of course, for example, acting dynasties have often been associated with the film industry; nonetheless, privileged access appears to be an ever more prevalent phenomenon in the current era.

Finally, we have the business programmes and competitions that promise a seat at the top table for those with the 'right stuff', feeding the dreams of young entrepreneurs of the future. However, the reality is that while a tiny number will get lucky enough to get through, as suggested, security, resources and connections will ensure that the privileged will smooth the way to the most lucrative futures for their own descendants.[19]

Co-opting the masses

Of course, as was noted earlier, those who can be kept onside through becoming part of the establishment themselves are evidently very few and far between. while the system could not be assured without a wider constituency. This, I would argue, is achieved through the creation of a descending hierarchy of *perceived inclusion*. In closest orbit and often dovetailing with the 1 per cent of high net-worth individuals are the 'courtiers' of this new *ancien régime*; the politicians, corporate managers, well-placed lawyers, accountants, agents, and sundry executives who serve but don't quite belong to the highest echelons of the elite themselves. The rewards of belonging to this group can, of course, be prodigious, also conferring enviable lifestyles upon its members. What defines this strata is that they are close enough to engage directly with those at the top, even to socialize to a greater or lesser extent, and to frequent many of the exalted and exclusive establishments occupied by the 'A listers'.

Beyond that is a wider group of those at arm's length who perform functions in relatively senior roles, but beyond the view of the big guns, except on limited and formal occasions. Similarly, there are the coterie of decorators, PR people, events organizers, high-end real estate agents, fashion gurus, jewellers, caterers and hoteliers, and sundry other facilitators who meet the elites' less direct needs. Here there appears to be a greater sense of unease in such relationships and a great deal of what might be described as courtly deference, a scenario that becomes very obvious when listening to some of the individuals offering services to the rich, who often exude an air of both unabashed snobbery linked with an air of fawning subservience, as evidenced on an expanding number of TV programmes concerning the lives of the elite. This may reflect both incorporation into the system of privilege, and ambiguity and unease regarding their own position as their personal prestige is simply by association and, hence, can be tenuous and temporary.

The vast majority of people, of course, live out their lives beyond these exalted circles and occupy a wide range of less well-rewarded and connected positions that, for many, still manage to bind them to the values of a system that rewards them unevenly and insecurely. Perhaps the best placed are the traditional and new professions, the non-elite lawyers, medics, business and IT professionals, academics, journalists and artists of various guises who continue to enjoy a decent and relatively secure income with benefits, together with a level of personal autonomy, status and sense of self-worth. While many of this group may not be particularly enamoured with the system and may rail against its flaws, they often have little pressing need to change it, as their potential losses may well exceed their gains. However, once again, this excludes the mass of people.

As was argued in Chapter 6, for the mass of those beyond the relatively insulated, allegiance to the system is largely maintained by a mix of fear, pragmatic accommodation, anxious enthusiasm or surly and fatalistic acceptance. For the vast majority, attempting to gain small advancements while keeping one's nose clean and playing ball is a means of gaining a foothold and avoiding being removed from an insecure position and falling into the abyss (for more on this, see the discussion later on). In many workplaces, including some of those that I occupied myself pre-academia, there are clear systems of control to ensure compliance and at least overt devotion to the firm and the values of those above, as was also discussed in Chapter 6. Middle and junior managers are evidently controlled through the promise of promotion if they reflect the right attitudes and values, often resulting in presentism and unpaid overwork as people seek advancement or merely to keep their positions where downsizing might be a recurrent possibility.

Advancement might also be used as a carrot for the lower orders, as Guy Standing notes in *The Precariat*, but may be more symbolic than financial, offering minor 'rewards' of status and prestige with minimal gains in terms of remuneration and benefits, through the 'uptitling' discussed earlier, where people are promoted by giving them a new role and standing in the firm rather than significantly more money or job security.[20] Finally, for those in the lowest ranks, control is exercised through often overwhelming (and expanding) systems of surveillance, generating an anxious and either deluded or grudging capitulation to the realities of lowly status and reward, only assuaged by the (often temporary) salve of having avoided joining those outside the system. The latter, of course, has become an ever-fearful and forbidding place by design since the onset of the neoliberal era. It is fear of the abyss that keeps many beyond the most secure and financially insulated in line and, paradoxically, as will be discussed in Chapter 11, when distress leads to incipient revolt, it is often cynically subverted and exploited in support of the very system that has generated these woes.

The abyss: reinventing the undeserving poor

One of the widely recognized hallmarks of the neoliberal era has been the marked shift in the way in which the poor in societies like the UK and the US have been perceived and treated by the wider society. This has been a long-running historical issue for these and, indeed, other developed economies, characterized by a changing landscape of poverty that has evolved historically in line with the shifting social, economic and moral climate. A shift towards more negative treatment of the poor that has affected many societies has arguably been more acute in Anglo-Saxon economies. Undoubtedly, this reflects the more intense application and embracing of the neoliberal credo in these nations. This has heralded a return to what were once thought to be anachronistic attitudes to poverty, but which have been disinterred with the revival of strident free market individualism and the belief that the poor, as with the rich, are largely responsible for their own fate. Such attitudes have allowed neoliberal governments to renege on the social contract and hard-won rights of citizenship that had been normalized in the postwar era, enabling the ever-evolving imposition of inequality, poverty and even destitution on increasing numbers of people, including children, in nominally rich societies:

> There has been a shameful increase in the level of destitution in the UK, with a growing number of people struggling to afford to meet their most basic physical needs to stay warm, dry, clean and fed. This has deep and profound impacts on people's health, mental health and prospects; it also puts strain on already overstretched services ... approximately 3.8 million people experienced destitution in 2022, including around one million children. This is almost two-and-a-half times the number of people in 2017 and nearly triple the number of children. Such high and increasing levels of destitution have no place in a country like ours.[21]

Poverty in the United States is extensive and deepening under the Trump administration whose policies seem aimed at removing the safety net from millions of poor people, while rewarding the rich, a U.N. human rights investigator has found. Philip Alston, U.N. special rapporteur on extreme poverty, called on U.S. authorities to provide solid social protection and address underlying problems, rather than 'punishing and imprisoning the poor'.[22]

With respect to the preceding pronouncement by Philip Alston, unsurprisingly he expressed a very similar view regarding welfare policy and poverty in the UK. Moreover, his successor, Olivier De Schutter, on a 2023 follow-up visit to the UK, asserted that the situation had worsened to the extent that the low level of welfare provision, particularly given resurgent inflation, effectively constituted a 'violation of international law' with respect to human rights and protection of the poor.[23] Against this background, under neoliberal governments welfare is gradually being outsourced to the growing number of food banks and other charity providers struggling to plug the growing gaps in contracting safety nets.

Confronting the poor

Historically, attitudes towards the poor in societies like the UK were heavily influenced by Christian values. In the Middle Ages, the poor were often viewed sympathetically with little sense that people were personally or morally deficient in having fallen on hard times. However, as was discussed in Chapter 2, the attitudes of the authorities began to change after the events surrounding the Black Death. The contraction of the medieval workforce and serfs leaving their employers to seek higher wages elsewhere became issues of contention, threatening the feudal social order. The Statute of Labourers and other legal moves introduced a strong element of compulsion in relation to work, wages and attitudes to idleness and poverty. All able-bodied people were effectively compelled to work without leaving their employers and were prohibited from demanding higher wages than were prevalent before the plague. Idleness, without good reason, was now viewed as contributing to the shortage of labour and was subject to punishment as a personal vice. Until the mid-1500s, unemployment and, in particular, begging and vagrancy were treated as criminal acts that were subject to harsh punishment. By the 1500s, however, many people were losing agricultural work as more land was taken from arable farming and used for sheep farming. At the same time, the dissolution of the monasteries under Henry VIII had reduced important avenues of support. Consequently, the authorities began to take more responsibility for the provision of work and for relief of the poor. This informed the institution of the English Poor Laws and the giving of outdoor relief in the early modern period. However, this was allied to the notion that everyone who was capable should be put to work. Where this had been arranged by the authorities, there was often little control over the nature of this work, while people were restricted from leaving employers without permission. By the 17th and 18th centuries, the Poor Laws had evolved to become a system where food and clothing were provided to those without work as a temporary measure intended to tide them over.[24] This was paid for by a tax on land and buildings that provided the means by which poor families could be helped through temporary hard times. In some ways this was rational for the better off, as it could be seen to sustain the rural workforce during lean times, leaving them available for work when things improved. It might also be argued that in small rural pre-industrial communities, people would tend to know one another, rendering poverty more visible and empathy more likely. However, this system did not survive the industrialization and urbanization of the 19th century.

In the industrial cities there appeared to be a further hardening of attitudes towards the poor. Much of this can be understood with the greater atomization of society and the emergence of a society of strangers. There were also increasing concerns regarding the aforementioned 'dangerous classes' in the cities, and that people should be industrious and work for themselves and their families, and should not be allowed to call easily on help from others. As such, the loosening of community bonds, together with motivating the new industrial workforce to accept more onerous working conditions and lives than they had experienced in the countryside, required intervention. It is interesting to note that in Britain, this led to the introduction of a new revised Poor Law in 1834 informed by the principle of *less eligibility* and focused on the urban workhouse as the main means of support for the destitute. The notion of less eligibility proposed that the lives of those who accessed public support should be more limited in terms of access to necessities than those available to the very poorest of the urban workforce, which was of itself very scant as exploitation was endemic. Again, the notion of compulsion to work was central, together with an association of poverty with vice and personal moral failure, a condition institutionalized in the form of the workhouse. The poorest came to greatly fear the privations of the workhouse, the default destination for England's 19th-century urban poor. In addition to meagre provision of food, there was a prodigious loss of freedom and dignity. Families were separated – husbands from wives and children from parents. Adults were engaged in long hours of mind-numbing hard work, breaking stones, picking oakum and so on, while many had to wear workhouse uniforms that emphasized the stigma of their position. Such was the fear and antipathy towards the system that a class of *crawlers* emerged in 19th-century London, referring to people who were so desperate, destitute, undernourished and exhausted by lack of sleep on the city streets that they would be observed around the poorer areas living on whatever scraps and assistance they could procure rather than accepting the tender mercies of the workhouse.[25]

Provision for the poor in America followed a similar pattern, given that it was highly influenced by the practices and values that had been prevalent in the mother country.[26] Outdoor relief was gradually replaced by the US 'poorhouse', a broad workhouse equivalent. However, in the US, the pioneering ethos and the fact that people could more readily move and potentially find opportunities elsewhere perhaps provided for a less intense and systematic regime of poverty, at least for a time.

Of course, as was described earlier, from the early 20th century onwards, a more enlightened system of relief for the old, the infirm and, eventually, the unemployed began to take shape in the UK, driven by Unionism, Chartism and a growing sense that there should be rights as well as obligations associated with citizenship. The shared experience of the 1930s depression and war provided the impetus for the further shift in attitudes and policy related to poor relief for both economic reasons, to sustain aggregate demand during slumps, and to maintain social and political stability. While there remained a distaste for wilful idleness, citizens of the UK and the US began to expect that their governments should look after them in times of trouble.

However, since the 1980s, of course, employers and the better off have demanded that governments should once more regulate the masses in their favour. While the impact on work, housing and related factors has already been addressed, the move away from redistribution and welfare was a key element of the new settlement. As well as anti-trade union legislation, the workforce was considered to require a curtailing of its power in other ways. As such, the age-old tried-and-tested methods described earlier of fear, necessity and compulsion have re-emerged together with familiar 'moral' arguments to support their implementation. To achieve this disciplining of the workforce, as well as looser employment protections, welfare had once more to become more threadbare and conditional. This is a critical point that is often overlooked in popular debates on rising insecurity and poor wages and conditions. While many poorer workers have been encouraged to view the unemployed as opponents and parasitical dependants, being subsidized from their hard-earned incomes via the tax system, there is a failure to understand the wider implications of the austerity policies that neoliberal governments have pursued. Firstly, increased conditionality and poorer provision of welfare for the needy, in and of itself, drives down wages and conditions for everyone as more people are forced by necessity to accept what is on offer. The real fear of destitution, homelessness, hunger and cold, which were once thought to have been vanquished in developed nations, but which has returned with a vengeance by design, may also be seen to operate as an instrument of control and oppression, instilling a sense of fear that is creeping up the social hierarchy. Secondly, the lack of a reasonable safety net subtly undermines the scope for the poor to escape the bottom end of the social hierarchy. As was noted earlier, a withered safety net together with increasing compulsion to take any employment that is available, under threat of sanctions that all support will be capriciously withdrawn, removes breathing space where people might previously have taken stock and explored alternative opportunities for career development or even started a business. Many an important career in the arts was also aided by the wherewithal to take some state-supported time out from the daily grind, a scenario associated with numerous well-known bands, actors, artists and writers. While none of the latter would have lived anything like a life of ease at that time, benefits would have provided a modicum of space to develop a career and get a foot on the ladder.[27] By contrast, the contraction of welfare and increasingly harsh conditionality may in some small way help us understand the aforementioned return of the better off to acting, popular music and other areas of cultural prominence.

Achieving a shift in public consciousness to allow for the denigrating of welfare has also followed a familiar pattern on both sides of the Atlantic, to persuade the public that the poor and unfortunate are largely lazy, fake and/or immoral and, critically, that they are 'different' from the majority. In the UK this rhetoric has employed imagery undeserving 'scroungers' or 'shirkers' living off of the largesse of their 'hard-working' contemporaries, with the clear implication that their call on state support is often illegitimate or fraud-ridden. It has also been a key feature of conservative pillorying of the poor, by right-wing politicians and the media, that the unemployed have chosen this lifestyle as it is more comfortable than the lives of the *hard working*. Of course, in the UK, this discourse also covered the tracks of the fact that Thatcherite neoliberal/monetarist policies aimed at squeezing out inflation had destroyed much of British industry in short order, adding millions to the unemployment statistics. Many, and particularly older men, were parked on disability benefits, never to re-enter the workforce. Nonetheless, the mantra of 'hard workers versus scroungers' was instilled in the public consciousness via a campaign of 'othering' and deliberate stigmatization aimed at the unemployed and the poor, becoming a longstanding neoliberal mantra. This re-invoking of the 19th-century discourse of 'less eligibility' described earlier can also be seen to have informed the narrative presented by the Cameron government's austerity Chancellor, George Osborne, with his introduction of ever more punitive sanctions and benefit caps.[28] This was the same government that fairly successfully shifted culpability for the 2007/2008 financial crisis from the underregulated banking sector – its actual source – to pin this on the previous Labour government's alleged overspending on the public sector and, mainly, welfare. As such, by sleight of hand, the poor were deemed culpable for the malfeasance of the rich, most of whom walked away unscathed.

In the US, welfare policy also became central territory of the neoliberal re-alignment, with welfare becoming even more piecemeal, degrading and time-limited than in the UK. One other difference in the way in which this was handled related to the particular version of the rhetoric aimed at demonizing the poor. Conservative politicians' depiction of so-called 'deadbeat dads' and 'welfare queens', while containing similar tropes relating to the unemployed living well on the backs of the majority, also had clearly racist overtones in the US. Once again, the poor were depicted as being lazy, feckless and parasitical, but with the clear implication that they were also more likely to be Black.[29] This has the effect of using pre-existing stigmas and disadvantage as a way into piling on more, while drawing a divide between poor Black, White and Latin Americans.

In contemporary neoliberal societies, stigmatizing imagery associated with poverty, unemployment and state support has become a central aspect of the common culture, reinforced through the media as much as the cult of competitive aspiration. TV documentaries depict the lives of the poor, often selecting the least relatable, respectable and appealing characters, sustaining dominant negative stereotypes. This 'poverty porn', a form of contemporary media output that presents the poor as beyond the pale, functions to sustain the neoliberal 'immoral' order in a variety of ways. As the theoretical framework presented here makes clear, difference can be both a source of curiosity or fear or both depending on the extent of that difference and how it is confronted. This is certainly the case with majority attitudes to those at the bottom of society. There is distaste but also prurient interest. This has been captured through an array of confrontational programming, like Jerry Springer's once-infamous talk shows or Jeremy Kyle's ill-fated daily diatribe in the UK. Here, the poor in general were depicted as being feral as well as feckless, leaving the audience with the vicarious pleasure of observing open conflict among the 'rabble', together with the reassuring satisfaction that the poor were not people like them.[30] This latter point is critical, as the harshest unempathetic treatment and disregard is much easier to apply to those who 'are not like us'.[31] This is a sharp form of the 'symbolic violence' that Pierre Bourdieu argued maintained unequal social structures.[32] It has also been a key feature of the campaign to divide potential allies against neoliberal exploitation and to co-opt those who remain compliant.

One further factor related to the re-emergence of vast structural inequalities and the pillorying of the poor rests on notions of 'dependency' and the various unrecognized ironies with which it is associated. Neoliberal politicians have long railed against the so-called 'dependency culture', the 'something for nothing' attitude that they ascribe to the poor. And yet, as we know, tax evasion and avoidance, tax breaks, government grants, financial bailouts and questionable public sector contracts, all of which benefit the rich, may place an infinitely greater burden on state finances than anything associated with the poor. Also, the notion of dependency itself is depicted as being morally corrosive in terms of the character and aspirations of the lower orders, as the largesse of meagre benefits received are alleged to ultimately only harm their prospects. However, the question that rarely seems to be asked is why the right are then so opposed to inheritance taxes and estate duties. By the same logic, the huge windfalls of unearned income received by the offspring of the rich would surely be much more corrosive and the state would only be assisting in rectifying this. However, as with much of the earlier discussion (and indeed with respect to many of the issues addressed throughout this book), the neoliberal moral framework undergoes whatever contortions are necessary to fit the interests of its architects and beneficiaries.

The damage done

While the preceding discussion sets out a number of the issues associated with the unequal and unjust society that has evolved since the implementation of the neoliberal model, the damage experienced for many across society is incalculable, as well as for the wider society and beyond, as will be set out in the final chapters. A central issue is that, as argued, insecure and divided societies are clearly more fearful and angry. People live ever more distant lives in secluded spaces, breaking down trust and security in the company of 'others'. Fear is expressed through the gating that now pervades our built environment. The rich defend the system often as much out of fear as greed, although the latter is a motivating factor while, as indicated earlier, fear of falling also makes greater accumulation and the exercise of influence to support that more likely. The levels of accumulation at the top have effectively entrenched the elite's position and have created social closure for most of the ranks below, while a balance of desperate aspiration, anxiety and despair is ever more pervasive the further down the ranks and the closer to the abyss people find themselves. The emotional consequences of this are profound and will be dealt with more directly in Chapter 12. However, one of the key issues for those at or near to the bottom or our society is the constant experience of both fear and shame. As *The Social Map* model proposes, living with constant fearful thoughts as to how you are going to maintain a job, avoid redundancy, meet elusive targets, manage punishing platform work, juggle the family finances and sustain accommodation places an intolerable burden of experiential overload. Eventually, a gnawing and, often, poorly articulated sense of injustice sets in that is constantly challenged by the ideological outpourings of the neoliberal media insisting that people's dire situation and disappointment is 'their own fault'.[33]

A sense of justice

As was noted earlier, amid rising inequality and within the context of the neoliberal settlement, UK and US politicians from the major parties began to subscribe to the view that inequality was not particularly problematic, with the caveat that New Labour and the Democrats retained some sense of obligation to mitigate excessive poverty. Policymaking was, hence, tailored towards providing some minimum wage guarantees and support low-income households. In short, the prior focus on redistribution and tackling intergenerational inequality had given way to a more laissez-faire approach with increasingly conditional assistance targeted at the poorest. However, beyond poverty, the problem is that inequality (and insecurity) is highly problematic in and of itself when it comes to negatively impacting on people and societies. This is something that was notably identified in Wilkinson and Pickett's 2009 work *The Spirit Level*.[34] As epidemiologists, Wilkinson and Pickett's exploration of the social determinants of health widened to apply the same principles to study the relationship between inequality and a range of other indicators of societal wellbeing, finding a similar relationship, suggesting that inequality seemed to be associated with a wide range of social problems. Of course, the work was widely critiqued by neoliberals. However, as I have argued elsewhere, there are good reasons as to why Wilkinson and Pickett's analysis is compelling. Firstly, as we engage with the world, we are constantly monitoring our experience in relation to the internalized model that has been shaped by the set of influences we've been exposed to throughout our socialization. Issues arise, however, when what has been internalized is significantly contradicted by experience. As was noted earlier, we are wired to detect anything that deviates from our normative expectations, triggering an emotional alarm. In terms of inequality, many people generally accept that their societies are unequal and, while they may not like this very much, it is often accepted as the way of the world and the dissonance is not too jarring. The degree to which we have accepted ideological tropes in terms of meritocracy evidently influences these responses. Yet, some instances of inequality seem to be more acceptable to most people than others, as we tend to accept relatively high rewards for individuals who we genuinely feel have very unique talents – admired actors, musicians, inventors, pioneering medics and so on. The key issue is perceived fairness, taking us back to some of the issues discussed at the outset of this chapter.

Robert Reich, among others, has notably pointed to the way in which neoliberalism has provided ample opportunity for those with wealth to 'rig the system' in their own favour.[35] As I argued in Chapter 5, there was perhaps no clearer example of this than the way in which those in the financial sector receive increasingly huge rewards that seem to be detached from any plausible rationale or real contribution. As with the increasingly lavish earnings enjoyed by corporate CEOs, the impression is given that reward is less related to individual skill and effort, but is more generally a consequence of individuals' power and proximity to sources of wealth, and the capacity to capture increasing amounts, thinly justified by some post hoc rationalization asserting that these are rewards for success and so on. However, these justifications tend to fall away when the rewards seem to keep coming regardless of performance and even in the midst of dramatic failure.

It is when people begin to see such rewards as being disproportionate and unjustly gained and distributed that appears to cause disquiet, particularly when their own efforts and aspirations seem to be unrecognized and under-rewarded. Of course, rightly or wrongly, most of us feel a bit like this from time to time. The real issue arises when the problem becomes systemic, as is increasingly seen to be the case after so many decades of increasingly bold appropriation. Those on the outside are provided with a vision of lifestyles to which they will never have access. As was discussed in Chapter 8, this has become ever more prevalent in the era of reality television and social media. The dissonance generated by internalized notions of how the world should be and the disjuncture between aspiration and desperation depicted in the media simply compounds such feelings. In darker moments, there may also be shame and self-reproach where a person entertains the notion that perhaps their less favoured situation is really down to being not quite good enough rather than the structural inequities that surround them, adding to the fear and frustration as nascent hopes are eroded by the reality of experience.[36]

Problems arise then when admiration falters and resignation turns to resentment, where growing numbers begin to question the negative assumptions around their own failings and begin to entertain the notion that the system is indeed rigged, and that they are no less deserving than the majority of the favoured. Anger and frustration quickly follow, of course, accompanied by declining trust and legitimacy regarding socioeconomic and political systems that produce and maintain the divisive and seemingly unfair aspects of contemporary societies. It can clearly be argued that this is where we are now for growing numbers in the UK, the US and many other developed economies, particularly since the financial crisis of 2007/2008, the austerity that followed and the way in which the COVID-19 pandemic and global conflict have further destabilized the lives of ordinary citizens, while those at the top seemed to prosper more than ever. Revelations around malfeasance of various forms that have been revealed over the last decade or so have also increasingly begun to pierce the patina of plausibility around neoliberal rhetoric, feeding popular discontent. However, the paradoxical manner in which this, together with the other psychosocial woes of living in neoliberal societies, has been exploited, channelled and redirected will be picked up in the next chapter.

Notes

1   'Income inequality', https://data.oecd.org/inequality/income-inequality.htm

2   Peters, M.A. (2018) 'The end of neoliberal globalisation and the rise of authoritarian populism', *Educational Philosophy and Theory*, 50(4): 323–325.

3   Milanović, B. (2020) 'Trump as the ultimate triumph of neoliberalism', *Global Policy Journal*, https://www.globalpolicyjournal.com/blog/14/05/2020/trump-ultimate-triumph-neoliberalism

4   Giroux, H.A. (2017) 'White nationalism, armed culture and state violence in the age of Donald Trump', *Philosophy & Social Criticism*, 43(9): 887–910, at 889.

5   Bell, T., Fry, E., Kelly, G., Murphy, L., Thwaites, G. and Tomlinson, D. (2022) *Stagnation Nation: Navigating a Route to a Fairer and More Prosperous Britain*, https://economy2030.resolutionfoundation.org/wp-content/uploads/2022/07/Stagnation_nation_interim_report.pdf

6   'Lord Brian Griffiths of Fforestfach (and Goldman Sachs) says his paychecks make you rich', *Time Magazine*, 22 October 2009, https://business.time.com/2009/10/22/lord-brian-griffiths-of-fforestfach-and-goldman-sachs-says-his-paychecks-make-you-rich/

7   Harvey, D. (2007) *A Brief History of Neoliberalism*, Oxford: Oxford University Press.

8   Kunda, Z. (1990) 'The case for motivated reasoning', *Psychological Bulletin*, 108(3): 480–498.

9   Hindy, Y. (2015) 'The "terrible simplifiers" of totalitarianism: how certainty can ruin a population', *The Stanford Freedom Project*, https://stanfordfreedomproject.com/what-is-freedom-new-essays-fall-2015/the-terrible-simplifiers-of-totalitarianism-how-certainty-can-ruin-a-population/

10 West, E. and Nelson, F. (2013) 'The strange death of the British middle class', *The Spectator*, 24 August.

11 Frank, R.H. and Cook, P.J. (1996) *The Winner-Takes-All Society: Why the Few at the Top Get So Much More Than the Rest of Us*, Harmondsworth: Penguin.

12 Galbraith, J.K. (2004) *The Economics of Innocent Fraud*, Boston: Houghton Mifflin.

13 Bourdieu, P. (1984) *Distinction*. London: Routledge.

14 Giroux, H.A. (2008) 'Beyond the biopolitics of disposability: rethinking neoliberalism in the new Gilded Age', *Social Identities*, 14(5): 587–620; Krugman, P. (2018) 'Why we're in a new Gilded Age', in H. Boushey, J. Bradford DeLong and M. Steinbaum (eds), *After Piketty*, Cambridge, MA: Harvard University Press, pp 60–72.

15 Piketty, T. (2014) *Capital in the Twenty-First Century*, Cambridge, MA: Harvard University Press.

16 https://ifs.org.uk/publications/reforming-inheritance-tax

17 Littler, J. (2017) *Against Meritocracy: Culture, Power and Myths of Mobility*, Abingdon: Taylor & Francis.

18 Bone, J. (2005) 'The social map & the problem of order: a re-evaluation of "homo sociologicus"', *Theory & Science*, 6(1): 1–20.

19 Littler, J. (2017) *Against Meritocracy: Culture, Power and Myths of Mobility*, Abingdon: Taylor & Francis.

20 Standing, G. (2011) *The Precariat: The New Dangerous Class*, London: Bloomsbury.

21 Fitzpatrick, S. et al (2023) *Destitution in the UK 2023*, York: Joseph Rowntree Foundation, p 1.

22 'America's poor becoming more destitute under Trump – UN expert', *Reuters*, 2 June 2018, https://www.euronews.com/2018/06/02/americas-poor-becoming-more-destitute-under-trump-un-expert

23 'UK "in violation of international law" over poverty levels, says UN envoy', *The Guardian*, 5 November 2023, https://www.theguardian.com/society/2023/nov/05/uk-poverty-levels-simply-not-acceptable-says-un-envoy-olivier-de-schutter

24 Quigley, W.P. (1996) 'Five hundred years of English Poor Laws, 1349–1834: regulating the working and nonworking poor', *Akron Law Review*, 30: 73–128.

25 Thomson, J. and Smith, A. (1877) *Street Life in London*, London: S. Low, Marston, Searle & Rivington.

26 Quigley, W.P. (1996) 'Five hundred years of English Poor Laws, 1349–1834: regulating the working and nonworking poor', *Akron Law Review*, 30: 73–128.

27 'Role of the dole: How benefits benefit artists', *Irish Times*, 4 August 2012, https://www.irishtimes.com/culture/art-and-design/role-of-the-dole-how-benefits-benefit-artists-1.530599

28 Pantazis, C. (2016) 'Policies and discourses of poverty during a time of recession and austerity', *Critical Social Policy*, 36(1): 3–20.

29 Cammett, A. (2014) 'Deadbeat dads & welfare queens: how metaphor shapes poverty law', *Boston College Journal of Law & Social Justice*, 34: 233–265.

30 'Jeremy Kyle Show "undermines anti-poverty efforts", says thinktank', *The Guardian*, 10 September 2008, https://www.theguardian.com/politics/2008/sep/10/thinktanks.socialexclusion

31 Garthwaite, K. (2016) 'Stigma, shame and "people like us": an ethnographic study of foodbank use in the UK', *Journal of Poverty and Social Justice*, 24(3): 277–289.

32 Bourdieu, P. (1984) *Distinction*, London: Routledge.

33 Littler, J. (2017) *Against Meritocracy: Culture, Power and Myths of Mobility*, Abingdon: Routledge.

34 Wilkinson, R. and Pickett, K. (2009) *The Spirit Level: Why More Equal Societies Almost Always Do Better*, vol. 6, London: Allen Lane.

35 Reich, R.B. (2020) *The System: Who Rigged It, How We Fix It*, New York: Vintage.

36 Littler, J. (2017) *Against Meritocracy: Culture, Power and Myths of Mobility*, Abingdon: Routledge.

11

Populism and the Politics of Primalization

> Things that for many decades were givens – the checks and balances on the executive, the role of the judiciary or the civil service, a media free from interference or vilification – now appear vulnerable. Things that once would have shocked us now seem commonplace. The ministerial code violated with impunity.[1]

The above could refer to any number of allegedly undemocratic or marginally democratic nations that people inhabiting the UK, dominated by the 'mother of parliaments' and adorned with the assumed hubris of being a model of democracy, would once have disparaged as authoritarian states. Now that slippage appears to represent a credible threat to the UK's own taken-for-granted 'rational' political organization. Similarly, across the Atlantic, that other global beacon of freedom and democracy experienced what to all intents and purposes was regarded by numerous commentators to be a potential coup attempt on 6 January 2021, as will be discussed in more detail later on.

Returning to the situation in the UK, the behaviour of Boris Johnson and his government during his relatively brief period in office was less dramatic, but also displayed a notable disdain and disregard for the conventions that had governed British political behaviour for most of the 20th and early 21st centuries. In addition to the headline 'offences' associated with so-called 'Partygate', there was a general sense that the loose constitution and tacit guidance that had been once taken for granted had been overridden by a populist Prime Minister who had less regard for rules and restraint than his predecessors, at least when applied to his own conduct and that of his inner circle. Rules appeared to be for the little people and were there to be gotten around by those who considered themselves 'born to rule'. While there had always been a sense of entitlement and hubris among Britain's traditional elite, forged and reinforced in the top public schools and prominent Oxbridge colleges, Johnson's degree of disregard for convention marked something of a departure. As with Trump, rather than gentlemanly condescension within the parameters of tacit longstanding rules, there was a sense of cynical opportunism, a disdain for longstanding norms, and a defiant unwillingness to accept responsibility when culpability for questionable behaviour was called out. In short, both of these politicians broke new ground in terms of how leading political figures in these mature democracies were expected to conduct themselves, often co-opting those around them to support the seemingly indefensible, while simultaneously coarsening and undermining the longstanding political cultures of their respective nations.

There are numerous questions that have arisen from the emergence of these disruptive figures in UK and US politics, including their appeal beyond their respective political parties' traditional constituencies, as well as the way in which their followers tended to overlook or even deny the significance or reality of numerous serious misdemeanours. Moreover, far from being isolated aberrations, this degradation of political conduct by right-wing populist politicians has been a growing global trend, including in other nations assumed to be mature and 'rational' modern democracies. In the UK, while the Conservative Party leadership after Johnson's departure may have been less colourful, in many ways it remains assiduously populist, while moving ever further to the right. Of course, Biden's presidency in the US appeared to mark a pushback against the march towards the consolidation of right-wing, authoritarian populism. However, this political hiatus in an increasingly polarized US was once again of the 'middle ground' flavour, cautious in challenging the excesses of neoliberalism in the face of an increasingly strident and illiberal right and a Republican Party further radicalized by Trump.[2]

Rational to charismatic authority and resurgent autocracy

In many ways, as suggested, Johnson and Trump can be viewed as emissaries of a phenomenon that has been sweeping the world more widely, where longstanding or nominally democratic states have been turning towards populist forms of increasingly anti-democratic authoritarian government, usually of the right. Aside from the world's longstanding and overtly totalitarian states – notably China, Iran and North Korea – Russia, Hungary, Serbia and Turkey have all moved decisively in this direction since the turn of the century, with others across Europe, including Italy, Germany, Sweden, the Netherlands and France, following in their wake to varying degrees. Even in these latter nations, where populists have not actually achieved or consolidated political control, once-marginal radical right-wing movements and parties have been gaining ground as a popular and electorally credible political force.[3] All of this runs counter to the expectations noted earlier that the future of the world would be one dominated by liberal economies and rational democratic government, eclipsing charismatic leaders and ideologically driven regimes.[4]

Until the early part of the 21st century, such claims, like those previously discussed in relation to Fukuyama's 'end of history' thesis, seemed potentially defensible to an extent, albeit that this was highly dependent on one holding a somewhat sanguine view of the neoliberal settlement. Across many nations, there had been an embracing or at least a growing acceptance and accommodation of neoliberalism, so much so that what would have been once considered to be a radically right-wing approach to political and socioeconomic affairs was, as argued, now being presented as the nonideological centre ground. This was very much the case for the triangulating, third way politics of the Clinton and Blair administrations. As was suggested in previous chapters, both had reconciled previously left-of-centre parties, especially in the case of the UK Labour Party, with the neoliberal consensus while effectively consolidating the neoliberal project by removing realistically electable alternatives. Policies were presented as being largely pragmatic, technocratic and rational, focusing on 'what works' as opposed to engaging in a serious social democratic challenge to the political and economic status quo set in train by the preceding conservative administrations they had replaced. This has been, in effect, a key source of the growing political disenfranchisement that will be discussed later on, removing potential channels for those who had lost out in neoliberal societies, and angered by its growing injustices, to express their dissatisfaction effectively via the ballot box. As was suggested in Chapter 4, acceptance of the main tropes of neoliberalism was presented as apolitical common sense, a perspective that the leading nations and supportive global corporations, institutions and media were keen to export globally.

As was noted in earlier chapters, in the discussion of the imperial ambitions of ancient civilizations, all dominant visions of the world, if successful for a time, have tended to view themselves as representing the pinnacle of reason and development that must be extended to educate, persuade or, as a final resort, conquer others to advance the cause and gain acceptance of their creeds. This 'will to power' has been no less evident among Western governments of the early 21st century. Notably, as well as attempting to establish liberal democracy and neoliberal economic management in the post-Cold War Eastern Bloc, there were clear ambitions to 'liberalize' developing economies and those of the Middle East. While the former appeared to be successful for a time in the 1990s, the latter seemed less pliable. Nonetheless, by various covert and overt attempts to undermine and/or otherwise supplant uncooperative governments, what had begun with the early neoliberal experiment in Chile continued in the form of adventures in Latin America, Iraq, Libya and elsewhere in the Middle East.

In part, the latter had been driven by the neoconservative and neoliberal ambitions associated with the Project for the New American Century in the late 1990s and early 2000s, which was informed by the assumption that the undermining of uncompliant regimes would produce a domino effect of Middle Eastern nations overturning autocracy to embrace Western-style democracy and (neo)liberal economies. However, as we now know, in recent decades the pendulum has moved in largely the opposite direction across the globe as, although neoliberal economics remains dominant, autocracy and radically ideological charismatic populists have increasingly challenged the confident consolidators of Western 'democratic' hegemony.[5]

Primalization, populism and post-truth politics

How then did we move so quickly from a period where it was confidently – or, as it turns out, overconfidently – predicted that we were moving towards a more peaceful, integrated and interconnected and consensual world, based on mutual economic interests and advancement, towards one that is increasingly, fractious, divisive and divided to an extent not seen since the 1930s?

The answer to that question may appear self-evident. As was set out in the preceding chapters, an evolving scenario with some important resonances has emerged, particularly since the turn of the new millennium, where we have disinterred many of the economic conditions and, to a degree, social and psychic ills prevalent in the 1930s with broadly similar effects on the political sensibilities of individuals and communities: 'Democracy's most dramatic setback, which came in the 1930s, when fascism spread over much of Europe, was partially driven by economic decline.'[6] Thus, rampant inequality and insecurity amid economic upheaval, fostered by laissez-faire economic policies that favour a licentious business and financial elite, and with little regard for the masses, have produced conditions for similar political turmoil. All of these factors are associated with experiential overload and, following from this, the condition of *primalization*, where reasoned, measured responses tend to become overridden by emotional thinking and reactions dominated by fear and anger, as outlined in Chapter 1.[7] In light of this, the appeal and rise of charismatic demagogues promising simplistic solutions, stability and order while offering a positive vision, identity and sense of solidarity and community to fractured, frustrated, demoralized and disenchanted peoples is perhaps unsurprising.

In qualification, this doesn't mean that the rise of contemporary populists is solely due to overwhelming support from the poor and dispossessed, as the picture is of course more complex than that. As was also noted at the end of the last chapter, these discontents and stressors in our own era have been further exacerbated by rising scepticism and distrust in relation to the legitimacy of 'the system' among growing numbers of the public. Hence, what has produced this phenomenon involves a complex of interests, insecurities, grievances, resentments and other motivations, which would presumably also have been the case in the 1930s.

At times of significant economic and social uncertainty, many of the better off and the relatively well heeled may also be drawn to right-wing populists who promise order and, in particular, defence and security regarding property rights as well as the protection and advancing of business and economic interests. In Johnson and, in particular, Trump's case, some elite and generally affluent support could also be seen to be a matter of simple self-interest as, while each has invoked the gallery of public prejudices and defence of ordinary 'Joe public', actual policy nonetheless appeared greatly geared towards the financial interests of big business and the wealthy.[8]

As to their broader appeal, in insecure and anxious times there is a tendency towards cultural defence and an aversion to the perceived 'contamination' represented by 'outsiders' – foreigners, ethnic minorities, immigrants and a variety of 'others', given that conditions of flux and uncertainty also entail an embracing of clarity and, at times, often a toxic quest for purification.

The latter relates to a tendency once highlighted by the anthropologist Mary Douglas, who pointed to the psychological binary between danger and contamination on the one hand, and safety and purity on the other.[9] This is consistent with the binary nature of human thought that is intrinsic to the construction of *The Social Map*, where the greater exposure to one dimension is often associated with a more insistent pull of the other. Put simply, and as was proposed earlier, in order to sustain a sense of balance, coherence and continuity in bewildering, insecure and frustrating circumstances, people will tend to lean towards strong leaders claiming to fight their corner and neutralize or expunge 'impurity', a state that has clear resonances with the current political direction of travel. As Inglehart observed:

> To a large degree, the shifts between democracy and authoritarianism can be explained by the extent to which people feel that their existence is secure. For most of history, survival was precarious. When food supplies rose, population levels rose with them. When food grew scarce, populations shrank ... During extreme scarcity, xenophobia was a realistic strategy: when a tribe's territory produced just enough food to sustain it, another tribe moving in could spell death for the original inhabitants. Under these conditions, people tend to close ranks behind strong leaders, a reflex that in modern times leads to support for authoritarian, xenophobic parties.[10]

This relationship between the insecurities and inequalities and the tendency towards support for anti-democratic, authoritarian figures, societal exclusion and rigidity is consistent with the deep psychosocial processes I have described thus far. The notion that societies under threat have a tendency to 'tighten' in this way also has clear resonances with Gelfand's previously mentioned work on tight and loose cultures.[11] Such conditions produce a leaning towards defensiveness and preparedness for attack that permeates societies. As was noted earlier, when this is understood in relation to the tendency for chronic stressors to induce a more primal, emotional state among large sectors of a population, the stage is set for personalities who, in more secure, stable and rational times, would most likely have been marginalized and regarded as too extreme to most people to enter the mainstream and achieve electoral credibility. In effect, populists like Johnson and Trump achieved electoral success via emotional appeals to a segment of the downtrodden whose longstanding exposure to experiential overload may have left them in precisely this primalized state; angry, fearful and susceptible to the simplistic, emotion-laden overtures of the populist.

Overall, it is through repetitive sloganeering, visions of re-creating an imagined idyllic past and positive and homogeneous collective identity, underscored by cult-like emotive mass rallies, that a sufficient segment of the alienated and angry working class has been co-opted, bolstering the ranks of the neoliberal right's natural constituency of the wealthy and aspirational middle class sufficiently to produce electoral success.

The regularly highly partisan and divisive rhetoric and policies of such demagogic figures, however, almost invariably create a yawning gulf among the electorate between the populist 'coalition' and the bemused moderates who cleave to the status quo, and who often only perceive the seriousness of the threat to democratic norms once it has reached an advanced stage. Meantime, such widening divisions in the political sphere often lead to the redefining of moderates as being enemies of the people, galvanizing the ire and emotional commitment of populist supporters. As has been argued elsewhere, overall, the budding autocrat appeals to people's fear, anger, their enmities and insecurities, promising a safe space, community and imagined triumphal future that, paradoxically, often relies on invoking sanitized imagery of a more economically orderly and culturally simpler imagined past. Again the resonances with the 1930s appear apposite:

> The readiness to place all hope in 'leadership', in the authority of a 'strong man', has in itself of course not been peculiar to Germany. Promotion by threatened elites and acceptance by anxious masses of strong authoritarian leadership, often personalized in one 'charismatic' figure, has been (and still is) experienced by many societies in which a weak pluralist system is incapable of resolving deep political and ideological rifts and is perceived to be in terminal crisis.[12]

As above, much of this was certainly consistent with the rise of Nazism from the ferment of defeat and the humiliating reparations of the First World War, the latter having greatly exacerbated Weimar Germany's experience of severe economic crises brought on by the Great Crash, while it must be borne in mind that the ailing nation had also been ravaged by the Spanish flu pandemic. In fear of inviting calls of 'Godwin's Law', there are of course differences with what has been happening in terms of the rise of contemporary right-wing authoritarian populism and the epochal events that led to the ascendancy of the Third Reich. Nonetheless, as argued, a number of the underlying and fundamental economic, social and cultural causal factors seem resonant, and not least in terms of disillusioned societies and peoples confronting long-term inequities, insecurity and profound cultural change.

Also, while the 'little corporal' had once been dismissed as a clownish figure, prior to the Nazi propaganda machine's construction of an iconic cult of personality, this also has echoes with public perceptions regarding the seriousness of Trump's entry into the 2016 electoral field, echoing my earlier remarks, where few would have anticipated his securing of the presidential nomination, least of all the presidency, nor would many have imagined the influence he would bring to bear in shaping a national insurgent movement and reforging the traditional Republican Party in his image.[13] Of course, we are not talking about Trump as head of a dictatorship, at least not yet, However, as will be discussed further on, it is now nonetheless clear that the disquieting developments at the end of his presidency, and intemperate noises off since, clearly suggest that US democracy may not be nearly as immune to such a trajectory as much of its population once presumed.

In the UK, Johnson's Brexit-based, albeit less fiery brand of populism did not fare quite so well, as the British establishment and public (including a segment of his own party) had not travelled so far from the norms of political business as usual that the 'unconventional' conduct of the former Prime Minister could be indulged beyond a certain point. Having bent the norms of parliamentary and extraparliamentary conduct well beyond what was customary, despite having weathered several storms due to his own conduct with the backing of his cabinet and many in his party, eventually there was one transgression too many and, as we know, he was forced to resign in the summer of 2022.

What is also interesting, however, is the level of support retained by Johnson, and most particularly Trump, despite their engaging in a wide range of repeated conduct that would, in more moderate times, have abruptly ended a political career. In fact, in Trump's case, his popularity has appeared to run counter to this longstanding trend.

In a sense, simply by assuming the mantle of disruptor, there appeared to be a perception that the normal rules do not apply to these figures.

At least in part, this may have been due to the fact that Johnson and Trump themselves seemed to believe that they were in fact exceptions, given that both had been born into privilege and appeared to retain a very strong sense of personal entitlement. This latter fact rendered their appeal beyond the wealthy and privileged even more puzzling. In Trump's case this could be partially reconciled with his public persona, which was much more New York hustler and wheeler dealer than the inheritor of a significant fortune that he really was. Johnson, however, appeared to be subject of considerable adulation from a significant contingent of the disenfranchised Brexit-embracing working classes who appeared to disregard his old Etonian, Bullingdon Club background, regarding him in terms of the (much cultivated) bumbling and clownish persona of 'good old Boris'. This 'good bloke, man of the people' schtick was also successfully played by former UKIP leader and Johnson's one-time Brexiteer partner Nigel Farage, who in 2023 appeared to declare an interest in assuming Johnson's mantle as populist head of an ever more right-wing Conservative Party.[14]

Of course, public image and personality has always been huge factors in the political realm, becoming ever more prevalent in our mediated age. This was also the case with respect to more centrist politicians such as Clinton, Blair and Obama. However, it can be clearly argued that cultivated personality and public image has never outweighed policy and political conviction in the UK and the US in the modern era to the degree witnessed since the emergence of Trump and Johnson.

The politics of impunity

Skulduggery, intrigue, ambiguity and, at times, even outright corruption have always been a feature of our political systems. However, as well as traducing the normal political cut and thrust to an unprecedented extent, and while politics has often been associated with dissembling and being 'economical with the actualité', in living memory there has perhaps never been such a blatant and unapologetic disregard for facts, evidence and truth within key developed democracies than has been displayed since the emergence of these political figures. Observations that Trump refuted statements he had clearly stated publicly on television[15] or seeing the look on White House Coronavirus Coordinator Dr Deborah Bix as Trump explained on camera that the notion of light inside the body and injecting disinfectant might be a treatment for COVID-19 appeared to represent a new and, at times, bizarre departure from rational political discourse.[16] Johnson's performances, of course, did not normally reach the same level of theatrical farce, Peppa Pig references aside. However, his serial denials of statements and facts that were widely supported by available evidence, and his cabinet's regular dissembling with explanations that went well beyond the regular duplicitous and evasive manoeuvres that were commonplace tactics of UK politicians, breached previous boundaries by some degree. In both cases what was unnerving was the extent to which what seemed clearly obvious and directly and unambiguously observed was directly denied. While, as was noted earlier, Johnson's career ended with a denial too far, this practice has been much more damaging when it comes to Trump.

There has perhaps been no more serious disjuncture between reality and asserted narrative, and indeed the greatest example as to how far political and legal normalcy has been undermined at the heart of Western democracies, than the events surrounding the US presidential election of November 2020 and the aforementioned storming of the US Capitol in Washington DC on 6 January 2021 in an attempt to impede the confirmation of the election result. Across the world's television news channels, we witnessed President Trump repeat his so-called 'big lie' that the election result was fraudulent, a claim he has been charged with knowing to be false,[17] while inciting his base to march on the capital with a view to preventing the confirmation of Biden's win. This, as many commentators observed, was backed by scenes of violence in which five people died and US law makers, including his own Vice President Mike Pence, were hiding in fear for their safety or even their lives.[18] When one considers the revelations that led to the impeachment and almost incarceration of Richard Nixon in the Watergate scandal in 1972, while serious, these seem to pale into insignificance in relation to the events that unfolded between November and January 2021. As Noam Chomsky noted in relation to Trump's unprecedented challenging of political convention:

[A] President who has said if he doesn't like the outcome of an election, he'll simply not leave office, and is taken seriously enough that, for example, two high-level, highly respected, retired military officers – one of them very well known, Lieutenant Colonel John Nagl – actually went to the extent of writing an open letter to General [Mark] Milley, the chairman of the Joint Chiefs of Staff, reminding him of his constitutional duties to send in the American military to remove the President from office if he refuses to leave.[19]

At the very least, what occurred represented a wholly unprecedented challenge to the US's longstanding democratic processes, instigated by its sitting President. As Democratic Representative Bennie Thompson, the chair of the committee investigating the events surrounding 6 January, put it: 'Jan. 6 was the culmination of an attempted coup, a brazen attempt, as one writer put it shortly after Jan. 6, to overthrow the government'. The departure from what had been regarded as normal political cut and thrust of democratic politics sent shock waves across the world, even against the backdrop of the liberties that Trump had already enacted during his term in office. Perhaps most shocking was the suggestion that this may not have been a spur of the moment gripe and galvanization of the disaffected prompted by genuine grievance over an unjust outcome. Rather, Trump's signalling prior to the election that the only way he could lose was if the vote was rigged had led to media commentary implying that the claims were part of a more orchestrated campaign for the 45th President to stay in office:

> President Trump is stepping up his attacks on the integrity of the election system, sowing doubts about the November vote at a time when the pandemic has upended normal balloting and as polls show former Vice President Joseph R. Biden Jr. ahead by large margins.
>
> Having yet to find an effective formula for undercutting Mr. Biden or to lure him into the kinds of culture war fights that the president prefers, Mr. Trump is training more of his fire on the political process in a way that appears intended to give him the option of raising doubts about the legitimacy of the outcome.[20]

Moreover, while Nixon's misdemeanours had fairly swiftly sealed his political fate, the fact that Trump had retained the support of most of his party in the aftermath of a much more serious challenge to democratic probity clearly indicated the degree of slippage from previous norms.

With the events of 6th January, growing divisions within the US appear to have become an open sore, with a significant segment of the population still wedded to if not Trump's MAGA movement per se, then at least the mindset that it fostered. In a real sense the lampooning, ridicule and derision that had once characterized educated liberals' response to Trump's numerous faux pas and indiscretions has given way to a much more serious set of concerns, as these events revealed something darker and more sinister emerging in US politics. The fact that Trump was able to go on to campaign for re-election after this monumental breach – and also continued to be supported by a large constituent of the Republican law makers who had run for cover in the face of their erstwhile leader's angry supporters – also raised alarm bells. This was particularly the case as many of the latter who had displayed dismay at the magnitude of the events on that day began to dissemble and reinterpret the experience as a regular variant of political cut and thrust, which it clearly was not.[21] The seriousness of Trump's threat to US democracy and what he has cultivated and unleashed was taken seriously by incumbent President Biden who, also in a clear break with the conventions that he has followed through a long political career, publicly cited Trump and his supporters as an existential threat and potential source of further anti-democratic activity and violent upheaval, a threat publicly echoed by retiring chair of the US Joint Chiefs of Staff Mark Milley in 2023.[22]

In light of this, we find ourselves in a situation where democracy appears to be substantially under threat by a form of, to some extent, nihilistic authoritarianism even in nations that have long prided themselves in having firmly rooted democracies founded on rational principles? Here it may be argued that politics both shapes and reflects the broader socioeconomic zeitgeist in a sort of feedback loop.

Charting the norms and standards of conduct of the political and business elite, an oligarchy has emerged that has grown ever more distant, unrestrained and self-assured as neoliberal deregulation increasingly pushed back and eroded the boundaries and prohibitions that once constrained their conduct. As was argued earlier, the fundamental mechanisms that contribute to conscience are also at work here, in that the dilution of internalised behavioural norms evidently reduces the potential for the associated emotional injunctions that arise when the latter are transgressed. Moreover, the trend towards deregulation and the licentious, hucksterish attitude that has prevailed in finance and business since the embracing of the neoliberal model can be seen to have accompanied a more general erosion of standards in public life. To some extent this erosion can be seen to have also influenced public expectations, normalising conduct that would have previously been regarded as being beyond the pale. In this climate, what were previously accepted rules and norms become minor hurdles to evade, work around or ignore in the pursuit of corporate profits or personal ambition. As was noted in Chapter 5, this was starkly evidenced in some of the practices that led to the financial crisis. In a very real sense, the equivocal nature of standards, perceived rewards and lack of consequences and accountability for questionable conduct has encouraged a cultural of shamelessness and mendacity that has proliferated across the oligarchic elite in neoliberal societies, while also infecting the political sphere. Johnson and Trump have been exemplars of the phenomenon among the major Western nations, albeit that this has been evident across many neoliberal and, indeed, underregulated nations, producing even more extreme protagonists. Again, it might also be argued that aforementioned personal histories and privileged upbringing of Johnson and Trump may have also doubtless compounded their lack of restraint:

> Johnson and Trump find themselves joining in a common crusade against liberal democracy, and using lies and falsehood to fight their battles. They believe that popular support ('the will of the people') gives them legitimacy to take on elected chambers, the rule of law, the civil service, and also the political parties they lead.[23]

Social media: mainstreaming the fringe

While the individual conduct of some of the central players has evidently contributed to the increasing denigration of democracy, the impact of social media on our identities, commercial and wider culture, as was discussed in Chapter 8, has of course also greatly contributed to the refashioning of political culture. The aforementioned 'filter bubbles' that Eli Pariser notably identified intensify a variety of political affiliations, enmities and prejudices in much the same manner as was discussed with respect to consumer identities and viral trends.[24] As we know, this has emerged in recent years as a critical issue with respect to the radicalization of political discourse and, it follows, of individuals and groups. Finding expression for the pent-up emotional injuries generated in our pressure cooker societies, within groups that offer affiliation and sense of belonging, is a heady mix. It's also the case that, in terms of influence, the repetition and emotionally charged nature of online debate, intensified by some of the mechanisms discussed thus far, leads to greater investment in the groups, beliefs and narratives to which people are regularly exposed.

A good deal of focus in recent decades had been applied to online Islamic radicalization and fear of the latter, particularly after 9/11, other terrorist acts, and the emergence of Al-Qaeda and then the Islamic State. For a time this tended to overshadow an increasing element of right-wing nationalism - growing in tandem with the expansion of so-called Alt and far-right discourse - that has been bound up with the MAGA and Brexit movements associated with Trump and Johnson respectively, with supporting roles played by Farage and host of other right-wing politicians and media pundits.[25] In the US, as noted in the last chapter, this has also been wedded to an increasingly politicised strand of right wing Christian Evangelical Nationalism.

What is critical is the way in which social media platforms' algorithms, in presenting individuals and groups with a stream of repetitive and emotive content related to their online activity and perceived interests, can distort and intensify allegiances and opinion, while spurring collective action.[26] This, of course, is not to overlook the fact that social media has also played a role in both mainstream debate and, indeed, far-left and 'identity politics', an issue to which I will return later on. Online debate, as argued, can be relatively benign or even highly positive, focused on emancipatory, progressive, egalitarian, prosocial and democratic ideals and sentiments. However, as we know, for angst-ridden, resentful and disaffected peoples, the stimulation of prejudice and hatred can be an easy path, providing focus for existential angst and affiliation through movements where it can find expression and release.

For the reasons outlined earlier, social media in our polarized societies can also provide fertile ground for manipulation by unfriendly states seeking to undermine the stability of competitor nations and regions, as was highlighted by the debate on Russia's alleged involvement in both the Brexit vote and the Trump election.[27] Of growing concern here is also the way in which AI technology can be used in tandem with social media to construct and disseminate disinformation in the form of deepfakes that can be used by nefarious foreign and domestic actors to spread convincing depictions of leading figures in scenarios that never actually occurred, at least not in anything like the way presented. This has led to concerns regarding the potential for such technologies to move public opinion to undermine democratic processes, generate confusion and profound distrust, with consequences even for national security.[28]

More commonly, social media is evidently associated with the increasing prevalence and take-up of conspiracy theories, like those related to so-called anti-vaxxers and the bizarre QAnon movement, both of which were also subgroups among Trump and Brexit supporters as well as being associated with far-right politics more generally.

The latter provides a particular example of the way in which *primalization* intersects with contemporary mediated discourse to pervade contemporary politics. Here, to recap, the long-term exposure to stress, change, insecurity and inequality impacts on people's capacity for critical, reflective and reasoned thought, as higher-level cognition and emotional inhibition and control (associated with the prefrontal cortex [PFC]) is disrupted and overridden.[29] Combined with the narrowing of attention that occurs with exposure to stressors, the result is that thought and action become increasingly narrow, rigid and driven by negative thinking and emotion, principally fear and anger associated with the amygdala and related regions, with the latter becoming more sensitized and more readily 'triggered'.[30] In this state, emotional stimulation and emotionally charged rhetoric trumps (no pun intended) the assumed business of politics of presenting arguments and evidence to a rational electorate, and accounts for the fact that reasoned argument and presented facts have appeared to have had less sway on voters in recent years, to the bemusement of centre-left and third-way parties attempting to counter populist opponents by this means. In neoliberal nations it might well be argued that many people's politics is defined by how afraid they have become and who their anger is directed towards, and which charismatic politician has channelled the latter, as opposed to any measured assessment of policies.[31] Biden's win in the 2020 US presidential elections can also be understood in terms of a fearful coalition of left and centre-left moderates rallying against the perceived threat of a further destabilizing Trump term, and the threat this posed to US democracy and stability, even if this may also be regarded as a rational position. Overall, in increasingly uncertain and polarized societies, ideology, unreason and emotion often appear to outweigh rational thinking, argument and calculation, at least beyond the relatively insulated who continue to vote for a spectrum of socioeconomic causes, spanning the liberal to the reactionary, including as suggested personal economic gain.

Democratic capture and 'inverted totalitarianism'

This issue is important as it goes to the heart of a key feature of the undermining of democracy in neoliberal states. In other words, when it comes to elections and voting patterns in nations like the US and the UK, emotion is highly important, but, as was argued previously, wealth evidently also matters. However, the way in which this plays out is complex and intertwined.

Firstly, it is clear that there is a left-leaning segment of the wealthy that will align with centre-left parties for ideological and pragmatic reasons as long as the party they are supporting does not challenge their economic position too assiduously. Some of this group are also driven by concern, even fear, being aware that pushing the inequality boat too far is not only economically detrimental, as was argued earlier, but also undermines social order and, consequently, may ultimately threaten their security and relative advantages:

> We are living in an age of extremes. Rising poverty and widening wealth inequality; the rise of anti-democratic nationalism; extreme weather and ecological decline; deep vulnerabilities in our shared social systems; and the shrinking opportunity for billions of ordinary people to earn a livable wage. Extremes are unsustainable, often dangerous, and rarely tolerated for long. So why, in this age of multiple crises, do you continue to tolerate extreme wealth? The history of the last five decades is a story of wealth flowing nowhere but upwards. In the last few years, this trend has greatly accelerated. In the first two years of the pandemic, the richest 10 men in the world doubled their wealth while 99 percent of people saw their incomes fall. Billionaires and millionaires have watched their wealth grow by trillions of dollars, while the cost of simply living is now crippling ordinary families across the world. The solution is plain for all to see. You, our global representatives, have to tax us, the ultra-rich, and you have to start now.[32]

In short, as above, there has been a growing awareness among a small, more enlightened segment of the elite that having a few less digits in already burgeoning offshore accounts is a worthwhile trade-off for security, stability, economic wellbeing for all and, critically, peace of mind.[33] This can be seen to be the case with those members of the elite willing to support Blair in the UK (but not Jeremy Corbyn) and who were supportive of Clinton (both Hilary and Bill) and Obama, but would presumably have been less likely to be wooed by Bernie Sanders. However, for the most part, the wealthy who hold significant assets tend to vote for parties that will help them sustain that wealth, gain more and avoid heavier taxation or redistributive policies.

> A growing body of research concludes, perhaps not surprisingly, that [asset] owners vote for centre-right parties such as the Conservatives in Britain, Republicans in the United States and the Liberals in Australia. Once in power, centre-right parties are most likely to advance policies aligned with the interests of the owners to prevent their wealth being expropriated through taxation. In contrast, centre-left parties strive to curry favour among those individuals whose chief asset is their own labour.[34]

Bound up with the impact of populist figures, the neoliberal elite in nations like the UK, the US and others can also be seen to have employed a range of time-worn strategies to neutralize the potential threat to their interests posed by real democracy. As was suggested in Chapter 4, in part this is simply achieved by using wealth to fund political campaigns, leaving incumbents indebted to and unwilling to upset their 'sponsors', as well as lobbying politicians either directly or indirectly through the activities of pro-neoliberal right-wing think tanks and institutes that also engage with politicians directly, offering 'advice' and holding policy-oriented events. A major activity of these organizations is also to feed the media with 'evidence' and a narrative that supports their patrons' interests, which often goes hand in hand with the right-wing political leaning of mass media outlets, given patterns of ownership. Of course, there are also left-leaning counterparts and news outlets presenting a counternarrative to neoliberal and elite-supporting discourse. However, understandably, in the battle to move public opinion, it is the more numerous and much more handsomely funded organizations and outlets in unequal neoliberal societies that often prevail in advancing and establishing of a political, economic and social 'common sense'.[35]

One of the key devices for achieving this, beyond the direct appeal to emotions, is to exploit the economic naivety and 'nudge' the inherent prejudices of segments of the public.[36] Firstly, as was discussed in the previous chapter, there are attempts, which are often successful, to persuade the public at large that, contrary to the real situation, policies that favour or, indeed, potentially challenge the interests of the rich are likely to affect the wider middle and aspirational public in the same way. The case of estate/inheritance taxes, and progressive taxation more generally, is a clear case in point. While middle-income earners and the poor are largely unaffected by estate or other wealth taxes – and would likely benefit from the reduced inequality and increased public spending made possible by more progressive taxation – they are nonetheless often persuaded that they will personally lose out. This is in line with the co-option narrative implying that 'you're one of us', which may also appeal to the misinformed hubris of the aspirational but modestly well off or, in some instances, even the relatively poor. The neoliberal narrative of individual worth, freedom and self-reliance addressed in the previous chapter is also brought to bear here, as arguments for state intervention, policies that help the poor or those on middle incomes are derided as being supportive of those who are individual failures, who can't stand on their own two feet and must remain 'dependent' on more worthy others. Mass media depictions lionize the winners as being smart, industrious and worthy, and stigmatize neoliberal society's losers as being feckless and, at times, uncivilized and feral, often including a barely concealed narrative that the poor are also deceptive and devious, and that their dependency is unnecessary and their lives less deprived than is claimed. This, as was also argued in the previous chapter, has been the most powerful narrative employed to support neoliberal assaults on welfare and wider public provision – that is, to rely on the state is a sign of personal inadequacy and confirmation that 'you're not one of us' and never will be.

This was also the tactic used to attack 'socialized healthcare' in the US that saw the aforementioned grossly misleading depictions of the UK's National Health Service (NHS) and the demonization of state provision play even among many of those whose lives, health and financial position would be greatly enhanced by the introduction of the Affordable Care Act (or Obamacare). The latter limited but significant step to extend more affordable healthcare coverage was greatly resisted by the corporate interests that have made US healthcare one of the most expensive services globally, delivering a five-star service for those who can best afford it while being precarious and potentially devastating for many of those who cannot. This has produced a scenario where healthcare costs are a leading cause of personal bankruptcy, particularly as people age, adding to the profound psychological and emotional burden that regularly accompanies declining health.[37] While Obama's reforms were aimed at tackling some of the more severe implications of healthcare policy, once again a significant sector of the needy was encouraged to decry this assault on their 'freedom' and capacity for self-reliance. On an interesting aside here, Trump's seeming adoption of some of the conspiracy theory rhetoric around the alleged shadowy 'deep state', as was argued earlier, also undermines the very notion of the state as a source of welfare, regulation and intervention that might curb the impunity of the corporate and financial elite and protect his own followers from hyperexploitation and socioeconomic exclusion.

Accompanying disinformation as a vehicle for distraction and domination, there has been the cultivation of 'grassroots' protest and resistance in what we have come to know as 'astroturfing'. This is a further strategy by which power and money has been applied to gaining influence and shaping public opinion, and can be one of the more underhand strategies that powerful political and corporate groups employ.[38] This is in addition to but in some ways aligned with the use of complicit academics and organizations to provide disinformation and muddy the waters in relation to issues that threaten corporate profits, such as providing 'evidence' and professional opinion to counter growing evidence, as arose with the risks associated with tobacco and, more recently, with respect to the threats to the climate, the environment and communities by the fossil fuel industry (see Chapter 9). Astroturfing takes this a step forward in the form of moves to infiltrate nongovernmental organizations (NGOs), to introduce paid agents to sway debate in public meetings, as well as instigating seeming grassroots campaigns and protest. The latter, of course, now also forms an important aspect of the sort of social media and other online persuasive activity. All of this is effectively aimed at sowing confusion over risky and hazardous but profitable corporate conduct, undermining public concerns around economic inequity and injustice as well as shoring up and advancing arrangements that support the neoliberal logic described earlier. Disparaging opponents and stigmatizing their causes, ideas and often the language they use are all means by which those who oppose neoliberal ideas are presented as 'out of touch', odd or inadequate in some way.

Corporate and elite actors also exert more overt influence by regularly presenting themselves as advocates for the general public interest through a variety of respectable guises. More moderately, such a sleight of hand takes the form of adopting innocuous, authoritative or misleading titles and presentation for what are effectively elite lobby groups and think tanks. Groups like the UK's Centre for Social Justice, the Centre for Policy Studies and the Taxpayer's Alliance, the latter of which assertedly campaigns for 'tax justice' (in effect lower and less progressive taxes and for neoliberal economic policies more generally) or in the US the Heritage Foundation, the Cato Institute and Partnership for America's Health Care Future (an industry lobby group broadly supportive of Obamacare, but against any move towards single-payer public healthcare) are examples of these numerous and diverse interest groups.

This domination and management of contemporary nominally democratic politics by a coalition of corporate interests, lobbyists and other segments of the elite led the political theorist Sheldon Wolin to argue that the US polity could be characterized as representing a form of what he termed 'inverted totalitarianism', as briefly mentioned in Chapter 4. The argument here was that differences between the major parties, and within them, represented a form of politics that, despite asserted political freedom, has presented the public with a narrowly limited agenda while assiduously managing information and debate, effectively neutralizing challenges to a political status quo that favours elite interests.[39]

As was noted earlier, the emergence of 'third way' politics and the ongoing rightward drift, together with the corporate domination of public information and content, indicates that this is a condition that is by no means particular to the US, but can also be applied to the UK and numerous other contemporary polities.

Evidence in support of Wolin's broad analysis can be observed in the establishment and media treatment of Corbyns' and Sanders' electoral forays. Both presented policy platforms that would have appeared as relatively mainstream, benign, centre-left agendas in the pre-neoliberal era. Nonetheless, Corbyn was branded as a dangerous 'lefty' in the UK for essentially having the temerity to challenge the political status quo and threaten the interests of the wealthy. While it might be argued that he was not a particularly personable candidate, significant opposition even from within his own party was largely fuelled by rejection of his politics, a fact underscored by Labour's return to a decidedly 'pragmatic' Blairite agenda under Keir Starmer's leadership. Sanders was also branded an extremist, despite his proposed administration including such eminent luminaries as Joseph Stiglitz, Paul Krugman and Robert Reich[40] – that is, highly regarded figures far from being irrational zealots – while his policy platform proposed numerous measures on education, healthcare, housing, labour markets and the economy that would have greatly benefited the less well heeled. However, the threat that this posed to wealthy vested interests could not be countenanced.

Of course, what remains of the 'real' left continues to resist the right-wing onslaught that is marked by a growing polarization between right and left in the UK and the US as mainstream politics continues to move ever rightward. However, left wing opposition has become fragmented to an extent as the multiplicity of disadvantage groups, in increasing recognition of racial, ethnic, gender, disability, age and other sectional inequities, have increasingly pursued their own distinct agendas marked by a decline in older class identifications and solidarities. As was briefly mentioned earlier and as will be discussed later on, identity and cultural inequity has become detached to an extent from class politics. As such, the battle between right and left has now morphed into the so-called 'culture wars' that have become a key platform for right-wing populist invective that has been exploited by the illiberal right to stigmatize and further fragment potential opposition.

Identity politics and populism

Since the 1980s, as has been widely recognized, there has been an increasing emphasis on individual rights and personal freedom, particularly in relation to minorities, following in the slipstream of the civil rights and emancipatory movements of the 1960s, to advocate for greater equality and restorative justice for marginalized groups. Now referred to (largely by its detractors) as identity politics, there has been an earnest and justified campaign (or in fact collection of campaigns) aimed at improving the lives, respect and dignity of a range of communities stigmatized and treated unequally due to their gender, sexual orientation, race or ethnicity. Identity politics as a concept has been associated with the Combahee River Collective (CRC), a group of 1970s Boston-based Black, feminist, lesbian and socialist activists who understood that the discrimination that they experienced encompassed both identity and economic factors.[41] This appears as a recognition of *intersectional* discrimination and disadvantage prior to Kimberle Crenshaw's cogent analysis and coining of the term.[42] However, as Asad Haider, a more recent commentator whose work I have drawn upon here, has argued, the CRC's challenge to racial, gender and sexual discrimination was also intrinsically bound up with its aim of challenging the political and economic structures that blighted the lives of themselves and all of those impacted by economic disadvantage. Collective solidarity across groups was seen as being as important as challenging prejudice based on identities. However, as Haider asserts, their understandable aim of challenging a multiplicity of inequities they witnessed and experienced was taken up by others who rightly expanded the challenge to discrimination based on identity, but increasingly lost sight of its relationship to economic inequity or the necessity of solidarity in challenging it. This dichotomy, he argues, obscures the fact that, in line with a point I made earlier, discrimination on any grounds within unforgiving neoliberal societies is regularly played out in economic terms, while the splitting of one form of inequity from another has allowed some 'moderate' neoliberal politicians to self-consciously support challenges to discrimination based on identities, while evading their intimate intertwining with economic injustice:[43]

> As Salar Mohandesi writes, 'What began as a promise to push beyond some of socialism's limitations to build a richer, more diverse and inclusive socialist politics' ended up 'exploited by those with politics diametrically opposed to those of the CRC'. The most recent and most striking example was the presidential campaign of Hillary Clinton, which adopted the language of 'intersectionality' and 'privilege' and used identity politics to combat the emergence of a left-wing challenge in the Democratic Party surrounding Bernie Sanders. Sanders's supporters were condemned as 'Bernie Bros', despite his widespread support among women; they were accused of neglecting the concerns of black people, despite the devastating effect for many black Americans of the Democratic mainstream's commitment to neoliberal policies. As Michelle Alexander wrote in the Nation, the legacy of the Clinton family was a Democratic capitulation 'to the

right-wing backlash against the civil rights movement' and 'Ronald Reagan's agenda on race, crime, welfare, and taxes'. The new brand of Clinton liberalism ended up 'ultimately doing more harm to black communities than Reagan ever did'.[44]

The increasing call for emancipation and challenges to longstanding prejudicial attitudes and practices concerning race, gender and other forms of marginalization that had blighted numerous lives have grown ever louder and more compelling. However, as we've witnessed recently, this call for progressive change on a number of fronts has been seized upon by the populist right, with any niceties abandoned, as a vehicle for forging their agenda and base particularly, as was noted earlier, among the traditional conservative constituency and disaffected segments of the White working and lower middle class. The insecurities of the latter groups especially, in line with the process of *primalization*, manifest in an increased emotional sensitivity to difference that is both invoked and, in a sense, sated by the scapegoating of 'others'. Populists, as was argued earlier, exploit these tendencies towards cultural defence in the face of chronic uncertainty and an associated desire for clarity, community and conformity. Haider also recognizes this general propensity, if not its biosocial foundations, as he quotes from a screenplay from a film (*My Son the Fanatic*) that addresses the appeal of fundamentalism and cultural conservatism as a defence against the threat of complexity and chaos and, as I have argued, the experience of experiential overload:

> Fundamentalism provides security. For the fundamentalist, as for all reactionaries, everything has been decided. Truth has been agreed and nothing must change ... Rationalists have always underestimated the need people have for belief. Enlightenment values – rationalism, tolerance, skepticism – don't get you through a dreadful night, they don't provide the spiritual comfort or community or solidarity.[45]

This neatly sums up some of the central contentions set out throughout this book, and one that needs to be restated here. The inherent complexities and stresses of modern living drive many towards rigidity and a desire for association more exclusively with those with whom they most closely identify and who share a similar sense of anger, fear and resentment, a condition cultivated by powerful charismatic actors. In the ranks of contemporary right-wing populist movements, victimhood is combined with a sense of fragile collective in-group superiority, which can be clearly observed in the mix of paranoia, loss and fiery egotism displayed by many of Brexit and Trump's MAGA supporters and most acutely by the various militia at the forefront of his insurgency. As Berlet and Lyons assert, much of this has taken a form where 'they combine attacks on socially oppressed groups with grassroots mass mobilization and distorted forms of anti-elitism based on scapegoating'.[46]

In a number of societies, politics has become a de facto battle between internally disparate groups, mobilized on the one hand by conservative ideologues, often backed by shadowy business interests defending their territory against the demands for social justice from the left-leaning segment of the multiply disadvantaged, those not persuaded by right-wing rhetoric, the latter being supported by an educated and progressive sector of the public, academic and political establishment. Among the other rhetorical weapons of choice employed by the right, the 'distorted forms of antielitism' to which Berlet and Lyons refer are deployed to obfuscate and conceal the real power base controlling and exploiting the masses, while those who advocate for something better for everyone are charged with representing a 'woke' elite threatening a way of life that has already been stolen.[47]

However, what Haider notes is that many on the contemporary left have been complicit in enabling this sleight of hand by neglecting the shared economic exclusion across a variety cultural, ethnic and other identities, while a commensurate focus on difference, and of the irreconcilability of experience, pushes those with the potential for collective resistance into silos. One of the key problems here, as Haider and indeed a range of other writers have pointed out, is that this approach to resisting disadvantage and prejudice has evolved into the form of exclusive, sectional campaigns that can be neutralized by turning potential allies on each other. Despite being advanced with the best of intentions and laudable aims, it always raises the potential for generating intergroup distance, distrust and potential conflict, presenting a barrier to the solidarity that is required to challenge the economic status quo that imposes itself on all but the rich and comfortable. This presents a conundrum as to how the profound injuries of the past and present, experienced by holders of a variety of marginalized identities and histories, can be confronted in a manner that prevents the potential for alienation and division that can be exploited from above. For Haider, this can only be achieved by the emergence of what he terms an 'insurgent universalism' that promotes solidarity and respect across identity divides in the shared endeavour of challenging the system (in his view, capitalism as a whole) that is the ultimate source of oppression and injustice.[48]

This also relates to the line of argument presented earlier in terms of how we respond to difference, cognitively and emotionally, effectively by default – that is, that classifying others as being similar or different has a significant impact on how we think and feel about them. Once more, this relates to the tendency for us to think about similar others in terms of how we think about ourselves, understanding their attitudes and actions in relation to our own thinking, emotions, internalized norms, values, attitudes and so on. By contrast, those who are classified as being different are understood through acquired stereotypes that reduce the cognitive burden when thinking about others with whom we don't readily identify. Correspondingly, our reflections on similar others entail a deeper emotional and cognitive engagement, while our response to others is 'colder'. There are also clear synergies with the overall framework informing the book in terms of recognizing our difficulty in dealing with difference and complexity more generally, and our strategies for reducing experiential overload, while these observations also fit with longstanding sociological perspectives, notably Erving Goffman's work on the roots of stigma, and particularly what he termed the 'tribal stigma' marked by division and prejudice:[49]

> To the extent that members of a social group other than one's own are viewed as dissimilar from oneself, the current results suggest that perceivers may actively deploy a different set of social-cognitive processes when considering the mental states of someone of a different race or ethnicity than a member of one's own ingroup. As such, prejudice may arise in part because perceivers assume that outgroup members' mental states do not correspond to their own and, accordingly, mentalize in a non-self-referential way about the minds of people from different groups. Without a self-referential basis for mentalizing about outgroup members, perceivers may rely heavily on precomputed judgments – such as stereotypes – to make mental state inferences about very dissimilar others. This view suggests that a critical strategy for reducing prejudice may be to breach arbitrary boundaries based on social group membership by focusing instead on the shared similarity between oneself and outgroup members.[50]

Further reinforcing the view, it has also been observed that thinking about self and others more actively involves different areas of the PFC: 'A functional distinction between ventral medial prefrontal cortex (VMPFC) and dorsal medial prefrontal cortex (DMPFC) is suggested by neuroimaging research implicating VMPFC in the representation of semantic knowledge about the self and DMPFC in the representation of social knowledge about others.'[51]

As was noted earlier, the suggestion that othering and discrimination may have deep neurological roots is a further reason why a collective, universalist narrative may be a significantly better route to confronting injustices than is currently offered by sectional identity movements that may, despite the very best of intentions, play into the hands of cynical politicians and unwittingly contribute to conditions where prejudice, distrust and conflict flourish. A recognition of these processes among progressives is critical at the present time, when our atomized and polarized societies seem ever more riven with competition, misunderstanding and conflict. Moreover, the implications of this go further than offering understanding perceived differences between national and ethnic communities and so on. The distinction of similarity and difference operates on a spectrum and might also be applied to distinctions of social class and economic standing. This has a bearing on what was discussed in Chapter 10 in relation to the growing economic divide in neoliberal societies, where distinctions of status lead to increasing stereotyping, and a lack of mutual identification, empathy and trust. While this has the potential to operate in both directions, elite control of sources of information allows for the presentation of positive impressions of the wealthy to counter negative stereotyping to an extent. Depiction of the poor through the media and in prejudicial political discourse, as was argued earlier, can by contrast be seen to deepen negative stereotyping, stigma, lack of empathy and social exclusion.

From neoliberalism to authoritarianism?

As has been argued from the outset of this chapter, while the tendencies discussed are ever-present, the stresses and inequities of living under neoliberal capitalism create a fertile environment for the cultivation of our baser instincts. As will be addressed in the next chapter, the injuries to our personal mental and physical health also go deeper than has been set out thus far, such that a specific discussion is necessary. Sadly, however, while there are some glimmers of light in terms of more progressive trends among upcoming generations, the prospect of a radical political and economic change of tack that might turn the tide of neoliberal capitalism and increasing right-wing extremism seems remote, as the latter remains a powerful obstacle and danger. Despite what the 'neoliberalism is dead' advocates suggest, the basic tenets of strident individualism and market fundamentalism seem highly resilient. While in the US, as noted, the Biden administration represented a return to the more moderate form of neoliberalism associated with Clinton and Obama, the stridently right-wing constituency mobilized by Trump looks to remain capable of regaining power.

It almost beggars belief that a mainstream establishment political party would continue to support such a divisive and erratic figure, one who has talked of politicizing the military, security and civil service, and who has spouted increasingly extremist and bizarre rhetoric via his Truth Social platform (it's almost banal to again draw an Orwellian connection here). Trump's claim on the platform that incumbent Presidents should have 'complete and total presidential immunity' from prosecution illustrates just how far he might be prepared to go in wielding autocratic power if he were to regain office.[52] In spite of being unequivocal in his intent to undermine and/or distort US institutions, pronouncements such as effectively accusing Democrats of infanticide, encouraging his supporters to believe that the 'deep state' is out to get them, as well as the 'big lie', have clearly shifted the boundaries of what is acceptable in US politics, leading to numerous claims that Trump is unfit for any public office, let alone the Presidency. And yet, as noted earlier, his brand of politics appears to have become entrenched due to the mobilization and electoral strength of his MAGA base. This may well be the case regardless of whether Trump himself reprises his leading role, as the mobilization of the angry and illiberal right in the US remains a potent political force with no shortage of pretenders willing to assume Trump's populist mantle. The advent of Project 2025 - the plan associated with the Heritage Foundation to support an extension of presidential powers and fundamental, right wing conservative reshaping of US governance - seems wholly consistent with this perspective. [53]

In the UK, Johnson's ignominious departure saw him replaced by the ill-fated Liz Truss administration, which, in spite of the economic and social ills generated by insecurity and inequality, doubled down to move even further to the neoliberal right than Johnson's administration. The new cohort effectively went back to strident neoliberal basics with a swift and unabashed red-in-tooth-and-claw programme of tax cuts for the very wealthy and corporations, removal of caps on bankers' bonuses and a resurrection of the trickle-down economics that has been seen to so evidently fail previously. This was allied to revival of support for expanded fossil fuel production, as a rebuff to environmental and climate concerns, further erosion of trade union and human rights, and greater punitive conditionality for those on welfare. In effect, the new administration marked a departure from the Johnson government by moving even further to the right while dispensing with any pretence to even-handedness or even the hollow redistributive rhetoric that had helped its predecessor garner votes from the pro-Brexit working classes. The advent of a Truss government marked the aforementioned *Britannia Unchained* cohort of right-wing neoliberal radicals' coming of age, while placing a bunsen burner under the unstable cocktail of a fragmenting union, economy and society.[54] Moreover, given the experience of the Truss administration, Johnson's mantle as being Britain's worst postwar Prime Minister appeared to be as short-lived as his premiership. The zealotry of Truss and co. was such that its raw and unvarnished application of free market dogma proved too much, or simply too brashly presented, even for a society that had travelled ever further to the right over the past four decades. Ensuing market volatility and public dismay saw a reversal of a controversial tax cut for the very rich in little over a week after it was announced and Truss' replacement by Rishi Sunak only a few weeks later. While this was enacted as a move to calm the markets and economic turmoil that had followed Truss' hamfisted policy interventions, from almost the outset Sunak came under pressure on a number of fronts from the far-right, Brexiteer wing of the party. This suggested that Truss' removal had been a calculated move to save Tory seats, given the inept implementation of her programme and public distaste for her hectoring style. Nonetheless, rabid neoliberalism and the call for tax cuts and further deregulation remained as a central plank of policy with continuing support among many in the party and the right-wing establishment more generally.

Across Europe, a similar trajectory has been evident with the right and the far right gaining further ground, for example, in Giorgia Meloni's Italy and the formerly Nordic social democratic Sweden, where the latter provided almost a test case for the corrosive social and political impact of the neoliberal turn. Sweden's turning away from the Nordic social democratic model and embracing of neoliberalism since the 1990s has seen greatly reduced taxes on income and wealth, substantially benefiting the rich, together with labour market and welfare 'reform'. The outcome has followed the familiar pattern outlined thus far of burgeoning inequality, the emergence of a wealthy elite detached from the rest of society, increasing social instability and associated ills, including a more volatile and febrile politics. Once again, ironically, the neoliberal destabilizing of society, the distress and anger of the disaffected and a lack of meaningful action from supine centre-left parties when they have gained office have been channelled by increasingly illiberal political movements offering utopia, but, in effect, intensifying the very conditions that have generated their followers' discontents and disorientation.

At the time of writing, the right also appears to have successfully challenged even Finland's exemplar of social democracy, with attacks on the welfare state and via the dog whistle of anti-immigration rhetoric. The success of Geert Wilders in the Netherlands' 2023 elections followed this ongoing trend. The threat to democracy in contemporary Germany was represented by an attempted far-right coup in December 2022 that was taken very seriously by the authorities, leading to arrests across the country, while there have been growing fears and subsequent public protests around the rise of the far right. On balance, however, while the trend towards normalizing the far-right, and divisive, unjust and increasingly authoritarian politics in major democracies is of clear and ongoing concern, there are some glimmers of light where populists have failed to gain office or have been rejected by their electorates following a term in office. Trump's losing of the 2020 election was notable, albeit very close (though not stolen) and as argued the threat remains. In the UK, the downfall of Johnson and Truss at the hands of their own party, and the poor standing of the Conservatives since, perhaps suggests that the tide may be turning to an extent, albeit that Labour's apparent aforementioned return to 'triangulation' and cautious and muted reform suggests that they may yet repeat the errors of the Blair/Clinton era, mildly ameliorating the neoliberal order rather than taking on the beast wholeheartedly.

On a final point here, it is important to note that while, in this and the preceding chapters, contemporary society has been characterized as being inherently disorderly, this is only the case up to a point. As Loïc Wacquant in his depiction of the *centaur state*[55] pointed out, there is such a thing as neoliberal order, while this chapter attempts to outline some of the ways in which it has been imposed and been sustained, through ideology supported by the sowing of division as well as the manipulation of the public angst and anger it has generated. It is a form of plutocratic order by and for the very few imposed on the many.

Of course, as indicated in Chapter 10, there are those nearer the top of the heap who support this settlement, as they have a stake in the game and enjoy relative security, for some supported by a cushion of inherited wealth. However, even among many of the 'achievers' there is often little awareness of how much of their lives have been blighted, and may be more so in future, by aligning themselves with this hyper-capitalist project. As to those further down the socioeconomic hierarchy, as noted, they are increasingly divided between various strata of the aspirational and the anxiously 'enthusiastic' and subservient, and, at the sharp end of our increasingly unforgiving societies, the despairing and desperate.

As will be addressed directly in the next chapter and as was the case for much of our history, the brief postwar hiatus aside, the comfort and security of a minority has been extended and consolidated by removing this from the majority incrementally over the last few decades, creating growing numbers for whom psychological and, increasingly, physical survival is an ongoing struggle. What is important here is that all but the most cosseted are subject to experiential overload to varying degrees, with profound negative consequences for their health and wellbeing. In the context of the general themes set out here, it is also important to note that the social and economic settlement that has been delivered can be viewed in relation to some of the arguments on evolutionary niche construction set out in Chapter 1.[56] Put simply, and as was noted earlier, as we shape society, we shape ourselves, while the epigenetic ramifications of this may well entail that our politics is about much more than defining the arrangements of the here and now, but how this will affect the biosocial constitution of current and, potentially, subsequent generations.[57] These issues will be taken up in the next chapter.

Notes

[1]   'When an agent of the Tory party decides the BBC's "bias", it's a huge problem', *The Guardian*, 25 August 2022,
      https://www.theguardian.com/commentisfree/2022/aug/25/bbc-agent-tory-party-bias-news-media-emily-maitlis-mactaggart-lecture

[2]   Herman, L. and Muldoon, J.M. (2018) *Populism in the 21st Century: From the Fringe to the Mainstream*, Abingdon: Routledge.

[3]   Inglehart, R. (2018) 'The age of insecurity: can democracy save itself?', *Foreign Affairs*, 97(3): 20–28.

[4]   Fukuyama, F. (1989) 'The end of history?', *The National Interest*, (16): 3–18.

5   Galston, W.A. (2018) 'The populist challenge to liberal democracy', *Journal of Democracy*, 29(2): 5–19.

6   Inglehart, R. (2018) 'The age of insecurity: can democracy save itself?', *Foreign Affairs*, 97(3): 20–28.

7   Bone, J. (2021) 'Neoliberal precarity and primalization: a biosocial perspective on the age of insecurity, injustice, and unreason', *British Journal of Sociology*, 72: 1030–1045; McEwen, B.S. (2005) 'Stressed or stressed out: what is the difference?', *Journal of Psychiatry and Neuroscience*, 30(5): 315–318.

8   ' "Trickle-down" tax cuts make the rich richer but are of no value to overall economy, study finds', *Washington Post*, 23 December 2020, https://www.washingtonpost.com/business/2020/12/23/tax-cuts-rich-trickle-down/

9   Douglas, M. (2003) *Purity and Danger: An Analysis of Concepts of Pollution and Taboo*, London: Routledge.

10 Inglehart, R. (2018) 'The age of insecurity: can democracy save itself?', *Foreign Affairs*, 97(3): 20–28, at 24.

11 Gelfand, M.J., Raver, J.L., Nishii, L., Leslie, L.M., Lun, J., Lim, B.C., Duan, L., Almaliach, A., Ang, S., Arnadottir, J. and Aycan, Z. (2011) 'Differences between tight and loose cultures: a 33-nation study', *Science*, 332(6033): 1100–1104.

12 Kershaw, I. (2001) *The 'Hitler Myth': Image and Reality in the Third Reich*, Oxford: Oxford University Press, p 13.

13 Burston, D. (2017) ' "It can't happen here": Trump, authoritarianism and American politics', *Psychotherapy and Politics International*, 15(1): e1399.

14 https://www.politico.eu/article/nigel-farage-leader-uk-conservative-party-2026/

15 'Fact check: Trump falsely denies saying two things he said last week', *CNN*, 30 March 2020, https://edition.cnn.com/2020/03/29/politics/fact-check-coronavirus-briefing/index.html

16 'Dr. Birx reacts as Trump suggests "injection" of disinfectant to beat coronavirus – NBC News NOW', *YouTube*, https://www.youtube.com/watch?v=d57zJr82dhQ

17 'Prosecutors say Trump knew his lies about 2020 election were false', *Associated Press*, 1 August 2023, https://www.pbs.org/newshour/politics/prosecutors-say-trump-knew-his-lies-about- e

18 https://wisconsinexaminer.com/2022/12/23/u-s-house-jan-6-panel-report-finds-trump-incited-insurrection-demands-accountability/2020-election-were-false

19 'Noam Chomsky believes Trump is the worst criminal in human history', *New Yorker*, 30 October 2020, https://www.newyorker.com/news/q-and-a/noam-chomsky-believes-trump-is-the-worst-criminal-in-human-history

20 'Trump's false attacks on voting by mail stir broad concern', *New York Times*, 24 June 2020, https://www.nytimes.com/2020/06/24/us/politics/trump-vote-by-mail.html

21 'What insurrection? Growing number in GOP downplay Jan. 6', *Associated Press*, 14 May 2021, https://apnews.com/article/politics-michael-pence-donald-trump-election-2020-capitol-siege-549829098c84b9b8de3012673a104a4c

22 'The patriot', *The Atlantic*, 21 September 2023, https://www.theatlantic.com/magazine/archive/2023/11/general-mark-milley-trump-coup/675375/

23 Oborne, P. (2021) *The Assault on Truth: Boris Johnson, Donald Trump and the Emergence of a New Moral Barbarism*, London: Simon & Schuster.

24 Pariser, E. (2011) *The Filter Bubble: What the Internet Is Hiding from You*, Harmondsworth: Penguin.

25 Goldberg, M. (2006) *Kingdom Coming: The Rise of Christian Nationalism*, New York: Norton.

26 Pariser, E. (2011) *The Filter Bubble: What the Internet Is Hiding from You*, Harmondsworth: Penguin.

27 Boyd-Barrett, O. (2019) *RussiaGate and Propaganda: Disinformation in the Age of Social Media*, Abingdon: Routledge.

28 Sayler, K.M. and Harris, L.A. (2020) 'Deep fakes and national security'. *Congressional Research* SVC Washington United States.

29 Arnsten, A.F. (2009) 'Stress signalling pathways that impair prefrontal cortex structure and function', *Neuroscience*, 10(6): 410–422, at 410.

30 Davis, M.C., Zautra, A.J. and Smith, B.W. (2004) 'Chronic pain, stress, and the dynamics of affective differentiation', *Journal of Personality*, 72(6): 1133–1160.

31 Bone, J. (2021) 'Neoliberal precarity and primalization: a biosocial perspective on the age of insecurity, injustice, and unreason', *British Journal of Sociology*, 72(4): 1030–1045.

32 https://costofextremewealth.com/

33 Hanauer, N. (2014) 'The pitchforks are coming … for us plutocrats', *Politico*, July/August.

34 Hellwig, T. and McAllister, I. (2019) 'Economic voting and party positions: when and how wealth matters for the vote', *Democratic Audit Blog*, https://www.democraticaudit. com/2019/02/27/economic-voting-and-party-positions-when-and-how-wealth-matt ers-for-the-vote/

35 Guardino, M. (2019) *Framing Inequality: News Media, Public Opinion, and the Neoliberal Turn in US Public Policy*, Oxford: Oxford University Press.

36 Thaler, R.H. & Sunstein, C.R. (2009) *Nudge: Improving Decisions About Health, Wealth, and Happiness*, London: Penguin.

37 Thorne, D., Foohey, P., Lawless, R.M. and Porter, K. (2020) 'Graying of US bankruptcy: fallout from life in a risk society', *Sociological Inquiry*, 90(4): 681–704.

38 Lee, C.W. (2010) 'The roots of astroturfing', *Contexts*, 9(1): 73–75.

39 Wolin, S. (2017) *Democracy Incorporated*, Princeton: Princeton University Press.

40 'Bernie Sanders hints at what a Sanders administration cabinet could look like', *Huffington Post*, 5 July 2015, https://www.huffingtonpost.co.uk/entry/bernie-sanders-cabinet_ n_7730208

41 Collective, C.R. (1983) 'The Combahee river collective statement', *Home Girls: A Black Feminist Anthology*, 1: 264–274.

42 Crenshaw, K. (2018) 'Demarginalizing the intersection of race and sex: a Black feminist critique of antidiscrimination doctrine, feminist theory, and antiracist politics', in K. Bartlett (ed), *Feminist Legal Theory*, Abingdon: Routledge, pp 57–80.

43 Haider, A. (2018) *Mistaken Identity: Race and Class in the Age of Trump*, New York: Verso.

44 Haider, A. (2018) *Mistaken Identity: Race and Class in the Age of Trump*, New York: Verso, p 9.

45 Haider, A. (2018) *Mistaken Identity: Race and Class in the Age of Trump*, New York: Verso.

46 Berlet, C. and Lyons, M.N. (2018) *Right-Wing Populism in America: Too Close for Comfort*, New York: Guilford Publications.

47 Berlet, C. and Lyons, M.N. (2018) *Right-Wing Populism in America: Too Close for Comfort*, New York: Guilford Publications.

48 Haider, A. (2018) *Mistaken Identity: Race and Class in the Age of Trump*, New York: Verso.

49 Bone, J. (2010) 'Irrational capitalism: the social map, neoliberalism and the demodernization of the West', *Critical Sociology*, 36(5): 717–740; Goffman, E. (1963) *Stigma: Notes on the Management of Spoiled Identity*, Harmondsworth: Penguin.

50 Mitchell, J.P., Macrae, C.N. and Banaji, M.R. (2006) 'Dissociable medial prefrontal contributions to judgments of similar and dissimilar others', *Neuron*, 50(4): 655–663.

51 Wagner, D.D., Haxby, J.V. and Heatherton, T.F. (2012) 'The representation of self and person knowledge in the medial prefrontal cortex', *Wiley Interdisciplinary Reviews: Cognitive Science*, 3(4): 451–470, at 454.

52 https://www.nbcnews.com/politics/donald-trump/trump-awaiting-ruling-says-preside nts-must-complete-total-immunity-rcna134483

53 https://www.nbcnews.com/politics/2024-election/donations-surged-groups-linked-conservative-project-2025-rcna125638

54 Kwarteng, K., Patel, P., Raab, D., Skidmore, C. and Truss, E. (2012) *Britannia Unchained*, London: Palgrave Macmillan.

55 Wacquant, L. (2010) 'Crafting the neoliberal state: workfare, prisonfare, and social insecurity', *Sociological Forum*, 25(2): 197–220.

56 Odling-Smee, F., Laland, K. and Feldman, M. (2003) *Niche Construction: The Neglected Process in Evolution (MPB-37)*, Princeton: Princeton University Press.

57 Lacal, I. and Ventura, R. (2018) 'Epigenetic inheritance: concepts, mechanisms and perspectives', *Frontiers in Molecular Neuroscience*, 292.

12

Public Issues as Personal Troubles: Individualizing Risk and the Health Costs of Turbocapitalism

> Neither the life of an individual nor the history of a society can be understood without understanding both.
>
> *C. Wright Mills*[1]

From the previous chapters, it seems clear that the perspective offered here on the effects of neoliberal arrangements on contemporary peoples is, to say the least, far from positive. In this chapter, however, I want to focus more closely on the effects on individuals and to argue that many of the very personal ills that we are experiencing can be attributed to life in neoliberal societies and the multifarious stressors to which we are subjected as a consequence of experiential overload. This, as was argued earlier, is a way of life that consistently denies us access to the conditions that support our cognitive and emotional balance. I also want to address the way in which personal tragedies in terms of damaged lives, as a number of commentators have argued, have often been misinterpreted by treating what are effectively societal ills as individual 'pathologies'.

Overall, experiential overload, inequity and primalization under neoliberalism contribute to a spectrum of damage, from an incipient sense of unease, fear, anger and paranoia discussed thus far, through a variety of forms of antisocial conduct, including the cultivation of the febrile political ferment discussed in the last chapter. However, turned inward, this is manifested in a growing epidemic of internal pain and anguish that is damaging our mental and physical health and wellbeing, while potentially impacting on successive generations.

Mental health: a growth industry

A whole public and private industry dealing with mental health issues has emerged to support the casualties of the neoliberal age, built on foundations that have been evolving for more than a century, but which has had a somewhat chequered history. To be fair, many of the interventions to tackle individual psychological problems have been advanced from an altruistic and empathic standpoint, albeit that there is growing debate as to the effectiveness of how we deal with people's inner psychic troubles. As will be argued here, the damage done has also been exploited commercially by a growing industry, with some earnest professionals being unwittingly complicit, as the desire to support the vulnerable has been distorted by the lure of professional prestige and profit.[2]

Sovereign individuals

A central theme that has emerged in the neoliberal era is that each of us is an individual island, which in one sense is not without foundation in our atomized societies. However, what is important is that we are islands beset by demands in an environment where we are often controlled rather than being in control. Contemporary individuals are expected to be compliant, eager and diligent workers who play by the rules, resilient in the face of multiplying demands, and avidly consuming contributors to growing the economy, while supporting and advancing the wealth and wellbeing of themselves and/or their immediate family. Our reward is, indeed, largely measured in our capacity to consume, as was noted in Chapter 8, to acquire and display the aspirational goods and lifestyle status markers that our consumer culture offers, once more contributing to economic growth. This is taken for granted as being the normative way of life under contemporary consumer capitalism and particularly under its stark neoliberal variant. In effect, our self-worth is largely measured in these terms, with aspects of personality and sociability seen as secondary incidental attributes, beyond those that can be marketed in the labour market as 'interpersonal skills' or as 'personality' that can be monetized via social or other contemporary media. As was argued earlier, the demands and stressors of living in a world like this, always being 'on', meeting deadlines, of having the individual resilience and 'can do' attitude that reflects the norms and values of neoliberalism, inevitably exacts a price:

> As recently as 2010, early retirement was a thing. We were writing about a 26-year old FX trader who thought she'd retire in 10 years and about Geraint Anderson, the ex-equity-researcher turned writer, who retired after 12 years aged 35 in 2009 with £2.5m in net assets.[3]

As was noted earlier, the big winners in this aspirational contest may earn enough to escape or to shift to a more leisurely means of wealth accumulation, aping the older moneyed class who have long sustained themselves through leisurely capitalism and collecting economic rents from land, property and investments. However, for most people, the scramble continues with the awareness of being consistently *performance managed* and monitored in the workplace, constantly called upon to demonstrate having the 'right stuff', with the residual fear of demotion, downsizing or dismissal if they are considered to be falling behind the pack. For those at the sharpest end of the job market, there is the experience of constant micromanagement and the awareness that, almost regardless of performance, the short-term risks and fluctuations in profitability of business tend to be managed by passing insecurity to the workforce, either through layoffs or the perpetual uncertainties of 'flexible' gig work. All of this is, of course, compounded by the endemic status anxiety that pervades our aspirational culture where economic and occupational 'failure', as was discussed previously, is feared as a place of personal shame and potential destitution for oneself and one's loved ones. For many, penury is often little more than a couple of pay cheques away, which may place not only one's status in jeopardy, but also the family home and access to food and other essentials in our increasingly unforgiving culture, given that the welfare safety net has now been decimated in line with neoliberal logic.

The way in which this fear has been exploited as a method of control was exemplified when Suella Braverman, the Conservative Home Secretary (in both the Truss and Sunak administrations), effectively argued at the party's 2022 annual conference that the UK's arguably already punitive welfare system needed to be more so, to 'encourage' people into work. Here Braverman suggested that 'we have got a lot of carrots to get people into work but we have got to add more conditionality and a bit more stick'.[4] In essence, one of the harshest welfare systems among the advanced nations was clearly not tough enough for the Home Secretary. The aim, of course, is not only to push people towards the low-pay and low-skill toil that, pre-Brexit, was often carried out by an exploited temporary workforce from the EU accession states, but is also part of the strategy that allows employers to consistently weaken terms and conditions and subjugate a workforce fearful of falling foul of the abyss, as was discussed in Chapter 10.

This mean-spirited approach to helping the less fortunate is also widely replicated in the US, while a notable example arose in March 2023 when Republicans in North Dakota's State Senate rejected a bill to provide free school meals for poor children while, a week later, they voted to raise their own meal allowances by $10 per day.[5]

Given these types of pressures in neoliberal states, compounded by economic turmoil in markets, the pandemic, the cost-of-living crisis and political and geopolitical conflict and upheaval, it is little surprise that there are numerous individual casualties whose problems go even deeper than those already addressed. For growing numbers, experiential overload has been consistent, incessant and intensive to a degree that leaves people in a state of chronically high negative emotional arousal, as one consequence of persistent stress, and with the absence of a manageable sense of control, clarity and consistency.

These factors are also compounded by deep-seated dissonance, firstly, in the very obvious way in which our societies continue to present highly inconsistent and conflicting images and narratives across the mass and social media. On the one hand, we are presented with a relatively cosy and benign image of middle-class life as being relatively comfortable, stable and accessible, in spite of the fact that sustaining this position has become increasingly arduous and stressful for professionals and effectively out of reach for many of the working classes. Despite this, increasing numbers of the 'frozen out' are consistently reminded that their lack of success is a personal rather than a societal failing and all, as was suggested in Chapter 10, are fed a continuous diet of 'rags to riches' narratives.[6]

On the flipside are the scare stories, where media output including news and advertising presents an ongoing diet of worries around becoming ill from dreadful diseases, experience of poverty and destitution, threats to the economy, personal finances and livelihoods and, of late in the US, the UK and elsewhere, climate breakdown, internal political instability, crime and the spectre of cataclysmic geopolitical conflict. As US President Biden noted in October 2022, the immediate threat from the Russia/Ukraine war had brought the world closer to Armageddon than at any point since the Cuban Missile Crisis of the 1960s, while simmering tensions between the West and, notably, North Korea and Iran, increasingly ambivalent relations with Xi Jinping's administration in China and, not least, serious renewed conflict in the Middle East have all added to more personal worries.

Against this background, a strong element of fear is clearly understandable, and one might even say rational, while the sense of injustice and frustration among those who find themselves disparaged due to their identity, while being politically disenfranchised and financially excluded from respect, exacerbates the anger and disaffection described thus far. This all sounds excessively gloomy of course, but I would argue that it is a reasonable reflection of where the avarice, disconnection and mendacity that has flourished in the neoliberal era has led us and which seems to merely get worse going forward. And yet, paradoxically, we are also constantly reminded that positivity is a normal and essential attitude for advancement in this precarious environment and that its absence is somehow a personal character flaw or even an individual pathology – psychological, or now potentially due to a 'chemical imbalance' in the brain, as will be discussed in more detail later on.[7]

Being a team player

The demand for positivity at all costs is now suggested to be psychologically harmful in and of itself, in line with a view that our efforts to suppress or struggle with our innermost emotions actually up the ante. As was discussed earlier with reference to the relatively recent psychological and therapeutic model, Acceptance and Commitment Therapy (ACT), the constant attempt to struggle with and evade our natural responses to negative feelings operates as an *emotional amplifier* that can lead to much worse than passing malaise. In effect, as will be discussed in more detail later on, contrary to much of the debate on mental health and wellbeing matters, struggling with our emotions and seeing our negative feelings as 'symptoms' to be fought with and overcome is, paradoxically, suggested to be at the root of many deeper and more serious emotional problems.[8] This is a notion that has a long pedigree, while an important forerunner was the pioneering work on emotional distress offered by the Australian physician Dr Claire Weekes. Weekes also argued that contrary to prevailing psychological and psychiatric perspectives, rather than seeing negative emotions as symptoms to be struggled with, the route to recovery was to do largely the opposite.

However, as we know, a whole tranche of online therapeutic and self-help culture has emerged over recent decades promising the prospect of happiness or at least a sense of security and contentment by following some interventionist strategy or other, together with the banishment of negative feelings. Some of this is aligned with various forms of positive psychology and the science of happiness championed by Richard Layard and taken up by numerous others. Once more, this is well meaning, and may have some benefits; however, this must be qualified, as this is dependent on the focus being on *realistic* positivity and taking action to improve one's circumstances in ways that might support a sense of meaning and wellbeing:

> Existing research has demonstrated that valuing happiness is generally related to decreased well-being outcomes (Mauss et al., 2011) as well as an increased risk of mood disorders (Ford et al., 2014). This negative relationship with well-being is suggested to be the result of a felt pressure to feel happy at all times, paradoxically decreasing positive emotion the more it is desired (Mauss et al., 2011).[9]

The notion that largely unwavering happiness is the default human state, and its absence must be struggled with and ultimately overcome and/or treated, may fall foul of the same misconceptions mentioned earlier in terms of the need to be always on point while stimulating the *toxic positivity* discussed in Chapter 6. For fear of inconsistency, as was argued earlier, we do all need to *perform* to some extent in modern societies, an observation that has a long pedigree within the social sciences. From Erving Goffman's work, pointing out that all of us are selective in what we present to the world, to the work of Arlie Hochschild discussed in Chapter 6 in relation to workplace performances, there has long been an awareness that in public we are rarely if ever wholly authentic selves. As these writers understood, we could never sustain anything approaching a social order if we were simply to let loose as the mood or inclination takes us. This also accords with the perspective that our biosocially mandated requirement for a sense of clarity, consistency and control necessitates that we present a constrained and socially recognizable version of ourselves to each other across a range of settings. As Goffman suggested, this makes a relatively manageable social life possible, as we draw on the content and information we're presented with to shape an appearance, persona and demeanour that we hope that others will recognize and accept. The question appears to be the extent to which we have to do this and how far the performances that society demands of us are removed from our sense of who we feel we really are and our real feelings. Modern business and service cultures, in particular, demand that we present a certain face and attitude. Hence, adding to the disorientation, dissonance and other stressors that contemporary individuals experience in turbocapitalist societies, an awareness that 'negativity' should be avoided at all costs and the chutzpah that was once the preserve of bumptious salespeople have become common currency in both the contemporary workplace and in our socially mediated culture. In fact, an air of confidence, eagerness and enthusiasm are often called for even in the most arduous and/or mind-numbing and humdrum occupations where we are required to present the best 'face' to colleagues and customers as a key feature of 'emotional labour'. However, in light of new understandings of the implications of emotion suppression and fabrication, the implications of Goffman and Hochschild and aligned works in the social sciences become even more significant.[10]

Placing this in context with the forgoing discussion, this does not mean that we should not be attempting to change our circumstances; on the contrary. However, the difficulties for many in the contemporary era are that, in feeling powerless to maintain a sense of balance and order in an emotionally toxic environment, effort turns to suppressing the resulting negative emotions and their public expression, generating internal struggle in lieu of positive action in an attempt to manage oneself and how one appears to others rather than tackling the real source of the malaise.

The virtual confessional

Related to some of the issues discussed in Chapter 8, one variant of contemporary controlled presentation of the self broadly relates to what Michel Foucault termed the 'confessional self', which has also emerged via social media in a manner that is seemingly paradoxical or oppositional to the cult of positivity. Here people present a self-image that appears vulnerable, where past trauma and other negative personal experiences are not only exposed in public but are also presented as a social performance. For most people, this may be done privately, but it has also been reflected in a particular form of individual 'psychodrama' that is a central feature of reality TV, online and social media self-presentation. In a sense, this is a presentational tendency employed by many people to simply to claim an element of significance in our atomized and potentially anonymous social landscape. It's a claim that states 'I'm here', 'I'm human', 'I'm complex', 'I've suffered' and, importantly, 'I'm authentic and my life has meaning'. This latter claim might be regarded as a response to the inauthenticity many people experience in our overly presentational culture and there is a sense in which public displays and confessionals can reveal very genuine emotional scarring. However, it is also the case that a form of staged and calculated authenticity can also be used as a device to attract followers and subscribers: 'Micro-celebrity is a mind-set and a set of practices that courts attention through insights into its practitioners' private lives, and a sense of realness that renders their narratives, their branding, both accessible and intimate.'[11]

As was identified in Chapter 8, the ostensibly deeply personal can be employed as a calculated device to create a sense of intimacy. For example, this can be seen in the way that online audiences follow the personal lives and revelations of celebrities and other influencers whose travails and trauma are often employed and monetized as they attract followers and subscribers. In short, for some, the contemporary confessional is an exercise in genuine soul baring, while for many others, it has become a mediated appeal for attention and/or economic gain. Here we often find social media and reality stars with ostensibly enviable lives get closer to their legion of fans, and to extend their appeal, through revealing their relationship problems, anxieties and their own psychic struggles.

Following on from this trend, the confessional presentation is at times bound up with the selling or advancing of a variety of self-help techniques, books and other content that has become a burgeoning industry in our unhappy times. The internet and social media are awash with almost every conceivable self-help strategy, from the banal to the bizarre, while this is also a key feature of reality television, where the personal 'reveal', alongside dramatic confrontation, is a familiar staple. This often takes the form of the aforementioned confessional followed by the asserted adoption of numerous forms of therapeutic intervention through which the celebrity has 'recovered'.[12] In part, the viewers of therapeutic content and confession are also seeking a solution to inner turmoil together with a feeling of community and, as was discussed earlier, the perceived security of connecting with others, even if this is only virtual.

The medicalization of misery

Of course, much of the preceding discussion can be characterized as being associated with 'para-therapy' or popular psychology, while the more authoritative purveyors of happiness and contentment are evidently among the burgeoning psychological and psychiatric professions, together with the vastly profitable pharmaceutical industry that has increasingly operated, and prospered, in tandem with the latter:

> Many psychiatrists and psychologists advocate for routine depression screening in the context of the economic burden of depression (Reynolds & Patel, 2017; Trautmann, Rehm, & Wittchen, 2016). In the US, despite a lack of evidence to support routine depression screening (Cosgrove, Karter, Vaswani, & Thombs, 2017; Thombs et al., 2017), it has been recommended by the United States Prevention Services Task Force (USPSTF) for everyone over 13, including for the first time during pregnancy and the post-partum period. It is noteworthy that the UK and Canada, looking at the same evidence as the US, made the explicit recommendation against screening because of concerns about over-diagnosis, overtreatment, and thus exposing people to the risks of treatment, particularly antidepressants and second generation antipsychotics, without enough evidence of benefit.[13]

Mental health issues have been rising precipitously, of course, and what is being argued in no way attempts to underplay the very genuine suffering that many people experience – on the contrary, given that this appears to be a burgeoning phenomenon across contemporary societies. The point being made here is that, in the first instance, the individualization of the causes of psychic distress is questionable at the very least, recognizing that the way in which this has been understood and approached is the subject of increasing criticism and controversy.[14]

In 2020, Dainius Puras, UN Special Rapporteur in the right to health, was criticized for an alleged 'anti-psychiatric' bias in his 2017 report.[15] This was due to his raising of some issues relating to the current approach to mental healthcare. In effect, Puras questioned the efficacy of the dominant biomedical model in psychiatry and the way in which psychiatric interventions could often override individual's human rights, through forced treatment, incarceration and so on. Of course, this is far from a new debate as psychiatry's and, to an extent, psychology's assumptions about mental health and its treatment have never been far from critique or controversy. While I'll return to issues with psychology later on, I think it's fair to say that psychiatry has come under particular scrutiny.

On the face of it, and as far as most of the public are aware, psychiatry is simply another branch of modern medicine much like any other: patients are seen, diagnoses are made and treatment programmes are advised, most commonly through drug programmes to 'correct' whatever malfunctioning part of the brain is deemed to be causing the patient's problems. However, it is this biomedical model of mental illness and mental health services that has attracted the most questioning and even opprobrium. The problem, its critics point out, is that in most other branches of medicine, for the most part 'diseases' tend to be roughly identifiable through very specific physical symptoms and verifiable through a variety of biological tests and scans. Of course, there are always some ailments that may present as being ambiguous or difficult to diagnose. However, even in these cases, it will normally be clear that the patient presents with an ailment that's physical in nature and origin, even if the precise process is unclear. This is not so for psychiatry, claim its critics.

Firstly, psychiatric diagnosis normally relies on applying labels to people's reported feelings, thinking and behaviour rather than evident physical symptoms. The subsequent diagnosis, rather than being the identification of a specific ailment, is based on a range of often ambiguous and overlapping 'disorders' that tend to be revised over time through succeeding generations of the psychiatric 'bible', the impressively titled *Diagnostic and Statistical Manual of Mental Disorders* (DSM), which is currently on its 5th edition. This contains a vast array of syndromes that people can suffer from with labels and criteria that have changed and expanded over time. Again, in qualification, other aspects of medicine evidently evolve with greater knowledge and understanding. The distinction here is that far more of psychiatric diagnosis and treatment is imprecise and based on shifting opinion, as well as being unreliable and largely unverifiable via clear evidence:

> The diagnostic system for psychiatry has also been increasingly noted as an impediment to progress. The problems have been extensively documented ... and do not need to be elaborated here, but *include excessive co-morbidity of disorders, marked heterogeneity of mechanisms and reification of disorders. In particular, the underlying validity of the disease entities has been questioned, in that the DSM and ICD categories do not map well onto emerging findings from genetics, systems neuroscience and behavioral science ...*; as a result, it becomes very difficult to translate research from basic studies, either in animal models or in humans, to a systematic understanding of pathology or to systematic treatments directed at mechanisms. (Emphasis added)[16]

DSM 5 was finally published in May 2013. Its architects had originally intended to introduce a radically new approach to diagnosing mental illness. At the outset, they had acknowledged the parlous situation they confronted: 'Despite many proposed candidates, not one laboratory marker has been found to be specific in identifying any of the DSM-defined syndromes. *Epidemiologic and clinical studies have shown extremely high rates of comorbidities among the disorders, undermining the hypothesis that the syndromes represent distinct etiologies.* Furthermore, epidemiological studies have shown a high degree of short-term diagnostic instability for many disorders.' But this time around, they promised, things would be different (Kupfer, First, & Regier, Reference Kupfer, First and Regier2002: xviii, 19). (Emphasis added)[17]

Such harsh criticism may be unfair in the sense that I'm sure that the majority of psychiatrists and, indeed, other mental healthcare professionals are earnestly committed to improving people's wellbeing. However, it has been argued that the 'disease' model of mental illness, the diagnostic criteria and the claims to biological foundations for mental illness represent a questionable basis for asserting equivalence of rigour and professional parity with other medical professionals. In a concise comment piece on these issues, Duncan Double, himself a psychiatrist, associates this trend with the neo-Kraepelin approach, associated with the highly influential psychiatrist Emil Kraepelin. For the latter, psychiatry was presented as a medical profession like any other – a biomedical discipline – through which rigorous diagnoses and treatment of disorders 'of the brain' could be managed.[18] As was noted earlier, this model came to significantly displace Freudian psychiatry with its talking cures, endowing the profession with a new confidence that mental illnesses were organic and likely innate in nature, and that they were capable of offering treatment in the form of an emerging class of drugs. However, it takes no great leap of the imagination to understand why this view of mental illness, while bolstering the psychiatrist's professional status, came to be vigorously promoted to the public (and to psychiatrists themselves) by global pharmaceutical conglomerates eyeing potentially huge profits emerging from the medicalization of human unhappiness and misery.[19]

One of the most vociferous and authoritative critiques levelled at contemporary psychiatry has been advanced by Allen Frances, an eminent psychiatrist himself who chaired and participated in the committees responsible for the compilation of earlier versions of the DSM. Frances takes aim at psychiatry's overdiagnosis and the medicalization of what he regards as normal feelings and behaviour. Again, there is no questioning the notion that human psychic suffering exists, including very serious suffering. Rather, the point Frances makes is that beyond the most serious problems, much of what psychiatry deems disorder is part of the normal features of living and is also a response to circumstances, such as those prevalent in our bewildering and stress-inducing societies, while the extent to which such 'maladies' require treatment has been significantly overextended.

He also recognizes that this is not only a highly profitable enterprise, but is also damaging on a number of fronts. In the first instance, treating people's understandable responses to adverse circumstances or experiences as diseases of the brain, without verification, risks 'patients' living their diagnosis.[20] Hence, people begin to see themselves as inherently damaged, a situation reinforced by the fact that much of psychiatry and psychology tends to suggest that psychic 'disorders' tend to be chronic – that is, they can be managed but not cured. The tendency for dependency, fatalism, hopelessness and 'repeat business' from this kind of narrative appears evident:[21]

> Anyone living a full, rich life experiences ups and downs, stresses, disappointments, sorrows, and setbacks. These challenges are a normal part of being human, and they should not be treated as psychiatric disease. However, today millions of people who are really no more than 'worried well' are being diagnosed as having a mental disorder and are receiving unnecessary treatment ... We also shift responsibility for our mental well-being away from our own naturally resilient and self-healing brains, which have kept us sane for hundreds of thousands of years, and into the hands of 'Big Pharma', who are reaping multi-billion-dollar profits. Frances cautions that the new edition of the 'bible of psychiatry', the Diagnostic and Statistical Manual of Mental Disorders-5 (DSM-5), will turn our current diagnostic inflation into hyperinflation by converting millions of 'normal' people into 'mental patients'. Alarmingly, in DSM-5, normal grief will become 'Major Depressive Disorder'; the forgetting seen in old age is 'Mild Neurocognitive Disorder'; temper tantrums are 'Disruptive Mood Dysregulation Disorder'; worrying about a medical illness is 'Somatic Symptom Disorder'; gluttony is 'Binge Eating Disorder'; and most of us will qualify for adult 'Attention Deficit Disorder' What's more, all of these newly invented conditions will worsen the cruel paradox of the mental health industry: those who desperately need psychiatric help are left shamefully neglected, while the 'worried well' are given the bulk of the treatment, often at their own 'detriment'.[22]

This perspective on psychiatry was also notably expressed in James Davies' 2013 book *Cracked: Why Psychiatry Is Doing More Harm Than Good*. Davies also takes aim at psychiatry's biomedical model, its diagnostic criteria, professional hubris, business model and relationship with the pharmaceutical industry.[23]

The sort of views expressed here have not been confined to psychiatry, as will be discussed later on, albeit that it is the branch of mental health provision that has attracted the majority of criticism. From the anti-psychiatry of Thomas Szasz and R.D. Laing to the poststructuralist critique of Michel Foucault and others, the discipline has been roundly challenged for the validity of some of its scientific claims and, notably, for its history of enforced confinement and treatments that could be seen to be seriously damaging, from electroconvulsive therapy to brain surgery. The latter notably captured the public imagination via Stanley Kubrick's nightmarish 1975 depiction of US psychiatric facilities in *One Flew Over the Cuckoo's Nest*. The horrific consequences of the lobotomy performed on Jack Nicholson's ill-fated lead character aside, perhaps equally disturbing was the way in which any 'sane' claim to autonomy or questioning of the organization was deemed to be symptomatic of mental illness, leading to some further sanction being applied to those who stepped out of line. This was reminiscent of what Erving Goffman described as 'looping' in total institutions, which arises where any sign of even the mildest verbal questioning or resistance can be turned back on the perpetrator, grossly escalating the extent of the challenge to authority and its basis as a means of instilling confusion and exerting control.[24] In effect, looping represents a form of institutional gaslighting that may be seen to pervade other areas of society and, not least, some workplace cultures.

Of course, all of this must be qualified, in that contemporary psychiatry has in the main stepped back from its more excessive historical practices, and there is little doubt that many practitioners act with good intentions and can be of help to some of those experiencing mental health issues. However, the legacy remains, as does the current practice of diagnosing and drugging the willing, and at times the unwilling, with a degree of confidence and hubris that does not seem to be warranted by the science. In many cases, the substances involved are applied inconsistently, with scant understanding of their impact on the complex functioning of the human brain and often with serious side effects that can cause longstanding damage to cognitive, emotional and even physical functioning.

As was noted earlier, criticism of current approaches to mental health issues are, of course, not confined to psychiatry, but have also been voiced against and even by clinical psychologists. While psychology and talking cures are often regarded as being much less questionable and more benign than some of the issues levelled against psychiatry, reservations remain in some areas. This is not to say that people do not benefit from therapy, as was suggested in relation to ACT previously, as many clearly do. Other talking therapies such as cognitive behavioural therapy (CBT) are also regarded as being beneficial. Evidently, being able to share and talk over personal troubles and gain some support is an important component of emotional aid, even aside from the clinical aspects of this. Nonetheless, the diagnostic and 'illness' model, and the normalcy issue, remain prevalent and have been subject to similar if lighter criticism. The issue is that psychology has tended to accept the classificatory model associated with psychiatry's DSM, which maintains that discrete syndromes can be identified with specific aetiology, morphing into disorders and diseases that require treatment, if not via psychiatry, then through the talking 'cures' offered by clinical psychology. As Frances asserts, and as was suggested earlier, while people undoubtedly suffer (and many very seriously), there remains a large question mark as to how we understand that suffering.[25]

As numerous neuroscientists have observed, McEwen included, when people suffer from fear and anxiety over a significant period, created by the environment and culture to which we currently expose them, they become generally more sensitized to negative emotional arousal.[26] In effect, they become emotionally trigger happy, while the impact of chronic negative emotional arousal on the PFC renders it more difficult for them to think clearly and inhibit these negative feelings. What I'm suggesting here is that much of what we regard as mental ill health might be ascribed simply to the fear and chronic stress imposed by our toxic socioeconomic environment. Outwardly expressed, this may present itself as the angry, intolerant, prejudicial and nativistic behaviour described in previous chapters. Internally, through ongoing rumination and psychic struggle, it may become a source of ongoing angst, distress and confusion that we associate with mental ill health. As to specific diagnosis and discrete conditions proposed by mental health diagnoses, are these merely defined by the specific focus of negative feelings, to whatever the individual has been thinking of and associated with their inner turmoil, as a form of misrecognition?

This is a view broadly consistent with ACT and some other perspectives, in the sense that the ultimate cause of serious mental trouble is fear of the experience of fear itself, particularly among the vulnerable and sensitized, rather than the specific objects or scenarios that have triggered that experience,[27] the latter being taken to be the grounds for a wide array of specific 'diagnoses'. Taking this line of argument further, might the very extreme distress and confusion we associate with psychosis also have some synergies, albeit with the application of a much greater degree of distress, with that experienced by a primalized mind that is increasingly susceptible to the acceptance of strange ideas, conspiracies and irrational allegiances, paranoia and prejudices? This is in line with a growing view that not only anxiety, depression and a range of other forms of psychic suffering but also psychosis may well have social causes.[28]

There is a further issue that presents itself when we think about contemporary mental health and its diagnosis and disease model. In other words, presenting mental health issues as innate diseases of the brain, as being enduring attributes rather than potentially recoverable responses to life's travails, has the danger that the person lives the label, regarding themselves as chronically damaged and unable to recover or improve their situation. In short, diagnoses may become destiny:

> [C]onceptualizing the distress that results from social, political, or economic injustice as a 'disease' is a thoroughly modern phenomenon based on the same attitudes toward knowledge, science, and subjectivity inherent in the neoliberal worldview. The disease burden framework is part and parcel of the neoliberalization of the subject – it 'responsibilizes' (Teghtsoonian, 2009) people for their distress and obscures the connection between social injustice and emotional suffering. While some have suggested that the disease framework might alleviate stigma, research on this topic has found that biomedical explanations increase social distancing and that, conversely, psychosocial explanations can be humanizing (Longdon & Read, 2017; Schomerus et al., 2012; Seeman, Tang, Brown, & Ing, 2016).[29]

Overall, in this view, the victims of the ills of living under frenetic contemporary capitalism become customers for one its most successful and growing industrial complexes, from self-help, psychology and psychiatry to pharmaceuticals, providing an alibi for those who benefit most from the system that its casualties are those susceptible or born to experience these conditions. In a real sense we are presented with the notion that the groundswell of human misery and angst that pervades our societies is due to inherently damaged individuals being unable to cope with the normal demands of everyday living, as opposed to simply normal human beings with regular emotional responses being exposed to the pressures and pathologies of everyday living in an increasingly inhuman world: 'Put crudely, the point of neoliberal ideology is not to convince us that Hayek was right; it is to console us that the sense of insecurity, of perpetual competition and individual isolation produced by neoliberal government is natural, because "that's what life is really like".'[30]

On a final point here, the tendency for contemporary psychiatry and psychology to discuss mental health issues in terms of 'symptoms', often pointing to how debilitating and disrupting the conditions they point towards can become, as well as enlisting clients, might also lead to the very 'fear of fear' discussed earlier, setting people up to be scared of their own emotions and to potentially view their normal upset and anxieties as signs of impending pathology. Might this broadly well-intentioned campaign to deal with psychic ills paradoxically end up instigating the kind of internal struggles that, as was noted earlier, are now considered to be key source of contemporary psychological problems, compounding the effects of their real source in demanding, bewildering, unequal, insecure and unjust neoliberal societies?[31]

From psychic ills to (un)healthy ageing

As was intimated in Chapter 1, our response to chronically challenging and stressful conditions has a negative effect on our emotional health and our capacity for rational thought, as well as having an impact on our neural plasticity, hormones and the expression of our genes. The latter is also implicated in the way we are affected by inequality, as this is a stressor that is deeply entangled with feelings of insecurity. In fact, there is growing evidence that low social status, in and of itself, damages our health via epigenetic changes that affect us neurologically and throughout the body, providing an explanation for the highly prevalent differences in vulnerability to illness and life expectancy (including healthy life expectancy) between wealthy and poor communities.[32]

One caveat here is that, in some primate and other species, in particular settings, the negative effects of social status can be more prevalent in high-status animals, and we might assume that this can also occurs in humans. This arises where the position of the dominant individual is highly insecure and there are consistent challenges and conflict.[33] Nonetheless, as was outlined earlier, for the most part, the wealthy and powerful in contemporary societies are insulated by wealth from the vagaries of the sea of insecurity that they have imposed on others. However – and this is also speculative – could the erratic and aggressive conduct of many authoritarian leaders be explained by the impact of the chronic stress of sustaining or pursuing individual dominance and power in ongoing conflictual circumstances? In short, might the tyrants, at least those heading up unstable societies and surrounded by potential rivals, be as vulnerable to *primalization* as those they harm and might this offer some insight into why, in line with the old maxim, that power appears to corrupt?[34]

However, returning to the issue at hand, while factors associated with negative emotions, such as substance abuse, poor diet and lifestyle practices, are often regarded as being the main cause of inequalities in terms of health and wellbeing, these also appear to be bound up in various ways with the epigenetic changes suggested here (and as was briefly flagged up in Chapter 1) of DNA methylation, histone modification and RNA changes that modify the expression of genes. As such, it is not only what people *do* in response to the stigma, shame and stress of losing out in highly competitive and status obsessed societies that matters, but the biological impact of people's social position and experiences can, in and of themselves, contribute to premature ageing, as well as a range of diseases.[35] As was also noted previously, in light of these discoveries, concern around inequality becomes much more acute in societies that have engaged in a renewed agenda in recent decades of not minding the gap between rich and poor as being an assertedly necessary and inevitable feature of the economy and society. The epigenetic as well as the synaptic impact on the brain and body surely necessitates a revision of the sanguine, even stridently uncaring attitude towards social inequity that has been normalized since the neoliberal turn.

However, if that were insufficient to generate a clamour for change, the prospect that this damage can be transmitted intergenerationally must focus the mind. As was addressed in Chapter 10, Pierre Bourdieu set out the means by which people's acquired *habitus*, the deeply engrained worldview, demeanour, accent and embodied habits that constitute a person, greatly affected their life chances. This he associated with cultural, economic and social capital, key experiences and resources acquired from one's background, contributing to life trajectories.[36] In a sense, *The Social Map* model is offered as an extension of the form of understanding of the individual that goes beyond the wholly social factors that Bourdieu and others extended to encompass our biological constitution and its intertwining with social life. Bourdieu considered social factors to be the key elements that explained the intergenerational transmission of inequality and as key impediments to social mobility. However, applying a further level of biological analysis, if epigenetic susceptibilities that without intervention to prevent them being realized further mar the limited 'opportunities' available to the less fortunate in highly unequal societies, this surely places the last nail in the coffin of the apologists for the neoliberal system and its claims to meritocracy, as it also opens up a new perspective on the social and the implications of social organization in terms of determinants of health.[37] As was noted earlier, the fact that a growing body of evidence indicating that negative emotional and health effects of social inequality can be inherited needs to be highlighted and taken very seriously by policymakers and publics. The implications for social justice here are fundamental if we consider that, as is the case at the time of writing, a compendium of ills, many of which were once thought to have been consigned to the past in major developed economies, such as hunger and poor diet, lack of secure and warm accommodation, rampant insecurity, shame and existential angst, injure both body and mind and, perhaps ultimately, the future health and happiness of subsequent generations.

Notes

[1]   Mills, C.W. (2023) 'The sociological imagination', in *Social Work*, Oxfordshire: Routledge, pp 105–108.

[2]   Sharfstein, S.S. (2008) 'Big pharma and American psychiatry', *Journal of Nervous and Mental Disease*, 196(4): 265–266; Scull, A. (2021) 'American psychiatry in the new millennium: a critical appraisal', *Psychological Medicine*, 51(16): 2762–2770.

[3]   'When bankers don't retire at 40. Or even 50', https://www.efinancialcareers.co.uk/news/2014/10/upset-as-40-something-bankers-find-themselves-unable-to-retire

[4]   'Suella Braverman claims "benefits street culture" still exists despite cost of living crisis', *Huffington Post*, 4 October 2022, https://www.huffingtonpost.co.uk/entry/suella-braverman-claims-benefits-street-culture-still-exists-in-britain-despite-cost-of-living-crisis_uk_633c3ccbe4b04cf8f366e35e

5 'North Dakota Senate votes to increase its own meal budget after rejecting free school lunch bill', *New Republic*, 7 April 2023, https://newrepublic.com/post/171716/north-dakota-senate-votes-increase-meal-budget-rejecting-free-school-lunch-bill

6 Lamont, M. (2019) 'From "having" to "being": self-worth and the current crisis of American society', *British Journal of Sociology*, 70(3): 660–707.

7 Esposito, L. and Perez, F.M. (2014) 'Neoliberalism and the commodification of mental health', *Humanity & Society*, 38(4): 414–442.

8 Harris, R. (2022) *The Happiness Trap: How to Stop Struggling and Start Living*, Boulder: Shambhala Publications.

9 Humphrey, A., Szoka, R. and Bastian, B. (2022) 'When the pursuit of happiness backfires: the role of negative emotion valuation', *Journal of Positive Psychology*, 17(5): 611–619.

10 Goffman, E. (1959) *The Presentation of Self in Everyday Life*, Harmondsworth: Penguin; Hochschild, A. (1983) *The Managed Heart: The Commercialization of Human Feeling*, Berkeley: University of California Press.

11 Khamis, S., Ang, L. and Welling, R. (2017) 'Self-branding, "micro-celebrity" and the rise of social media influencers', *Celebrity Studies*, 8(2): 191–208.

12 King, B. (2008) 'Stardom, celebrity and the para-confession', *Social Semiotics*, 18(2): 115–132.

13 Cosgrove, L. and Karter, J.M. (2018) 'The poison in the cure: neoliberalism and contemporary movements in mental health', *Theory & Psychology*, 28(5): 669–683.

14 Roberts, M.T. (2021) 'Globalization and neoliberalism: structural determinants of global mental health?', *Humanity & Society*, 45(4): 471–508.

15 Dharmawardene, V. and Menkes, D.B. (2019) 'Responding to the UN Special Rapporteur's anti-psychiatry bias', *Australian & New Zealand Journal of Psychiatry*, 53(4): 282–283.

16 Cuthbert, B.N. and Insel, T.R. (2013) 'Toward the future of psychiatric diagnosis: the seven pillars of RDoC', *BMC Medicine*, 11(1): 1–8.

17 Scull, A. (2021) 'American psychiatry in the new millennium: a critical appraisal', *Psychological Medicine*, 51(16): 2762–2770, at 2762.

18 Double, D. (2002) 'The limits of psychiatry', *British Medical Journal*, 324(7342): 900–904.

19 Esposito, L. and Perez, F.M. (2014) 'Neoliberalism and the commodification of mental health', *Humanity & Society*, 38(4): 414–442.

20 Frances, A. (2013) 'Saving normal: an insider's revolt against out-of-control psychiatric diagnosis, DSM-5, big pharma and the medicalization of ordinary life', *Psychotherapy in Australia*, 19(3): 14–18.

21 Rozental, A., Kottorp, A., Boettcher, J., Andersson, G. and Carlbring, P. (2016) 'Negative effects of psychological treatments: an exploratory factor analysis of the negative effects questionnaire for monitoring and reporting adverse and unwanted events', *PloS one*, 11(6): e0157503.

22 Frances, A. (2013) 'Saving normal: an insider's revolt against out-of-control psychiatric diagnosis, DSM-5, big pharma and the medicalization of ordinary life', *Psychotherapy in Australia*, 19(3): 14–18.

23 Davies, J. (2013) *Cracked: Why Psychiatry Is Doing More Harm Than Good*, London: Icon Books.

24 Goffman, E. (1961) *Asylums: Essays on the Social Situation of Mental Patients and Other Inmates*, Harmondsworth: Penguin.

25 Frances, A. (2013) 'Saving normal: an insider's revolt against out-of-control psychiatric diagnosis, DSM-5, big pharma and the medicalization of ordinary life', *Psychotherapy in Australia*, 19(3): 14–18.

26 Kaul, D., Schwab, S.G., Mechawar, N. and Matosin, N. (2021) 'How stress physically re-shapes the brain: impact on brain cell shapes, numbers and connections in psychiatric disorders', *Neuroscience & Biobehavioral Reviews*, 124: 193–215.

27 Harris, R. (2022) *The Happiness Trap: How to Stop Struggling and Start Living*, Boulder: Shambhala Publications.

28 Read, J., Bentall, R.P. and Fosse, R. (2009) 'Time to abandon the bio-bio-bio model of psychosis: exploring the epigenetic and psychological mechanisms by which adverse life events lead to psychotic symptoms', *Epidemiology and Psychiatric Sciences*, 18(4): 299–310.

29 Cosgrove, L. and Karter, J.M. (2018) 'The poison in the cure: neoliberalism and contemporary movements in mental health', *Theory & Psychology*, 28(5): 669–683.

30 Frances, A. (2013) 'Saving normal: an insider's revolt against out-of-control psychiatric diagnosis, DSM-5, big pharma and the medicalization of ordinary life', *Psychotherapy in Australia*, 19(3): 14–18.

31 Hayes, S.C., Wilson, K.G., Gifford, E.V., Follette, V.M. and Strosahl, K. (1996) 'Experiential avoidance and behavioral disorders: a functional dimensional approach to diagnosis and treatment', *Journal of Consulting and Clinical Psychology*, 64(6): 1152–1168; Esposito, L. and Perez, F.M. (2014) 'Neoliberalism and the commodification of mental health', *Humanity & Society*, 38(4): 414–442.

32 Palma-Gudiel, H., Fañanás, L., Horvath, S. and Zannas, A.S. (2020) 'Psychosocial stress and epigenetic aging', *International Review of Neurobiology*, 150: 107–128; Gottschalk, M.G., Domschke, K. and Schiele, M.A. (2020) 'Epigenetics underlying susceptibility and resilience relating to daily life stress, work stress, and socioeconomic status', *Frontiers in Psychiatry*, 11: 163.

33 Anderson, J.A., Johnston, R.A., Lea, A.J., Campos, F.A., Voyles, T.N., Akinyi, M.Y. and Tung, J. (2020) 'The costs of competition: high social status males experience accelerated epigenetic aging in wild baboons', *Biorxiv.*

34 Becker, J.C., Hartwich, L. and Haslam, S.A. (2021) 'Neoliberalism can reduce well-being by promoting a sense of social disconnection, competition, and loneliness', *British Journal of Social Psychology*, 60(3): 947–965.

35 McEwen, C.A. (2022) 'Connecting the biology of stress, allostatic load and epigenetics to social structures and processes', *Neurobiology of Stress*, 17: 100426; Meloni, M. (2014) 'The social brain meets the reactive genome: neuroscience, epigenetics and the new social biology', *Frontiers in Human Neuroscience*, 8: 309; Guidi, J., Lucente, M., Sonino, N. and Fava, G.A. (2021) 'Allostatic load and its impact on health: a systematic review', *Psychotherapy and Psychosomatics*, 90(1): 11–27.

36 Bourdieu, P. (1984) *Distinction*, London: Routledge.

37 Notterman, D.A. and Mitchell, C. (2015) 'Epigenetics and understanding the impact of social determinants of health', *Pediatric Clinics*, 62(5): 1227–1240; Loi, M., Del Savio, L. and Stupka, E (2013) 'Social epigenetics and equality of opportunity', *Public Health Ethics*, 6(2): 142–153; Meloni, M. (2014) 'The social brain meets the reactive genome: neuroscience, epigenetics and the new social biology', *Frontiers in Human Neuroscience*, 8: 309; McEwen, C.A. (2022) 'Connecting the biology of stress, allostatic load and epigenetics to social structures and processes', *Neurobiology of Stress*, 17: 100426; Lacal, I. and Ventura, R. (2018) 'Epigenetic inheritance: concepts, mechanisms and perspectives', *Frontiers in Molecular Neuroscience*, 292.

Conclusion: Where to Now?

It's fair to say that the scope of this book is wide-ranging and ambitious, one might argue overly so in places. To begin with, a central contention of this work, as outlined in the earlier chapters, is that engaging with an understanding of where we are now is best approached by trying to gain a richer appreciation of our development and constitution. Firstly, this has been undertaken to illustrate some of the recurrent patterns and consistencies in our historical development that have brought us to this point and, secondly, it is argued that a much fuller appreciation of key aspects of the latter must include an appreciation of the interaction of both the social and the biological in shaping our development. In short, as I have argued, while ahistorical and abiological analyses have produced a vast range of important insights with respect to society and the human condition, failing to include both a historical and a biological perspective removes the potential for a critical level of understanding of the past and the present, particularly given that the crucial role of our biological needs and propensities as a key factor shaping our historical and current engagement with the world has been largely overlooked or downplayed. As has been identified, throughout much of our history, the drive to make sense of our world, to impose control over the environment and to accommodate other people can be understood, at least in part, in terms of a contest to shape our reality in a way that meets with not only our requirement for fundamental resources, but also our deep biologically defined psychosocial as well as physical needs. Missing this not only impoverishes understanding, but also provides space for ungrounded, ultimately misleading and, at times, opaque and obscure 'understandings' of who we are and where we are going. Overall, what I've set out to do here is to apply a more grounded and holistic perspective to offer a particular a way of thinking about the society we've produced, as well as applying this to exploring a critical stage in terms of our development.

One of the key issues addressed throughout has been in terms of the way in which we understand ourselves and the type of societal organization that is conducive to our health, wellbeing and development, both individually and collectively, and how in this regard we have come to lose our way. We are eminently capable of great feats of creativity, kindness, charity and cooperation, which, when we are at our best, continue to be widely in evidence, even amid the darkness of the present. Drawing on a range of works, it seems very clear that it is within an environment of cooperation and stability that we are at our happiest and healthiest, as this is intrinsic to our better nature. The problem, however, is that as we also know we have a darker side where our need for control, clarity and predictability, rather than moving us towards sense making, creativity, discovery and solidarity, has led us in the direction of competition, conflict and domination, subjugation and even obliteration of others who stand in the way of a less enlightened way of meeting our needs. It is only by appealing to the former and overcoming the latter that we can move forward and evolve, both socially and indeed to a degree biologically, in a progressive direction.

As was argued earlier, the very long road towards modernity was marked by an ongoing struggle between these polarities, from the consensual, rational and enlightened to the dogmatic, prejudicial, avaricious and, all too often, bloody. However, it was not so long ago that we appeared to be reaching a point where we were beginning to realize at least some possibility of the former eclipsing the latter as a critical step in our maturation. For this short period between the end of the Second World War and the early 1970s, a glimpse of a better world seemed possible or at the very least worth aiming for. However, the turn to neoliberalism, and all that this implies in terms of our culture, social arrangements and understanding of ourselves, has derailed and resurrected a regressive set of arrangements and darker zeitgeist, dismantling the fledgling progressive effort that not so long ago seemed to be moving us tentatively in the direction of greater democracy, peace and optimism for the future. Of course, as has been discussed, this was very far from being a complete project. The dark side was far from being conquered and remained very much in evidence. Nonetheless, a more progressive mindset was emerging and there was at least the beginning of hope and a belief that this might become the more general direction of travel. However, over the last few decades, such optimism has been unravelling apace, impacting on our lives from the personal to the geopolitical, where current trends threaten not only our personal happiness and contentment, economic wellbeing and societal cohesion, but also potentially our very existence, constitution and the sustainability of the planet.

While critique and polemic are widespread and understandable, and I readily concede that there is a good deal of that here, it is impossible to seriously engage with these matters and remain wholly impassive. However, since the dawn of the neoliberal era, that is precisely what we've been encouraged to do; to accept as normal a form of society that denies many of us basic needs and resources while encouraging our worst impulses. We have been persuaded to lionize and protect the interest and values of a diminishing coterie of winners, almost regardless of how just and/or questionable their good fortune has been acquired, and to condemn and vilify the impoverished and the losers for having failed to overcome the often insurmountable impediments to changing their fortunes. Seduced by a shallow consumerism, a disposable and often vitriolic public sphere, as well as depthless mediated connections in place of real relationships and the supportive communities we need, we are kept in place by a deluded aspiration that we have a stake in an inherently rigged and grossly uneven contest.

As was argued earlier, our co-option to this way of life can be seen as a concerted campaign, particularly in the neoliberal UK and US, mounted by a coalition of politicians, right-wing think tanks, media and corporations to advance an agenda that conceals the profound injustice at its heart and denies the damage it has generated, even in terms of the economic aims by which it is justified. Writing this on the approach to Christmas, and with apologies for being trite, it's clear that we have been encouraged to side with the unreconstructed Scrooge in Dickens' *A Christmas Carol* or the noxious Potter in Frank Capra's perennial Christmas favourite *It's a Wonderful Life*. It is interesting that both of these still-popular works were offered as literary and filmic challenges to precisely the type of economy, society, culture and mindset that the UK and the US have foisted on most of the world and have persuaded many to support. In a sense, we have re-created Pottersville and have left the contemporary George Bailey's of this world to their fate.

Despite this, it seems clear that this agenda has never been wholly successful, and often goes against the grain, given the very continuing popularity of this kind of fictional content and also the way in which publics often rally in times of crisis or when they are made aware of clear injustice. As will be argued towards the end of this chapter, I would suggest that while we can be too readily encouraged to be selfish and nasty, for most it doesn't take very much to turn the tide. As such, the ideologues and apologists for this toxic form of society have had to work consistently to sustain our increasingly unjust and uncaring societies, aided by the cognitive and emotional delirium imposed via insecurity and inequality-induced *primalization* that has 'softened up' many of those who are often the victims of the movements that they have rallied to, from the centre and far right to radical religious and other variants of irrational and angry extremism for the most disaffected. Moreover, the division and isolation that have emerged due to our way of life, coupled with the influence of mass and social media, have provided fertile ground for political manipulation that has possibly never been more effective. As such, many have been kept in a state of permanent dissonance, further compounding the psychological burden that has been addressed throughout this work. While the evidence and diagnosis are clear and, as I have argued here, the consequences immensely more far-reaching than has been currently understood, what can be done to recover our society and ourselves from our currently destructive path and to 'take back control' from the narrow interests that continue to undermine our individual and collective wellbeing?

Firstly, there are some very obvious actions that will need to be taken to move us towards a more positive track and to confront many of the serious problems and developments that potentially threaten our individual and collective wellbeing, albeit that the obstacles currently seem almost insurmountable, not least due to the deterioration of relations at the global level and the resistance of powerful financial and corporate interests to meaningful change.

Evidently, as was outlined in Chapter 9, we must firstly secure the future of our planet and confront those powerful vested interests that continue to cynically subvert meaningful action on climate change, as they seek to keep the lucrative cash cow of fossil fuels going for as long as possible while dragging their heels over the move to sustainable and renewable energy sources. As the hesitant international agreements from Paris to COP were affected by the impact on energy by the war in Ukraine, the latter was seized upon by fossil fuel companies as a rationale and opportunity for undermining even the agreed and limited but necessary steps towards net zero. This has also been exploited by politicians on the right and presented as a feature of the contemporary culture wars, a device for garnering support from a substantial segment of disaffected publics.

Those who continue to engage in pollution and environmental degradation, which has been growing apace in the neoliberal era, must be also brought to book and the costs of this kind of activity must be made to substantially outweigh the current profits that can be gained from overlooking environmental destruction. These are very obvious, even banal points, but are nonetheless critical as we cannot begin to engage with the other serious issues that confront us if efforts towards restoring a semblance of stability and progress are undermined by catastrophic climate breakdown and the conflicts large and small that may inevitably ensue in a scramble for remaining resources and liveable environments.

Related to this, as was identified in Chapter 5, finance must evidently be constrained in terms of its capacity to distort and misdirect reward while encouraging anti-planet and wider antisocial activity through much of its activities. It is now clear that when financial sector power, influence and activity is not kept sufficiently in check, a range of social, economic and political problems soon follow. The experience of both 1929 and 2007/2008 make this abundantly clear. The tendency towards speculation and footloose capital, as well as the almost unfettered ability to create and extend credit, and hence debt, has distorted the cost of living for billions across the globe while profiting a minority. Stagnating wages, insecure work, exorbitant housing costs and housing insecurity, economic instability and, consequently, political and geopolitical tensions as well as environmental degradation – much of this can be traced back to the activities of underregulated finance. What also often goes unrecognized is that 'assistance' to the general public in the form of underregulated money creation and loose credit often simply drives up the prices of essential assets and goods, profiting corporates and rentiers, while locking the masses into a condition of subjugation as effectively indentured servants of this system. While, of course, part of the issue here is that the influence of the financial sector, which has grown ever more powerful under neoliberalism, now undermines the capacity of polities to bring it back under control, challenging the dominance and the unjustified rewards for gambling with intangibles in financial markets and, more critically, with the speculative price setting of life's essentials. Given all of these environmental, economic, social, personal, political and health 'externalities', re-regulation is essential, including a shift away from the emphasis on short-term profitability, and the exploitation that goes with it, as a key socioeconomic and political focus, and perhaps even the removal of essential commodities from speculative markets altogether (for more of this, see the discussion further on).

In terms of sustaining ourselves within modern economies, we are now being presented with the prospect of a further source of unprecedented upheaval. Since the Industrial Revolution, we have deeply installed an economic model where most of us are dependent on selling our labour to survive, even when arrangements were more benign, to the extent that this has become common sense such that even raising this as an issue seems almost radical. However, as was argued in Chapter 6 and as has been identified in an expanding range of works, what if this is in fact no longer possible for many or even most of us, despite sanguine politicians' and economists' insistence that all technological advances create more new jobs than they destroy? As was argued earlier, an increasingly workless, highly insecure or piecemeal working future seems a likely possibility for many people with the advent of AI and automation, while finance-driven businesses are highly unlikely to willingly pass on advances in productivity and profitability to maintain employment and pay at sustainable levels, given recent experience. At present, demographic change and older workers leaving the workforce early, often through ill health, have kept employment levels up, even if pay, job security and prospects have been diminishing. However, how might we address a scenario where the current stresses imposed by stagnating incomes and insecure work move towards unemployment on an unprecedented scale? If we look at what is happening in manufacturing, commerce and even the creative and high-tech industries with the increasing capability of AI, this no longer seems fanciful.

In addition, the effects of digitalization on services and consumerism may undoubtedly further narrow options for routine employment, further threatening the foundations of contemporary capitalism. Indeed, what happens should a lack of demand through reduced incomes combine with a lack of motivation to consume? Might this arise as the 'retail apocalypse' and the move to mainly online shopping potentially erode consumerism as a leisure pursuit by removing the environments in which it was initially cultivated and sustained? Of course, as was noted in Chapter 8, one obvious positive from this may be some respite from the overconsumption that must contract as a necessary condition for tackling climate change and protecting our environment. However, all of this would evidently entail a radical downward shift in our way of living and place a large question mark with respect to our means of subsistence, while removing much of the consumerist activity that keeps many wedded to this system. It seems clear that such a scenario would present a further profound threat to political and social stability, so much so that it is difficult to see how this might be accommodated (and widespread social unrest averted) not only within neoliberal capitalist societies but also under any form of capitalism that we have seen thus far.

As was also argued earlier, aligned with the need for income, we have, of course, the essential need for shelter. However, as was outlined in Chapter 7, the combination of the erosion of secure work and the inflation of housing costs adds another level to profound difficulties here. Deregulated banks and other lenders' competition to extend as much credit for house purchases as could possibly be serviced by borrowers inflated a price bubble, leading to banks and other lenders capturing an ever bigger slice of homebuyers' earnings, reaching an unsustainable level when this 'Ponzi scheme' collapsed in 2007/2008, only to be reinflated for a time via ever lower interest rates and other interventions by central banks. As was also noted earlier, the move towards two income families together with this provision of more credit provided little economic benefit to the public, despite the necessary expansion of career opportunities for women, given that it now largely takes two full-time incomes leveraged to the margins of affordability to buy a house, or in many cases to rent in inflated private markets. As interest rates return to something like normal, and the servicing of housing costs becomes ever more unaffordable for both owner occupiers and private renters (as the landlords who entered the market as a get-rich-quick scheme push up their rents to try and stay ahead of the game), what happens when this coincides with falling incomes? Of course, as with the threat to paid work, this is already happening to an extent. Increasing numbers of individuals and families are facing eviction and destitution, while many young adults who would have flown the nest and set up homes of their own remain in student-style flat shares and living with parents well beyond the age of previous generations. This not only takes a toll on mental health, personal growth and life chances, but is also having an impact on demographics, as many young people are forced to defer or abandon the notion of parenthood. However, while this is already a serious scenario, the further erosion of the labour market, income and job security described earlier would surely render this position wholly untenable, where housing might become ever more dependent on the lottery of inheritance. In the past, of course, one way of squaring the circle when the market rendered work too insecure and housing too costly was for the losers to become live in domestic servants for the winners. This was a way life for around 4 per cent of the UK population in 1900. However, in a world of cheap automated assistance, and indeed housing that is less capable of accommodating live-in servants, this is evidently no longer a viable solution for very practical reasons, obvious questions of social acceptability aside.

These latter issues also resonate with Thomas Piketty's identification of a move away from open, ostensibly mobile societies, as the capacity of people to move forward through paid work is outpaced by accumulated wealth. Piketty was already pointing towards more rigidly stratified societies in the West, echoing that of the pre-industrial age, while this would clearly greatly intensify if, as seems likely, the preceding situation is realized even to some degree from where we are now.[1] Hence, a further significant reduction in the availability of paid work and access to decent affordable housing will mean that any rhetoric around social mobility via this route becomes ever more redundant, meaning that even the currently threadbare defence against unequal transfers of wholly unearned income and property fall away

A number of writers, commentators and businesspeople have raised similar concerns, with one of the main solutions to a relatively workless future being the provision of universal basic income (UBI) by right of citizenship. In apparently recognizing the implications of their work, OpenAI, have also proposed this as a potential 'necessity':

> [I]t is possible that advances in artificial intelligence could lead to significant changes in the job market and the economy. If AI were to replace a large number of jobs, it could potentially lead to widespread unemployment and economic disruption. In such a scenario, it is possible that some form of universal basic income (UBI) may be implemented as a way to provide financial support to people who are unable to find employment.
>
> There are a number of different ways that UBI could be funded. One possibility is that it could be funded by taxes on businesses or high earners. Another possibility is that it could be funded by the profits generated by AI and automation, if these technologies are widely adopted and become a significant source of income.[2]

This is of course laudable, and something along these lines may well be necessary to avert social, political and economic meltdown should AI and automation follow a significant labour-supplanting trajectory. Notably, Guy Standing, author of *The Precariat*, is a strong advocate for such a move motivated by an equally strong sense of social justice.[3] However, I would note that while I have great respect for Guy and his work, and while UBI might be made to work very well under some conditions, I have some residual concerns as to how this might play out in practice, at least if UBI was offered without certain conditions. Firstly, if Piketty's highly stratified society is realized, where paid work becomes scarce, then we may move towards a semi-feudal scenario where the moneyed inheritors continue to enjoy a gilded lifestyle while the masses live a subsistence existence on a minimal level and/or a diminishing level of UBI, and where currently contracting social mobility is no longer a realistic prospect. As such, it may be that some form of uneasy status quo is only sustained through manipulation, fatalistic acceptance, division, tight surveillance and oppression, potentially through the application of the technologies that have brought about this scenario. Such a dystopian future is not impossible and may only require a moderate shift from where we are now.

However, from a more practical standpoint, in addition to scepticism regarding studiously tax-averse neoliberal societies and shareholder value-oriented corporations agreeing to fund such largesse, there is a concern that the provision of a basic income to most of the population in an underregulated capitalist economy could realistically lead to whatever funds being available tending towards a very basic subsistence level, if that. Even where the rollout of basic income might initially be set at a reasonable level and may provide an initial support and even an economic boost, given the example of what has happened in housing markets, additional spending power often simply translates into higher prices for essential goods and services, as capital will tend to raise prices towards the limits of what can be sustained, securing as large a proportion of earnings as possible. The earlier discussion of the way in which companies have tended to exploit inflation expectations to increase their prices and profit margins also has a bearing here. Without price controls, it is not inconceivable that this is what might arise with a turn to mass basic income, where much of the provision is appropriated and added to corporate bottom lines through price gouging. It may also be the case that whatever resources and accommodation provided by underregulated markets that are affordable to those wholly dependent on UBI are inadequate or unacceptable, as is increasingly the case for those dependent on welfare benefits at present in neoliberal societies like the UK and the US.

However, an allied welfare model, Universal Basic Services (UBS), may offer a workable alternative or more likely an important adjunct to UBI, as a 2021 paper by Büchs proposes, while dealing with some of the issues identified earlier.[4] UBS is in some ways self-explanatory; the idea would be for the basic provision of essentials such as food, energy, housing, healthcare, transport, and communications services to be provided by the state. The provision of the latter may be made possible through taxing corporate profits and wealth, particularly that generated by automation and AI, to compensate and support those displaced. This would avoid some of the pitfalls suggested previously in relation to UBI, as companies would be unable to use their market position to impose high costs on the public, as is currently the case, for goods and services that are effectively nondiscretionary. This would also ensure that provision would have the potential to be publicly mandated and designed to meet with decent standards, as opposed to the current scenario where there can often be only limited market competition and, at times, collusion to sustain high prices for less than optimal goods and services. The market might then continue to operate for the provision of additional products and non-essentials. This would most likely also have the effect of driving up standards while tempering pricing for market provision, given the availability of reasonable quality public alternatives, while limiting the potential for the aforementioned price inflation that might arise from providing UBI alone in an unregulated market.

Büchs, citing a wide range of sources, also indicates that this would only work well if it satisfied four criteria; 'a) planetary boundaries, b) needs satisfaction, c) fair distribution, and d) democratic governance'.[5] This seems like a plausible set of necessary criteria for such an arrangement to be successful, while also being potentially progressively transformational. Firstly, as was noted in Chapter 9, the first of these criteria may be essential to our future in a world where our overuse of natural resources and impact on the environment and climate threatens our food supplies, our habitat and, ultimately, our very existence. The other criteria are obviously connected in that they are all dependent on a form of functional democracy that radically improves upon the current model in the UK and the US where, as was identified earlier, the agenda is often set and monitored by powerful interests and the real needs of the majority and marginalized are sidelined, managed and manipulated. In short, implementing this type of arrangement would require considerable and widespread buy-in across and, potentially, between societies, given the interconnectedness of the global economy and, not least, the fact that the redistributive elements would presumably be dependent on curtailing capital flight and some nations adopting beggar-thy-neighbour policies to offer low tax and low regulation to attract inward investment. Similar to what has arisen in recent decades in terms of competitive lowering of capital gains and other taxes to attract corporates, without a move back towards some sort of international consensus and regulatory framework (a form of Bretton Woods plus?), the capacity for progressive state intervention will remain highly constrained by the power of the global financial and corporate sector under neoliberal governance.

Of course, while work may become less central to people's lives, much will still go on, perhaps with a greater emphasis on prosocial, intellectual and creative activities as many mundane and routine tasks are delegated to AI, albeit that, as was indicated earlier, generative AI now appears to pose a challenge even to many creative and artistic industries to a degree that seemed unimaginable just a short time ago. Where work continues, this could operate on a platform or gig economy model, with the important proviso that the public were genuinely released from dependence on paid work as a means of sustaining a decent and socially inclusive standard of living. With respect to the latter, this would also necessitate clamping down on the engines of inequality that pervade our societies at present. Rather than winner takes all, work might be rewarded on a form of partnership model and one where rewards are much more aligned to contribution, as opposed to the current arrangement where corporate executives and senior managers largely set their own salaries, and obtain outlandish bonuses largely by squeezing the incomes of much of their workforce and raising prices wherever possible to maximize short-term profit and shareholder value.

It seems to have largely been forgotten, but as far back as the 1970s J.K. Galbraith (with apologies as it may have become clear that he was an early formative influence of mine) argued that some form of fixed and not too wide differential between the people at the top and bottom of a company was a way forward to tackling inequality and providing fair and workable incentives within firms.[6] On this latter point, as was noted in Chapter 7, human beings are highly sensitive to and motivated by quite small differences in terms of prestige and reward, while the current system may produce simply rentier parasitism and not much effort beyond that at the top, together with apathy, fear and disaffection at the bottom. The wider impact of a more measured system of reward would retain incentives, but with a greater sense of fairness and a society where people did not inhabit radically different worlds, viewing each other as alien objects of distrust and enmity. In order to achieve this, the legacy of past injustice would also evidently need to be confronted, observing but overcoming discrimination and inequalities of race, ethnicity, gender, age and class that continue to scar our societies.

As to pre-existing economic inequities, dismantling the dynastic accumulations of wealth and power that are on the rise at present would also need to feature in order to avoid the latter being used to politically undermine a more consensual and egalitarian society, and retain a position of privilege that many of the comfortably off would be ill-disposed to relinquish, as was the case at the onset of the muted rebalancing of the New Deal era.

A more balanced and communitarian social order would clearly be helpful in reducing some of the growing mental health issues that, as argued in Chapter 12, much of which have their roots in insecurity, inequality and injustice coupled with social atomization and estrangement. Beyond those experiencing severe psychic difficulties, we might return to being healed by the positives of our experience in living a decent life, and by our community with others, rather than costly and damaging pharmaceuticals or individualized 'treatment' that attempts to repair and sustain us in a toxic environment. As was also noted previously, given our growing understanding of social epigenetics, the health benefits for us and for subsequent generations may be a critical outcome of turning away from our current path, as life expectancy (and healthy life expectancy) and our constitution have been compromised by our current trajectory of development.

On this point, of course another major fly in the ointment that currently confronts us is the corrosive effects of the internet and, more particularly, social media, whose original promise has been distorted by greed and manipulation in a manner that is destroying our health, happiness, social stability and communities, while debasing our culture, invading our privacy and curtailing our freedoms. That being said, as was argued in Chapter 8, on balance there is a great deal that is positive about this technology, in providing instant and easy access to a wealth of information (albeit sadly together with confounding misinformation) and to each other, as well as providing a platform for a range of prosocial advocacy and protest to counter its darker influence. Of course, the genie is out of the bottle here and it is hard to envisage a return to a society where the internet and social media are not a central feature of everyday life. However, reform is feasible, as proposed by initiatives such as Demos' Good Web Project.[7] This would, of course, once more require greater progressive state involvement (as opposed to some of the more insidious state involvement we have seen in recent years) with an allied effort to removal of the bots that distort and manipulate online discourse for profit or nefarious political ends. According to Demos, a challenge to the scale and influence of the tech giants who have overseen and benefited from current arrangements would also be a critical feature of returning an element of these technology's original promise. This would also entail recognizing the threat to democracy and governance that 'Big Tech' organizations pose should their growing influence be allowed to continue unchecked.

The scale of the task

Moving towards any kind of resolution of the huge problems that currently confront us, including something like the form of radical re-alignment of the political and socioeconomic contract suggested previously, may seem like a virtually intractable scenario at present. Given the scope of our difficulties, as was noted earlier, progress can surely only come from cooperation between stable democratic societies that cannot be divided and played off against each other by financial and corporate interests. On any account, a return to a more stable world system of cooperating democratic states would evidently require, as well as much greater trust than exists at present, the active engagement and commitment to democracy of a workable majority of informed and reasoning citizens across the major nations, and displacement of the conflict-prone populist autocrats who are currently on the rise. While the reader might be forgiven for thinking that this is utopian pie-in-the-sky nonsense given the state of the world order at present, this is essential if a decent life in a sustainable world is going to be a possible for subsequent generations. However, this may not be such a tall order as we assume from the standpoint of the present.

Mark Fisher's *Capitalist Realism* addressed the notion that the system is so entrenched that it is almost impossible to imagine significant change, as I would argue it is deeply engrained in our collective *social maps*. Nonetheless, fundamental change is simply a fact of history, often arising despite few imaginings of the transformations that might arise over a few decades. From the rise and fall of Rome, the eclipsing of the feudal system and the emergence of modern societies to the prosocial, technological and structural developments that emerged between 1900 and the 1960s, few would have conceived of the scale and impact of these changes much before they had occurred. Of course, our cognitive conservatism contributes to a strong element of inertia, where we often cleave to business as usual for long after arrangements have served their usefulness or have even become recognizably harmful. However, as we know, profound change arises at pivotal moments, often following crises, where the habitual is no longer tenable and there is a window where the desirable becomes possible and, with hindsight, inevitable and essential. With many of the social, political, technological, economic and environmental developments that are emerging, we are surely approaching such a moment. The outcome can, of course, be positive or negative, as the transition from the brief progressive era to the regressive neoliberal age attests. Not many people in the 1950s and 1960s, I might suggest, would have imagined the social, economic and cultural impoverishment that neoliberalism has delivered despite technological advances, while the potential for things to get much darker still, as was argued earlier, remains a very clear prospect at present.

Thus, turning around our divided and fractious world will take concerted global action just as the geopolitical direction of travel seems to be going unnervingly in the opposite direction.

While it's a hackneyed expression, there may be something in the maxim that it's always darkest before the dawn. Our species has regularly only moved forward once the dire consequences of one situation or another has forced our collective hand. While we currently seem to be rushing headlong into a form of 'Blade Runner' society; of deepening division, mass surveillance, subjugation and angry, nationalistic autocratic rule, there is also growing evidence that many of the young, those yet to be deeply scarred and demoralized by the injustices and inequities of our societies, have recognized many of these issues and there are signs of a growing impetus for positive change. This is occurring even in regimes where dissent poses great risk. Among a host of other nations, including our own, the trend towards growing hate, anger and fear is prevalent, but is also being countered by fledgling calls from many among emerging generations for greater democracy and a much better way of life. It is surely critical that this prosocial mobilization achieves its aim before it is distorted, harnessed and exploited by disaffection, shattered hopes, and the fear and dark, destructive anger of *primalization* sets in.

While this is the scenario in the Global North, there may also be ever-increasing pressure in the Global South as reductions in offshored manufacturing jobs, due to automation and reshoring, are compounded by dramatic changes in climactic conditions, depleting already very low incomes while also rendering many of the very basic and insubstantial forms of shelter endured by the poor unliveable, piling further tensions on already critically fractious societies.

Overall, there is a window and some hope, even if the road forward remains narrow, while the importance of getting it right cannot be underestimated as, aside from the very obvious threats that currently present themselves, continuing on our current path will undoubtedly do further untold damage in the medium to longer term in ways that, as was argued previously, go very deep and are much more difficult to readily identify than immediate consequences. We need to ensure that the profound changes that are currently underway across our societies and environment take us in a more human-friendly direction, towards a just transition in its fullest sense, as contrary to some thinking we are not infinitely malleable and we need to find a way of living that meets our fundamental needs rather than, as was noted in Chapter 12, for numerous casualties to be consigned to an emotion-shredding psychic struggle to manage in a world that, once more, has returned to a form of order largely serving the needs and desires of a gilded and insulated minority. We have capitulated and been seduced to accept a socioeconomic system where many people do not readily fit and which is fatefully undermining our health, development, social stability and ecosystems. Hence, another swing of the pendulum is desperately needed to devise, push for and install a new form of order, and to nurture a social, economic, political and environmental niche that meets the needs of the majority in tandem with the sustainable, peaceful and progressive development of life on our planet.

Notes

[1] Piketty, T. (2017) *Capital in the Twenty-First Century*, Cambridge, MA: Harvard University Press.

[2] 'Open AI CEO predicts universal basic income necessity', https://ainewsbase.com/open-ai-ceo-predicts-universal-basic-income-will-be-paid-for-by-his-company/

[3] Standing, G. (2011) *The Precariat: The New Dangerous Class*, London: Bloomsbury.

4   Büchs, M. (2021) 'Sustainable welfare: how do universal basic income and universal basic services compare?', *Ecological Economics*, 189: 107152.

5   Büchs, M. (2021) 'Sustainable welfare: how do universal basic income and universal basic services compare?', *Ecological Economics*, 189: 107152.

6   Kenneth, G.J. and Nicole, S. (1978) *Almost Everyone's Guide to Economics*, Harmondsworth: Penguin.

7   https://demos.co.uk/project/the-good-web-project/

Index

References to figures appear in *italic* type.

Printed and bound by CPI Group (UK) Ltd, Croydon, CR0 4YY

27/10/2024

14580559-0004